COST MANAGEMENT OF DEPOSITS

COST MANAGEMENT OF DEPOSITS

A STUDY OF URBAN BANKS

By

Shirish R. Kulkarni

ANMOL PUBLICATIONS PVT. LTD.

NEW DELHI-110 002 (INDIA)

ANMOL PUBLICATIONS PVT. LTD.
4374/4B, Ansari Road, Daryaganj
New Delhi - 110 002

Cost Management of Deposits

First Edition, 2000

ISBN 81-261-0622-0

PRINTED IN INDIA

Published by J.L. Kumar for Anmol Publications Pvt. Ltd., New Delhi and Printed at Mehra Offset Press, Delhi.

Contents

Acknowledgements

Dr. S. G. Deobhankar, my research guide has been the inspiration to take up the present work. His expertise in the field of Business studies added with vast experience in other relevant fields has enabled me to understand intricacy in Banking Sector. I am very much grateful to him.

I thank Prof. V. G. Patel, Head of the Department, Business Studies, S. P. University for providing help as and when asked for.

I am grateful to Prof. J. K. Shyan, Dean, Faculty of Commerce, M. S. University of Baroda

Prof. J. R. Khedkar Head, Dept. of Accounting and Financial Management, M.S. University of Baroda and one of my senior colleague Shri. M.R.Vyas. All has been instrumental for constant inspiration to carry out the research. They have been kind to provide help at various levels.

I would like to express my sincere thanks to Prof. Kiran Joshi, Faculty of Management, M.S.University of Baroda for giving constructive suggestion at each level during the course of research.

I forward my sincere thanks to Mrs. Alka Lasenia, Dr. Sanjeev Joshi for helping me during collection of references and data. I thank all Managers and his Staff from the Co-operative Banks for providing necessary information.

I am grateful to Mr. Mayank Ray and Dr. Vipul Kalamkar for their help during analysis of the dataset.

Finally the support of my family and well wishers have helped me to achieve my targets in the stipulated time.

Shirish Kulkarni

1

Introduction

"Co-operative movement in India is one of the largest voluntary movements in the world dedicated to benefit the people of small means and having common economic needs. The primary aim and objectives of these banks are to inculcate habit of thrift, savings and mutual aids leading to better economic conditions of those who joins co-operatives."[1]

"In view of satisfying the needs and requirements of all strata of Urban and Semi- Urban population in their social and economic upliftment, particularly the amelioration of weaker sections of the community and also for the development of trade and small industries, the Urban Co-operative Banks are expected to function far more effectively and efficiently."

Banking Definition

Section 5 (c) of the Banking Regulation Act 1949, defines Banking as "Accepting, for the purpose of lending or investment, of deposits of money from the public repayable on demand or otherwise and withdrawal by cheque, draft, order or otherwise."

H. Wolf has defined a "Co-operative Bank as an agency, which is in a position to deal with small man on his own terms accepting the security he has without drawing on protection of the rich. That agency must not be a channel for pouring charity or subsidising the small man out of the public funds, instead the material help must be backed by moral improvement and strengthening the fible."[2]

"Mutual or Co-operative Credit Society, as its name indicates, consists of number of individuals, who join together to pool their surplus savings with the purpose of eliminating the profits of the Bank or Moneylender. A Credit Association is a Co-operative Institute; the profits of which is more or less equally divided between depositors and the borrowers. The character of the society depends entirely on character of the members." [3]

Co-operative Banking has three important pre-requisites, which are not found in Commercial Banks:

i) Democratic Management
ii) Responsiveness to felt needs and
iii) Self and Local participation.

Co-operative Banking is a special form of business organisation aiming at the economic upliftment of the members and laying a great emphasis on moral principles and human values.

A statutory definition of the Co-operative Banks has been laid down for the first time in the Banking Laws (applicable to Co-operative Societies) Act 1965. This Act seeks to extend certain provision of the Reserve Bank of India Act 1934 and Banking Regulation Act 1949 to the State Co-operative Banks, Central Co-operative Banks and primary Non-Agricultural Credit Societies as well as Urban Co-operative Banks.

The Co-operative Banks gave a special cheratem of taking up the responsibility of helping the economically weaker and poor as well as other marginal sector of the society. However, they still involved in the other banking operations with the changing times and demand of the society.

Changing Role of Urban Co-operative Banks

"There has been over the years a sea change in the functioning of the Urban Co-operative Banks, with an initial leaning towards the low income groups, primarily for consumption type of credit, these banks have gradually diversified their activity in consonance with national objectives and priorities, in providing credit for productive investment with special emphasis on the weaker sections of society."[4]

Presently the emphasis of the credit policy of the Urban Co-operative Banks is as follows:

- i) Employment generation,
- ii) Self employment and
- iii) Financing of small and medium size business and industry.

These Banks provide 60 per cent of their advances to the priority sector as compared to 40 per cent of the Commercial Banks. Along with the banking operation for the allocation of priority sector, these Banks are discharging their social responsibility by allocating 25 per cent of the lending to weaker sections of society. Out of total 1400 Urban Banks, 42 are Women Banks, solely owned and managed by women and helping in raising women's socio-economic status.

Resources of the Urban Co-operative Banks

One of the important features of the Urban Co-operative Banks has been to rely on its internal resources. The source of funds of these banks comprises of the following types:

- i) Owned funds,
- ii) Deposits and
- iii) Borrowing from financial institutions.

The deposits constitute a bulk of loanable funds, while borrowings of the Urban Co-operative Banks constitute an insignificant proportion of their working capital. The owned funds comprises of:

i) Share capital and
ii) Reserves.

The Reserve Bank of India constituted a Standing Advisory Committee for Urban Co-operative Banks in 1983. The report of committee is based on the study of ten years data between 1974-75 and 1983-84, which reflects the proportion of own funds to working capital of Urban Co-operative Banks as under:

TABLE 1.01

PROPORTION OF DEPOSITS AND OWN FUNDS TO WORKING CAPITAL OF URBAN CO-OPERATIVE BANKS IN INDIA

Sr. No.	*Year*	*% of Deposits to Working Capital*	*% of Own Funds to Working Capital*
1	1974-75	70.68	15.00
2	1975-76	71.30	16.00
3	1976-77	70.60	16.28
4	1977-78	72.90	15.80
5	1978-79	72.00	14.90
6	1979-80	73.00	13.90
7	1980-81	72.80	12.50
8	1981-82	72.00	12.20
9	1982-83	71.00	12.20
10	1983-84	73.56	11.80
11	1988-89	76.77	10.15
12	1993-94	83.90	13.62
13	1994-95	83.79	13.81
14	1995-96	83.99	13.37
15	1996-97	85.03	13.17

Source: Report of Standing Advisory Committee on Urban Co-operative Banks- RBI - 1984. And Report on Trends and Progress of Banking in India RBI 1996-97.

It can be observed from the data that the proportion of owned fund to working capital ranges between 10.15 per cent and 16.28 per cent, the trend of proportion of the owned funds to working capital is continuously declining from 1976-77 to 1983-84 and also in 1988-89.

For the year 1989, the owned funds of Urban Co-operative Banks were Rs. 905.28 Crores while working capital of Urban Co-operative Banks was Rs. 8916.39 Crores. The proportion of own funds to working capital has further gone down to 10.15 per cent.

The banking activity of Urban Co-operative Banks has shown a promising growth ever since their inception. A look at the data from 1993-94 to 1995-96 has indicated a significant progress in the deposits, working capital and increase in the advances, table 1.02. The owned funds have risen from Rs. 2723 crores to Rs. 3848 crores, the deposits during these years have been increased from Rs. 16769 crores to Rs. 24165 crores. The deposits have always remained seven times more than the owned funds, indicating attraction for deposits in these banks.

Borrowings

The proportion of borrowings in financial sources of the Urban Co-operative Banks has remained steady as seen in the data from 1993-1996. The percentage of borrowing towards the working capital has remained between 0.024 and 0.026 during the period of 1993-96, table no. 1.02.

Similarly the data of table 1.04 for Gujarat Urban Co-operative Banks reflects similar growth of these funds. The data shows an increasing trend for all types of sources towards working capital of these banks. Increase in the share capital indicates growth in the membership, whereas growing deposits is an indicator of preference of the investors for their banks i.e. for both, members as well as non-members.

TABLE 1.02

PROGRESS OF URBAN CO-OPERATIVE BANKS

(Rs. in Crores.)

Items	*1993-94*	*1994-95*	*1995-96*	*1996-97*
No. of Banks	1400	1431	1501	1653
Owned funds	2723	3312	3848	4541
Deposits	16769	20101	24165	29313
Borrowing	496	577	758	618
Advance	12172	14795	17908	20613
Working capital	19988	23990	28771	34472
Per cent of owned funds to W.C.	13.62	13.80	13.37	13.17
Per cent of deposits towards W.C.	83.89	83.78	83.99	85.03

Source: Statistical Tables of RBI.

The data under study reveals that the deposits are a key resource for the working capital, the present work is intended to workout the cost management of the deposits. The available information shows poor attention being paid to this important aspect of the banking business, so it is logical to highlight the costs of deposits in order to make Urban Co-operative Banking a more efficient and professionally managed and viable institution. The previous studies on the aspects of costing are on the costs of loanable funds and total costs of banking operations, etc.; these can be easily grouped as:

i) Cost of loanable fund,

ii) Cost of credit and

iii) Cost of bank's services.

The available information shows the costing works being done in the commercial and public sector banks, whereas the Co-operative Banks are grossly neglected for such studies.

Cost Management

Importance

Cost management in Urban Co-operative Banking industry is a recent development; the banking industry has widely understood its importance as a tool for cost analysis of banking services. The cost of a product or service is a key factor in price fixation and profit margin determination.

The technique of ascertaining the cost of a product in any industry depends upon the type of industry. Urban Co-operative Banking industry being a service industry, the product of this industry is considered as the service made available to its members and customers. The cost of a product depends upon the cost of "inputs" i.e. raw material, labour and other overheads but in case of Urban Co-operative Banks, inputs are in the form of deposits. These depositors are mainly paid interest and by rendering services. Urban Banks are providing various services to its customers and members to attract deposits. In a manufacturing organisation, the cost of product is ascertained by the composition of various cost elements such as:

i) Cost of material,
ii) Cost of labour, and
iii) Cost of the overheads.

In the service sector, the principles underlying the process of costing are the same but their application differ. The cost of loanable funds for Urban Co-operative Banks is same as the cost of sales in the manufacturing industry. The cost of sales in Urban Banks i.e. cost of loanable funds per rupee (unit) are not directly related to the amount of advances provided, further it is not related to the rate charged on advances.

The Institute of Cost and Management Accountant of England had given the definition for cost accountancy, "The application of costing and cost accountancy principles, method and practice of cost control and ascertainment of information derived there for the purpose of managerial decision making."

Cost accountancy is a science, owing to the facts that, it is systematic methodology based on certain fundamental principles and empirical observations. Consequently, looking at the other aspects like application of techniques, methods and requiring skills, the cost accountancy is as an art also.

Objectives

i) *Ascertainment of cost:* Cost of product or cost of banking services can be ascertained with the help of cost accounting. Various techniques of costing like standard costing, marginal costing, absorption costing, uniform costing, etc. are being used.

ii) *Determination of selling price:* Profit is a major objective of any business. It is necessary that the revenue is greater than cost. Cost accounting provides desired cost for determining the selling price for banking services. It helps in analysing total cost under variable costs and fixed costs.

iii) *Controlling cost:* Cost accounting involves the study of different processes of banking services, which will facilitate measuring the efficiency of operation of the department and or division of a bank. Many techniques or methods have been evolved to exercise control over banking service costs.

Advantages

Advantages of cost accounting to the Urban Bank Management are:

i) Usefulness in recession, depression or seasonal variation,

ii) Aids in preparing estimates of project finance,

iii) Elimination of wastage,

iv) Measuring and improving efficiency,
v) Provides data for periodic profit and loss accounts,
vi) Aids inventory control like in cash management,
vii) Aids control over staff cost, and
viii) Helps in managerial control.

Considering above-mentioned advantages of cost accounting, the role of Urban Banking in Indian economy can be better appreciated if Urban Banks are—

i) Financially sound and operationally efficient and
ii) Strengthening and managing its resources professionally.

As mentioned earlier, the objective of this study is to analyse the cost of deposits. Deposits are the inputs of banking industry, whereas advances and other services are the outputs of the banking industry. Pricing of outputs depends on external variables in a manufacturing industry. The price of a product cannot be determined only on the basis of cost of sales but market price for similar products should also to be taken into account. During the period of recession and depression, manufacturing industries may not earn any profit. Even if it may not cover the cost of sales, the industry may continue its production taking into consideration a future revival of the market. They may not close down production even after making losses. Selling price may not cover the fix costs but selling prices which covers only the variable cost would allow the production to continue. Manufacturing industry would like to continue production and sale the product by covering variable cost to survive in the market even though they are incurring losses. Market forces compels the industry to reduce prices due to the competition in the market, therefore output prices are governed by external forces i.e. market forces. These external forces are beyond the control of manufacturing industry and other industries.

Profit Cost Relationship

To attain the goal of maximisation of profit either the industry has to increase the selling price or reduce the cost of sales. In other words, to increase the profit, either raise the selling price or control the cost of sales. The rise in selling price will adversely affect on total sales and sales will go down. Reduction in sales will reduce the profit. So, it is not advisable to raise the selling price. This is quite in conformity with the law of supply and demand.

Profit maximisation depends upon the external variables, which are highly uncertain, as understood from the market. Unpredictability exists owing to many socio-economic factors. However, the internal factors of cost of a product are very much under control. So, the emphasis should be to work out the costs of inputs in such a way that the product is to be able to sell in the market, ensuring a certain amount of profit at any given point of time. The process of reducing the costs has to be undertaken to meet this goal. Reduction in costs will definitely increase the profit, if the input costs are under check. For such costing, following parameters are to be dealt with:

i) Cost of input,
ii) Cost of labour,
iii) Cost of other overheads,
iv) Cost as administrative expenses and
v) Cost as financial expenses.

"Any objective and rational cost analysis on accounting system of commercial Banks must cope up with these two aspects of the problem of choice of the proper "output" variable - the unit of - "output" of the bank for cost accounting purpose.

A commercial bank conventionally visualised as a financial intermediary or agency—making loans and investments to business and individuals with the help of deposits and capital funds mobilised, again from individuals and business.

The conventional cost analysis or accounting ideas and techniques as relating to commercial banking stem from such a visualisation of the commercial bank — its "output" mainly constituted by the volumes of loans and investment and its "inputs" or "raw material" constituted by the deposits and capital funds mobilised and employed in loan and investment extension."[5]

As stated earlier, the major functions performed by Urban Co-operative Bank are:

i) Accepting deposits and
ii) Making loan and investment

Out of these, accepting deposits becomes "input" or "raw material" for Urban Banks, whereas making loan and investment becomes 'output' or "final product". Pricing of 'output' or "final product" extremely depends upon external forces. Cost of "output" i.e., loans and advances are not much under the control of Urban Banks, however the "input" of Urban Banks can be manipulated for the cost of deposits.

Interest payable on deposits has greater share in total cost of deposits of Urban Co-operative Banks. Earlier Urban Banks were permitted to pay one per cent higher rate of interest and later on from 1985 onwards these banks were allowed to pay only half per cent more interest compared to the commercial banks. The Reserve Bank of India allowed this advantage to the Urban Co-operative Banks to attract more depositors, so that the laid down social objectives of these banks can be fulfilled, without depending upon other funding agencies.

The Economic Reforms

The ongoing financial sector reforms since 1990, have changed the equations for the financial sector business.

"The financial sector reforms currently underway in India must be seen as a component of the over all scheme of structural reforms. The overall package is aimed at enhancing the productivity and efficiency of the economy as a whole and also increasing international competitiveness. The reforms are comprehensive in scope covering besides financial sector reforms, several other components of economic policy including liberalisation and deregulation of domestic investment. Opening up of key infrastructure areas hitherto reserved for public sector for private sector participation, opening up of economy to foreign competition by reducing protective barriers."[6]

Deregulation of Interest Rates

The Reserve Banks of India started simplifying structure of interest rates since September 1990. For the banking sector a gradual approach has been adopted in reforming interest rate structure in India and therefore the advantage of rate of interest was allowed to the Co-operative Banks which came under review. RBI deregulated the interest rates on term deposits of Urban Co-operative Banks from 1st October 1995. Interest rate structure on domestic deposits prescribed by RBI for the year 1995-96 was as under:

TABLE 1.03

RATE OF INTEREST ON DOMESTIC TERM DEPOSITS OF URBAN CO-OPERATIVE BANKS

Sr. No.	*1st October, 1995*		*2nd July, 1996*	
	Term of Deposits	*Maximum Rate of Interest Allowed*	*Term of Deposits*	*Maximum Rate of Interest Allowed*
1.	46 day and up to 2 year	12%	30 days & up to 1 year	10%
2.	More than 2 year	Free	More than 1 year	Free

The rate mentioned above are applicable to all the banks. Ceiling of interest rates on term deposit was kept at 10 per cent per annum for duration up to 1 year from July 1996 onwards. But there is no maximum rate prescribed by RBI for the term deposits for more than one year. This clearly indicates that commercial and other banks can offer attractive interest rates to get more deposits. Thus the Co-operative Banks will no longer enjoy the advantage of offering higher rates of interest on the deposits. Commercial banks, being more wide spread will also take the advantage of these returns and will be in position to attract more deposits.

These reforms will have far reaching repercussions for the growth of Co-operative Banks. Since not only Indian commercial banks but also foreign banks will have the opportunity to enter in the Indian monetary market. Thus there is a real threat to the Co-operative Banks, which works with a social objective in attracting the deposits.

Deposits to GDP—Comparison

"The extension of banking stands out a significant achievement. As a ratio of GDP at current prices, bank deposits increased from 18 per cent in 1969-70 to 45.3 per cent by end March 1995. All the indicators of financial development such as finance ratio, financial inter relation ratio and intermediation ratio have significantly increased implying the growing importance of financial institutions in the economy and growth of financial flows in relation to economic activity." [7]

As stated above, the financial sector is gaining importance in the growth of any economy. With liberalisation and reforms under way, the deposits worth 45.3 per cent of GDP till 1995, will have more partner to share i.e. Foreign Banks and Indian Banks. The Co-operative Banks are going to be in a great disadvantage, since the public sector commercial banks as well as foreign banks are in a better position to attract the saving compared to the Urban Co-operative Banks owing to the deregulation.

Under this complex scenario, the Urban Co-operative Banks, called as the bank of "small man" operating normally in local areas having democratic local and largely untrained management, finds itself faced with the total take off professional management compared with other banks.

Urban Banks are not operating for maximisation of profit. Till 1995, these banks were allowed to pay more interest on deposits and to charge less interest on loans and advances. Urban Banks were protected under Reserve Bank of India's regulated structure of interest rates. With the change of rules of financial market, these banks have to workout a strategy for their survival to fulfill their social commitments.

Under the changed market scenario, to attract the deposits, these Co-operative Banks also have to adopt a similar interest payment strategy as compared with the other banks. In other words, in order to survive in the market, these banks would have to become like other commercial banks. There are many odd comings in the way of Co-operative Banks in achieving these market goals.

"Indian Banking is now on the threshold of a major transformation and much of its success in meeting the challenges of change would depend on how the individual banking institution gear and brace themselves up organisationally, operationally and functionally with desired degree of operational and competitive efficiencies."[8]

Banking is a very different type of business. A high measure of conservatism is involved and bears very high risks and can not be considered to earn high profit. That is why, at no time in the history of our country or even elsewhere, have banks become high profit earners?

Sources of fund of Urban Co-operative Banks in Gujarat are increasing continuously during past four decades. Owned funds which comprise of share capital and reserves were Rs. 1.1 crores on 30th June 1960 which has grown up to Rs.

TABLE 1.04

PROPORTION OF DEPOSITS REGARDING OWNED FUNDS AND BORROWINGS WITH THE WORKING CAPITAL OF URBAN CO-OPERATIVE BANKS IN GUJARAT

(Rs. in Crores)

Items	*30th June 1960*	*30th June 1974*	*30th June 1987*	*30th June 1988*	*30th June 1989*	*30th June 1990*	*30th June 1991*	*31st Mar 1992*	*31st Mar 1993*	*31st Mar 1998*
Deposits	5.67	91.02	1327	1561	1745	2072	2342	2593	3160	9948
Own funds	1.1	15.3	251	273	322	385	451	541	659	1736
Borrowings	0.76	16.22	241	297	351	401	467	523	527	1494
W.C.	7.53	122.54	1819	2131	2418	2858	3260	3657	4346	13178
% of Own funds to W.C.	14.6	12.48	13.8	12.8	13.3	13.5	13.8	14.8	15.16	13.17
% of Deposits to W.C.	72.3	74.28	72.95	73.25	72.16	72.5	71.84	70.9	72.71	75.49
% Of Borrowings-to W.C.	10	13.24	13.25	13.9	14.5	14	14.3	14.3	12.12	11.33

1736 crores in the year 1998. Deposits of Urban Banks in Gujarat stood at Rs. 5.67 crores in 1960, which increased to Rs. 9948 crores on 31st March 1998. Working capital which was just Rs. 7.53 crores in 1960 increased to Rs. 13, 178 Crores in the year 1998.

Composition of deposits, owned funds and borrowings as the sources of funds of Urban Co-operative Banks as observed at all India level found similar at Gujarat. Capital of Urban Co-operative Banks during last four decades is ranging from 12.48 per cent to 15.16 per cent to working capital. Deposits to working capital, minimum 70.09 per cent on 31March 1992 and maximum 75.49 per cent on 31 March 1998. The share of Borrowings in working capital of Urban Co-operative Banks is between 10 per cent in 1960 and 14.5 per cent in 1989.

Contribution of deposits to sources of funds to Urban Co-operative Banks at All India level as well as at Gujarat level is ranging between 70 per cent to 80 per cent. In other words borrowings and owned funds taken together are just between 20 per cent to 30 per cent of working capital of Urban Co-operative Banks at Gujarat and all India level.

Though the scene is not yet clear but one can foresee alarm bells for these banks. These Co-operative Banks have been caught in the contradiction of social responsibility and global market economy. Profit making is not the ultimate goal of these Co-operative Banks. However in the present scenario of free market the issue is debatable.

Research Design

Scope of the Study

This study aims to deal with complex situation in which Urban Co-operative Banks have been dragged into. To sustain in the competitive banking industry, Urban Banks will have to be viable. To uplift the small man, a member of Urban Banks, these banks will have to make profit, even when urban bank does not aim to maximise the profit. Make profit and survive in the banking industry, Urban Banks can not increase its lending interest rate but it can only consider lowering down it's cost of deposits.

For the scope of the study as stated above, a ten years data from 1987-88 to 1996-97 has been taken for ascertaining the impact of deregulation in the financial sector. The time period chosen is divided into regulated phase up to 1995-96 and post regulation phase from 1996 onwards.

For studying the Urban Co-operative Banks' cost management of deposits, these ten years are divided into two :

i) Regulated interest rates era i.e. protected atmosphere from 1986-87 to 1995-96.

ii) Deregulated interest rate era i.e. free economy from 1995-96 to 1996-97.

Objectives of the Study

i) To examine the performance of deposits and deposits mobilisation of Urban Co-operative Banks.

ii) To analyse the fixed cost components of Urban Co-Operative Banks and to identify main determinants of fixed cost components of Urban Co-Operative Banks.

iii) To ascertain the variable cost of deposits of Urban Co-Operative Banks.

iv) To analyse the nature and components of other costs of banking activities of Urban Co-Operative Banks.

v) To evaluate the impact of financial sector reforms on costs of Urban Co-Operative Banks.

vi) To compare inter bank cost ratios and to suggest model for cost efficiency in Urban Co-operative Banks.

vii) To compare the costs with earnings and review the major determinants of profit and profitability of Urban Co-operative Banks.

Selection of Sample Banks

Ten Urban Co-operative Banks have been selected throughout Gujarat out of which three Urban Banks namely (1) Kalupur Commercial Bank (2) Surat People's Co-operative Bank and (3) Rajkot Nagarik Bank are scheduled Banks. The Surat People's Co-operative Bank and The Sardar Bhiladwala Bank are from South Zone of the Gujarat State. The Anyonya Sahayakari Bank, The Baroda People's Bank and The Anand Mercantile Bank are from the Central Zone of Gujarat State. Whereas The Dahod Urban Bank is entirely covering the tribal area. The Kalupur Commercial Bank and The Natpur Co-operative Bank are from the North Zone of Gujarat. The Rajkot Nagrik Bank covers the entire Saurashtra Zone of Gujarat State. The banks for study are selected at random.

Following Urban Co-operative Banks from Gujarat have been selected for the study:

i) Sardar Bhiladwala Co-operative Bank, Valsad district.
ii) The Surat People's Co-operative Bank, Surat City, Surat district.
iii) Anyonya Sahayakari Mandali Co-operative Bank Ltd., Vadodara city.
iv) Baroda People's Co-operative Banks, Vadodara city.
v) The Anand Mercantile Bank, Anand city, Anand district.
vi) Dahod Urban Co-operative Bank, Dahod city, Dahod district.
vii) The Natpur Co-operative Bank, Nadiad city, Kheda district.
viii) The Kalupur Commercial Bank, Ahemadabad city.
ix) Sarvodaya Nagrik Bank, Visnagar, Sabarkatha district North Gujarat.

x) The Rajkot Nagrik Bank, Rajkot city, Rajkot district.

These banks are well spread throughout Gujarat State. The study, which involves cost of deposits, used the data of these banks having three cost components namely:

i) Fixed costs,
ii) Variable costs, and
iii) Social and other costs.

The study reflects how these ten banks have managed their cost of deposits, what is the difference between regulated interest rates period and deregulated interest rates-period. Keeping the goal of co-operative movement in practice and matching the deposits and total cost of operating the banks.

In the following chapters, we would deal with these components of costs and finally a synthesis of the data interpretation on the objectives will be presented in order to understand the impact of post deregulation era and subsequently the importance of costs of deposits will be highlighted. Since this is the only parameter, which can help Co-operative Banks to become viable, keeping their social objective intact.

Source of Data

This is a compilation of primary data collected from various sources like annual reports of selected Urban Co-operative Banks, Gujarat Urban Co-operative Banks' Federation, National Federation for Urban Co-operative Banks. This is supported by reports of certain committees, study groups, workshops appointed by The Reserve Bank of India. Primary data is collected by personal visit to the selected Urban Co-operative Banks and the discussion with the branch managers. Annual Reports of Gujarat Urban Co-operative Banks' Federation were available only for the years 1986-87 to 1993-94 and 1997-98.

Methodology

It was decided to construct average balances of various items of assets and liabilities. The data for this purpose were taken for two consecutive years from the annual reports of the selected banks. The data regarding fixed costs variable costs and other costs is taken from the profit and loss accounts of the banks and were arranged according to the requirements to get the better framework for computation and analysis.

Statistical tools like mean, standard deviation, co-efficient of determination are used to analyse the data. Multivariate Analysis of Variance (MANOVA) is used to test the hypothesis. Maps, Graphs, Pie charts are used for some supportive and meaningful interpretations. The trend analysis and ratio analysis are used to derive growth and also the determinants of costs.

Organisation of Study

The study is divided into nine chapters:

Chapter 1 defines the problem and spells out the objectives and focuses on relevance of the study. It also describes the research methodology including the choice of sample.

Chapter 2 discusses the past studies in the field of cost analysis of banking activities. Also reviews the related literature.

Chapter 3 deals with overall progress of Urban Co-operative Banks in India as well as in Gujarat.

Chapter 4 covers discussion of deposits mobilised by Urban Co-operative Banks in India and in Gujarat.

Chapter 5 analysis the various components of fixed costs and the total fixed cost of selected Urban Co-operative Banks. Also reviews the relevance of fixed costs with deposits.

Chapter 6 examines in detail the interest paid on deposits

as variable cost of deposits.

Chapter 7 brings out the impact of fluctuations in CRR and SLR on the banks' earnings. This chapter also deals with the social banking, social cost and the influence of non-performing assets on banks' profits.

Chapter 8 presents cost management of deposits by way of preparing the formats of cost sheet of selected Urban Co-operative Banks and proposes the standard cost.

Chapter 9 covers the summary of earlier chapters in the form of conclusions and offers the suggestions for reducing the cost and improving banks' profitability and recommends the areas for further research.

REFERENCES

1. *Dashabdi Year Book*, 1985.
2. H. Wolf, Co-operating Banking, No. 2, p. 3.
3. Sannechoen, *Consumers Co-operation*, pp. 182-183.
4. RBI, Report - 1984, p. 86 — by Standing Advisory Committee for Urban Co-operative Banks, 4th meeting.
5. V Kalyanaram, RPC, Cost Accounting in Commercial Banking Industry., p. 32, published by ICWA 1972.
6. C. Rangarajan, *Banking Sector Reforms Rational and Relevance*, pp. 18 and 19, published by AF, Delhi.
7. C. Rangarajan, Banking Sector Reforms Rational and Relevance, p. 19, AF, Delhi.
8. A.K. Roy, Chief Manager, Dena Bank, Head Office, Mumbai. *IBA Bulletin* Vol. XV Sept., 1993 p. 6.

2

Review of Literature

"Indian Banking is now on the threshold of a major transformation and much of its success in meeting the challenges of changing would depend on how the individual banking institution gear and brace, themselves up organisationally, operationally and functionally with desired degree of operational and competitive efficiencies."[1]

Banking is a very different type of business. A high measure of conservatism is involved and bears very high risks that can not be taken to earn high profit. That is why, at no time in the history of our country or even elsewhere, have banks earned huge profits and their shares have never been sold as blue chip shares. In terms of profit, a bank cannot compete with the companies like Reliance or Indian Petro-chemicals Corporation Limited. They have always been at best moderate profit earners. Some banks may earn above average and some others below average profit. However, in recent years, profit performance of Indian Banks has been under pressure. The pressure on profits and profitability of Indian Banks had surfaced in early 1960 itself, much before the nationalisation of major commercial banks.

In order to understand the viability of a bank many experts engaged in the field of banking have studied the complexity of a banks' profit and profitability. Even though banks do not function with an objective of maximisation of profit. "Economic viability is also essential for the survival of any business activity and banking industry is no exception to it."[2]

"It is to be recognised that maximisation of profit is not and it should not be the main objective of public sector banks, otherwise there would be no justification for their nationalisation. But, to argue that, profit is irrelevant for public sector banks is to miss some important points. Profit and profitability are important factors to a bank for the twin purpose, i.e.,

i) Providing a cushion for loan losses and risks arising from foreign exchange and interest rate change and
ii) Generating internal capital."

Both these factors are equally important for Indian banks, as it is so, for the banks in foreign countries. Free availability of capital and reserves less fixed assets, will be able to provide a cushion to meet loan losses until appropriate policy and strategy changes have taken sufficient time to work out their effects on profitability and profit.

"It is necessary for the banks to build up internally generated capital and reserves. This can be done only if their current profits are sufficiently high. Since the mandatory purchases of securities under SLR and also higher CRR and priority sector financing at concessional rates affect the profitability of banks adversely, the ability of the banks to generate internal capital is very limited."[3]

"It is now accepted principle that these banks are not to run solely or even mainly with the objective of making maximum profit. However, this does not mean that they are not to make any profit at all. In particular there is substantial investment of public funds, in the banks and a reasonable return on this investment would be expected by the government."[4]

The National Banks are not running with the object of earning maximum profit as they have to make their due contribution towards the fulfillment of the economic and social objectives lay down by the government. This does not, however, mean that there should be no profit motive at all. Nationalisation of Banks does not absolve the banks from their obligation to maintain proper financial and monetary discipline. There is a substantial investment of public funds in these banks and the Government would expect a reasonable return on these investments. The method of cost control and pricing policy should be such as to ensure a reasonable return on the funds invested by Government in the National Banks.

Obviously Urban Co-operative Banks have been working to achieve the goal of Co-operative movement in India. They have to help the small men to uplift themselves but it does not mean that they should not earn any profit, but they may not aim for maximisation of profit. These banks do earn a reasonable profit in order to carry out the banking activities.

Banking Commission Report for the year 1972 has provided the following data regarding cost of Urban Banks (on p. 285).

TABLE 2.01

COSTS OF AN "ALL INDIA AVERAGE OF URBAN CO-OPERATIVE BANK"

Activities	*Average Balance (Rs. in Lacs)*	*Cost Per cent Per Annum of Average Balance (Including Interest Paid)*
Currant Deposits	5.84	3.37
Savings	13.70	4.64
Fixed	27.54	6.38
Other	3.85	—
Total Deposits	50.43	5.52

Of the total deposits more than 50 per cent is a fixed deposit. Cost of fixed deposits is also higher than that of any other type of deposits. Current deposits are not paid any interest till operating cost of the current deposits is very high."[5]

A well-known equation of profit is

Profit = Price – Cost.

Fixation of prices of banking services plays an important role for earning the profit. In any commercial organisation, every increase in price, keeping cost constant, will increase the profit. But "The task of evolving an optional price structure for the banking industry has to satisfy not only the profit requirements of the industry but has also to fulfil the overall objectives in regard to deposit mobilisation. Pattern of bank credit and its costs to the various sectors of the society as well as the general development of banking facilities and saving habit all over the country."[6]

Committee on production, efficiency and profitability (PEP committee) observed the limitation in development of commercial banking. "While the operational cost of banking system has increased steadily, partly owing to factors beyond the control of the bank management, no systematic attempt has been made so far to adopt scientific methods of improving productivity and efficiency in the banking system. Individual efforts made in this connection are few and sporadic and their impact is marginal. Banking has to emerge as a viable and not subsidised means of achieving the national policy objective."[7]

Historical Background

The costing of bank services received considerable interest in United States of America, United Kingdom and other western countries during early forties, but no serious thought was given to this subject in India till 1970, though individual banks were conducting ad-hoc cost studies from time to time. However the first study, at the macro level, was initiated by the Banking Commission in the year 1969 and completed in 1972. Thereafter it was State Bank of India, which took up regular cost studies. The need for a systematic and regular arrangement for a study of a cost structure and other related areas in commercial banks on an on-going basis was stressed by the working group on productivity, efficiency and profitability, committee, constituted by the Reserve Bank of India in April 1976."[8]

The year 1982, declared as "The Year of Productivity", the need for cost effectiveness in service organisations like banks where the cost of service is a key parameter of productivity, assumed considerable importance.

Costing Manual

At the Banks' Economists meet in 1986, Shri Bagchi, of Punjab National Bank emphasized that the "Improving profitability is important to Nationalised Banks. Because social obligations which have been a cost on them can not be performed without adequate profit subsidisation of priority sector cannot be carried unless the overall profitability is there."[9]

In the seminar organised by Banker's Training College, the then Deputy Governor of RBI, Dr. C. Rangarajan said, "Improving profitability of banks has been an area of great concern, both to the RBI and the Government of India. The performance of Financial Institutions can be judged by its allocational and operational efficiency. Allocational efficiency refers to efficient allocation of funds by an institution among competing demands. Operational efficiency refers to the difference between the rates at which funds are raised and deployed. Gains accruing to the banks on account of measures may be called as environmental profit because the accrue on account of external factors and not due to improved internal efficiency of banks."[9]

In past studies on economies of scale, in banking, have indicated that in case of cost output relationship, the measurement of output assumes importance. The studies wherein a bank is viewed as a collection of liabilities or what produces bank revenue, as output variable.

The reasons responsible for declining profitability of commercial banks are:

i) It is argued that the deterioration in the profitability of commercial banks is due to the movement in the spread and burden (The difference between average return on earning assets and average cost of raising deposits or borrowing). The earning of the bank on the one hand is declining on account of deployment of funds in low yielding advances i. e. food procurement, priority sector advances, differential interest rate (DIR) advances etc. while on the other hand, the wages—salary costs goes on increasing on account of inflation and massive recruitment of additional staff in view of heavy rural and semi-urban branch expansion programme.

ii) Rapid expansion of branches and share of priority sector lending have negative influence on profitability behaviour and in later case this is statistically significant too. Thus decline in profitability is attributed to the social responsibilities assigned to a bank.

iii) The monetary policy of the RBI is also one of the reason for declining profitability of commercial banks. The statutory and net liquidity requirements, the interest rates policy on deposits and advances etc. undoubtedly affected the profitability of commercial banks

iv) Heavy competition for deposits from non-banking financial institutions has also negative impact on bank profitability.[10]

"The review of previous costing studies in Indian banks brings out the fact that the assessment of cost of various activities and evolving cost based pricing strategies received little attention till recent years.

The major factors that influence the decisions on pricing are cost, competition and quality. The cost is the prime factor in pricing. The price must recover cost and generate sufficient profit so as to realise a fair rate of return on capital and to impart stability to organisational growth even in a competitive environment, it is more important to know accurate cost to meet the competition efficiently. The price and quality should go to hand in hand and customers expect the increase in price should accompany in improvement in quality of services."[11]

"Since the banking sector reforms have been set in motion, the priorities in banking operations underwent far reaching changes. There had been shift of emphasis from development or social banking to commercially viable banking. Profitability became the buzzword and the prime mover of the financial strength and performance of banks. Unlike in past all banking operations gradually came to be measured in terms of their ability to generate profits.

One of the crucial factors in maintaining profitability of a bank is its ability to control cost of operations. The cost to income ratio should be kept at minimum possible levels reducing overheads on an on-going basis but without adversely affecting the quality of services. Closing down of loss making rural branches, reducing staff cost through adaptation of technology and improving their productivity etc., goes a long way in cutting overheads in this inflationary environment."[12]

These studies include Ahadeff (1964) Schweiger ar McGee (1961) Horvitz (1963) Grebler and Brighan (1963).

The definition of bank output still remains a major problem confronted by researchers and no consensus on the adequate measure of output is reached. In majority of studies on economies of scale, cost was defined as total operating cost, which excluded interest cost. Most of the studies assume constant cost elasticity. The equation price, i.e., variable price cannot increase the output of the bank for two reasons i.e. (a) It is an external function and (b) Banks have to attain the social and national goals. Then ultimately to make the banking operation viable the another variable cost can be operated. Cost has an inverse relation with profit. Every reduction in cost while keeping prices constant can lead to a rise in profit. Therefore cost control becomes important.

"One of the important advantage of cost analysis is that it provides useful information for involving rational price structure. In the banking industry, it can form the basis for computation of service charges for measuring the profitability of different activities and for adopting proper interest rate policies. In the past, the need for knowledge of the costs and profitability of each one of the bank's services was not keenly felt as long as the profits earned by banks were high. In the banking industry in India, there have been practically no attempts made at analysing cost. The banks have been generally working on the principles that so long as they make a reasonable profit on their overall operations, it does not make much difference whether some operations were profitable or others resulted in loss. With the increasing costs of banking operations, the need has arisen for scientific determination of both the servicing costs and interest rates, which involves determination of profit objectives as a first step."[13]

Until the year 1969, Government of India did not pay much attention to the cost analysis of banking business. The "Banking Commission" setup in the same year and had studied the aspect of cost analysis over and above several others in the banking operations.

"In the context of decreasing profitability of banks' operations, profit planning assumes crucial importance in the efforts made towards efficiency improvement, profit planning is based on fund management, work management and cost management techniques. It necessitates locating profit and cost centers, identifying elements that determine income and cost structure of each center and the organisation as a whole. Finding out the extent to which these factors can be influenced by policy and planning, evolving means to wide spread between cost and returns, and developing supplementary / alternative sources of income or profits.

There is growing realisation to control operational costs due to expansion of non-remunerative branches in rural areas, growth in employment, rise in wages due to pay revision and cost of living indices and a general increase in overheads and other costs. Cost increases through rational system of pricing financial services and revision service charges, rationalising lending and investment policy and realistic interest rate structure.

The need for cost analysis was not felt by banking industry until the year 1969 when Government of India appointed "Banking Commission". This Commission, one of them being the cost aspect, studied several aspects of the Banking Industry.

In evolving a programme for profitability improvement concentrated attention has to be given to costs of staffing pattern. Operational workflow, wastage removal analysis, well developed management information system, social obligation accounting, cost and performance control, decentralised supervision and cost benefit analysis."[14]

In April 1976, the Reserve Bank of India had constituted a working group to examine the question of cost control, operational efficiency and bank profitability. A study of banking costs was organised by the group, covering nearly one thousand branches of 21 selected banks. The objective of the study was to estimate the cost of servicing of various activities of banks. The study reflects the procedure for collection of data through suitably designed schedules on costs and output data from selected branches and time spent on various activities by staff members in each of the selected branches. The study group has tried to find out the solution to a short-term problem and long term action plan in future. Working group recommended the steps for banking cost, operational efficiency and profitability of Banks.

"The business of the bank may be classified in two broad groups – a) Fund activities comprising of Deposits and Advances, and b) Other activities including all other services like remittances, cheques and bill collection, foreign exchange dealing etc. In 1984, funds activity accounted for 72.6 per cent of the total servicing cost, 42.2 per cent for deposits and 30.4 per cent for advances. Among other activities, remittances and bills accounted for about 17.6 per cent, foreign exchange about 3.1 per cent and other activities including government business balance 6.9 per cent."[15]

Even if there are certain problems of analysis and appropriation of costs in banking industry serious efforts have been made in several countries to develop methods of costing suitable to the bank operations.

In the United States of America, in early twenties, number of articles were published in the banking journals highlighting the importance of careful analysis of the relationship between revenue cost and profits of different bank activities. In 1940, Willian C. Remper first developed scientific methods of cost analysis. The president of the first National Bank of Parkston, South Dakota (USA) and the Chairman of the Bank Management Committee of the South Dakota Bankers Association defined "Bank Cost Analysis". It is defined "as a method of allocating a portion of all expenses of a bank to each of the activities in order to determine the cost of each item transaction."

The Federal Reserve Bank of USA, through their functional

cost analysis programme, developed a system of complete cost analysis." To bring effective cost accounting within the reach of even the smallest banks, the Federal Reserve Bank of New York in 1958, began developing a simplified functional cost analysis, which has since been greatly expanded and is now available to member banks in all twelve Federal Reserve districts."[16]

Banks are performing fund activities as well as non-fund activities. Banks are providing several services to their customers. They earn the revenue from both fund and non-fund services. In activities, interest is the major revenue but banks also charge non-fund services. The pricing of such services is based on the cost of services.

Pricing of services is an area of management and in absence of scientific pricing system, the present practice of pricing of services in Indian banks is mostly arbitrary and not based on costing exercise.

The cost estimates have to be the basis for pricing the services. As generation of profit is must for any commercial organisation, cost factor cannot be ignored in pricing of services. However, considering the Indian banks' commitment to social banking, the profit factor can not be the sole guiding factor in pricing. The principle of cross subsidisation in pricing should continue to be of relevance and at the same time, each activity cost has to be recovered from the respective activity income. In this context, the activity-wise cost benefit analysis assumes great importance.

In the changing environment, the importance of customers' satisfaction and the cost awareness has to percolate to all layers of the bank. Effective customer education would be very useful in convincing the customers to pay a higher price for improved quality of service.

The emerging scenario calls for radical changes in

functioning of commercial banks towards their service activities in a big way during the years ahead to strengthen their profitability. In this regard, service based income is far superior to fund based income as there is no need to have larger capital for earning similar amount of income through fund based activities and there is no need to make large provisions against erosion of non performing assets.

Banks abroad earn huge income from their diversified services (Non fund activities). The ratio of ancillary service activities' income to total income is 49 per cent in Swiss banks, 38 per cent in US banks, 41 per cent in the UK banks and 36 per cent in German banks. However, the Indian Banks earn only 12 per cent of their income from their ancillary services.

"Costing of bank services and products is a technique and process of ascertaining cost of various bank services and product. The major aims of costing are:

i) Ascertainment of cost,
ii) Control of cost,
iii) Determination of selling price,
iv) Guidance to frame business policy.

The financial reforms implemented in the Indian Banking Sector have created intense competition and reduced the profit margins of banks. These developments call for decisions based on quantitative techniques, which have made costing of bank services and products very important. The pricing process also has become very important. The pricing process environment and scientific costing analysis will product in the years ahead."[17]

Certain studies cover economies of scale in banking, i.e. size and cost relationship—

"If there is a relationship between the total operating

costs of banks and the size of banks, an understanding of this relationship will enable us to determine the most desirable size of banks, at least from the cost angle. If the relationship is such that the marginal cost is constant at all levels of output then it implies that there is no limit to size. If on the other hand, marginal cost declines and then rises it is possible to obtain the least cost size."[18]

Broadly, the method adopted is to estimate the total cost function of banks from a cross section sample. From the estimated total cost function, marginal cost curve and average cost curve is derived, which enables to draw conclusion on the impact of size of banks on operating expenses.

Dr. C. Rangarajan and Paul Mampilly studied top thirty banks' data in which ratio of interest to total expenditure varied between 70 per cent to 80 per cent. But, interest was excluded from total costs, as there could not be any scale economics in this element. The other elements in the cost considered are:

i) Printing and stationery,
ii) Postage telegrams and telephones,
iii) Rent for premises,
iv) Depreciation of physical assets.

Level of Deposits is taken as variable representing all activities of the bank to compare with cost. The findings of the study were:

i) Cost was minimum at the level of deposits' amounting to Rs. 300 crores,
ii) Marginal cost increased slowly between deposits level ranging from Rs.300 crores to Rs.400 crores,
iii) Sharp increase in marginal cost occurred after deposits crosses Rs. 500 crores."[19]

Alhadeff and Howitz in the year 1965 analysed the relation between size of the bank and its total operating cost as a per cent of loans and investments. Both have found that costs as a per cent of loans and investments decline for banks with less than approximately $5 million of total deposits remaining fairly constant for banks holding $5 and $25 to $50 million in deposits and then again decline for larger banks.[20]

"Gramely used multiple regression technique to examine the relationship between size and cost of banks from a sample of 270 member banks of Tenth Federal District. He found that the co-efficient for the logarithm of total cost to total assets fell as bank size increased. Bank size and other characteristics are namely:

i) Ratio of time deposits to total deposit,
ii) The ratio of total loans to total assets,
iii) The ratio of consumer loans to total loans and
iv) The percentage growth of assets from 1956 to 1959 accounted for 62 per cent of the variation in total cost."[21]

"To meet the higher cost of operations, the banks have to naturally mobilise a larger volume of business which alone could bring in adequate income despite lower interest margin available on advances. The need for larger working capital and lending business becomes all the more necessary when viewed in the context of all-round increase in the salaries and allowances. In order to effectively compete with the other segments of the banking system, a bank has to necessarily go in for duly trained and well qualified staff operate from adequately furnished premises located in decent locality, incur higher rentals for premises, particularly in larger metropolitan center, energy charges etc.

It may be observed that no provision has been made for the costs that have to be incurred by the banks, particularly those operating in metropolitan centers, towards mechanisation for clearing house operations. Similarly, the expenditure that a bank has to incur towards training of its staff, setting up of training establishment, internal and branch inspection machinery has also not been provided for in the above exercise. In the context of higher cost, the banks' have to incur on the various aspects, their earnings have also to be commensurate with such costs. The banks have to necessarily strive to increase the volume of business to maximise their earnings to meet the above costs."[22]

Costs of funds include mainly interest component and establishment expenses. Studies have taken both components separately as well as jointly. In raising funds for banking, the sources are deposits, borrowings and owned funds of the bank. For all these sources cost of fund is not same. Only deposits constitute current, saving and term deposits. Cost of all types of deposits is different. In some of the studies these all sources taken together is called "common pool approach". Junare expressed that the banks can lower the costs of funds by managing the mix of funds in favorable position.[23]

First Approach—Common Pool Approach

"All funds both cost bearing and non cost bearing received through different resources make a common pool."

Mathematical Representation

$$\text{Effective Rate of Funds' cost} = \frac{\text{Cost of cost bearing funds}}{\text{Volume of cost bearing funds} + \text{Volume of non cost bearing funds}}$$

Second Approach - Cost Of Loanable Funds

Mathematical Representation

$$\text{Cost of loanable funds} = \frac{\text{Interest paid} - \text{Interest earned on CRR and SLR}}{\text{Total funds} - \text{Funds Blocked in CRR and SLR}}$$

In a hypothetical example, interest paid on deposits of Rs. 100 is Rs. 10 but the cost of loanable fund is Rs.12.5 as calculated because of SLR 25 per cent with interest 5 per cent and CRR 3 per cent without interest.

"A commercial bank keeps raising funds from various sources. Conceptually all these funds enter into a common pool of funds. And then the rest of the problem of funds management is basically the deployment of these funds or asset management. This is done in such a manner that the criteria of profitability, liquidity, safety and national priorities for credit allocation are satisfied. However banks do not enjoy full freedom in this regard. A part of total funds entering the common pools has to be used for carrying cash reserves and other highly liquid assets including investment in government and other eligible bonds and securities. These assets on an average earn lower rates of interest compared to what a commercial bank is ordinarily able to earn on its loans and advances portfolio. The same logic can be extended to concessional lending to certain borrowers which are accorded a favored treatment under national property guidelines issued by Government or Central Monetary Authority. In India a certain percentage of loans and advances is being stipulated for this purpose."[24]

"Cost of funds is considered to be most appropriate for all types of comparisons and decisions, this is based on following reasons:

i) Cost needs to be defined for the bank as a whole taking all funds raised by the bank during the period such that total funds raised from different sources equal total funds deployed in cash inventory and reserves, investments, loans, and advances and other assets including fixed assets,

ii) All funds are assumed to flow into a common pool, no source of fund is related to any specific use or uses of funds,

iii) Cost of funds needs to be calculated totally separately and independently of the revenues arising from deployment of funds at no stage while measuring cost of funds they should get mixed up with each other,

iv) Interest cost needs to be calculated in terms of effective rates by relating average outstanding to actual amount of interest paid and not in terms of nominal rates,

v) Cost needs to be reckoned as total cost by adding manpower and all other operating costs to the interest cost to arrive at the over all cost of funds to the bank and similarly related service charges recovered need to be deducted."[25]

The methodology can be developed by any individual bank within the framework of uniform parameters provided by the Reserve Bank of India. While foreseeing the success of such a system, some issues deserve deliberation. On the expense side, around 65 per cent of total is constituted by interest costs. Since the interest rates are decided and revised by the RBI, what is left to the bank is to make efforts to change the deposit—mix in favour of current deposits, which are apparently least costly. However, the process of changing the deposits mix has been historically gradual and slow. It is likely to be equally slow, so that annually visible gain in terms of saving of interest cost may not be attainable.

The other major component of total expenses is staff cost, which normally accounts for around 20 per cent. The comparative positions of some bank reveals that around 2 per cent of working funds during last decade are represented as staff cost.

"The banks have been called upon to enhance the profitability when the deployment pattern of resources is as under:"[26]

Resources	Rs. 100
SLR / CRR	Rs. 49
Priority sector	Rs. 22
Residual	Rs. 29

In Banking Industry, the major costs are interest on deposits and establishment expenses. This must be covered by proper deployment of funds. The attempt, therefore, should be to ensure that the costs are minimised and incomes are maximised while rendering banking services satisfactorily.

Management of Deposit Mix

"One of the method of cost reduction would be to have a proper mix of different kinds of deposits. The banks ought to plan for appropriate distribution of deposits into current, where there is no interest cost but may be high servicing cost; savings bank, where there is low interest cost; and time. In case of time deposits, while the interest rate varies according to the range of maturity periods, more of even such deposits in shorter maturates will tend to reduce the interest cost. Given the structure of interest rates the choice left to the bank is to have a proper composition of its deposits and accordingly, evolve a suitable strategy for mobilising deposits with a view to maintaining a favorable deposit mix to minimise the costs of its funds."[27]

"Banks' expenditure on staff is estimated to be about 20-25 per cent of their total expenditure."[28]

"The servicing cost of small accounts is very high. The deposit mix in recent years has changed more in favour of term deposits with longer maturity, which carry higher interest costs.

Term deposits with a maturity of over 5 years form over 61.8 per cent of total deposits in 1980 as against 38.4 per cent in 1976 and 6.2 per cent in 1970. Thus the cost of resources in going up the earnings have been reduced with increasing proportion of low yielding assets."[29]

"The banking industry differs from other industry in several respects. Three important characteristics of the banking industry are worth noting:

i) It is a multiproduct service industry,
ii) It is extremely labour intensive in the sense of a very low ratio of fixed assets to labour and
iii) Borrowed funds form the bulk of capital employed and hence interest cost of these funds are an important constituent of costs."[30]

Assessing the profits and profitability of banks in general and Indian Banks in particular, can be complex exercise. The accounting standards governing the disclosure and presentation of information exempt banks in India giving meaningful details of their financial positions. No meaningful information relevant for systematic analysis of performance of banks is made available in their balance sheets and Profit and Loss Accounts. In contrast, much detailed disclosures are made by commercial banks in foreign countries either voluntarily or due to statutory disclosure requirement.

"The main determinants of the interest earning and interest costs are:

i) The structure of the interest rates on deposits and advances including investments,
ii) The structure of deposits, i.e., the proportion of current savings and time deposits in total deposits.,
iii) Monetary policy measures particularly CRR, SLR, Priority sector credit allocations etc., and
iv) Proportion of various categories of advances.

Non-priority, priority sectors, the government fixes foods and banks in India have very little control over them. Even the structure of deposits over which bank are believed to have some influence, in practice by interest differential as between various types of deposits and the level of overall interest rates, rather than by the marketing efforts of the bank. As customer becomes aware of the potential for improving their yield by more efficient management of their funds, the scope for the banks to have large interest free current account deposits or low interest bearing savings bank deposits as hither to enjoyed by them will become increasingly limited. A close examination of the trend of the yield on investment, yield on advances and interest cost will throw light on the factors responsible for the decline in net interest earning."[31]

"The main conclusion that emerges from the analysis is that the difference between the average costs of funds and the effective yields on funds is much more than what is reflected in the conventional spread analysis. This means that a good part of the financial surplus generated by the financial intermediation activities of commercial banks in India went to government kitty in the form of subsidised funds and special interest tax. The proportion of total financial surplus generated by the banks that went to the government in the form lower cost of funds."[32]

"The cost of loanable funds is determined by the cost of deposits, establishment expenses and other administrative costs and also proportion of DTL pre-empted by way of CRR and SLR, taking into account the earnings on such pre-emptiness. For a bank to be in a lending business must meet the statutory and other monetary prescription determined by the RBI from time to time. Thus the balance after meeting these pre-emptiness only would be available for lending. In any case, banks have to keep certain minimum cash balance with them to meet operational liquidity requirements. During the period 1970-79 the cash in hand averaged to about 2 per cent of the DTL and to that extent their SLR investments could have been reduced as cash in hand is also reckoned as a part of SLR. Taking all these factors into account, the cost of loanable funds during 1970-79 has been worked out. The cost of loanable funds steadily increased from 8.59 per cent in 1970 to 13.7 per cent in 1975 but after a slight fall in 1976 rose again to 14.56 per cent in 1977. In 1978 and 1979 it stood at 12.98 per cent and 1988 respectively."[33]

"One of the important problem encountered in cost analysis in banking industry is the association of cost with output. In other words, the problem is that of allocating and apportioning cost over time and product in cost investigation. The problem of time period arises when an output is produced in one period and the costs of its production are recorded in another period. The problem is likely to be greater when the time period is shorter. So most cost analysis have employed annual cross section figures, a procedure that reduces the problems relating to allocation and apportionment over time period and provides a sufficient number of observations for a meaningful accounting analysis. In multi-product firms, the identification of costs with a particular type of output is difficult. The banking industry in India does not involve in great problems of joint production and joint cost for broad groups of output, such as demand deposits and consumer loans. Therefore allocation and apportionment of operating cost of each type of its broad categories of output is possible."[34]

"Complex and difficult problem of cost analysis regarding apportionment of overhead cost is supervisory and administrative expenses. The more highly a bank is departmentalised, the more ready can a major portion of its income and expenses be objectively distributed to clear cut departments and functions. In a very small bank only a few (three or four) employees participate actively in nearly all the bank operations, making precise cost distribution virtually impossible."[35]

"Another important costing consequence resulting from the composition of bank cost is the difficulty of allocating the cost of funds to specific revenue areas. Unlike a manufacturing enterprise, a bank has difficulty in identifying the specific uses of its major inputs — the funds. It is often difficult to trace the cost and source of funds of the particular loan. For instance, current account funds of customers' cost significantly less to obtain that 'bought' funds from the money market. When money is re-lent to customers, it becomes impossible to match the funds lent with those bought, borrowed or obtained as deposits on current account. Management must realise the costing problems inherent in allocating the cost of funds and effect of the same on profit allocation, evaluation of efficiency having pricing, production and marketing strategies."[36]

"From the foregoing analysis of empiric, it emerges that while the supply of credit by bankers is elastic to the lending rates, the demand for credit is not. This finding has a crystal clear implication for an excellent use of interest rate weapon for effective policy purpose. While it is expected that an increase deposit interest rates would substantially raise the volume of deposit supply, the study seems to reveal that a simultaneous increase in advance rates which is necessary to pay higher deposit rates, will not curb the demand for credit to any significant extent. In other words, if the banking assets and the lending capacity of the banks is to increase sharply, it can be achieved by simultaneously raising the deposit rates and advance rates.

Concluding, we may say that when national income is rising and state of business in the country is good, there is a great deal to be gained in terms of expansion of banking services. Bank capabilities to render more and better services, if deposits rates and lending rates were simultaneously increased."[37]

It should be viewed as an opportunity to convert Indian banking into a strong sound and vibrant system capable of playing its role efficiently and effectively and making due contribution to the growth and progress of the rural sector of the Indian economy.

"Competition in the banking industry has become more keen and intense than ever before with the entry of new private sector banks and more foreign banks. Competition among banks may be based on price, quality of service, products, offer of specialised services, technology, skill, location advantages and strategy of early entry.

Earlier, in an era of fully administered interest rates on deposits and advances, price based competition was not prevalent in the banking industry. However, with the phased deregulation of interest rates on advances as well as on deposits, banking industry will witness competition based on product pricing. It will not be long before the service charges on ancillary services too will be freed from regulated pricing mechanism and once that happens, banks' vying with each other to step up their fee-based income would accentuate price based competition in the banking industry."[38]

"No doubt under deregulated, globalised environment margins are expected to become thinner and thinner. It is a situation where the fittest and the fastest will survive. The environment will weed out weaker units. How to face the challenges is more important than identifying measures to remedy the reducing margins. Banks having lower spread are expected to immediately hurt by the competition.

Gradual deregulation of interest rates has resulted in a rate-war where each bank is trying to offer better rates both to depositors and borrowers. As a result the gap between maximum term deposit rate and minimum lending rate on advances over Rs.2 lac limit has come down from 7 per cent in 1991 to 5 per cent in 1994 and 2 per cent in 1996. A scenario has been created where only strongest and fittest will survive. Banks with high cost of deposits, low yield on advances and investments, lower ratio of other incomes to total income, high Non-Performing Assets (NPA) are expected to hit severely. All banks should join together to ensure ethical banking so that weaker one get time to improve themselves. Better assets liability management favourable deposit mix, high yield on advances and investments, low level of NPAs, improved non-interest income etc. will hold the key to survival in the immediate future."[39]

"In order to study cost benefit analysis of any proposition or scheme, the cost of different functions and services rendered by the bank should be available. It is in the fitness of the things that the RBI had initiated certain costing exercises for the industry as a whole and directed all the banks to open separate costing sells for taking up subsequently the exercises themselves. In the near future, each individual bank is expected to have a well designed cost information system for assessing the servicing costs of various functions performed by banking."[40]

REFERENCES

1. Ref.: A. K. Roy, chief manager Dena Bank Head office Bombay *IBA Bulletin* Vol. XV Sep. 1993 p. 6.
2. Ref.: Cost of Banking Services, *RBI Bulletin*, April 1978, p. 224.
3. Ref.: S. K. Verghese, *Profits and Profitability of Indian Commercial Banks in Seventies*, National Institute of Bank Management, pp. 72 and 73.
4. Ref.: Report of Study Group on banking cost, Banking Commission Government of India, Bombay, 1971 p. 164.
5. Ref.: Shri R. G. Saraiya, chairman Banking Commission report Government of India publication 1972.
6. Ref.: Shri R. G. Saraiya, chairman, Banking Commission, Report of the Banking Commission, Government of India Publication 1972.
7. Ref.: Report of committee on PEP, p. 45.
8. Ref.: Manual on costing by RBI 1989, p. 1.
9. Ref.: R.N. Malhotra, Ex-Governor, Reserve Bank of India said "Bank should make special efforts to improve their productivity and creating cost consciousness at all levels.
10. Ref.: Vipin Shah, *Cost and Efficiency in Banking*, p. 3.

11. Ref.: R. Elan, Manager United Bank of India Article Costing of Bank services and products,' *IBA Bulletin*, Vol. XVII, No. 12 December 95, p. 13.
12. Ref.: P.P. Pathless, Manager, The Federal Bank, Always profit planning by Banks strategies for the 21st Century, *IBA Bulletin*, December 1998, pp. 28, 30.
13. Ref.: R. G. Saraiya Chairman, Banking Commission, Report of the Banking Commission, Government of India, 1972, p. 296.
14. Ref. S.D. Tripathi, Indian Banking towards 21st Century issues and perspectives, Deep and Deep Publications, pp. 27 and 28.
15. Ref.: Sureshchand Garg, *Indian Banking: Cost and Profitability*, Anmol Publications Pvt. Ltd., Delhi, p. 66.
16. Ref.: Crossc, Howard D. and Heupel George H., *Management Policies for Commercial Banks*, Prentice Hall, p. 103.
17. Ref.: R. Elango, Manager United Bank of India, Costing of Bank services and products, *IBA Bulletin*, Volume XVII, No. 12 December 1995, p. 8.
18. Studied by Ex-Governor of RBI Dr. C. Rangarajan and Paul Mampilly.
19. Ref.: C. Rangarajan, Indian Institute of Management, Paul Mampilly National Institute of Bank Management Economies of scale in Banking, Technical studies prepared for Banking Commission Volume - I published by RBI in 1972.
20. Alhadeff David — A Monopoly and Competition in Banking, University of California Barkeley 1954 and Horvtz Paul M. Economies of scale in banking, *The Journal of Finance*, May 1965.
21. Ref.: Gramely Lyle E. A study of scale of Economics in banking, Federal Reserve Bank of Kansas City, 1962.
22. Ref.: Standing Advisory Committee for Urban Co-operative Bank, Reserve Bank of India 1985, p. 68.
23. S. O. Junare, Faculty Member, Udaybhansinhji Institute of Co-operative Management Gandhinagar. Article " Concept of Cost in Urban Co-operative Banks". *Journal of Institute 'Sahayog'*.
24. Varsha S. Varde and Sampat P. Singh, *Profitability of Commercial Banks*, National Institute of Bank Management, p. 72.
25. Varsha S. Varde and Sampat P. Singh, *Profitability of Commercial Banks*, National Institute of Bank Management, p. 80.
26. Shri K. Kannan General Manager (0/5) BOB Workshop on iProfit Planning February 4 to 6, 1988 proceeding. Banker Training College, RBI Bombay pp. 45, 46 and 47.

27. Dr. P.D. Ojha, Dy. Governor of RBI, Workshop on Profit Planning proceeding 4 to 6 Feb 1988. Bankers Training College, RBI, Bombay, p. 7.
28. *Statistical Tables*, RBI 1982, p. 31.
29. Sureshchand Garg, *Indian Banking: Cost and Profitability*, p. 38.
30. Report of Study Group of Banking Commission, Govt. of India on Banking Cost, 1971, p. 10.
31. Report of Study Group of Banking Commission, Govt. of India on Banking Cost, 1971, pp. 28 and 29.
32. Report of study Group of Banking Commission, Govt. of India on Banking Cost, 1971, pp. 41 to 42.
33. S. R. Verghese, pp. 46 & 47.
34. Dr. P.V. Ramana Murty, *Cost and Profitability of Public Sector Banks*, p. 59.
35. *Cost Accounting in Banking Industry*, ICWAI Culcutta, 1979, p. 80.
36. S.C. Garg, *Indian Banking: Cost and Profitability*, p. 44, 45.
37. H. S. Sandhu and RPS Hundal, Guru Nankdev University Amritsar, An empirical Model of Commercial Bank Credit in India, Indian Banking Towards 21st Century, Deep and Deep Publications, New Delhi, p. 128.
38. Ref.: K.S. Gopal Senior Manager, The Vysya Bank, Banglore, *IBA Bulletin*, January 1997 p. 11.
39. Ref.: N. Parameshwar, Manager BOB Baroda, *IBA Bulletin*, January 1997, p. 41.
40. Ref.: Prof. B. Satyamurty, NIBM, Profitability and Productivity in Banks Concepts and Evaluation Workshop on Profit Planning, Feb. 4 to 6 1988 proceedings. Bankers Training College, RBI Bombay, p. 81.

3

Profile of Urban Co-operative Banks

BRIEF HISTORY

Introduction

As stated in the previous chapters, there are many aspects to be dealt in, in order to understand the contribution of Urban Co-operative Banks in India. It is worthwhile to document a profile of Urban Co-operative Banks in India. These banks hold the social responsibility to fulfill the financial and investment needs of "Small Man" of Indian society.

Brief History

Germany is called the birthplace of Urban Co-operative Credit Movement in the world. Francis Haeck established first Co-operative Credit Society in Belgium, in 1848. This credit society operated as an investment organisation rather than co-operative. In 1850, Schulze Delitszch started Urban Credit Society with a view to inculcating the habit of thrift among the members and to grant them credit for variety of purposes on personal security and at lower rate of interest. The pioneer experiment of Urban Co-operative banking became successful in the year 1855 in Germany. Then the concept of Urban Co-operative banking spread from Germany to Italy. Professor Luigi Luzzatti's dedication proved useful in Italy.

The Co-operative Credit Societies Act was passed in 1904, which helped in organising Co-operative Credit Movement in India. This act laid special emphasis on promotion and development of Agricultural Co-operative Credit Societies. But, soon after the passing of this act, at the initiative and efforts of local leadership, some Urban Co-operative Credit Societies were registered. In the year 1904 at Kanjeevarm, Madras Urban Co-operative Credit Society was registered. Later in the year 1905, two co-operative credit societies were started:

i) Betgiri Co-operative Credit Society, Dharwar district in Bombay province,
ii) The Bangalore City Co-operative Credit Society at Mysore State.

The report of committee on co-operation published in 1915 says "Urban Co-operative Societies might serve a useful purpose in training the upper and middle urban classes to understand ordinary banking principles." As per the report of the committee, Urban Co-operative Banks were operating in Madras, Bengal, Bihar, Orissa, Punjab and Assam. Subsequently several Banking Inquiry Committees also recommended for developing Urban Co-operative Banks. In the year 1930, Baroda State Banking Inquiry Committee and in the year 1931, Bombay Provincial Banking Inquiry Committee underlined the importance of these banks in promoting banking habits among urban people and granting them credit on easy terms.

In the year 1931, the report of Indian Central Banking Inquiry Committee was published. It has stated " The duty of these urban banks should be to try to do for small traders, the small merchants and the middle class population what commercial banks are doing for the big traders and the big merchants."

In an important development in the year 1935, The Reserve Bank of India was established. Agriculture Credit Department of RBI recognised the importance of Urban Co-operative Banking in India and started publishing the important statistics related to working of Urban Banks.

Under the Chairmanship of Shri R.G. Saraiya, the Committee on "Co-operative Planning" in 1946 reported that "Joint Stock Banks are not interested in developing the business of small loans because cost of advancing and recovering them is high. Further, as Joint Stock Banks are not likely to have, under ordinary circumstances, full and intimate knowledge of the standing and resources of a person of moderate means. They will not advance loans on personal security. On the other hand, there are, in urban areas, number of persons with small means, like traders and merchants, artisans, factory workers, street hawkers, motor drivers who resort to moneylenders and similar agencies for small loans and obtain them at high rate of interest. Ex-servicemen like technicians and skilled workmen like carpenter, blacksmith, mechanics etc. will also require credit for setting up their own business in small work shops. Co-operative Urban Banks qualify by establishing personal and intimate relationship with people of this class as the most suitable agencies for serving their credit need."

The Reserve Bank of India surveyed and studied all aspects of Urban Co-operative Banks during the year 1957-58. The report published in 1961 made valuable suggestions on how to develop urban banks on sound lines. The report stated "The general picture of Urban Co-operative banking which emerges out of this study is one of a fairly widespread, financially sound, expanding useful framework of banking institution which have their own place of importance in banking structure of a large part of the country."

Again the Reserve Bank of India appointed the working group on Industrial Financing through co-operative banks in 1968. This working group assigned new role to these banks by urging them to provide financial assistance to Small-Scale Industries.

In the year 1971, for the first time, Reserve Bank of India conducted a seminar of Chief Executive Officers of Urban

Co-operative Banks. Seminar was convened at Banker Training College, Poona. The seminar made useful contribution to the development of Urban Co-operative Banks.

First All India Conference of Urban Co-operative Banks and Credit Societies was organised at Ahmedabad in March 1978. This was organised jointly by National Federation of Urban Co-operative Banks and Credit Societies and Gujarat Urban Co-operative Banks' Federation. Conference was well attended by delegates from different States of India and top-level policy makers in the field of urban banking.

Growth Profile

Brief Background

The year 1848 saw a birth of first co-operative credit society in Belgium, soon after this in the year 1889, people of Vadodara formed their own credit society and named it as Kavathekar Mandali. Later on this Mandali was known as The Anyonya Sahayakari Mandali Co-operative Bank Ltd. Opening of this co-operative credit bank in Vadodara has a historical significance. With this, Vadodara City earned the reputation of being the first city to have a co-operative credit society not only in the entire Indian sub-continent but also in Asia. Credit for this historical achievement goes to Prof. V.L. Kavathekar, an eminent Professor of Economics in the princely State of Gaekwads. He could very well visualise the financial difficulties faced by middle and lower income groups as well as economically and socially marginalised masses in the urban and rural areas for their day-to-day economic needs. These people were easy prey in the hands of private moneylenders. Often these strata of people used to live a life long economic and social slavery under these private moneylenders popularly known as "Sahukars".

The Jambusar People's Co-operative Bank Ltd. located in Bharuch district was the next such bank opened in the year 1909 and is formerly recognised as the first Urban Co-operative bank in Gujarat State.

Big financial institutions rather failed to fulfil the task of catering to the needs of economically weaker sections. Therefore the idea of credit co-operative banks became an immanent objective need. A look at the data of The Anyonya Sahayakari Bank, Table 3.01 indicates a phenomenal growth of the bank since 1889 onwards. Its growth over the years is an indication of the faith of people expressed in the bank. There is a great rush for the membership in most of these banks, a direct reflection of credit co-operative movements' success.

TABLE 3.01

PROGRESS OF THE ANYONYA SAHAYAKARI MANDALI CO-OPERATIVE BANK LTD.

Particulars	*Year 1889 Rs.*	*Year 1998 Rs.*
Share Capital	75	24178490
Deposits	763	1260522258
Advances	325	631863678
Profit	15	14280888
Branches	NIL	10

Source: Annual reports of Anyonya Co-operative Mandali Co-operative Bank Ltd.

The Urban Co-operative movement started in India with the objective of helping small traders, artisans, factory workers and fixed income salaried masses. These Co-operative Banks served two main purposes, firstly to free the large low income and poor population from the clutches of private money-lenders and secondly to inculcate the habit of thrift and saving.

The review report of Reserve Bank of India in the year 1939-40 acknowledges the prominent role of these credit Co-operative banks in serving the credit needs of urban masses. From time to time, reviews on the progress of these banks have been undertaken in order to strengthen the functioning and also to make the services of these banks more socially relevant, thereby necessitating the reforming of the objectives of these banks. However, the main function of these banks remains to accept the deposits from the members and non-members as well as advancing loans to its members in need.

These Urban Co-operative Banks were brought under the provisions of the Banking Regulation Act 1949, in the year 1966. Prior to this, these credit Co-operative banks were considered as co-operative societies, thus covered under the preview of Co-operative Societies Acts of the respective States. These banks were required to apply to the RBI, for a license to conduct the banking business. The RBI didn't interfere with the powers of these banks regarding organisation, registration, management and winding-up of the business. These banks are continued to be under the Co-operative Societies Acts of the concerned State for these matters.

Government of India appointed a study group, in the year 1963, on "The Credit Co-operatives in the Non Agriculture Sector", known as Varde Committee. The important recommendations of Varde Committee are worth mentioning here:

i) The committee suggested one bank for one area of operation, else there would be increased competition for the deposits if the numbers of banks were more. The study suggests restriction of the area of operation to certain ward or same categories of person so that there is no overlapping of jurisdiction of different banks,

ii) These banks should ensure to have only one class of members and the practice of nominal membership should be abandoned. In case where a member is allowed for the nominal membership due to his inability to purchase shares in the initial stage, such type of members should be persuaded to become permanent members at the earliest by purchasing the required shares of the bank,

iii) The Board of Directors should be elected by adopting election once in a three-year or each year or by rotation for one third of the Board. The committee rates the later system more desirable,

iv) The depositors should be persuaded to become members in order to have a Board of Directors of higher confidence,

v) To strengthen the fund position of new banks or for the banks in need of funds, the State may contribute up to Rs.25,000 on a matching basis in order to make-up a minimum level of share capital of Rs. 50,000 per Urban Bank. This contribution should be recovered within one year. To safeguard its financial interest the State Government may nominate up to 3 directors but not exceeding one third of the total strength of directors,

vi) Banks showing promising progress and efficient management should be allowed to receive the investments of surplus funds of local bodies, educational bodies, etc.,

vii) Before permitting any branch of any of the Commercial Banks in the operational area of any Urban Credit Co-operative Banks, the capacity and the scope of development of the Urban Co-operative credit banks should be considered,

viii) The apex co-operative should finance the Urban Co-operative Banks as and when needed for their development. There should be a representation of these banks in the Board of Directors of Central Co-operative Banks,

ix) There should be a diversification of loans in order to widespread the financial market for these urban credit co-operative banks,

Membership

The membership of an Urban Co-operative bank is limited

to the persons residing in city and town; they may be salaried employees, factory workers, small traders or artisans etc.

Variations are seen with regard to the average members per bank in the different States. Tamil Nadu has the highest membership of 7000 per bank (128 Banks) followed by Maharashtra - 3000 members (358 banks) and Orissa 1800 members (13 banks). However, the average membership in Madhya Pradesh and Rajasthan was found at the lowest i.e. 1000 members (42 banks) and 300 members (23 banks) respectively.

The total shareholders of all the Urban Co-operative Banks in the State stood at 12.11 lacs at the end of June 1983 against the urban population of 106.02 lacs, as per census 1981. Thus the urban banks have covered about 11.42 per cent of urban population of the State. Membership increased by 9.25 per cent in the year 1983, later from the year 1989 to 1993 approximately there is an increase of four per cent every year. Whereas in the year 1998 total number of members were 28.13 lacs. A constant increase reflects that the people of Gujarat seem to be more interested in active participation of Urban Co-operative Banks' functioning. But on the other side of the coin, the study reflected that the Urban Co-operative Banks covers only 39 per cent of the urban population. Thus there is still wide scope for Urban Co-operative Banks to increase the membership in urban area of Gujarat. In the said study, it is assumed that from one family there is one member of Urban Co-operative bank and one family is assumed to be of five members.

There is a wide disparity in the membership figures from different districts of Gujarat state, Vadodara attains first position by having 70 per cent membership of the Urban Co-operative Banks of the district. The membership figures are based on the assumption that at least one member from each family would avail the membership in these banks.

Areas of Operation

As per its byelaws, an Urban Co-operative Bank is expected to function within the municipal jurisdiction or in the town. The study group on credit co-operative has recommended that "Normally, it is advisable for the Urban Co-operative Banks to restrict its areas of operations to the Municipality or Taluka town." [1]

Management Structure

The apex body of an Urban Co-operative bank comprises of the general body of its members. For the regular routine affairs of the bank, the Board of Director(s) is / are elected from the members of the bank. The tenure of the directors varies in different States. Normal practice to appoint the directors is to hold election every year by rotation for one third of the Board of Directors. The Varde Committee (1963) has observed that the large number of directors continued to get elected on term after term basis in most of these banks. To get new Directors in the Board, the committee suggested to insert a clause that "No director should be allowed to contest for more than two consecutive terms." This is to prevent the same members from getting re-elected term after the term. The findings of the committee also highlighted the advantages of continuance of senior members in the Board for better management as well as to ensure commitment to the service. The staff in these banks should be professionally trained for its growth as well as service to its members.

Mobilisation of Deposits

In the time span from 1983 to 1992, a seven-fold increase in the deposits of Urban Co-operative Banks is observed.[2] The tally of deposits stood at Rs. 813.35 lacs in the year 1992, as against Rs. 187.05 lacs in the year 1983. The average deposit per bank is also in conformity with the growth of the deposits. In the year 1983, the average deposits per bank was Rs. 1,84,536,52 lacs, which rose to Rs. 10,64,672.17 lacs in the year 1992. During three financial years i.e. 1995-96, 1996-97 and 1997-98 deposits of Urban Co-operative Banks have again increased steadily alongwith an increase in number of bank offices. The bank offices in the year 1995-96 of Urban Co-operative Banks were 1327 which rose to 1363 in the year 1996-97 a net increase is 36 bank offices. Subsequently for the year 1997-98 this increase in the Urban Co-operative Bank is about 53.

TABLE 3.02

DEPOSIT MOBILISED BY URBAN CO-OPERATIVE BANKS IN INDIA

Sr. No.	*Items*	*Financial Years* 1995-96	1996-97	1997-98
1	No. of Banks reporting	1,327	1,363	1,416
2	Deposits	24,165	30,714	38,472
3	Growth	4,064	6,549	7,758
4	Per cent Growth	20.2	27.1	25.3

Source: *Report on Trend and Progress of Banking in India 1997-98*, p. 24, RBI Publication.

Similarly deposit of these 1416 Urban Co-operative Banks in the financial year 1998 amounted to Rs. 38,472 crores, a record increase of 25.3 per cent in 1997-98.[3]

These figures reflect the confidence that banks have earned from its members and non-members. There is a clear increase in the money flow from non-members over the period mentioned. These banks are allowed to have deposits in the current, saving and fixed accounts. The bulk about 63 per cent of deposits are in the fixed deposits accounts. The remaining 37 per cent consist of current and saving accounts.

The increase in deposit mobilisation during 1966 to 1977 was about 239 per cent and during 1983 to 1992 were about 323 per cent. This increase is attributed to two factors; one is growth in the branches of these banks as a result reaching to more and more segments of society; Secondly, the overwhelming confidence expressed by the people as seen in the increase in the membership and thus contributing in the deposits. There is also a significant increase in the deposits from non-members.

TABLE 3.03

AVERAGE DEPOSIT MOBILISED BY URBAN BANKS IN INDIA

Sr. No.	*Year*	*No. of Banks*	*Total Deposits Mobilised (Rs. in Crores.)*	*Avg. Deposit Mobilised Per Bank (Rs.)*
1	1983	1175	157.05	1,84,536.52
2	1984	1208	207.94	2,51,196.00
3	1986	1241	297.49	3,69,183.42
4	1988	1275	431.40	5,50,031.21
5	1990	1283	533.17	6,84,502.51
6	1991	1305	741.46	9,67,609.80
7	1992	1309	813.35	10,64,672.17
8	1996	1327	24165	18,21,024.8
9	1997	1363	30714	22.53 Crores
10	1998	1416	38472	27.17 Crores

Source: *Year Book of Gujarat* Urban Co-operative Banks Federation and RBI 1996, 97, 98.

Financial Resources of the Urban Co-operative Banks

These banks would have the sources of finance from their own funds consisting of paid-up share capital and accumulated profit in various forms. The borrowings from central co-operative as well as the deposits from the members and non-members constitute the borrowed funds of these banks. To enable low-income group for membership, the face value of a share is kept at Rs. 10 per share. These members have to maintain ten per cent amount of borrowings in the form of share capital as per the bylaws.

TABLE 3.04

OWN FUNDS OF URBAN BANKS IN INDIA

Sr. No	*Year*	*Share Capital*	*Total Reserve*	*Own Fund*
1	1983	11,782.49	17,671.67	29,454.16
2	1984	14,010.77	22,942.53	36,953.30
3	1986	18,075.69	34,109.49	52,185.18
4	1989	24,325.67	53,917.43	78,243.10
5	1990	27,652.59	68,276.20	95,928.79
6	1991	34,976.66	97,603.07	1,32,579.73
7	1992	37,267.77	1,23,978.65	1,61,246.42
8	1996	397 crore	3451 crore	3848 Crore
9	1997	547 crore	4148 crore	4695 Crore
10	1998	606 crore	5053 crore	5659

Source: *Year Book of Urban Banks Federation* and *Report on Trend and Progress of Banking in India*, RBI Publication.

The State Government's share in these banks is baring a minimal amount. The reserves as have shown a 60 per cent increase from 1983 to 1992.

The loanable funds of the urban banks constitute the total resources available out of the above. Various factors such as statutory requirements for maintenance of cash reserve and liquid assets as under section 18 and 24 of Banking Regulation Act, 1949 limits the extent of actual funds available for loaning operations. Under the present Reserve Bank of India's directives, Banks are required to maintain 15 per cent CRR of their total demands and time liabilities, cash with The Reserve Bank of India. In total 36 per cent SLR in cash, treasury bills and investment in Union Government and State Government securities and other approved securities. Thus the amount available for lending is restricted to 49 per cent of the total resources of urban banks. (CRR – Cash Reserve Ratio; SLR = Statutory Liquidity Ratio). CRR and SLR requirements have fluctuated during these years. SLR reduced to 31.5 per cent and CRR to 10 per cent of DTL.

Loans and Advances

Advances play an important role in the gross earnings of Urban Banks and promote the economic development of the country. The basic function of credit is to enable individuals and business enterprises to purchase goods and or services. Demand for credit by business firm arises because of time process. Consumers demand credit to acquire goods in advance for which they pay later. The time gap between production, distribution and consumption gives scope for wide use of credit.

Among all the functions of banking, the lending of funds with or without security is most important. Balance sheets of Urban Co-operative Banks reflect about 85 per cent of their total revenue arises from interest and discount. Similarly the share of advances in total assets of the urban banks is about 70 per cent and thus advances act as the backbone of banking business. The strength of banking depends upon soundness of advances.

The power to create money is with Urban Co-operative Banks. Banks' loans are to be called as the indirect agents for productivity and activity. Urban Banks through their consumer loan contribute to consumption activity — creating constant demand for consumer goods like houses, furniture etc.

Classification of Advances

Bank credit may be classified in a variety of ways according to security, maturity, method of repayment and purpose. Generally banks' advances are classified as follows:

i) Cash credits,
ii) Overdraft demand loans,
iii) Term loans,
iv) Bills purchased,
v) Bill discounted.

i) *Cash Credits:*

It is a credit given in cash to business firms. The borrowers have to operate the account within a given limit as and when required. Cash credit is generally allowed against the pledge or hypothecation of goods against book debts or personal security.

ii) *Overdrafts:*

It is fluctuating account indicating the aggregate amount by which the depositors have over drawn. This facility is given to current account holders only. This enables the customers to draw over and above their balance up to the extent of the limit stipulated. The security for an overdraft account may be personal, shares, debentures, government securities etc.

iii) *Term loans:*

Normally term loan maturity period is longer than one year. A term loan provides the borrower with intermediate or long term capital funds. The maturity period is more than one year but less than ten years. This facility of term loan is designed to meet the borrowers' needs for credit for longer period. Next to cash credit, term loans have assumed great importance in advance portfolio of the banking system in the country.

iv) *Bills purchased:*

Bills are sometimes purchased from approved customers in whose favour regular limits are sanctioned. In this transaction bank holds the bill only as security for the advances.

v) *Bills discounted:*

The bills maturing within 30, 60 days or more are

discounted by the banks for approved customers. Bills of exchange discounted by the Banks are credited to customers account. In this type of advance, banks rely upon the credit worthiness of the endorser and the drawer.

There are other types of advances like demand loans, consumer credit, clean advance etc.

The resources of the banks as discussed earlier are not entirely available for loans and advances. The statutory reserve fund of Urban Co-operative Banks, as a rule, is to be invested. These investments are mainly in the Government Bonds and other Government Securities to maintain the Statutory Liquidity Ratio (SLR) as prescribed by The Reserve Bank of India from time to time.

The funds available for the loans are generally utilised for the following purposes:

i) Purchase of instruments and or materials required by the artisans,
ii) Petty trade and small industry,
iii) Payment of prior dues,
iv) Purchase of foodgrains and other necessities of life,
v) Ceremonial expenses,
vi) Educational expenses,
vii) Purchase of National Saving Certificates and other national bonds, marketable securities, etc.,
viii) Payment of Insurance Premiums,
ix) Medical expenses, and
x) Housing.

Following table 3.05 reveals the loans and advances of Urban Co-operative Banks.

TABLE 3.05

LOANS AND ADVANCES AND WORKING CAPITAL OF URBAN CO-OPERATIVE BANKS (Rs. in Lacs)

Sr. No	*Year*	*Loans And Advances*	*Working Capital*
1.	1983	1,60,825.38	2,61,179.39
2.	1984	1,97,285.97	3,33,089.46
3.	1986	2,78,742.73	4,81,827.43
4.	1988	4,24,235.18	7,22,313.04
5.	1989	53,54,057.17	8,91,639.53
6.	1991	7,37,921.70	12,54,938.14
7.	1992	8,12,265.26	13,93,452.49
8.	1994	12,17,200.00	19,98,800.00
9.	1995	14,79,500.00	2,39,900.00
10.	1996	17,90,800.00	28,77,100.00
11.	1997	20,61,300.00	34,47,200.00

Source: RBI, UBD Co. Bombay and Report on trends and progress of banking in India, RBI Publication 1996-97.

Urban Co-operative Banks allowed 61.58 per cent of working capital credit in the year 1983. This proportion reduced to 58.8 per cent in the year 1991, which marginally increased to 59.8 per cent in 1997. Growth rate of advances during the period of 1983 to 1992 was 400 per cent whereas from the year 1994 to 1997 it observed at 70 per cent. This shows healthy sign for Urban Co-operative Banks.

Financing Small Scale Industries

In the year 1959, a seminar was organised at Hyderbad on Financing of small-scale industries. In this it is observed that these industries are strategically important in Indian economy, hence adequate finance for their development must be provided. It was concluded that Urban Co-operative Banks are appropriate agencies to cater the credit needs of these industries.

Government of Gujarat amended the Gujarat Co-operative

Societies Act to facilitate financial assistance to small-scale industries owned by partnership or joint stock company. Urban banks have also amended their byelaws permitting small-scale industries to become the members in the form of partnership / joint company.

Progress of Urban Banks in Gujarat

Gujarat has been a place of co-operative movements in different spheres of social and economic activities mainly in the agricultural and allied fields of production. White Revolution is a landmark achievement of Gujarat, binding the small farmers by forming their own milk co-operative society. This revolution has influenced other strata of Indian society. As mentioned earlier, the birth of first co-operative bank was also in Gujarat and Vadodara happens to be the proud of city to earn this reputation. In the year 1889, first Urban Co-operative bank known by the name The Anyonya Sahayakari Co-operative Mandli Ltd. was opened. This was a historical development during British rule; post independence, India has encouraged the growth of Urban Co-operative Banks from sixties onward.

Gujarat State was formed on 1st May 1961. Even though first co-operative bank was formed in Gujarat, the state has to work hard to take the leading position in India. Since formation, Gujarat has been promoting the industries as well as modernisation in agriculture sector. The entire population of the state is active participant in the growth of the small-scale industries and variety of co-operatives. Normally people have used their own resources and indigenous skills for the progress of the state as well as their own improvement in living standards. The Urban Co-operative Banks have a big stake in this growth of the state.

The opening account for the Gujarat State was a mere 41 Urban Co-operative Bank with 18 branches in the year 1960. These banks had 1,13,219 members, the number of depositors and borrowers in the same year stood at 58256 and 17259 respectively. These banks had share capital of Rs. 73 lacs and a total reserve of Rs. 37 lacs only. The deposits were Rs. 567 lacs and the working capital was about Rs. 753 lacs and the total advances were of the tune of about Rs. 375 lacs.

In the year 1975, Gujarat Urban Co-operative Banks' Federation was established. By this time Gujarat had 208 Urban Co-operative Banks with 68 branches.

TABLE 3.06

PROGRESS OF URBAN CO-OPERATIVE BANKS IN GUJARAT

Sr. No.	*Indicators*	*1960*	*1989*	*1990*	*1992*	*1998*
1.	No. of Banks	041	288	288	288	321
2.	No. of Branches	018	290	298	325	615
3.	Membership (Lacs)	1.31	19.09	19.05	21.85	28.13
4.	W.C. (Crores)	7.53	2418.93	2858.57	3657.48	13178.85
5.	Advances (Crores)	3.75	1431.49	1646.61	2150.21	6622.79
6.	Share Cap (Crores)	0.73	75.16	83.79	99.97	250.83
7.	Deposits (Crores)	5.67	1745.18	2072.04	2593.32	9948.25
8.	Reserves (Crores)	0.37	247.51	301.97	441.39	1485.61
9.	Profit (Crores)	0.07	40.39	42.20	65.06	220.74
10.	Staff Members	667	5886	1768	12832	14761
11.	No. of Depositors (Lacs)	0.58	489.5	49.88	55.43	NA
12.	No. of Borrowers (Lacs)	0.17	7.39	7.58	8.19	NA

Source: Year Book of Gujarat Urban Co-operative Banks Federation years.

Above table 3.06 shows the growing different indicators in the number of banks and the branches.

The data shows that, since 1962 the number of Urban Co-operative Banks have steadily increased. However from 1989 onwards, the numbers of banks have not been changed, instead of branches of these banks have increased, a steady increase is seen in the membership standing at 28.13 lacs till 1998 that is an encouraging growth.

The socio-economic conditions are conducive for the co-operative sector in Gujarat as can be seen from the success of various co-operative banks operating in the state. Greatly influenced by the Gandhian philosophy, Gujarat State has all the subjective and objective conditions needed for the growth of co-operative sector. Historically, land of Gujarat has been a trading place, involving small-scale industries and artisan workers of all kinds. These people are always in need of money.

The Urban Co-operative Banks in Gujarat are steadily sharing progress and in fact are proving to be highly competitive. The fulfillment of financial needs through these banks have been unmatchable compared with the commercial banks for the middle and low income groups from all 'n' routs of life in Gujarat. Lot of more efforts required to be done to improve the growth of Urban Co-operative banks in Gujarat.

Reserves

These banks have also shown a total reversal in the share capital compared to the total reserves. There is a general growth in the share capital of their banks owing to the increased participation from the members and non-members.

One significant information in table 3.06 tells that till the year 1960, share capital of Urban Co-operative Banks was more than its total reserves. Afterwards total reserves of Urban Co-operative Banks in Gujarat were more than the share capital. Such a situation is an indicator of sound financial position of a bank. Another aspect is that the Urban Co-operative Banks in Gujarat have not to depend upon outside borrowings. Their own funds and deposits are enough to run the business. The profit earning capacity of the bank is improving and if this trend continues for more than ten years then the profit of Urban Co-operative Banks in Gujarat may be more than their share capital.

Deposits Mobilised

The growth of deposits in the Urban Co-operative banks of Gujarat has been quite satisfactory. There is a growth of about 28 per cent in the number of banks' offices during 1983-1998 and the deposits in the banks have increased to 330 per cent which is a good indicator of the people's faith in these banks.

In pre plan era, deposit mobilisation was not the problem as deposits credited to the banks in the normal course were more than sufficient to meet the limited demands for credit to be made. Ability of bank officer judged on the basis of advances, he could make.

In view of the long-term objective of The Reserve Bank of India's Monetary Policy bank should mobilise more deposits. Banks are assumed to include banks to rely on their own deposits, to satisfy increasing credit needs of the community rather than to depend on The Reserve Bank of India for resources. Monetary authority expects banks to occupy vital position in the economy to counter inflanatonary pressure by mobilising more and more savings of the people.

Banks have little to do with the activity of saving as it neither direct the people to save nor it can increase their income so that they may set apart something out of their income but they do help in stimulating savings by providing the incentives like:

i) Interest on deposits,
ii) Cheap remittance of funds,
iii) Safe custody of valuables,
iv) Financial consultation.

Out of the above, Co-operative banks were able to offer higher rate of interest on deposits than the Commercial Banks and majority of the banks have got their safe custody for depositors' valuables.

Urban banks are facing tough competition in maintaining the growth rate in mobilisation of deposits. They have to make concentrated efforts. Urban Banks have compete commercial banks and financial institutions like—Unit Trust of India, Public Provident Fund, The Life Insurance Corporation of India, National Development Banks, National Savings Certificates, Post Office Deposits, Shares and Debentures etc. The financial assets other than bank deposits including commercial banks have grown at compound growth rate of 16.5 per cent between 1969-70 and 1986-87. This clearly indicates an increasing preference of savers in favour of financial assets other than bank deposits.

Interest Rate Structure

The Countries in the world having free economy, rate of interest is an important determinant of bank deposits. However, in India interest rate structure have been rigidly administered till 1995. It is linked to the maturity parameter of term deposits. Reserve Bank of India reviews its interest rate policy from time to time.

Till 1995 interest rates on nationalised commercial banks' deposits were uniformly applicable at any given time, but The Reserve Bank of India allowed Urban Co-operative Banks to keep its interest rate higher by 1 per cent more than Commercial Banks to provide the incentive and to develop the co-operative movement.

Types of Deposit

Traditionally, banks have been accepting three types of deposits from the public, namely — current, savings and fixed deposits. Commercial Banks as well as Urban Co-operative Banks do no pay any per cent of interest on current deposits. Also on savings deposits Commercial Banks and Urban Co-operative Banks pay 4.5 per cent interest. On fixed deposits, rate of interest differs with the term of deposits.

A high deposit rate will mean a high lending rate, in the turn it will raise the capital formation, more investment more income and finally more savings and more deposits. Because of Urban banks, deposit mobilisation is possible for local credit needs. Urban area can become self-reliant.

TABLE 3.07

MOBILIZATION OF DEPOSITS BY URBAN CO-OPERATIVE BANKS IN GUJARAT DURING 1982-83 TO 1997-98

Sr. No	*Year*	*No. of Banks*	*Deposits*	*No. of Banks' Offices*	*Deposits per Bank*
1	1982-83	275	60,253.67	479	125.79
2	1983-84	283	75,474.60	506	149.16
3	1984-85	285	90,470.06	528	171.34
4	1985-86	285	1,09,430.55	545	200.79
5	1986-87	287	1,32,731.48	563	235.76
6	1987-88	288	1,56,128.56	571	273.43
7	1988-89	288	1,74,517.92	578	301.93
8	1989-90	288	2,07,204.44	586	353.59
9	1990-91	288	2,34,259.86	593	395.04
10	1991-92	288	2,59,331.57	613	423.04
11	1997-98	321	9,94,824.00	615	1617.60

Source: Year Book of Gujarat Urban Co-operative Banks Federation, Ahemdanad.

The deposits vary from bank to bank, it is worth while to know the average deposits per bank. Surprisingly the figures are again quite encouraging i.e. 238 per cent increase in the deposits per bank office for the period 1982-83 to 1991-92 and 282 per cent growth observed during 1991-92 to 1997-98. Among the different category, fixed deposits constitute the highest (54.17 per cent) followed by saving (21.40 per cent) and lastly the current deposits (13.48 per cent).

Working Capital Growth of Urban Banks in Gujarat

The working capital growth is determined mainly by the own funds and deposits growth of the respective bank(s). In case of Urban Co-operative Banks in Gujarat for the period 1983-1998, working capital has grown in conformity with the own funds growth and the growth of deposits. The increase in working capital is about 320 per cent during the period of 1983-84 to 1991-92 whereas working capital increased by 260 per cent during 1991-92 to 1997-98 as calculated from table 3.08. Working capital and profit of the Urban Co-operative Banks in Gujarat during 1982-1998 are:

TABLE 3.08

COMPARISON OF PROFIT WITH WORKING CAPITAL. (Rs. in Lacs)

Year	*Working Capital*	*Profit*	*Profit percentage of working capital*
1983-84	87,155.65	2,131.82	02.45 per cent
1991-92	3,65,747.74	6,505.39	01.78 per cent
1997-98	1317885.00	22,074.00	01.67 per cent

Source: Annual Reports of Urban Co-operative Banks Federation, Gujarat.

The figures available for the period further reveals that there are very few banks having working capital less then one crore rupee. Out of 288 banks, 280 banks have shown a working capital amount of more than one crore rupee. However the proportion of profit to working capital shown a decline trend from 2.45 per cent to 1.78 per cent for the financial years 1982-83 to 1991-92 respectively. Further declined in the year 1997-98 to 1.67 per cent. This is an issue to be concerned about these banks that one has to deal with the various parameters which may directly or indirectly influence the profit of a bank and work for the improvement in the profit.

Loans and Advances

The capacity of these banks to give loans is steadily increasing as well as the advances given for different purposes to different section of society is also on increasing trend which implies the success in the desired role of these banks in Gujarat. The loans have increased to 27 per cent for the period 1983-1998. The advances about 43 per cent were given for the purpose of trade and commerce, for the industry investment about 20 per cent and for the consumption purpose about 15.72 per cent, the remaining amount were utilised for social purposes.

TABLE 3.09

PURPOSE-WISE DISTRIBUTION OF ADVANCES OF URBAN CO-OPERATIVE BANKS ON 31ST MARCH, 1992 AND ON 31 MARCH, 1993

Sr. No	*Purpose*	*Advances*		*Percentage of Advances to Total*	
		1991-92	*1992-93*	*1991-92*	*1992-93*
1	Domestic appliances	6,194.52	7,512.27	02.88	03.18
2	Social purpose	4,476.89	5,043.26	2.08	02.14
3	Repayment of old debt	626.79	1,062.65	0.29	00.45
4	Medical expenses	2,147.97	2,281.53	1.00	00.97
5	Others	20,054.16	21,922.56	9.33	09.29
	Total consmp. Purpose	33,800.33	37,822.27	15.72	16.02
6	Trade & Commerce	92,619.16	1,00,982.38	43.07	42.78
7	Industrial purpose	42,635.03	46,382.14	19.83	19.65
8	For self employment	21,193.13	23,635.50	9.86	10.01
9	Education purpose	1,606.77	1,839.69	0.75	00.78
10	For purchase of property	23,166.24	25,374.13	10.77	10.75
	Grand total of Advances	2,15,020.66	2,36,036.11	100.00	100.00

Source: Year Book of Gujarat Urban Co-operative Banks' Federation, Ahemdabad.

Audit Class

The Reserve Bank of India allotted Audit class from A to D based on functioning of Urban Co-operative Banks for the year ended on 31st March 1992. The criteria taken into consideration for allotting the audit classes are financial positions, management aspects and maintenance of books of accounts after following the norms guided by RBI from time to time. Out of 288 Urban Co-operative Banks in Gujarat 241 Banks were allotted 'A' class; 28 Banks got 'B' class, 13 Banks were rated 'C' class and only 6 Banks were rated 'D' class. It seems that out of 288 Banks, 83.68 per cent i.e. 241 banks got 'A' audit class, which is prestigious and encouraging achievement for Gujarat Urban Co-operative Banks.

Regional Imbalance

There are 5 distinct regions in Gujarat State viz. i) South Gujarat, ii) Central Gujarat, iii) North Gujarat, iv) Saurashtra, and v) Kutch.

It is observed that more than 160 banks constituting approximately 55 per cent are located in Central Gujarat region. Although in terms of urban population, the coverage of this region works out to 44 per cent of total urban population nearly 110 lacs, as per 1981 census. Kutch has only 1 per cent, Saurashtra has 17 per cent, South Gujarat account to nearly 9 per cent. It reflects clear-cut imbalance in the growth of Urban Co-operative Banks in the State. This imbalance will have to be rectified and efforts must be made to ensure development of urban banks in undeveloped and underdeveloped areas in the interest of long term and sound growth of urban banking.

Commercial Bank Compared

Urban Co-operative Banks provide financial assistance and other non- fund services to its members and customers. In this sense urban banks are similar to the commercial banks. Basic difference between commercial banks and urban banks is in respect of objectives, method of work, location and credit policy. Commercial banks normally avoid lending of small loans whereas urban banks provide credit to small man, petty loans. Commercial banks used to open branches in the area where big volume of business is expected, but urban banks are being opened by people themselves in their own area irrespective of size of business as it is their own bank. Therefore urban banks provide banking facility to the people at a time suitable to its members and in a way familiar to local people.

REFERENCES

1. Ref.: *Varde Committee Report*, 1963.
2. Ref..: *Annual Reports of GUCBF*, 1983 to 1992.
3. Report on Trend and Progress of Banking in India, 1997-98, p. 24, RBI Publication.

4

Deposit Performance of Urban Co-operative Banks

Introduction

The growing public confidence in the working of Urban Co-operative Banks in India has succeeded in attracting deposits even from non-members. An urban bank generally accepts current deposits, savings deposits and fixed deposits. Bulk of total deposits of the Urban Co-operative Bank comprises of the fixed deposit mobilised by bank. On an average the deposits collected by them at all over in India satisfy more than 50 per cent of working capital needs.

In pre plan era, deposit mobilisation was not a problem. Deposits credited to the banks in the normal course were more than sufficient to meet the limited credit demand. The ability of a bank officer was judged on the advances he could make. The situation now is different; the biggest challenge faced by the banking industry today in the context of economic planning is the mobilisation of adequate resources.

Need for increased mobilisation of deposits by banks assume importance in view of the long-term objectives of the Reserve Bank's monetary policy. Banks must rely on their own deposit resources, so as to satisfy increasing credit needs of the community rather than to take credit from the Reserve Bank of India. Monetary authority expects banks to occupy vital position in the economy to counter inflationary pressure by mobilising more and more savings of the people.

Banks have little to do with the activity of saving as it can neither direct the people to save nor can motivate them to increase their incomes so that they may be able to set a part something out of their income. But they do help in stimulating savings by providing incentives like:

i) Interest on deposits,
ii) Cheap remittance of funds,
iii) Safe custody of valuables and
iv) Financial consultation.

Mobilisation of Deposits in India

Nationalisation of Commercial Banks and Deposits Mobilisation

The activity of deposit mobilisation by banks came into shape and rather attained credibility only after the 14 major commercial banks were nationalised in 1969. The banking prior to nationalisation was the privilege of a few bigwig only i.e. big industrialists, big businessmen and big landlords. More deposits and more advances from and to, such a business house was an easy circle for the banks, which now looks like a lazy dream for the banks. In the pre nationalisation period banks were like a joint stock company and mainly under the influence of big business houses. These business houses used to muster up resources required by them through their banks, by routine operations only. The banks had neither national goal to fulfil nor social obligation to perform. The public in universal was not made aware of the facilities provided by the banks.

Establishment of State Bank of India in 1955 with nationalsation of 14 commercial banks set the ball rolling for drastic changes in banking operations. The banks' resources are now being used in the national development. Parameters have been laid down for deployment of funds like priority sectors and weaker sections. Every bank had to advance at least 40 per cent of its total credit to priority sector at concessional rate of interest i.e. agriculture, small scale industries and small business, also one per cent of its total advances to the weaker section at the rate of four per cent interest under DRI scheme. Further, about 15 per cent of its advances should go to agriculture sector directly.

Apart from the above, The Reserve Bank of India with a view to keep the inflationary tendencies under check and to keep the funds with the banks under their control, have a device of Statutory Liquidity Ratio (SLR) and Cash Reserve Ratio (CRR). Nearly 40 per cent of the deposits of banks are required to be kept in liquid form i.e. either with The Reserve Bank of India or investment in Government securities and or in cash. Deposits with RBI and investment in govt. securities earn very less return compared to the advances given to industries or business.

In order to satisfy all above requirements, banks need more funds in the form of deposits so that they can invest in non- priority sectors to earn profit. Survival and development of banks is influenced by their ability to attract deposits from different segments of the society rather than by the volume of their capital resources. Banks purchases deposits, produce and sell loans and advances. In other words deposits are the main inputs for loan outputs. Hence mobilisation of deposits is very much needed in view of tough competition encountered by other banks and financial institutions like:

i) Public sector: Unit Trust of India (UTI), Public Provident Fund (PPF), National Development Bonds, National Saving Certificates etc.

ii) Private sector: Joint Stock Companies' deposits, equity shares, debentures and chit funds etc.

TABLE 4.01

DEPOSITS WITH NON BANKING CORPORATE SECTOR

(Rs. in Crore)

Sr. No	*Category of Company*	*Deposits*	
		1995-96	*196-97*
1	Non Financial Companies	2,95,344.7	3,57,153.0
2	Financial Companies	99,725.3	1,16,635.4
3	Other Non Banking Companies	8710.2	16,644.5
	TOTAL	4,03,780.2	4,90,432.9

Source: RBI Annual Report, 1997-98.

Non Financial companies' deposits have increased by Rs. 79,809 crore at 21 per cent of growth rate. Financial companies' deposits rose from Rs. 99,725.3 crore to Rs. 1,16,635.4 crore, the rise is Rs. 16,910.00 crore at 17 per cent. Other non banking companies' deposits increased from Rs. 8710.2 crore for the year 1995-96 to Rs. 16,644.5 crore in the year 1996-97, the increase is of Rs. 7,934 crore. The overall increase in deposits with non banking corporate sectors companies is 21 per cent. The deposits mobilised by commercial banks after nationalisation are as under:

TABLE 4.02

DEPOSITS MOBILISED BY COMMERCIAL BANKS AFTER NATIONALISATION

(Rs. in Crore)

Year	*Deposits*	*Year*	*Deposits*
1969	5148	1990	173515
1970	5690	1992	23599
1975	13711	1993	274995
1976	17698	1994	312340
1982	52250	1995	364724
1984	69804	1996	449151
1986	91336	1997	504595
		1998	601348

The deposits in August 1986 were amounting to Rs. 91336 crore as against monetary resources amounting to Rs. 124474 crore. Banks have adopted special schemes to suit the budget of different strata of the society such as salary saving, insurance linked deposits, recurring deposits, term deposits etc. These schemes brought large amount of deposits to the banks. There has been a significant increase in the deposits of scheduled commercial banks in post bank nationalisation period.

TABLE 4.03

DEPOSITS AND PER CAPITA DEPOSITS OF SCHEDULED COMMERCIAL BANKSIN POST NATIONALISATION PERIOD

	Years							
Particulars	*1969*	*1973*	*1978*	*1980*	*1985*	*1990*	*1994*	*1998*
Deposits in crore	4646	5165	23133	30377	77075	173515	323632	601348
Per Capita deposits	88	160	361	494	1026	2098	3596	N.A.

Source: 'India 1995' Reference Manual. Ministry of Information and Broadcasting and Report of Trends and Progress of Banking, RBI - 1997-98

Since the nationalisation of banks from 1969 to 1973 deposits of scheduled commercial banks increased by 11 per cent, while per capita deposits increased by 81 per cent. It implies that propensity to save of an individual increased during this period. During the five years from 1973 to 1978 the deposits of scheduled commercial banks. Then onwards both deposits as well as per capita deposits are showing continuous rise. It means in the initial period of post nationlisation the increase in the banks' deposits is uneven but from 1978 there is uniform growth.

The deposits of commercial banks reached to the peak of Rs. 601348 crore in the year 1998, the increase in the deposits compared to previous year is Rs. 97753 crore at 19 per cent. The annual growth rate of deposits for the period from 1992 to 1997 is; 17 per cent in 1992-93, 14 per cent in 1993-94, 18 per cent in 1994-95, 23 per cent in 1995-96 and12 per cent in 1996-97. From this detail, it becomes clear that in the year 1995-96 – 23 per cent is highest growth, which declined to 12 per cent in the year 1996-97 but again there is rise of 19 per cent in the year 1998.

Financial Sector Reforms and Deposits Mobilisation

The freeing of money market called for banks to adopt a new approach to deposit mobilisation from passive acceptance of deposits to active management of deposits. In this context, rising of funds through the issue of certificate of deposits deserves special attention. The main advantage of CD's is, bank can raise wholesale deposits at market related rates, which enable them to tailor the inflow of deposits to match the seasonal amount for wholesale credit. For instance there is a definite cycle of ebb and flow of food procurement credit. The Reserve Bank of India indicates the projections for food credit in its credit policy announcement. Based on these projection banks can plan deposits acceptance of proper maturities so that return flow of food credit is matched by maturities of deposits. Since the minimum lending rate applicable on the food credit, banks can offer attractive rates on such tied deposits.

Another area of deposits-management is choosing a proper profile of the term deposits. Successive survey on banks' deposits conducted by the Reserve Bank of India indicates large portion of banks term deposits is at maximum maturity of over three years. Apart from incurring higher cost of funds, this creates rigidity in the liability/management specially when there are revision in deposit rate structure. Hence it would be productive for banks to evolve suitable marketing strategy to encourage term deposits of proper maturity mix. In this context, the recent revision in the deposit rate structure has given an opportunity to banks to overhaul the maturity pattern in favour of short-term deposits as the rate of interest on term deposits is deregulated completely.

Private sector expects liberalisation of the economic activities in financial sector. Government of India has already announced its intention to allow mutual funds in private sector. Although Money Market Mutual Funds (MMMF's) are to be floated by banks and their subsidiaries, even these areas may eventually be opened to non- bank entities. There is already a flight of term deposits from banks to non- bank financial institutions. There is a need for new types of products which banking system must come out to compete effectively with non-bank entities. Money Market Deposit Account (MMDA's) is one of the product which can be considered by banks. MMDAs are deposit accounts maintained by banks on which money market related rates are offered to the depositors and at the same time depositors are given limited withdrawal facilities by cheque without notice. In the developed countries, MMDAs have effectively counted the competition from MMMFs and other deposit taking institutions. There is no reason why such facility cannot be made available to bank depositors in India.

Bank Deposits and Savings

Bank deposits are important macro economic variables. Banks have been and will continue to remain the most powerful instrument for collection of savings. At a micro level, deposits constitute an important profit centre in a bank. Inspite of this, it is observed that bank deposits have received much lesser attention of researcher compared to advances of banks. In 1994, banks' deposits reached to the peak of around 51.8 per cent of national income.

Bank deposits constitute a vital component of national savings. To understand the behaviour of bank deposits, it is necessary to understand behaviour of savings. Saving is nothing but non-utilised income. In other words, saving is any excess of income over consumption. An individual saves a part of their income for meeting future needs. Symbolically S = Y – C, where 'S' denotes savings. Y for income and 'C' for consumption. Keyns said, "Saving is function of income i.e. S = f (Y)". It means that as income increases savings will also increase and vice-versa. Saving depends on propensity to save, which is derived from propensity to consume. Symbolically, it is $\Delta S/\Delta Y = 1 - \Delta C/\Delta Y$. According to Keyns, the consumption function is a stable function of income. It means that normally change in income does not bring any change in consumption in short period. Hence change in income will obviously bring change in savings. Marginal propensity to save is the ratio of DS/DY, which is always less than one.

"Capital formation is the most significant variable of economic growth. At the macro level the banking system is main component of the machinery which converts savings of the machinery which converts savings into capital "[1]

It is interesting to study domestic savings pattern compared to Gross Domestic Product.

TABLE 4.04

GROSS DOMESTIC SAVINGS AS A PERCENTAGE OF GDP

Sectors	*1993-94*	*1994-95*	*1995-96*	*1996-97*	*1998-99*
Public	0.5	1.5	1.9	1.5	1.0
Private	21.3	22.7	22.2	22.9	22.1
Total	21.8	24.2	24.1	24.4	23.1

Source: *Indian Economic Survey*, 1998-99.

Total gross domestic savings declined to 23.1 per cent of GDP in 1997-98 from 24.4 per cent of GDP in 1996-97. Public savings contributed 0.5 per cent and Private savings 21.3 per cent of GDP for the year 1993-94. In the year 1998-99, the public savings declined progressively to 1 per cent of GDP from recent peak of 1.9 per cent in 1995-96.

Realising the importance of saving in the process of economic development, Government of India made concentrated efforts over three decades for developing financial intermediaries of all possible types for mobilising savings from various segments of the community. The Government of India has emphasised on mobilisation of savings in all the five-year plans. Several legislation have been passed from The State Banks of India Act, 1955 to The Regional Rural Bank Act, 1979. Promotion and mobilisation of savings are consciously directed towards the achievement of socio-economic objectives.

During the post bank nationalisation period, banks' deposits in India have grown at growth rate of more than 17 per cent per annum. Bank deposits constitute one of the important monetary variables of the Indian economy. It was 51.8 per cent of national income in the year 1993-94 as stated earlier.

TABLE 4.05

DEPOSITS AS A PERCENTAGE OF NATIONAL INCOME

1969-70	*1973-74*	*1978-79*	*1980-81*	*1985-86*	*1990-91*	*1992-93*
15.5	21.4	29.4	35.9	43.6	48.3	50.5

Source: 'India 1995' A Reference Manual, Ministry of Information and Broadcasting and Report of Trends and Progress of Banking, RBI - 1997-98.

National income is, total of income generated by the all the four factors of production viz.; (i) Land, (ii) Labour, (iii) Finance and (iv) Enterprenurship. It is a good variable to compare with the deposits. Above table represents the deposits as a percentage of national income. Since nationalisation, it is continuously growing and in the year 1993-94 it reached at the peak of 51.8 per cent.

It will be worth noting the behavior of deposits' rate with scheduled commercial banks in India during 1981 and 1995. The total deposits have registered an average annual growth of 17.90 per cent and fixed deposits have shown an increase of 17.95 per cent. The gross domestic savings during the period of 1981 and 1995 have increased by 15.40 per cent.

TABLE 4.06

AVERAGE ANNUAL GROWTH RATE OF TOTAL DEPOSITS, FIXED DEPOSITS AND GROSS DOMESTIC SAVINGS PER CENT CHANGE

Particulars	*1981-95*	*1981-85*	*1986-90*	*1991-95*
Total deposits	17.90	17.78	18.38	17.54
Fixed deposits	17.95	18.12	19.07	16.78
Gross domestic savings	15.40	12.61	16.88	16.74

Source: Annexure Report on Currency and Finance various issues of RBI Bulletin.

During the period of 1981–1990, total as well as fixed deposits increased with the gross domestic savings. On comparison with the period of 1991-95 the total deposits' growth rate shows decline of 17.54 per cent and fixed deposits' growth rate has also reduced to 16.78 per cent. It certainly pin points that commercial banks are less preferred for mobilizing the deposits. But, still, before coming to the above conclusion the fact must be noticed that there is a relative fall in gross domestic savings during 1991-95.

Khusro and Sidharthan in early seventies undertook a study on determinants of banks' deposits (An econometric model of banking in India). They identified interest rates as the only variable influencing the demand for banks' deposits. Further demand and time deposits were separated for the study. The demand for demand deposits was found to be inversely related to the rate of interest on time and saving deposits whereas demand for time deposits was directly related to the interest rates on time deposits.

Challenge for Banking Industry

From the beginning of 1980's, the banking sector is facing intense competition from other financial and non-financial institutions prominently the corporate sector, Life Insurance Corporation of India, Unit Trust of India and Post offices. It is widely known that household sector contributes over 70 per cent of total savings in the country. The two third of total deposits with banks are contributed by this household sector. In the recent years, the amount of savings deposited in the banks is reducing but before 1976-77 the percentage of household savings with the banks has increased, it was 35.7 per cent in the year 1969-70 as compared to 56.8 per cent in the year 1976-77 i.e. nearly 20 per cent increase. But again it reduced by 20 per cent from 1976-77 to 1981-82. Household savings with banks were only 36 per cent in 1981-82.

In the last decade, corporate sector has been able to mobilize considerable portion of household saving. In the year 1977, the amounts of public deposits with corporate sector were to the tune of Rs. 587 crore. These have been consistently increasing since then and stand over Rs. 10, 000 crore by now. Thus corporate sector became a challenge for the banking industry in their traditional fort. Financial intermediation by corporate sector between the user and suppliers of funds is by passing the banking system.

Non-Banking Financial Companies (NBFC) have emerged as an important part of the financial sector. There were 7,000 NBFC's in the year 1981, the number rose to 25,000 in 1991 and then to 41,000 in 1996. In July 1997 there were 37,000 applications for re-registration of NBFC's. The total deposits of NBFC's were of about Rs. 3,000 crore in 1984, which increased to Rs. 20,000 crore in 1996. NBFCs now have entered into leasing on hire purchase, consumer and auto finance, investment, banking and bills discounting and so many other forms of financing. These all have made them a crucial part of financial markets and will intensify the competition with banks in mobilising the deposits. NBFCs mobilise the savings of small investor by offering them attractive returns and have become a challenge to the banks in mobilising the deposits.

Deposits Mobilised by Urban Banks in Gujarat

As discussed earlier, Urban Co-operative Banks are banks of 'small man'; their area of operation is normally limited to where they are located. Therefore these banks are expected to be self-reliant and collect their loanable funds from deposits. In accepting deposits, responsibility to pay interest also increases hence the funds collected in the form of deposits are required to be efficiently invested or advanced or used for other alternative purposes so that it balances the liquidity and profitability. In 1986, Gujarat experienced that the deposits up to Rs. 1000 contributed 11 per cent of total deposits. This implies that majority of those deposits are from 'small man'.

Now a days, savings of 'small man' is attracted by stock market, mutual funds post office etc. offering higher rates of interest schemes. In the changed scenario urban banks have to face the competition. In past, it was easy to get deposits by offering only 1 per cent interest more than commercial banks. But now in deregulated structure of interest, to maintain the growth rate of deposits, urban banks have to make efforts. Other financial institutions and commercial banks provide better services to customer in comparison to urban banks. Even then urban banks are successful in obtaining trust of the people.

In past higher rate of deposits mobilised by urban banks may be for two reasons:

i) Personalised services rendered by urban banks and
ii) 1 per cent higher rate of interest on savings and term deposits compared to commercial banks.

One important characteristic of these deposits was nearly 45 per cent of total deposits constituted by term deposits. Secondly, approximately 60 per cent of total deposits came from small depositors, in which deposit amount was up to Rs. 5000.

In the time span from 1983 to 1992, a seven-fold increase in the deposits of Urban Co-operative Banks was observed.[2] The total of deposits stood at Rs. 813.35 lacs in the year 1992 as against Rs. 187.05 lacs in the year 1983. The average deposit per bank is also equally in conformity with the growth of the deposits. In the year 1983, the average deposit per bank was Rs. 1,84,536.52 lacs which rose to Rs. 10,64,672.17 lacs in the year 1992. During three financial years 1995-96, 1996-97 and 1997-98 deposits of Urban Co-operative Banks have again increased steadily and simultaneously with increase in number of bank offices. The Urban Co-operative Banks' offices in the year 1995-96 were 1327, which rose to 1363 in the year 1996-97, a net increase is 36 bank offices. Subsequently for the year 1997-98 this increase in the Urban Co-operative Banks is about 53.

TABLE 4.07

AVERAGE DEPOSIT MOBILISED BY URBAN BANKS IN INDIA

Sr. No.	*Year*	*No. of Banks*	*Total Deposits Mobilised (Rs. in Crore)*	*Average Deposit Mobilised Per Bank (Rs.)*
1	1983	1175	157.05	1,84,536.52
2	1984	1208	207.94	2,51,196.00
3	1986	1241	297.49	3,69,183.42
4	1988	1275	431.40	5,50,031.21
5	1990	1283	533.17	6,84,502.51
6	1991	1305	741.46	9,67,609.80
7	1992	1309	813.35	10,64,672.17
8	1996	1327	24165	18,21,024.8
9	1997	1363	30714	22.53 crore
10	1998	1416	38472	27.17 crore

Source: Year Book of Gujarat Urban Co-operative Banks' Federation and *Reports on Trends and Progress of Banking*, RBI 1997-98.

TABLE 4.8

DEPOSIT MOBILISED BY URBAN CO-OPERATIVE BANKS DURING THE YEARS 1995-96 1996-97 AND 1997-98

(Amount in Crore)

Sr. No.	*Particulars*	*Financial Year*		
		1995-96	*1996-97*	*1997-98*
1	No. of Banks Reporting	1327	1363	1416
2	Deposits	24,165	30,714	38,432
3	Growth	4064	6549	7758
4	Per cent growth	20.2	27.1	25.3

Source: Report on Trend and Progress of Banking in India 1997-98 Page 24 RBI Publishes.

Similarly deposits of 1416 Urban Co-operative Banks amounted to Rs. 38,472 crore recording an increase of 25.3 per cent in the financial year 1997-98.

These figures are a reflection of the confidence that banks have earned from its members and non-members. There is a clear increase in the money flow from non-members over the period mentioned. These banks are allowed to have deposits in the current, saving and fixed accounts. The bulk about 63 per cent of deposits are in the fixed accounts. The remaining 47 per cent consist of current and saving accounts.

The deposit mobilisation during the period from 1966 to 1977 was about 239 per cent and 323 per cent during the period from1983 to 1992. This increase is attributed to two factors. One is growth in the branches of these banks, as a result, reaching to more and more segments of society and secondly the overwhelming confidence expressed by the people as seen in the increase in the membership and thus contributing in the deposits. There is also a significant increase in the deposits from the non-member.

The growth of deposits in the Urban Co-operative Bank of Gujarat has been quite satisfactory. There is a growth of about 28 per cent in the number of banks' offices during the period from 1983 to 1998 and corresponding an increase in deposits in the banks to 330 per cent, which is a good indicator of the people's faith in these banks.

TABLE 4.09

MOBILISATION OF DEPOSITS BY URBAN CO-OPERATIVE BANKS OF GUJARAT DURING 1982-83 TO 1997-98.

Sr. No.	*Year*	*No. of Banks*	*Deposits*	*No. of Banks Offices*	*Deposits per Bank*
1	1982-83	275	60,253.67	479	125.79
2	1983-84	283	75,474.60	506	149.16
3	1984-85	285	90,470.06	528	171.34
4	1985-86	285	1,09,430.55	545	200.79
5	1986-87	287	1,32,731.48	563	235.76
6	1987-88	288	1,56,128.56	571	273.43
7	1988-89	288	1,74,517.92	578	301.93
8	1989-90	288	2,07,204.44	586	353.59
9	1990-91	288	2,34,259.86	593	395.04
10	1991-92	288	2,59,331.57	613	423.04
11	1997-98	321	994826.00	615	1617.60

Source: *Year Book of Gujarat Urban Co-operative Bank Federation,* Ahemadabad.

The above table reveals that deposits vary from bank to bank, it is worthwhile to know the average deposits per bank, the figures are again quite encouraging, i.e., 236 per cent, increase in the deposits per bank for the period mentioned in the table 4.09. Among the different category, fixed deposits constitute the highest (54.17%) followed by saving (21.40%) and lastly the current deposits (13.48 per cent).

Deposits Per Bank Office

Commercial banks are having widespread network throughout India. Commercial Banks' Management is professional, so obviously deposits mobilised by commercial banks will be large. Following table reflects comparision of deposits mobilised by commercial banks and the Urban Co-operative Banks in Gujarat.

TABLE 4.10

PER BANK OFFICE DEPOSITS MOBILISED BY THE URBAN CO-OPERATIVE BANKS IN GUJARAT AND THE COMMERCIAL BANKS IN INDIA

Sr. No	*Year*	*Deposits Per Bank Office*	
		Urban Banks in Gujarat	*Commercial Banks in India*
1	1980	90.14	124.03
2	1981	104.10	137.43
3	1982	125.79	156.80
4	1983	149.16	164.27
5	1984	171.34	149.30
6	1985	200.79	159.41
7	1986	235.76	187.92
8	1987	273.43	211.99
9	1988	301.93	243.29
10	1989	353.59	276.66
11	1990	395.04	308.80

Source: Year book of Gujarat Urban Co-operative Banks' Federation and statistical tables relating to banks in India by the Reserve Bank of India.

Above-mentioned table compares only 11 years' deposits per bank office during the year 1980 and 1990. These 11 years are selected for comparision because within that period; initially up to the year 1983, per bank office deposits of urban banks are less than the commercial banks. As the urban banks were under development, the mobilizing deposit performance was poor as compared to commercial banks. But it is reverse from the year 1984 to 1990 and it is again expected to continue same trend. From this, it seems that the urban banks were becoming popular amongst people of Gujarat. The deposits mobilised from the year 1984 and onward are self-explanatory, that urban population prefers urban banks compared to commercial banks.

At the end of June 1960, deposits aggregated to Rs. 4646 crore. By the end of March 1993 they had increased to Rs. 2,74,938 crore and to Rs. 3,23,632 crore by the end of March 1994. Deposits with public sector banks were Rs. 3871 crore in June 1969. At the end of March 1993 deposits were Rs. 2,39,614 crore and further increased to Rs. 2,80,908 crore by the end of March 1994.

TABLE 4. 11

GROWTH OF DEPOSITS OF URBAN CO-OPERATIVE BANKS IN GUJARAT

(Rs. in Crore)

Particulars	*Urban Banks' Growth of Deposits During the Years*					
	June 1960	*June 1980*	*June 1985*	*June 1990*	*March 1993*	*March 1998*
Deposits	5067	295.61	904.7	2072.04	3160.61	9948.24
Depositors	NA	1560859	3461036	4988246	5878586	NA
Deposits per depositor	NA	1894	2614	4154	5376	NA
Annual growth rate	NA	28%	19.82%	10.21%	21.88%	214%

Source: Year book of Gujarat Urban Co-operative Banks' Federation - growth rate stated is compared to previous year.

Deposits of Urban Co-operative Banks in Gujarat have increased from Rs. 2072.04 crore for the year 1989-90 to Rs. 3160.61 crore for the year 1992-93. Similarly depositors also have increased from 498824 for the year 1989-90 to 5878586 for the year 1992-93. If we look at the deposits per depositor from the year 1980 i.e. Rs. 1894, which has increased nearly by three, times and reached up to Rs. 5376, but growth rate is uneven during 1980 to 1998.

TABLE 4.12

THE TOTAL DEPOSITS (C+ S +F+O)

Sr. No.	Name of the Banks	87-88	88-89	89-90	90-91	91-92	92-93	93-94	94-95	95-96	96-97
1	The Kalupur Bank	6,418.99	6,968.08	9,610.75	10,822.62	11,762.50	17,285.10	30,426.85	33,182.10	36,879.17	41,866.57
2	The Rajkot Nagrik Bank	15,326.76	12,216.53	14,000.64	15,432.27	16,512.87	18,446.53	21,076.77	22,828.45	28,073.33	32,933.33
3	Anyona Saharakri Bank	2,146.78	2,370.12	2,789.96	3,166.13	3,461.17	3,957.40	4,514.10	5,282.56	7,089.67	9,798.10
4	The Surat Peoples's Bank	9,017.15	8,149.52	9,253.43	10,375.37	11,245.19	13,636.97	15,239.82	17,398.35	19,546.20	25,421.60
5	The Natpur Co-op. Bank	2,014.52	1,393.74	1,699.89	1,950.46	2,167.30	2,521.78	2,872.26	3,454.70	5,056.79	6,595.10
6	The Anand Mercantile Bank	843.21	1,763.55	2,130.43	2,518.10	3,019.16	3,034.23	3,789.40	4,068.01	5,397.69	6,026.01
7	Dahod Urban Bank	1,605.67	1,799.63	1,986.14	2,202.05	2,410.95	2,691.14	3,053.61	3,415.28	4,444.11	6,032.17
8	Sarvodya Nagrik Bank	523.73	638.57	718.59	809.49	889.55	1,048.92	1,135.25	1,285.53	1,573.54	1,720.45
9	Baroda People's Bank	562.09	1,210.83	1,473.32	1,782.24	2,095.95	2,626.07	3,003.66	2,000.98	4,468.95	5,905.10
10	Sardar Bhiladwala Bank	3,079.71	3,588.95	4,162.37	4,575.30	4,919.56	5,766.23	6,920.97	7,950.84	9,188.26	11,098.17

Deposits play an important role in financing resources of Urban Co-operative Banks. Share deposits in working capital of Urban Co-operative Banks are not equal for all the states in India. Deposits' share of Gujarat in all India deposits of Urban Co-operative Banks is 26 per cent. There are total 8 Urban Co-operative Banks in India having deposits more than 100 crore. Which includes 2 from Gujarat. Total deposit of Urban Co-operative Banks in India on 30-6-89 were Rs. 6845 crore, out of which, deposits of Rs. 1745 crore were from Gujarat.

TABLE 4.13

NUMBER OF TIMES DEPOSITS INCREASED WITHIN 10 YEARS OF SELECTED URBAN CO-OPERATIVE BANKS

Sr. No.	*Name of Banks*	*No. of Times Deposits Increased Within 10 Years*
1	The Kalupur Commercial Bank	6 times
2	The Rajkot Nagrik Bank	2 times
3	The Anyonya Sahayakari Bank	3.5 times
4	The Surat People's Bank	3 times
5	The Natpur Co-operative Bank	4 times
6	The Anand Mercantile Bank	3 times
7	The Dahod Urban Bank	3 times
8	The Sarvoday Nagrik Bank	2 times
9	The Baroda People's Bank	5.5 times
10	The Sardar Bhiladwala Bank	2.5 times

As per Table 4.12 sizeable increase in the deposits of selected Urban Co-operative Banks. Continuos rising trend is observed in all the ten banks. If growth of deposits among ten banks is compared, the following picture is emerging. Table 4.13 showing number of times deposits of selected Urban Co-operative Banks have increased between the year 1987-88 and the year 1996-97 i.e. for ten years. One of the scheduled Urban Co-operative Bank, i.e., Kalupur Commercial

Bank shows 6 times rise in their deposits within ten years. Normally to maintain audit class, RBI guideline is suggesting 20 per cent rise

Rajkot Nagrik Bank is a scheduled bank, shows rise 2 times i.e. nearly 200 per cent increase within ten years. While other scheduled bank i.e. Surat People's Co-operative Bank's deposits have rose 3 times within ten years. But one non-scheduled Bank, The Baroda People's Co-operative Bank's deposits has increased rapidly by 5.5 times within ten years. The deposits of Kalupur Commercial Bank in the year 1986-87 were Rs. 6115.03 lacs, which rapidly increased to Rs. 41897.92 lacs in the year 1996-97 and maintained nearly 30 to 40 per cent increases every year. Which again highest in selected ten Urban Co-operative Banks. Similar type of rise has been shown by The Baroda People's Co-operative Bank, its deposits were of Rs. 1021.19 lacs and Rs. 6717.44 lacs in the year 1996-97. Rise stood approximately at 550 per cent in 10 years. But in 10 selected banks, the highest deposits are mobilised by Rajkot Nagrik Bank and within ten years deposits increased by 2 times and in the year 1996-97 they stood at Rs. 32368.43 lacs. Second highest deposits are mobilised by Surat People's banks, deposits growth is three times in ten years i.e. from 1986-87 to 1996-97. In the year 1996-97, total deposits of The Surat People's Bank are Rs. 27870.85 lacs. The bank which started first in Asia continental; The Anyonya Sahayakari Mandli Co-operative Ltd., its deposits in the year 1996-97 amount to Rs. 9798.43 lacs; looking to the age of this bank, its total deposits are not significant. The deposit growth is 3.5 times within 10 years.

Current Deposits

These deposits are also called as demand deposits. Earlier 0.5 per cent interest was paid on balance of these deposits. Looking to the administrative work involved in maintaining current deposit accounts, now a days no interest is paid on any amount of balance. So, current deposits have become interest free deposits. Available cost data regarding current deposits shows that these deposits are the cheapest deposits. Only establishment expenses are incurred on current deposits.

Annual Growth Rate

As per Table 4.14, current deposits of selected Urban Co-operative Banks are showing the rising trend throughout the 10 years' period i.e. 1987-88 to 1996-97. Only four banks out of ten show fluctuation in the trends of increasing current deposits. The Kalupur Commercial Bank for the year 1990-91, 1994-95 and 1995-96 reflects decline, compare to pervious year in current deposits; for The Dahod Urban Co-operative Bank thrice, The Sarvodaya Nagarik Bank once and The Baroda People's Co-operative Bank had four times such reduction in current deposit. On the other hand The Surat People's Bank's current deposits for the year 1988-89 shows 14 times increase compared to the year 1987-88. The Kalupur Commercial Bank's current deposits of 1993-94 increased by 360 per cent compared to previous years. Remaining year's annual growth rate of current deposits ranging between 8 per cent and 98 per cent as compared to pervious year.

As per table 4.15, proportion of current deposits to total deposits is lowest for The Sarvodaya Nagarik Bank i.e. ranging from 0.02 per cent to 0.07 per cent for each year. On the other hand it is highest in case of The Kalupur Commercial Bank. Current deposits are 20 per cent to 31 per cent of total deposits of this bank during the year 1987-88 and 1996-97. Current deposits are considered to be cheapest from cost point of view. For most of the years, for nine banks, except The Kalupur Commercial Bank, current deposits are less than 10 per cent of the total deposits. It is observed that the current deposits are more with commercial banks than that of urban banks.

Saving Deposits

As per table 4.16, these deposits are compared with current deposits of any bank. Further, interest cost is incurred on

TABLE 4.14

ANNUAL GROTH RATE OF CURRENT DEPOSITS

Sr. No.	*Name of the Banks*	*87-88*	*88-89*	*89-90*	*90-91*	*91-92*	*92-93*	*93-94*	*94-95*	*95-96*	*96-97*
1	The Kalupur Bank	1.00	1.22	2.01	0.76	1.36	1.21	3.60	0.64	0.72	1.94
2	The Rajkot Nagrik Bank	1.00	1.19	1.13	1.27	1.26	1.17	1.29	1.10	1.06	1.14
3	Anyona Saharakri Bank	1.00	1.15	1.42	1.17	1.32	1.11	1.15	1.06	1.36	1.53
4	The Surat Peoples's Bank	1.00	3.01	1.06	1.12	0.97	1.60	1.04	1.05	1.10	1.21
5	The Natpur Co-op. Bank	1.00	1.21	1.16	1.07	0.95	1.55	1.07	1.03	1.48	0.91
6	The Anand Mercentile	1.00	1.13	1.21	1.33	1.07	0.90	2.04	0.74	0.98	1.19
7	Dahod Urban Co-Op Bank	1.00	0.94	1.37	1.20	0.62	1.10	1.20	1.56	0.88	1.51
8	Sarvodya Nagrik Bank	1.00	1.36	1.57	0.90	1.30	1.23	1.23	1.56	0.88	1.06
9	Baroda People's Bank	1.00	1.39	1.36	1.15	0.92	4.87	0.82	0.49	0.56	1.45
10	Sardar Bhiladwala Bank	1.00	1.38	1.29	1.31	1.04	1.44	1.24	1.39	1.01	1.15

TABLE 4.14 A

THE CURRENT DEPOSITS

Sr. No.	Name of the Banks	87-88	88-89	89-90	90-91	91-92	92-93	93-94	94-95	95-96	96-97
1	The Kalupur Bank	846.86	1036.47	2084.95	1592.49	2158.63	2604.37	9370.40	6025.89	4357.59	8454.03
2	The Rajkot Nagrik Bank	460.72	549.30	623.10	791.22	999.01	1173.41	1510.55	1655.71	1759.32	2001.95
3	Anyona Saharakri Bank	57.98	66.77	94.62	110.60	146.13	161.78	185.42	197.28	268.91	412.30
4	The Surat Peoples's Bank	450.64	1355.36	1438.38	1609.29	1564.19	2495.20	2597.98	2732.79	3017.37	3662.90
5	The Natpur Co-op. Bank	63.59	76.81	88.85	95.26	90.46	140.13	149.26	153.63	227.53	206.05
6	The Anand Mercantile Bank	98.60	111.64	135.08	179.58	192.33	172.91	353.48	260.15	255.45	305.14
7	Dahod Urban Bank	63.59	60.02	82.07	98.22	61.38	67.77	80.99	126.58	110.78	167.03
8	Sarvodya Nagrik Bank	21.21	28.78	45.05	40.74	53.01	64.97	79.67	124.57	109.10	116.16
9	Baroda People's Bank	24.25	33.64	45.77	52.70	48.54	236.29	193.66	94.67	53.41	77.47
10	Sardar Bhiladwala Bank	210.47	289.43	374.10	491.49	512.99	737.95	915.78	1274.07	1292.27	1491.14

TABLE 4.15

PROPORTION OF CURRENT DEPOSITS TO TOTAL DEPOSITS

Sr. No.	Name of the Banks	87-88	88-89	89-90	90-91	91-92	92-93	93-94	94-95	95-96	96-97	AVG
1	The Kalupur Bank	0.13	0.15	0.22	0.15	0.18	0.15	0.31	0.18	0.12	0.20	0.18
2	The Rajkot Nagrik Bank	0.03	0.04	0.04	0.05	0.06	0.06	0.07	0.07	0.06	0.06	0.06
3	Anyona Saharakri Bank	0.03	0.03	0.03	0.03	0.04	0.04	0.04	0.04	0.04	0.04	0.04
4	Surat Peoples's Bank	0.05	0.17	0.16	0.16	0.14	0.18	0.17	0.16	0.15	0.14	0.15
5	Natpur Co-op. Bank	0.03	0.06	–0.05	0.05	0.04	0.06	0.05	0.04	0.04	0.03	0.05
6	Anand Mercantile Bank	0.12	0.06	0.06	0.07	0.06	0.06	0.09	0.06	0.05	0.05	0.07
7	Dahod Urban Bank	0.04	0.03	0.04	0.04	0.03	0.03	0.03	0.04	0.02	0.03	0.03
8	Sarvodya Nagrik Bank	0.04	0.05	0.06	0.05	0.06	0.06	0.07	0.10	0.07	0.07	0.06
9	Baroda People's Bank	0.04	0.03	0.03	0.03	0.02	0.09	0.06	0.05	0.01	0.01	0.04
10	Sardar Bhiladwala Bank	0.07	0.08	0.09	0.11	0.10	0.13	0.13	0.16	0.14	0.13	0.11

these deposits. It is worth noting that till today the interest rate of saving deposits are regulated by The Reserve Bank of India. Today 4.5 per cent interest is payable on saving deposits. Saving deposits of the Kalupur Commercial Bank are less than those of its current deposits. The Kalupur Commercial Bank is the only bank in selected urban banks having such situation throughout study period of ten years. Remaining all nine co-operative banks' saving deposits are higher than that of their current deposits for all the ten years. Rajkot Nagrik Bank amongst selected banks is mobilising highest saving deposits than that of any other bank for all the study period.

Marginal reduction in saving deposits of the Kalupur Commercial Bank is noticed in the year 1990-91, i.e., Rs. 1150.23 lacs which was Rs. 1183.31 lacs in the year 1989-90. Similarly the Anand Mercantile Bank's saving deposits are reduced by just Rs. 7 lacs in the year 1995-96, but The Sarvodaya Nagarik Bank has experienced this decline for three years. Except these five incidents, there is a continuous rise revealed by all ten banks for all ten years.

Annual Growth Rate of Saving Deposits

As per Table 4.17, in the year 1994-95, The Kalupur Commercial Bank has registered 51 per cent annual growth in saving deposits and 48 per cent in the year 1989-90. Conversely The Rajkot Nagrik Bank has registered just one per cent increase in the year 1988-89, which stands lowest in the table. For another two years i.e. 1989-90 and 1990-91, saving deposits of the same bank has registered growth less than 10 per cent. Similarly overall weak growth and fluctuations in saving deposits of The Dahod Urban Co-operative Bank is noticed.

Saving Deposits to Total Deposits

As per Table 4.18, proportion of saving to total deposits indicates share of saving deposits in the total deposits. It is

TABLE 4.16

THE SAVING DEPOSITS

Sr. No.	Name of the Banks	87-88	88-89	89-90	90-91	91-92	92-93	93-94	94-95	95-96	96-97
1	The Kalupur Bank	634.67	800.58	1183.31	1150.23	1424.79	1608.97	2070.14	3131.73	3866.72	4364.62
2	The Rajkot Nagrik Bank	2560.33	2585.29	3046.01	3327.80	3479.93	3816.82	4302.99	5470.90	6790.63	7707.78
3	Anyona Saharakri Bank	526.49	565.96	663.98	733.62	804.54	834.30	951.23	1163.29	1408.31	1940.44
4	The Surat Peoples's Bank	2021.69	2313.50	2784.80	2943.57	3283.29	3486.07	4183.29	5139.55	5642.57	6612.07
5	The Natpur Co-op. Bank	226.20	248.45	313.49	383.36	419.35	451.88	551.65	703.05	718.36	802.63
6	The Anand Mercantile Bank	211.42	243.70	308.43	369.80	425.58	379.35	452.79	557.29	552.59	689.29
7	Dahod Urban Bank	372.22	433.33	495.26	533.15	577.59	572.71	629.53	790.80	818.81	910.58
8	Sarvodya Nagrik Bank	95.13	107.45	141.97	180.09	193.41	245.41	240.18	344.75	321.34	310.16
9	Baroda People's Bank	226.20	288.00	387.35	465.12	566.59	638.20	696.16	833.78	983.05	1195.34
10	Sardar Bhiladwala Bank	810.58	929.4	1,137.63	1,172.98	1,328.46	1,566.44	1,941.95	2,319.93	2,651.12	3,188.45

TABLE 4.17

ANNUAL GROWTH RATE OF SAVING DEPOSITS

Sr. No.	Name of the Banks	87-88	88-89	89-90	90-91	91-92	92-93	93-94	94-95	95-96	96-97
1	The Kalupur Bank	1.00	1.26	1.48	0.97	1.24	1.13	1.29	1.51	1.23	1.13
2	The Rajkot Nagrik Bank	1.00	1.01	1.18	1.09	1.05	1.10	1.13	1.27	1.24	1.14
3	Anyona Saharakri Bank	1.00	1.07	1.17	1.10	1.10	1.04	1.14	1.22	1.21	1.38
4	The Surat Peoples's Bank	1.00	1.14	1.20	1.06	1.12	1.06	1.20	1.23	1.10	1.17
5	The Natpur Co-Op Bank	1.00	1.10	1.26	1.22	1.09	1.08	1.22	1.27	1.02	1.12
6	The Anand Mercentile	1.00	1.15	1.27	1.20	1.15	0.89	1.19	1.23	0.99	1.25
7	Dahod Urban Co-op. Bank	1.00	1.16	1.14	1.08	1.08	0.99	1.10	1.26	1.04	1.11
8	Sarvodya Nagrik Bank	1.00	1.13	1.32	1.27	1.07	1.27	0.98	1.44	0.93	0.97
9	Baroda People's Bank	1.00	1.27	1.34	1.20	1.22	1.13	1.09	1.20	1.18	1.22
10	Sardar Bhiladwala Bank	1.00	1.15	1.22	1.03	1.13	1.18	1.24	1.19	1.14	1.20

TABLE 4.18

PROPORTION OF SAVING DEPOSITS TO TOTAL DEPOSITS

Sr. No.	*Name of the Banks*	*87-88*	*88-89*	*89-90*	*90-91*	*91-92*	*92-93*	*93-94*	*94-95*	*95-96*	*96-97*	*AVG*
1	The Kalupur Bank	0.10	0.11	0.12	0.11	0.12	0.09	0.07	0.09	0.10	0.10	0.10
2	The Rajkot Nagrik Bank	0.17	0.21	0.22	0.22	0.21	0.21	0.20	0.24	0.24	0.23	0.21
3	Anyona Saharakri Bank	0.25	0.24	0.24	0.23	0.23	0.21	0.21	0.22	0.20	0.20	0.22
4	Surat Peoples's Bank	0.22	0.28	0.30	0.28	0.29	0.26	0.27	0.30	0.29	0.26	0.28
5	The Natpur Co-op. Bank	0.11	0.18	0.18	0.20	0.19	0.18	0.19	0.20	0.14	0.12	0.17
6	Anand Mercantile Bank	0.25	0.14	0.14	0.15	0.14	0.13	0.12	0.14	0.10	0.11	0.14
7	Dahod Urban Bank	0.23	0.24	0.25	0.24	0.24	0.21	0.21	0.23	0.18	0.15	0.22
8	Sarvodya Nagrik Bank	0.18	0.17	0.20	0.22	0.22	0.23	0.21	0.27	0.20	0.18	0.21
9	Baroda People's Bank	0.40	0.24	0.26	0.26	0.27	0.24	0.23	0.42	0.22	0.20	0.27
10	Sardar Bhiladwala Bank	0.26	0.26	0.27	0.26	0.27	0.27	0.28	0.29	0.29	0.29	0.27

TABLE 4.19

THE FIXED DEPOSITS

Sr. No.	Name of the Banks	87-88	88-89	89-90	90-91	91-92	92-93	93-94	94-95	95-96	96-97
1	The Kalupur Bank	2,755.11	3,252.66	4,098.92	5,301.27	5,157.50	10,108.84	18,799.45	23,945.94	28,573.59	28,940.00
2	The Rajkot Nagrik Bank	6,598.29	7,014.69	7,840.19	8,593.91	9,175.99	10,474.49	12,178.88	11,916.74	15,091.24	18,079.69
3	Anyona Saharakri Bank	1,562.31	1,737.39	2,031.36	2,321.91	2,510.50	2,961.32	3,377.45	3,921.99	5,412.45	7,445.36
4	Surat Peoples's Bank	2,938.97	3,257.26	3,649.44	4,059.53	4,203.72	5,385.80	5,654.67	5,634.29	6,662.48	9,153.18
5	Natpur Co-op. Bank	934.53	1,064.83	1,290.93	1,462.46	1,650.31	1,929.32	2,171.00	2,597.67	4,110.90	5,422.96
6	Anand Mercantile Bank	533.19	687.94	930.18	1,169.55	1,523.92	1,679.90	2,256.80	2,564.83	3,955.29	4,116.38
7	Dahod Urban Bank	1,169.86	1,306.28	1,408.81	1,570.68	1,771.98	2,050.66	2,343.09	2,497.90	3,514.52	4,954.56
8	Sarvodya Nagrik Bank	407.39	482.11	531.57	588.66	643.13	738.54	815.40	816.21	1,143.10	1,294.13
9	Baroda People's Bank	311.64	434.32	425.54	517.87	556.94	747.83	918.58	926.13	1,717.00	2,104.24
10	Sardar Bhiladwala Bank	2,058.66	2,370.12	2,650.64	2,910.83	3,078.11	3,461.84	4,063.24	4,356.84	5,244.87	6,418.58

The Kalupur Commercial Bank again whose saving deposit ratio to total deposits is less than all other nine banks. The ratio ranges between just 7 per cent and 16 per cent. Whereas The Baroda People's Bank's saving deposits proportion to total deposits is higher, ranging between 35 per cent and 47 per cent, second highest bank for such proportion is The Surat People's Bank, remaining banks' saving deposits are on an average of 20 per cent to 25 per cent.

Fixed Deposits

As per Table 4.19, fixed deposits are highly preferred by the urban people. But from the viewpoint of banks, the fixed deposits are costlier than that of current and saving deposits. They are also called as term deposits. Urban banks were allowed to pay 1 per cent higher interest on fixed deposits; therefore obviously fixed deposits are costlier to urban banks than that of commercial banks. This is one of the reasons that urban people were giving preference to Urban Co-operative Banks rather than commercial banks. Establishment expenses are less required but interest cost on fixed deposits is very high. The Reserve Bank of India regulated interest rate on fixed deposits up to 1996. Fixed deposits of the entire ten banks under the study period are uninterruptedly rising at a faster growth rate, the exception to this growth rate is for The Kalupur Commercial Bank in the year 1991-92 and The Baroda People's Bank in the year 1989-90. Fixed deposits of The Baroda People's Bank reduced by just 6 lacs whereas The Kalupur Commercial Bank's declined nearly of Rs. 150 lacs in respective years.

As revealed from the Table 4.20, Fixed deposits' growth registered by The Kalupur Commercial Bank is 96 per cent and 86 per cent for the year 1992-93 and 1993-94 respectively. Lowest growth registered by The Sardar Bhiladwala Bank is ranging from 6 per cent to 22 per cent. The entire progress in fixed deposits is fluctuating. All the banks during ten years of study period are showing ups and downs in the growth rate of fixed deposits.

TABLE 4.20

ANNUAL GROWTH RATE OF FIXED DEPOSITS

Sr. No.	Name of the Banks	87-88	88-89	89-90	90-91	91-92	92-93	93-94	94-95	95-96	96-97
1	The Kalupur Bank	1.00	1.18	1.26	1.29	0.97	1.96	1.86	1.27	1.19	1.01
2	The Rajkot Nagrik Bank	1.00	1.06	1.12	1.10	1.07	1.14	1.16	0.98	1.27	1.20
3	Anyonya Sahayakari Bank	1.00	1.11	1.17	1.14	1.08	1.18	1.14	1.16	1.38	1.38
4	The Surat People's Bank	1.00	1.11	1.12	1.11	1.04	1.28	1.05	1.00	1.18	1.37
5	The Natpur Co-op. Bank	1.00	1.14	1.21	1.13	1.13	1.17	1.13	1.20	1.58	1.32
6	The Anand Mercantile Bank	1.00	1.29	1.35	1.26	1.30	1.10	1.34	1.14	1.54	1.04
7	Dahod Urban Bank	1.00	1.12	1.08	1.11	1.13	1.16	1.14	1.07	1.41	1.41
8	Sarvodya Nagrik Bank	1.00	1.18	1.10	1.11	1.09	1.15	1.10	1.00	1.40	1.13
9	Baroda People's Bank	1.00	1.39	0.98	1.22	1.08	1.34	1.23	1.01	1.85	1.23
10	Sardar Bhiladwala Bank	1.00	1.15	1.12	1.10	1.06	1.12	1.17	1.07	1.20	1.22

Table 4.21 shows share of fixed deposits in total deposits is very high compare to current and saving deposits as revealed in the table. The Natpur Co-operative Bank's ratio of fixed deposits to total deposit is ranging between 75 per cent and 84 per cent during the period of 1987-88 and 1996-97. Except The Baroda People's Bank, all the banks' proportion of fixed deposits to total deposits is more than 50 per cent.

Other Deposits

Other deposits comprise of recurring, daily saving or any other scheme of deposits. Normally these deposits are considered as time deposits or fixed deposits. Some banks are merging these deposits with fixed deposits, therefore table 4.22 shows very low amount of other deposits or some banks like The Anyonya Sahayakari Bank, The Dahod Urban Bank and The Sardar Bhiladwala Bank are showing nil for other deposits. But The Kalupur Commercial Bank and The Rajkot Nagrik Bank show sizeable amount of other deposits. The Kalupur Commercial Bank is showing sudden decline in other deposits from the year 1992-93. Table 4.23 is showing the proportion of other deposits to total deposits. From the year 1988-89, The Rajkot Nagrik Bank shows the stable share of other deposits in total deposits.

Total Deposits

Total deposits comprise of current, saving. fixed and other deposits. As discussed earlier, current deposits are without interest cost, saving deposits, which are regulated interest rate bearing and fixed deposits are deregulated interest. As we have seen, individually saving, current and fixed deposits are continuously increasing naturally then total deposits must be rising continuously. The increase can be observed from the table 4.25 of total deposits of urban banks and the table of annual growth compared to previous year. Significant rise in total deposits is of The Kalupur Commercial Bank i.e. the total deposits for the year 1987-88 were amounting to Rs. 4236.64 lacs which increased to Rs. 41,901.91 lacs for

TABLE 4.21

PROPORTION OF FIXED DEPOSITS TO TOTAL DEPOISTS

Sr. No.	Name of the Banks	87-88	88-89	89-90	90-91	91-92	92-93	93-94	94-95	95-96	96-97	AVG
1	The Kalupur Bank	0.43	0.47	0.43	0.49	0.44	0.58	0.62	0.72	0.77	0.69	0.56
2	The Rajkot Nagrik Bank	0.43	0.57	0.56	0.56	0.56	0.57	0.58	0.52	0.54	0.55	0.54
3	Anyona Saharakri Bank	0.73	0.73	0.73	0.73	0.73	0.75	0.75	0.74	0.76	0.76	0.74
4	The Surat Peoples's Bank	0.33	0.40	0.39	0.39	0.37	0.39	0.37	0.32	0.34	0.36	0.37
5	The Natpur Co-op. Bank	0.46	0.76	0.76	0.75	0.76	0.77	0.76	0.75	0.81	0.82	0.74
6	Anand Mercantile Bank	0.63	0.39	0.44	0.46	0.50	0.55	0.60	0.63	0.73	0.68	0.56
7	Dahod Urban Bank	0.73	0.73	0.71	0.71	0.73	0.76	0.77	0.73	0.79	0.82	0.75
8	Sarvodya Nagrik Bank	0.78	0.75	0.74	0.73	0.72	0.70	0.72	0.63	0.73	0.75	0.73
9	Baroda People's Bank	0.55	0.36	0.29	0.29	0.27	0.28	0.31	0.46	0.38	0.36	0.36
10	Sardar Bhiladwala Bank	0.67	0.66	0.64	0.64	0.63	0.60	0.59	0.55	0.57	0.58	0.61

TABLE 4.22

THE OTHER DEPOSITS

Sr. No.	Name of the Banks	87-88	88-89	89-90	90-91	91-92	92-93	93-94	94-95	95-96	96-97
1	Kalupur Bank	1,878.37	2,243.57	2,778.63	3,021.58	2,962.92	186.86	78.54	81.27	107.92	139.25
2	Rajkot Nagrik Bank	2,067.25	2,491.34	2,719.34	2,857.94	2,981.81	3,084.35	3785.10	4432.14	5143.91	4535.49
3	Anyona Saharakri Bank	0.00	0.00	0.00	0.00	0.00	0.00	0.00	0.00	0.00	0.00
4	Surat Peoples's Bank	1,223.40	1,380.81	1,762.98	2,193.99	2,269.90	2,803.88	3,891.72	4,223.78	5,993.45	8442.69
5	Natpur Co-op. Bank	3.65	6.62	9.38	7.18	0.45	0.35	0.35	0.00	163.46	0.00
6	Anand Mercantile Bank	720.27	756.74	799.17	877.33	802.07	726.33	685.74	634.36	915.20	1460.73
7	Dahod Urban Bank	0.00	0.00	0.00	0.00	0.00	0.00	0.00	0.00	0.00	0.00
8	Sarvodya Nagrik Bank	20.23	0.00	0.00	0.00	0.00	0.00	0.00	0.00	0.00	0.00
9	Baroda People's Bank	454.87	614.66	746.55	923.88	1,003.75	1,195.26	146.40	1,715.49	2,528.05	3335.37
10	Sardar Bhiladwala Bank	0.00	0.00	0.00	0.00	0.00	0.00	0.00	0.00	0.00	0.00

TABLE 4.23

PROPORTION OF OTHER DEPOSITS TO TOTAL DEPOSITS

Sr. No.	*Name of the Banks*	*87-88*	*88-89*	*89-90*	*90-91*	*91-92*	*92-93*	*93-94*	*94-95*	*95-96*	*96-97*	*AVG*
1	The Kalupur Bank	0.34	0.27	0.23	0.26	0.26	0.17	0.01	0.00	0.00	0.00	0.15
2	The Rajkot Nagrik Bank	0.37	0.17	0.18	0.18	0.17	0.16	0.15	0.17	0.16	0.16	0.19
3	Anyona Saharakri Bank	0.00	0.00	0.00	0.00	0.00	0.00	0.00	0.00	0.00	0.00	0.00
4	Surat Peoples's Bank	0.40	0.15	0.15	0.17	0.20	0.17	0.18	0.22	0.22	0.24	0.21
5	The Natpur Co-op. Bank	0.39	0.00	0.00	0.00	0.00	0.00	0.00	0.00	0.00	0.02	0.04
6	The Anand Mercantile Bank	0.00	0.41	0.36	0.32	0.29	0.26	0.19	0.17	0.12	0.15	0.23
7	Dahod Urban Bank	0.00	0.00	0.00	0.00	0.00	0.00	0.00	0.00	0.00	0.00	0.00
8	Sarvodya Nagrik Bank	0.00	0.03	0.00	0.00	0.00	0.00	0.00	0.00	0.00	0.00	0.00
9	Baroda People's Bank	0.00	0.38	0.42	0.42	0.44	0.38	0.40	0.07	0.38	0.43	0.33
10	Sardar Bhiladwala Bank	0.00	0.00	0.00	0.00	0.00	0.00	0.00	0.00	0.00	0.00	0.00

TABLE 4.24

PROPORTION OF TOTAL DEPOSITS TO WORKING CAPITAL

Sr. No.	Name of the Banks	87-88	88-89	89-90	90-91	91-92	92-93	93-94	94-95	95-96	96-97	AVG
1	The Kalupur Bank	0.70	0.67	0.71	0.68	0.68	0.83	0.79	0.75	0.70	0.71	0.72
2	The Rajkot Nagrik Bank	1.15	0.82	0.80	0.81	0.80	0.79	0.77	0.76	0.77	0.79	0.83
3	Anyona Saharakri Bank	0.80	0.80	0.81	0.80	0.80	0.79	0.78	0.81	0.81	0.84	0.80
4	Surat Peoples's Bank	0.95	0.73	0.70	0.69	0.69	0.67	0.65	0.67	0.64	0.65	0.70
5	The Natpur Co-op. Bank	1.41	0.80	0.80	0.81	0.78	0.83	0.81	0.80	0.88	0.88	0.88
6	Anand Mercantile Bank	0.49	0.79	0.78	0.75	0.74	0.72	0.88	0.86	0.79	0.84	0.76
7	Dahod Urban Bank	0.73	0.72	0.72	0.72	0.72	0.72	0.66	0.66	0.72	0.84	0.72
8	Sarvodya Nagrik Bank	0.68	0.72	0.71	0.66	0.67	0.66	0.65	0.70	0.73	0.70	0.69
9	Baroda People's Bank	0.45	0.73	0.76	0.74	0.74	0.73	0.67	0.40	0.64	0.66	0.65
10	Sardar Bhiladwala Bank	0.86	0.81	0.80	0.78	0.75	0.74	0.74	0.74	0.75	0.74	0.77

the year 1996-97, the rise is 8.89 times during these ten years. Compared to any other bank under the study, The Rajkot Nagarik Bank has mobilised remarkably highest deposits during ten years of study. The Anand Mercantile Bank and The Baroda People's Bank registered nearly 500 per cent increase in total deposits during ten years.

Total Deposits to Working Capital

Working capital comprises of owned funds, deposits and borrowings of the banks. As discussed earlier. major share in working capital is of deposits. In the table, same position is revealed for the total deposits to working capital of selected Urban Co-operative Banks during ten years of study. As revealed from the table 4.24, total deposits of Rajkot Nagarik Bank in the year 1987-88 amounted to Rs. 11686.59 lakh and working capital amounted to Rs. 13378.53 lacs, so total deposits constitute 87 per cent of the working capital. Only Baroda People's Bank and Anand Mercantile Bank's total deposits forms nearly 50 per cent of working capital during ten years, other eight banks' two third of the working capital is constituted by total deposits.

Composition of Total Deposits

It is interesting to study the composition of total deposits of ten selected Urban Co-operative Banks in Gujarat for ten years' averages of current, saving, fixed and other deposits. Total deposits are assumed to be Rs. 100, and then the chart is showing composition of:

i) Average current deposits to average total deposits,

ii) Average saving deposits to average total deposits,

iii) Average fixed deposits to average total deposits and

iv) Average fixed deposits to average total deposits are drawn for each individual bank.

TABLE 4.25

ANNUAL GROWTH RATE OF TOTAL DEPOSITS.

Sr. No.	Name of the Banks	87-88	88-89	89-90	90-91	91-92	92-93	93-94	94-95	95-96	96-97
1	The Kalupur Bank	1.00	1.09	1.38	1.13	1.09	1.47	1.76	1.09	1.11	1.14
2	The Rajkot Nagrik Bank	1.00	0.80	1.15	1.10	1.07	1.12	1.14	1.08	1.23	1.17
3	Anyonya Sahayakari Bank	1.00	1.10	1.18	1.13	1.09	1.14	1.14	1.17	1.34	1.38
4	The Surat People's Bank	1.00	0.90	1.14	1.12	1.08	1.21	1.12	1.14	1.12	1.30
5	The Natpur Co-op. Bank	1.00	0.69	1.22	1.15	1.11	1.16	1.14	1.20	1.46	1.30
6	Anand Mercantile Bank	1.00	2.09	1.21	1.18	1.20	1.00	1.25	1.07	1.33	1.12
7	Dahod Urban Bank	1.00	1.12	1.10	1.11	1.09	1.12	1.13	1.12	1.30	1.36
8	Sarvodya Nagrik Bank	1.00	1.22	1.13	1.13	1.10	1.18	1.08	1.13	1.22	1.09
9	Baroda People's Bank	1.00	2.15	1.22	1.21	1.18	1.25	1.14	0.67	2.23	1.32
10	Sardar Bhiladwala Bank	1.00	1.17	1.16	1.10	1.08	1.17	1.20	1.15	1.16	1.21

The graph 4.01 to 4.10 are showing the composition of average current, saving fixed and other deposits to average total deposits. Larger current deposit share to total deposit is of Kalupur Commercial Bank. It has maximum of 19 per cent of average current deposits to average total deposits. Second position obtained by mobilising higher current deposits is The Surat People's Bank registering 15 per cent and 12 per cent by Sardar Bhiladwala Bank; remaining banks have registered current deposits less than 10 per cent. Lowest share of current deposits amongst 10 selected banks is of The Dahod Urban Co-operative Bank and The Baroda People's Bank is just 3 per cent of average current deposits. It is desirable to use the current deposits as they are bearing lower costs. Ten selected urban banks are the representative banks for all the urban banks of Gujarat. It may be concluded that urban banks of Gujarat are unable to take advantage of this low cost source of current deposits. Hence proportion of current deposits is lower as compared to commercial banks.

Conversely the fixed deposits contribute more towards the total deposits of selected Urban Co-operative Banks. Higher contribution of fixed deposit is of The Anand Mercantile Bank i.e. 82 per cent. Only The Surat People's Bank's Average total deposits include lowest i.e. 58 per cent of fixed deposits. Largely each bank except Surat People's Bank amongst selected banks registered more over 70 per cent or more of average fixed deposits to total deposits.

As mentioned earlier, term deposits as costly source of funds contributes large share in total deposits, is negative facto on the part of Urban Co-operative Banks of Gujarat.

Average saving deposits of The Baroda People's Bank constitute 22 per cent of average total deposits during the year 1987-88 to 1996-97. The Sardar Bhiladwala Bank is placed at first position for having 28 per cent more average saving deposits. Simultaneously this is the bank amongst ten selected banks having second lowest average fixed deposits to the tune of 60 per cent to total deposits. The Kalupur Commercial Bank contributes only 10.7 per cent of average saving deposits to average total deposits, which is the lowest contribution amongst all ten banks.

Profit Deposits Compared

Table 4.26 showing ratio of profit to the total deposits of selected Urban Co-operative Banks reveals the behavior of profit with increasing deposits throughout the study period. Eye-catching fact is that no bank out of ten banks and for no years has registered the profit more than 10 per cent to total deposits. The Rajkot Nagarik Bank and The Anyonya Bank for all the ten years have shown only one per cent of total deposits, Baroda People's Bank shows 5 per cent to 6 per cent of profit to total deposit. Except few years resultant ratios of profit to total deposit are even less than 5 per cent.

Constant ratio of profit to deposits also reveals that urban banks of Gujarat are in a position to maintain it. Earlier we have studied that growth rate of deposits are very high. Even in rising deposits, urban banks keeps on earning profit constantly. Additional deposits obtained by urban banks are utilised in such manner that the profits are not reduced. Other sides of the fact are that profitability of the urban banks has reduced and rising deposits do not bring significant rise in profit.

TABLE 4.26

PROPORTION OF PROFIT TO TOTAL DEPOSITS

Sr. No.	*Name of the Banks*	*87-88*	*88-89*	*89-90*	*90-91*	*91-92*	*92-93*	*93-94*	*94-95*	*95-96*	*96-97*	*AVG*
1	The Kalupur Bank	0.02	0.02	0.02	0.01	0.01	0.01	0.01	0.02	0.02	0.03	0.02
2	The Rajkot Nagrik Bank	0.01	0.01	0.01	0.01	0.01	0.01	0.01	0.01	0.01	0.01	0.01
3	Anyona Saharakri Bank	0.01	0.01	0.01	0.01	0.10	0.01	0.01	0.01	0.01	0.02	0.01
4	The Surat Peoples's Bank	0.02	0.03	0.03	0.03	0.06	0.03	0.03	0.03	0.01	0.01	0.03
5	The Natpur Co-op. Bank	0.02	0.04	0.04	0.04	0.04	0.05	0.04	0.04	0.03	0.04	0.04
6	Anand Mercantile Bank	0.04	0.02	0.03	0.02	0.02	0.03	0.03	0.03	0.02	0.03	0.03
7	Dahod Urban Bank	0.02	0.02	0.02	0.02	0.02	0.02	0.02	0.02	0.02	0.01	0.02
8	Sarvodya Nagrik Bank	0.01	0.01	0.02	0.02	0.01	0.02	0.01	0.01	0.01	0.02	0.02
9	Baroda People's Bank	0.05	0.03	0.03	0.03	0.03	0.03	0.04	0.06	0.03	0.03	0.04
10	Sardar Bhiladwala Bank	0.03	0.03	0.02	0.04	0.05	0.04	0.02	0.03	0.05	0.06	0.04

GRAPH 4.01

COMPOSITION OF AVERAGE CURRENT, SAVINGS AND FIXED PLUS OTHER DEPOSITS OF THE KALUPUR BANK

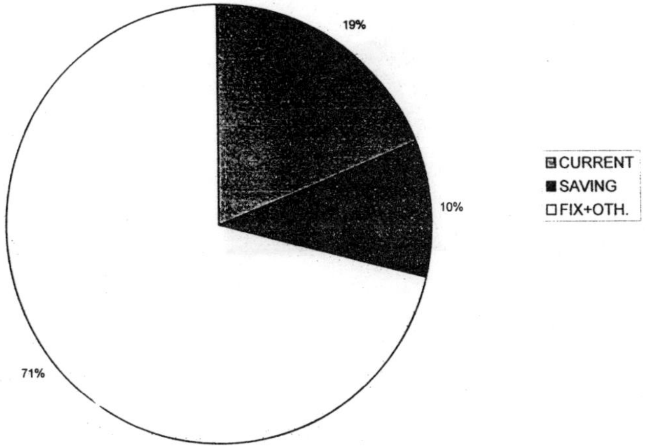

GRAPH 4.02

COMPOSITION OF AVERAGE CURRENT, SAVINGS AND FIXED PLUS OTHER DEPOSITS OF THE RAJKOT NAGARIK BANK

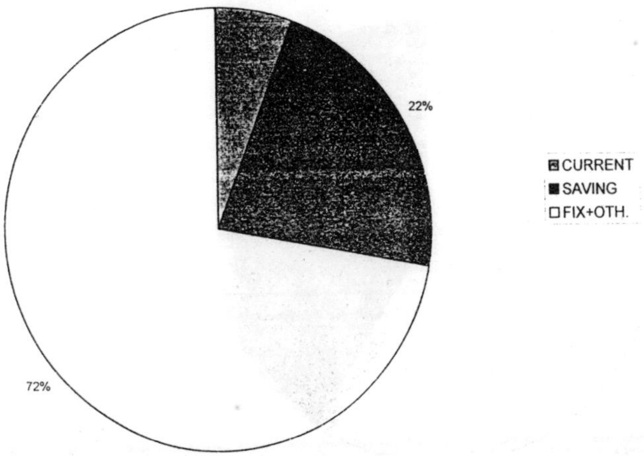

GRAPH 4.03

COMPOSITION OF AVERAGE CURRENT, SAVINGS AND FIXED PLUS OTHER DEPOSITS OF THE ANONYA SAHAYAKARI BANK

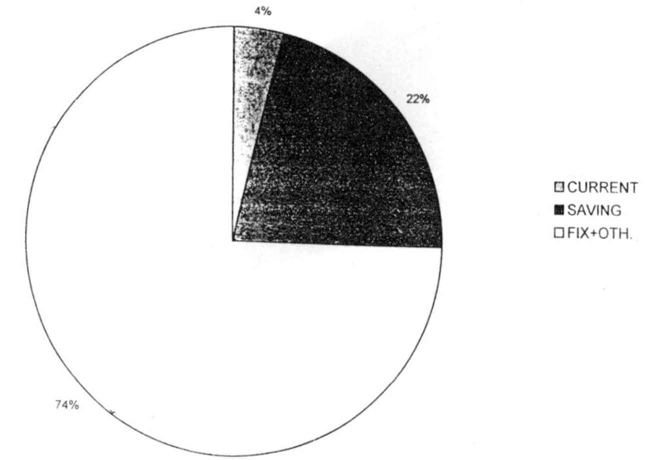

GRAPH 4.04

COMPOSITION OF AVERAGE CURRENT, SAVINGS AND FIXED PLUS OTHER DEPOSITS OF THE SURAT PEOPLE'S BANK.

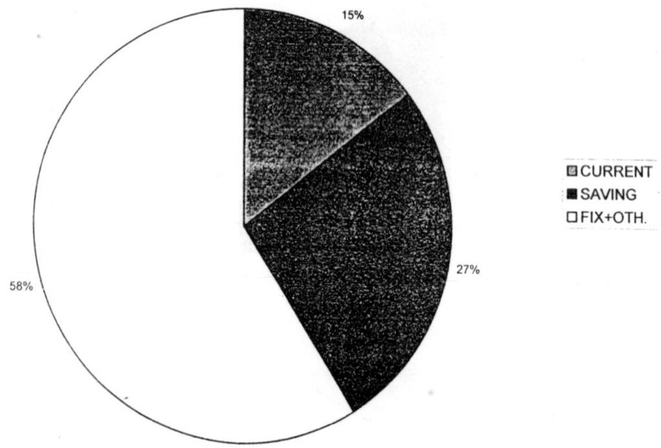

GRAPH 4.05

COMPOSITION OF AVERAGE CURRENT, SAVINGS AND FIXED PLUS OTHER DEPOSITS OF THE NATPUR CO-OP. BANK

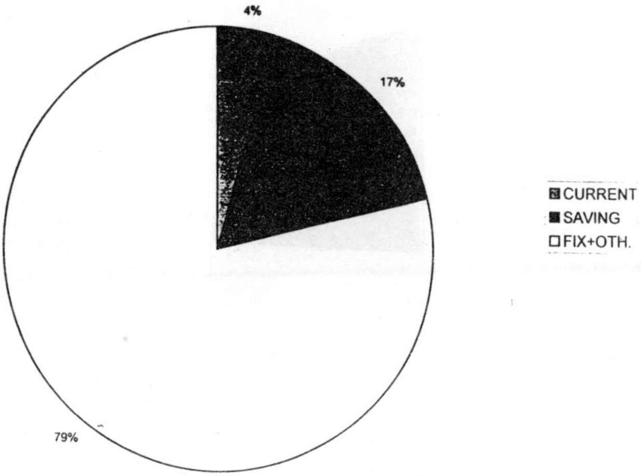

GRAPH 4.06

COMPOSITION OF AVERAGE CURRENT, SAVINGS AND FIXED PLUS OTHER DEPOSITS OF THE ANAND MERCANTILE BANK

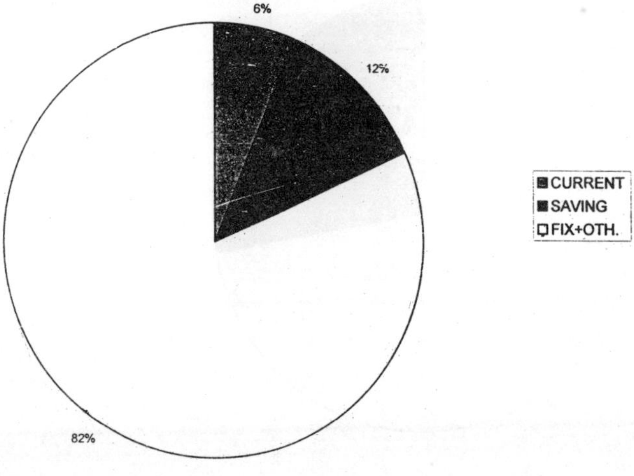

GRAPH 4.07

COMPOSITION OF AVERAGE CURRENT, SAVINGS AND FIXED PLUS OTHER DEPOSITS OF THE DAHOD URBAN BANK

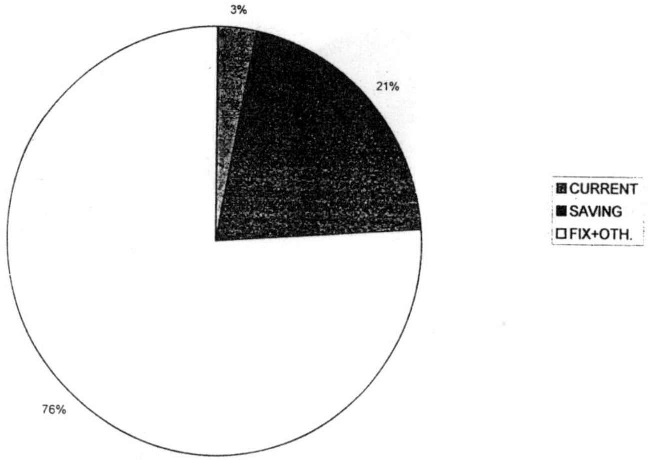

GRAPH 4.08

COMPOSITION OF AVERAGE CURRENT, SAVINGS AND FIXED PLUS OTHER DEPOSITS OF THE SARVODAYA NAGARIK BANK

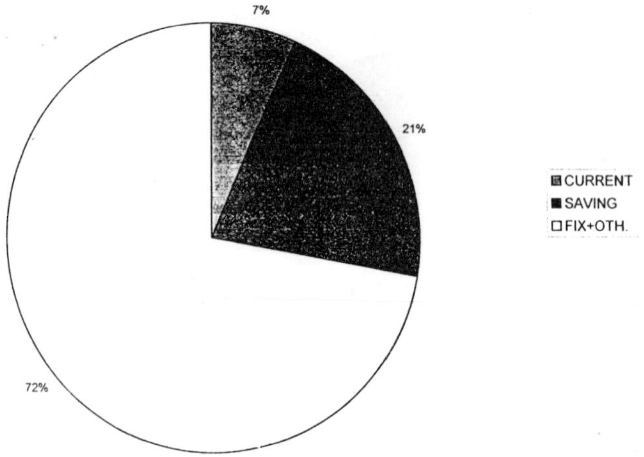

GRAPH 4.09

COMPOSITION OF AVERAGE CURRENT, SAVINGS AND FIXED PLUS OTHER DEPOSITS OF THE BARODA PEOPLE'S BANK

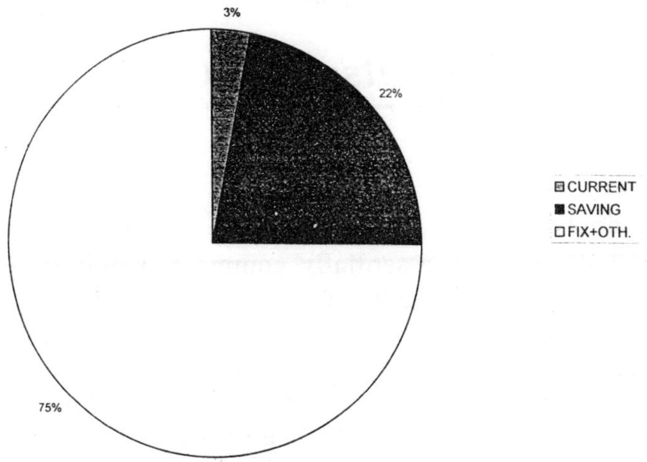

GRAPH 4.10

COMPOSITION OF AVERAGE CURRENT, SAVINGS AND FIXED PLUS OTHER DEPOSITS OF THE SARDAR BHILADWALA BANK

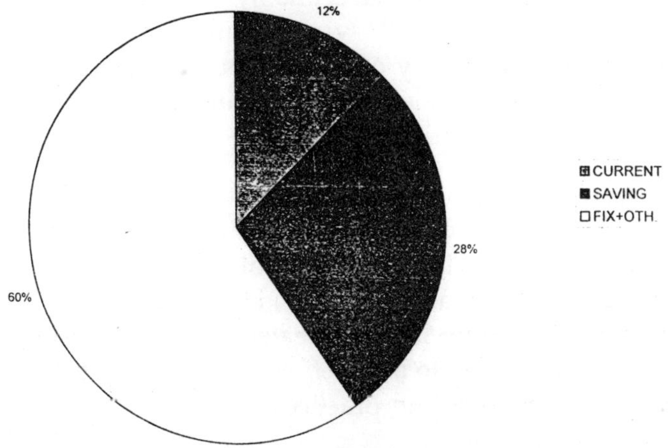

5

Deposits: Fixed Cost

Introduction

The banks are essentially commercial organisations, therefore profit is considered as an important indicator and measure of their efficiency. The declining trend of profitability in the public sector banking industry has become a sensitive and embracing issue for management of the banks. Public sector banks are expected to balance "Profit object" with "Service motive" which is a crucial and difficult task too. Both "Service" and "Profit" are contradictory with each other in nature.

As a result of financial sector reforms, banks have to face new challenges in the Indian economy. The viability of banks depends upon three "P" viz., profit, profitability and productivity. Adequacy of profit should be determined in such a manner that losses incurred in new areas may be absorbed without difficulties.

The banks are playing a very important role in the national development and economy of India. Therefore it has become important to develop a degree of cost consciousness. Deregulated interest rate structure and increasing establishment expenses will further lead to greater cost consciousness on the part of banks and to make efforts to reduce costs through improved operations and practices.

The Bank Administration Institute, USA, submitted a

report on "Cost in Commercial Banking" in the following language:

> "Costing has had its great use and development in the manufacturing field. Consequently there is a natural tendency to apply manufacturing cost concepts to banks. For the proper application of the costing process to the banking field, it is necessary to understand the characteristics of cost in banks. Cost characteristics strongly influence the validity of certain cost technique."[1]

The cost of funds in a bank is very similar to the cost for sales in a manufacturing industry. In case of industry involved in manufacturing, the cost of sales represents the cost required to manufacture a product plus the cost factor incurred for selling a product (funds). However in a manufacturing industry, there is a trend for reduction in cost per unit of a product as volume of production increases. The factors that control reduction in cost are, purchasing of raw material in large quantity, more efficient use of labour and manufacturing facilities / technology. While in case of bank, although the interest cost is a substantial part of "cost of sales", the amount of loans rendered by a bank does not directly affect the cost i.e. the interest per unit deposits. Therefore, reduction in unit cost must come from better utilisation of resources categorized as a non-interest cost of deposits. Further, the Banks are also influenced by external factors, such as money market. This external factor controls the trend of interest cost and the general effect of being looked into fixed price for fixed period of time. This external factor controls the trend of interest cost and the general effect of being looked into fixed price for fixed period of time. Better management of cost helps to overcome this external factor.

Complexity of banking industry is due to generation of multi product outputs. Also banking is a labour intensive service industry. This has made many researchers to study cost management of banking industry by various methods and techniques as under:

Methods and Techniques of Costing

Process Costing

Process costing is defined as "The form of operation costing where standardised goods are produced under a method where the product passes through two or more processes before it becomes a final product."[2] In this method, costs are collected according to departments or processes, which is further divided by the quantity of the production so as to arrive at the product cost at each process, operation or stage of manufacturing. A separate account for each process is to be opened and all expenditure of that particular process or operation is to be charged thereon. In process costing of a finished product, output of a previous process becomes the 'Raw material' or 'Input" of the subsequent process. This method is suitable for industries involved in continuous process of production of a product or products through the same process or processes e.g. rubber product, bread, medicines, battery, chemicals, textiles, sugar, oil etc. Each process account is debited by the amount of direct material, labour and with proportionate establishment expenses. When the product(s) is/are being processed in more than one-department then the cost of one department is to be transferred to the subsequent department.

Process costing can be highlighted as:

i) The production is continuous,
ii) The output of previous process becomes input of subsequent process,
iii) The products are homogeneous, standardised and an identical,
iv) Average cost per unit is determined for a given period for each process. The unit cost is obtained by accumulating all manufacturing costs and dividing it by numbers of units produced.

Banking is a service industry and as discussed earlier, its

'Inputs' or "Raw material" is "deposits", whereas "output" i.e. finished product is "advances". Process costing technique is used by some of the researchers for valuing the cost of services provided by banking industry. But in my opinion, it is not suitable to apply due to following reasons:

i) Production of services is not continuous e.g. in banking, interest cost is a substantial part of "The cost of sales" but the amount of loans and advances i.e. "output" do not affect the interest cost per unit of funds i.e. input obtained,

ii) The output of initial process does not form a part of input of subsequent process e.g. funds so collected by way of current, savings or fixed deposits may form part of cash credit, over draft, call money, term loan or even any investment,

iii) The product of banking industry is not an identical one as required for process costing.

Operating Costing

Few researchers have found operating costing best suitable for banking industry. Operating costing is a method used to ascertain the cost of services as distinguished from the cost of manufacturing of the products. ICMA, London defines operating costing as "the form of operation costing where standardised services are provided either by an undertaking or by a service cost centre within an undertaking". The principle of operation costing is to accumulate costs incurred in a period under convenient headings and relate them to the units of services rendered in the same period to obtain the average unit cost.

The services of operating cost method used are as under:

i) Transport services: Passenger Transport, Goods Transport, Air Transport, Water Transport, Railways etc.,

ii) Supply services: Gas, Electricity, Water,
iii) Social services: Hospitals, Hotels, Canteens ,
iv) Public utilities: Libraries, Laboratories,
v) Municipal services: Street lighting, Road and Drainage maintenance.

The special features of operating costing are:

i) It enables for selection of suitable cost units such as Cubic meter for gas. The gallon or liter for water supply, Mile or kilometer for transport / passengers, Kilo watt per hour for electricity supply and for Hospitals — per patient a day or per bed or per room. In these cases, the unit of cost is not the job, product or process but the services rendered and also they are all different units to measure the services,
ii) The costs can be collected under fixed cost (Costs for providing services) variable cost (Cost of actually rendering services in running) and semi variable cost (costs for maintaining services - maintenance). Further total cost (fixed + variable + semi variable) for specific period can also be obtained,
iii) The average unit cost can be obtained by dividing Costs so collected by total number of cost units.

Procedure or Steps of Operating Costing System

i) Determine the unit of service: The unit may be composite unit as a passenger kilometer or simply as a unit cost per kilometer,
ii) The division or classification of expenses as fixed and variable,
iii) Allocation of costs to the units.

As defined by ICMA London, operation costing is suitable where standardise services are provided. But, neither a Bank nor its any single department provides standardise services that can be considered as the cost centre. Banks are engaged in processing various types of financial services such as acceptance of public deposits, lending and transfer of fund.

The product line of public deposits includes:

i) Current deposits,
ii) Saving deposits,
iii) Fixed deposits.

The product line of lending includes:

i) Short term loans. (cash credits, overdrafts, foodgrain loans etc.),
ii) Long term loans,
iii) Discounting of bills.

While the product line of transfer of funds includes:

i) Collection of bills,
ii) Issuing Gift cheques or travelers cheques,
iii) Collecting electricity bills, telephone bills or insurance premium,
iv) Remittance of funds by different tools etc.

Essentially, therefore Banks are multi product firms.

According to C. Rangarajan "The earlier approach, while theoretically sound, runs into severe problems in estimation. The number of variables is quite large as compared to sample number of Banks for which data are available. In earlier approach, we broke down the functions of Bank into various separate lines and introduced one or two variables to represent the size of each line of business. Alternatively, we felt that the size of deposits in a Bank could represent the level of activity in all other lines of business such as advances and miscellaneous (consisting of Bills, Remittances, Letter of credit etc.) and therefore decided to introduce only a level of deposits as a variable, to introduce only a level of deposits as a variable representing all other activities. We are conscious of the shortcoming of this approach. This method implies that a change in the mix of advances will have no influence on cost. In other words, the assumption that the amount of deposits determines the total cost, ignores other ways in which a given amount of deposits can be dispersed as loans and advances. We were not able to obtain meaningful results when a large number of variables which were closely related were introduced."[3] This reflects the shortcoming of operating costing used for Banking industry.

Uniform Costing

Uniform costing is to be adopted by private and urban banks as suggested in "Manual on costing in Private Sector and Urban Banks."[4] It simply suggests uniformity to be followed in costing principles and/or practices by several organisations/institutions. It is not a separate method of costing such as job costing or process costing. Thus the main feature of uniform costing is—it is used and applied uniformly in a number of firms in the same industry. The nature and degree of uniformity depends upon the nature of the industry and the extent to which the Management is willing to adopt it.

Uniform costing implies the adoption of uniformity in following principles or approaches.

i) The method of costing to be adopted,
ii) The technique of costing applied such as marginal costing, standard costing etc.,
iii) Uniformity in classification of expenses and their allocation to the respective accounting heads,
iv) Method of valuation of materials, issues of pricing and valuation of stock,
v) Classification of overheads among productive administration, selling and distribution,

vi) Basis of apportionment and absorption of overheads,

vii) Method and rate of depreciation,

viii) Inclusion or exclusion of rent on freehold property and interest on capital,

ix) Method of remuneration to workers,

x) Manner of compilation of costs and other data,

xi) Statement, form and other records,

xii) Definition of items to be categorised as fixed and variable expenses,

xiii) Coding of accounts to maintain uniformity.

Uniform Costing Aims to

i) Provide basis for cost comparison between different concerns of same industry and,

ii) To help trade associations in regulating production capacity, utilising surplus productive capacity, deciding price policy and fixation of reasonable prices.

Advantages of Applying Uniform Costing are

i) Comparison of costs like salaries, rent, postage and telegrams, printing and stationery etc. is made possible. If any concern's expense is excessive as compared to others, corrective action can be taken,

ii) Services of cost experts and consultants may be utilised jointly by all concerns in the same industry,

iii) Unhealthy competition can be converted to healthy competition,

iv) Smaller units can share the benefits of research and development carried out by bigger units,

v) Efficiency of different methods of production can be compared,

vi) It is useful tool for managerial control. The data of one bank can be compared with others' data and weak points can be detected,

vii) Efficiency can be compared within the departments,

viii) Creates cost consciousness among the concerns within same industry and provides the best method of cost control.

A seminar on "Costing in Banks" organised by The Reserve Bank of India at Bombay in 1988, concluded with the following common agreements namely:

i) "In light of the experience gained and the benefits derived by the public sector banks from the costing exercise, it was felt that introduction of similar uniform costing system in the licensed scheduled private sector banks and scheduled Urban Co-operative Banks on and on going basis would be useful.

ii) Taking into consideration the advantages of cost data in controlling expenses and improving profitability, it was felt that the uniform costing technique may be fruitfully adopted by the Banks in the Private Sector and Urban Co-operative Banks also.

iii) The operations of a large number of small Banks in these sectors are located in certain areas. The business is mixed and volume of operations of these banks is different from that of public sector banks. It was therefore felt that the requirements of private sector banks and urban banks have to be studied in detail to bring out suitable set of guidelines to enable them to adopt a uniform approach and work out comparable results.

iv) The Reserve Bank of India constituted a committee representing different Banks in December 1988. The committee studied the uniform costing exercises in vague in the public sector banks and their experience is based on the interaction with banks and the needs of different banks' in-group.

The committee finalised the recommendations and submitted its report in the form of "Manual on costing in Private Sector and Urban Banks." The manual was circulated among all the scheduled licensed private sector banks and scheduled Urban Co-operative Banks.

v) The meeting of the banks was held in June 1989 at The Reserve Bank of India, Bombay that discussed the comments and the suggestions from the Banks; the draft was suitably modified. The manual provides for uniform input and output formats, definitions and meaning of terminology used in exercises. Guidelines for data collection processing and analysing the data and also action points for Bank Management to make exercise successful have been incorporated in the manual. The manual aims to meet the needs of all those concern with costing exercises in Banks."[5]

The private sector banks and Urban Co-operative Banks were asked to set up the "costing cell" immediately in their Head office or Central office. The uniform costing system is very much suitable for costing exercised in Banks, but it requires exhaustive framework to study the costs of Banks. Constant support by Banking staff can make uniform costing a success. An individual will not have enough means to go for uniform costing.

Direct Costing

"Direct costing is also popularly known as marginal costing, In direct costing, the total cost is divided into Fixed cost and Variable cost. Fixed costs are treated as a separate pool and are met by contribution margin of all services. The contribution margin is worked out by subtracting the variable cost of a service from the revenue earned on those services. Direct costing attracts & has certain limitations. In the banking industry there are very few costs, which can be treated as variable cost. All the items of expenses for a given period of time appear to be fixed. Moreover, staffs cost and other establishment expenses are to be maintained irrespective of work load fluctuations. This is more or so, as most of ancillary services rendered by the banks do not have a regular flow of business. Since cost parameters changes their status as direct cost, fixed cost or semi variable cost, it is therefore difficult to bifurcate fixed cost from variable costs. Further a part of the fixed cost which is not directly associated with any service may not be included anywhere while calculating costs for individual services. As most of the elements of fixed cost can be directly traced to different services, isolating all items of fixed cost may vitiate activity wise total cost, if the size of costing unit changes." [6]

Direct and Indirect Costs

Costs which can be traceable or identifiable with a cost centre, unit of output or a segment of business operation are called as 'Direct cost' and costs not so traceable or identifiable are referred to as 'Indirect costs'. For example, the cost of the services of the clerk directly engaged for preparing and issue of the draft is direct cost, whereas the cost of the services of the Branch Manager engaged in multi and various duties is treated as indirect cost. The direct or indirect costs are essentially related to the size of a costing unit. This is the overview of the direct cost. If remittances as a whole is treated as a costing unit then the Branch Manager's salary may be taken as direct cost, in case he is directly involved in the activity of different ways of remittances.

The direct cost should not be confused with direct costing. In absorption costing, direct cost refers to the cost which is attributable to a cost centre or cost unit For example—direct labour, direct material and direct expenses including traceable fixed expenses i.e. the fixed expenses which are directly chargeable. In direct costing factory variable overhead is taken as direct cost while in the absorption costing it is indirect cost

Incremental Costing

Incremental costing relates to the incremental or differential cost represented by increase or decrease in total cost resulting from any variation in operation. Incremental costing measures the change in total cost that results from alternate courses of action. Incremental costs are generally variable costs but may include fixed cost. In case, where more facilities or equipment are added to complete the objective, there is an increase in volume of services. In such situation, incremental costing approach is more appropriate as the volume changes in short period of time. This helps banking industry to make short term tactical decisions. Further, it helps the management to find out ways to recover the fixed cost by utilising idle facilities. It highlights each rupee earned over and above the incremental cost from the use of otherwise idle capacity recovers the fixed costs and increases the profit. This approach is generally relevant when there exist idle or unused capacity in short run.

Absorption Costing

Absorption costing is also termed as Traditional or Full cost method. In absorption costing, fixed cost as well as variable cost is taken into account to determine the cost of production. Variable costs such as direct material, direct labour, direct expenses etc. are directly charged to the product, while the fixed costs are apportioned on some reasonable basis over different products produced during the period. Thus absorption costing is a technique that assigns all cost i.e. fixed and variable costs to product cost or cost of services rendered under absorption costing. The management is interested in knowing whether or not a product can earn sufficient return after absorbing its share of total cost.

This approach is opposite to direct costing. It assigns the total cost, consisting of fixed and variable costs, to different services and is also known as "Actual cost" or "True cost"; it is the total cost as used in this approach, guides managerial decisions in long run.

Full absorption costing approach would reflect the actual cost of rendering banking services taking into account not only the branch level cost but also administrative offices' cost.

Banking Commission setup by Government of India analyzed the cost data of Urban Co-operative Banks and came out with cost of deposits of different types.

TABLE 5.01

COSTS OF DEPOSITS, ALL INDIA AVERAGE OF URBAN CO-OPERATIVE BANKS

Indicators	*Average Balance In Lacs of Rs.*	*Cost Per cent Per Annum of Average Balance (Including Interest Paid)*
Current deposits	5.84	3.37
Saving deposits	13.70	4.64
Fixed deposits	27.54	6.38
Other deposits	3.35	—
Total deposits	50.43	5.52

Source: Report of Banking Commission setup on February 3, 1969 by Govt. of India.

The Reserve Bank of India constituted a Standing Advisory Committee in January 1983 for Urban Co-operative Banks. It had studied the norms for viability of Urban Co-operative Banks and its branches. Committee had studied total operative cost of Urban Banks, following table representing fixed and variable costs of Urban Banks which is published in their report.

Total operative costs would vary for each slab of rise in working capital at Rs. 10 lacs in proportion to the increase in variable cost.

TABLE 5.02

THE TOTAL COST OF OPERATIONS EXCLUDING THE COST OF RESOURCES WOULD WORK OUT AS UNDER

Nature of Operative Costs		*Larger Metro Centres*	*Other Metro Centres*	*Urban Centres*	*Semi Urban Centres*
	Fixed cost on establishment	1.74	1.35	1.04	0.68
Fixed cost	Other fixed costs on Rent, Rates, Taxes, Board Meetings	0.95	0.67	0.42	0.20
	Total	2.69	2.02	1.46	0.88
Variable Cost	For each slab of increase at Rs. 10 lacs in working capital	0.29	026	0.23	0.21

Table 5.03 relates to financial year, as published in The Reserve Bank of India Bulletin comprising of directors' fees, rent, postage, stationery, law charges etc.

Fixed Cost

Fixed Cost Defined

Kohler's dictionary for Accountant's on page No. 217 has defined fixed cost (or expenses) as "cost for plant capacity or other long-term assets or obligations, which have already been incurred and hence cannot be changed." An operating expense or operating expenses as a class do not vary with business volume as seen in few cases such as, interest on bonds, rent, property tax, depreciation, minimal amounts of selling and general overheads. A cost designated as fixed is often a function of capacity, and thus, although fixed with respect to volume, varies with the size of the plant, which can be altered over a time. In this sense, it varies with time (the long run) rather than production volume (in short run). However, other usage also needs to be allowed for, one department of a plant may bear a monthly service charge

TABLE 5.03

COST OF DEPOSITS OF SCHEDULED COMMERCIAL BANKS IN INDIA AMOUNT IN CRORES

Sr. No	*Particulars*	*1961*	*1962*	*1963*	*1964*	*1965*	*1966*	*1967*	*1968*
1	Average deposits on weekly basis	1573	1768	1919	2167	2449	2857	3225	3651
2	Interest paid on deposits	36.23	44.45	5.20	59.33	86.24	115.34	132.35	147.48
	Percentage of deposits	2.30	2.51	2.62	2.74	3.52	4.04	4.10	4.04
3	Int. paid on borrowings	1.92	1.23	1.71	2.93	6.08	4.29	5.08	5.84
	Percentage of deposits	0.12	0.07	0.09	0.14	0.25	0.15	0.16	0.16
4	Establishment Expenses	30.60	37.04	42.94	52.07	65.50	80.80	100.25	116.09
	Percentage of deposits	1.95	2.10	2.24	2.40	2.68	2.83	3.11	3.18
5	Other working expenses	8.91	11.33	12.70	14.78	17.63	21.02	22.91	26.72
	Percentage of deposits	0.57	0.64	0.66	0.68	0.73	0.74	0.71	0.73
6	Total operating expenses	78.82	95.48	109.28	131.14	177.96	224.38	264.08	300.17
	Percentage of deposits	5.01	5.40	5.69	6.05	7.27	7.86	8.19	8.22

originating in another department, to the former. The charge is looked upon as a fixed cost beyond its immediate control to the latter; the charge may in large measure derive from variable costs over which it has primary control. Fixed costs' are not fixed in the sense that they do not fluctuate or vary; they vary, but from causes independent of volume. Although usually defined with respect to volume, the term fixed costs may also be applied when some other factor is the independent variable, and cost the dependent variable.

As stated earlier in the definition of a fixed cost given by Kohler, fixed costs remains constant in total regardless of changes in volume upto a certain level of output. They are not affected by changes in volume of production. There is an inverse relationship between volume and fixed cost per unit. Thus total fixed costs do not change with change in volume but vary per unit of volume. Here a fixed cost is compared with deposits. It will be observed that the fixed costs of banks do not vary with change in volume of deposits. In other words, there is inverse relation between fixed cost and amount of deposit. Thus fixed cost per unit of deposit will vary inversely with amount of deposits. Every increase in amount of deposit will reduce the fixed cost per unit of deposits. But, it must be remembered that fixed cost will remain constant upto a certain level of amount of deposits.

Deposits are on "X" axis and cost is on "Y" axis. Fixed cost curve remains unchanged irrespective of amount of deposits.

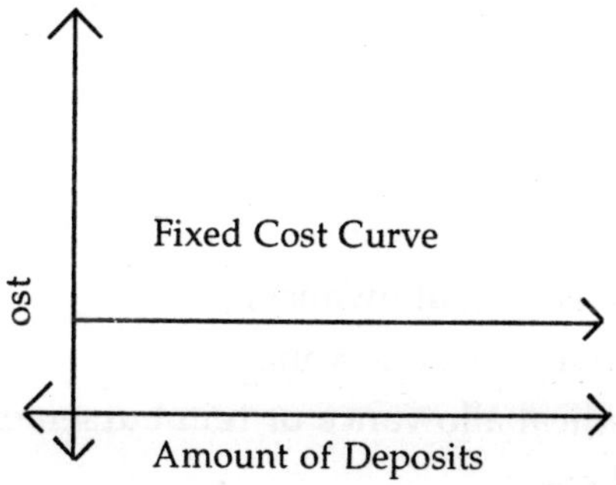

Elements of Cost

Analysis of profit and loss account shows following items constituted as cost of Urban banks

— Interest paid on deposits, borrowings etc.
— Salaries and allowances, provident fund and gratuity contributions.
— Directors' and committee members' fees and allowances.
— Rents, taxes, insurance, lighting etc.
— Legal fees, law charges.
— Postage, telegrams, telephone etc.
— Auditors fees.
— Depreciation and repairs of banks' property. etc.
— Printing, stationery, advertisements, etc.
— Other miscellaneous expenditure.

In above mentioned elements of banks' costs, interest cost is variable cost as it has a direct positive relation between amount of deposits and interest, therefore interest do not form a part of fixed cost. Interest as a variable cost is discussed at length in subsequent chapter VI. Profit and loss account is debited with these expenses. The profit and loss account of ten selected Urban Co-operative Banks in Gujarat includes this fixed cost, which are presented in tabular form.

Salaries, Allowances, Provident Fund and Gratuity Contributions

Every Bank pays to its employee an amount on monthly basis under the head of "Salaries" like:

i) Basic pay,
ii) Dearness allowance,
iii) House rent allowance,
iv) Conveyance allowance,
v) Medical allowance or reimbursement,
vi) Others.

In addition to these, banks' contributes for provident fund and gratuity. Basic pay depends upon pay scale but the dearness allowance is fixed according to changes in wholesale price index number. House rent is payable as per percentage of basic pay and class of city/town. Conveyance allowance and medical allowance are of fixed amount. Revision in basic pay takes place nearly at every five years of interval. Bank Pay Commissions' are revising these pay scales taking into consideration the demand of the Union of Bank employees. Banks being an employer under provident fund act has to contribute for provident fund of the employees.

There is no relation prevailing between salary and volume of business of the Bank. Change in amount of banks' deposits and advances will not bring any change in the salaries of bank employees. In other words, increase in bank deposits and advances will not increase salaries of banks' employees but conversely decrease in deposits or advances will not reduce the salaries of banks' employees, so salaries are independent volumes of overall business of the bank. The reasons for increase in salary of an individual employee are:

i) Promotion of an employee to higher class,
ii) Yearly increments in salary,
iii) Revision in pay scales.

Again these reasons for increase in salaries are in no way related with any change in the volume of Banks' deposits and advances. There are certain reasons, which brings changes in total salary of Bank employees, which are having relation with volume of Bank business.

Firstly when Bank opens new branches for expansion purpose, which requires additional staff to run the new branches.

Secondly Bank starts providing new Banking services to its customer then also addition will take place in the existing strength of the staff.

Thirdly continuous increase in banks' business, workload will increase, for which existing banks' employees would have to perform more.

The Reserve Bank of India constituted Standing Advisory Committee for Urban Co-operative Banks in January 1983. The study of the staffing pattern presented in the sample Banks, which enable them to achieve the result. As it was seen, 14 Banks reported a loan business exceeding Rs. 7 lacs, while 19 Banks reported working capital exceeding Rs. 10 lacs per clerk. The Banks having working capital per clerk above Rs. 9.50 lacs numbered 22. Therefore it was felt proper to assume at least a workload of Rs. 10 lacs in terms of working capital per clerk, similarly it was observed for Accountants, Section Officers and Cashiers. Taking into account major factor, the following staffing is considered essential for Bank to function on efficient lines and to be in a position to tap the available business potentials in its area of operation to the maximum level

Staffing Pattern

TABLE 5.04

STAFFING PATTERN SUGGESTED BY STANDING ADVISORY COMMITTEE, RBI

Cadre	*Minimum staff required by a Bank at least at the end of five year*		
	Number of posts		
	Metropolitan	*Urban*	*Semi Urban*
Manager	1	1	1
Asstt. Manager	1	1	-
Accountant	1	1	1
Section Officer	1	1	-
Cashier	1	1	1
Clerk	2	2	2
Typist	1	1	-
Peon	2	2	2
Security Guard	2	1	1

Standing Advisory Committee for Urban Co-operative Banks suggested that:

i) Additional Accountant's post for every increase of Rs. 100 lacs in working capital,

ii) Additional Section Officer for every increase of Rs. 75 lacs in working capital,

iii) Additional Cashier for every increase of Rs. 50 lacs in working capital,

iv) Additional Clerk for every increase of Rs. 10 lacs in working capital.

For a certain level of working capital, the existing staff of the bank can perform efficiently but any increase in working capital beyond a threshold level would demand a corresponding increase in the bank's staff. Additional employment will increase the salaries that in turn increases the fixed cost. In other words, salary cost is related with volume of business. Therefore salary cost includes two components — fixed cost as well as semi variable cost.

The standard deviation for all the elements of fixed cost is calculated as per following formula.

$$SD = \sqrt{\frac{S\,(Xi - X)^2}{n - 1}}$$

Here SD = Standard deviation

N = Number of years

Xi = Fixed cost each year

X = Average if fixed cost

$\Sigma\,(Xi - X)$ = Summation of difference taken from mean.

Coefficient of variation can be calculated as under:

$$CV = SD \div X \times 100$$

Here CV = Coefficient of variation

SD = Standard deviation

X = Average audit fees.

Table 5.05 shows the salaries and allowances as one of the elements of fixed cost of selected Urban Co-operative Banks in Gujarat. The highest salary-paying Bank in the sample is Surat People's Bank during all the ten years. For the year 1987-88, salaries and allowances paid by Surat People's Bank is Rs. 121.68 lacs. It is at the peak for the year 1995-96 amounting to Rs. 598.44 lacs. But then for the year 1996-97, it has declined to Rs. 551.87. It can be observed that Kalupur Bank and Rajkot Nagrik Bank are also paying the salaries and the allowances between the range of Rs. 110 lacs and Rs. 460 lacs during the ten years of the study.

Table 5.06 reflects the proportion of salaries with the total fixed costs of selected Urban Co-operative Banks. This element of fixed cost has a major share in total fixed costs, on an average it is more than 70 per cent for all the banks in a sample. Within the sample of ten banks, a share of salaries and allowances in total fixed cost is nearly 90 per cent of Sarvoday Nagrik Bank. This Bank becomes highest salary paying bank as in the year 1995-96, the proportion stands at 91.66 per cent. The Kalupur Commercial Bank having highest deposits in the sample of ten Urban Co-operative Banks but comparatively it has very low proportion of salaries and allowances in total fixed cost. For the year 1987-88, Kalupur Commercial Bank's salary payments were 69.75 per cent of the total fixed cost whereas in the year 1993-94 it was 80.16 per cent. For remaining years, the proportion has remained between 70 and 75 per cent. Compared to Kalupur Commercial banks, deposits of Rajkot Nagrik Bank's are slightly low but the payment for salaries and allowances as proportion of fixed costs is on an average of 80 per cent.

Out of 8 elements of fixed cost compared with total cost of selected Urban Co-operative Banks, it is observed that share of salaries and allowances is highest in total cost.

TABLE 5.05

SALARIES AND ALLOWANCES AS AN ELEMENT OF FIXED COST

Sr. No.	Name of the Bank	87-88	88-89	89-90	90-91	91-92	92-93	93-94	94-95	95-96	96-97	AVG	SD
1	The Kalupur Bank	112.59	134.18	175.35	202.30	158.26	237.75	268.71	343.53	414.96	451.95	249.958	118.229
2	Rajkot Nagrik Bank	123.30	135.18	156.12	215.55	186.01	276.70	305.34	338.91	375.64	456.64	256.939	112.059
3	Anyona Sahakari Bank	41.13	46.35	52.04	74.18	56.95	90.22	105.50	131.47	163.43	203.21	96.448	54.599
4	Surat People's Bank	121.68	138.08	198.16	218.66	209.04	307.19	387.86	484.42	598.44	551.87	321.540	174.141
5	Natpur Co-Op Bank	13.32	17.34	21.88	26.77	21.39	36.98	40.13	49.91	72.67	76.77	37.716	22.483
6	Anand Mercantile Bank	17.15	18.93	21.11	27.40	23.16	30.98	37.19	44.23	60.81	86.06	36.702	21.940
7	Dahod Urban Bank	17.47	19.69	30.61	30.52	26.89	41.41	46.66	62.04	66.91	74.36	41.656	20.219
8	Sarvodya Nagrik Bank	12.65	15.12	18.89	21.85	22.69	36.97	45.23	58.68	68.03	76.11	37.622	23.239
9	Baroda People's Bank	17.03	20.01	29.62	34.51	30.51	52.25	56.06	98.27	109.85	133.59	58.170	41.225
10	Sardar Bhiladwala Bank	48.95	67.78	98.25	81.76	63.35	126.54	145.15	159.51	186.29	260.22	123.780	65.886

TABLE 5.06

PROPORTION OF SALARIES AND ALLOWANCES WITH TOTAL FIXED COST

Sr. No.	Name of the Bank	87-88	88-89	89-90	90-91	91-92	92-93	93-94	94-95	95-96	96-97	AVG	SD
1	The Kalupur Bank	0.697	0.724	0.767	0.776	0.769	0.789	0.802	0.768	0.728	0.703	0.752	0.036
2	Rajkot Nagrik Bank	0.815	0.783	0.794	0.818	0.815	0.813	0.805	0.801	0.809	0.830	0.808	0.013
3	Anyona Sahakari Bank	0.827	0.809	0.829	0.890	0.843	0.836	0.795	0.866	0.809	0.818	0.832	0.028
4	Surat People's Bank	0.760	0.792	0.830	0.809	0.839	0.816	0.829	0.833	0.822	0.808	0.814	0.024
5	Natpur Co-Op Bank	0.637	0.696	0.699	0.728	0.671	0.753	0.687	0.691	0.726	0.699	0.699	0.032
6	Anand Mercantile Bank	0.682	0.639	0.684	0.732	0.692	0.672	0.680	0.720	0.724	0.746	0.697	0.033
7	Dahod Urban Bank	0.782	0.815	0.859	0.827	0.833	0.822	0.833	0.828	0.767	0.855	0.822	0.029
8	Sarvodya Nagrik Bank	0.840	0.801	0.834	0.841	0.829	0.859	0.896	0.897	0.917	0.899	0.861	0.038
9	Baroda People's Bank	0.723	0.737	0.790	0.737	0.594	0.679	0.721	0.828	0.749	0.665	0.722	0.065
10	Sardar Bhiladwala Bank	0.825	0.833	0.823	0.815	0.732	0.817	0.834	0.838	0.843	0.833	0.819	0.032

Table 5.07 gives proportion of salaries and allowances with total cost of selected Urban Co-operative Banks. For the year 1994-95, Sardar Nagrik Bank's share of salaries and allowances in total cost stands at 25.05 per cent of total cost. Rajkot Nagrik Bank has the lowest proportion in the year 1889-90 at 6.17 per cent of the total cost. The highest proportion of Rajkot Nagrik Bank is 8.44 per cent. Rajkot Nagrik Bank has maintained its proportion of salaries and allowances with total cost at a very low level during ten years. Sardar Bhiladwala Bank and Sarvoday Nagrik Bank has the higher share of salaries and allowances in total cost for all the ten years.

Director's Fees

At a regular interval, meeting of banks' directors is being arranged. For attending the Board's meeting, Directors are being paid directors' fees and conveyance allowances. For both the fees and allowances, amounts are fixed or may differ on the basis of director coming from a distant place by different mode of transportation. This is an expenditure of Directors' fees, which will not increase or decrease because of change in amount of Bank's deposits or advances. It remains constant, therefore this element of cost is included in fixed cost.

1. Cost Accounting in Commercial Banks, ICWAI,
2. ICMA, London,
3. C. Rangarajan RBI Bank Commission Report 1972,
4. Published by RBI on August 2, 1989,
5. Seminar on 'Costing in Banks' arranged by RBI, Bombay in December 1988,
6. RBI manual 1989.

For attending Board's meeting, Members of the Board i.e. Directors are being paid fees or conveyance allowances. Table 5.08 includes the Directors' fees paid by selected Urban Co-operative Banks in Gujarat i.e. Kalupur Bank, Natpur Co-operative Bank and Sarvodya Nagrik Bank's directors' fees

TABLE 5.07

PROPORTION OF SALARIES AND ALLOWANCES WITH TOTAL COST.

Sr. No.	Name of the Bank	87-88	88-89	89-90	90-91	91-92	92-93	93-94	94-95	95-96	96-97	AVG	SD
1	The Kalupur Bank	0.090	0.106	0.117	0.149	0.121	0.145	0.117	0.098	0.099	0.079	0.112	0.023
2	Rajkot Nagrik Bank	0.072	0.072	0.062	0.084	0.082	0.083	0.084	0.084	0.071	0.074	0.077	0.008
3	Anyona Sahakari Bank	0.152	0.152	0.150	0.184	0.175	0.174	0.188	0.213	0.189	0.164	0.174	0.020
4	Surat People's Bank	0.135	0.139	0.160	0.157	0.134	0.153	0.169	0.199	0.197	0.137	0.158	0.024
5	Natpur Co-Op Bank	0.080	0.107	0.113	0.123	0.108	0.116	0.113	0.123	0.133	0.093	0.111	0.015
6	Anand Mercantile Bank	0.108	0.089	0.079	0.084	0.072	0.066	0.086	0.098	0.093	0.101	0.088	0.013
7	Dahod Urban Bank	0.080	0.080	0.109	0.097	0.090	0.093	0.094	0.115	0.095	0.081	0.093	0.012
8	Sarvodya Nagrik Bank	0.159	0.147	0.177	0.177	0.191	0.193	0.192	0.250	0.241	0.183	0.191	0.032
9	Baroda People's Bank	0.147	0.123	0.146	0.135	0.125	0.131	0.106	0.180	0.161	0.141	0.139	0.021
10	Sardar Bhiladwala Bank	0.148	0.130	0.222	0.166	0.143	0.184	0.190	0.181	0.191	0.200	0.176	0.028

are included with some other head, hence not shown separately. Average Director's fees paid by Anyonya Bank and Baroda People's Bank is amounting to Rs. 39, 000 and Rs. 36, 000 respectively. Surprisingly, both the Banks' business is not more than Surat People's Bank and Rajkot Nagarik Bank whose average Director's fees are Rs. 17,000 and 14,000. One more factor is worthwhile to note that eventhough Anyonya Bank's all Directors are having residence at Baroda, still Directors' fees are high whereas Rajkot Nagrik Bank has it, branches all over Gujarat and whose Directors are coming from different parts of Gujarat, eventhen the Directors' fees are less. The Annyonya Sahayaki Bank and The Baroda People's Bank requires controlling this cost. Standard deviation in directors' fees of all the Banks is less than 0.25, so it could be stated that directors' fees as an element of fixed cost remains unchanged. It does not vary with the increase or decrease in the business of banks. C.V. for Dahod Urban Bank is lowest i. e. 14.87.

Postage Telegram and Telephone

Table 5.09 presents the expenses on postage and telegrams incurred by selected Urban Co-operative Banks in Gujarat. The Rajkot Nagarik Bank's expense on postage is the highest at Rs. 12.26 lacs for the year 1995-96 amongst selected banks. Lowest average postage and telegram expense is Rs. 74, 000 of Dahod Urban Bank. Intra Bank's postage and telegram expenses can be compared by standard deviation. Kalupur Commercial Bank's average expense is Rs. 4.33 lacs, with standard deviation of 1.96, which indicates that during ten years postage and telegram expenses have remained stable. These expenses of The Rajkot Nagarik Bank may be high but the standard deviation is just 2.57. Remaining Banks' standard deviation is still lower than Kalupur Bank and Rajkot Nagarik Bank. Co-efficient of variation of Natpur Co-operative Bank is 17.57 minimum amongst 10 selected Banks whereas maximum CV is 54.09 of Anyonya Bank.

TABLE 5.08

DIRECTOR FEES EXPENSE AS AN ELEMENT OF FIXED COST.

Sr. No.	Name of the Bank	87-88	88-89	89-90	90-91	91-92	92-93	93-94	94-95	95-96	96-97	AVG	SD
1	The Kalupur Bank	0.00	0.00	0.00	0.00	0.00	0.00	0.00	0.00	0.00	0.00	0.000	0.000
2	Rajkot Nagrik Bank	0.13	0.12	0.12	0.13	0.10	0.14	0.15	0.16	0.18	0.18	0.141	0.026
3	Anyona Saharakri Bank	0.22	0.42	0.38	0.16	0.33	0.55	0.50	0.27	0.31	0.80	0.394	0.186
4	Surat People's Bank	0.02	0.02	0.03	0.20	0.11	0.22	0.24	0.21	0.18	0.42	0.165	0.125
5	Natpur Co-Op Bank	0.00	0.00	0.00	0.00	0.00	0.00	0.00	0.00	0.00	0.00	0.000	0.000
6	Anand Mercantile Bank	0.15	0.13	0.11	0.13	0.16	0.23	0.27	0.27	0.27	0.29	0.201	0.071
7	Dahod Urban Bank	0.19	0.15	0.15	0.21	0.16	0.21	0.22	0.22	0.21	0.21	0.193	0.029
8	Sarvodya Nagrik Bank	0.00	0.00	0.00	0.00	0.00	0.00	0.00	0.00	0.00	0.00	0.000	0.000
9	Baroda People's Bank	0.20	0.21	0.23	0.40	0.35	0.45	0.41	0.38	0.47	0.45	0.355	0.104
10	Sardar Bhiladwala Bank	0.42	0.54		0.00	0.14	0.00	0.00	0.00	0.00	0.00	0.122	0.210

TABLE 5.09

POSTAGE AND TELEGRAM EXPENSES AS AN ELEMENT OF FIXED COST

Sr. No.	*Name of the Bank*	*87-88*	*88-89*	*89-90*	*90-91*	*91-92*	*92-93*	*93-94*	*94-95*	*95-96*	*96-97*	*AVG*	*SD*
1	The Kalupur Bank	2.22	2.76	3.15	3.30	2.75	3.77	4.55	6.06	6.65	8.08	4.329	1.963
2	Rajkot Nagrik Bank	5.18	6.67	7.56	8.29	6.92	8.36	11.53	12.17	12.26	11.28	9.022	2.573
3	Anyona Saharakri Bank	0.53	0.70	0.63	0.80	0.88	1.09	1.29	1.49	2.07	2.47	1.195	0.646
4	Surat People's Bank	1.33	1.75	1.73	2.68	2.60	3.31	3.34	3.88	3.41	4.51	2.854	1.025
5	Natpur Co-Op Bank	0.52	0.66	0.72	0.86	0.64	0.85	1.14	1.18	1.40	1.55	0.952	0.348
6	Anand Mercantile Bank	0.80	0.79	1.18	1.10	0.79	1.05	1.12	1.31	1.11	1.14	1.039	0.183
7	Dahod Urban Bank	0.36	0.36	0.38	0.53	0.44	0.68	1.00	1.06	1.26	1.33	0.740	0.387
8	Sarvodya Nagrik Bank	0.44	0.72	0.96	1.01	0.80	1.19	0.85	1.75	1.50	1.46	1.068	0.404
9	Baroda People's Bank	0.72	1.35	1.16	1.77	1.27	1.89	1.91	2.09	2.49	2.79	1.744	0.632
10	Sardar Bhiladwala Bank	1.29	1.54	1.70	2.37	2.15	2.63	2.62	2.74	3.73	5.07	2.584	1.121

Rent, Taxes, Insurance, Lighting etc.

Rent is being paid for the use of premises to its owner regularly. Taxes are paid to the local authorities annually. The amount of rents and taxes are fixed for a regular interval. Similarly is the case of insurance premium is based on the sum assured. Lighting charges are based upon the consumption of units of electricity. In no way these expenses are related to volume of Bank's business. Therefore, it is added to fixed costs.

Table 5.10 is showing the expenses of Rent, Rates and Taxes of selected Urban Co-operative Banks. The Kalupur Bank and the Rajkot Nagarik Banks are scheduled banks and have the branches in different parts of Gujarat. Urban Banks may not have own premises for their branches in different cities of Gujarat, then the only option is to hire the premises. Higher the premises hired, more will be the rent to be paid, therefore average of Rent, Rates and Taxes of Kalupur Bank and Rajkot Nagarik Bank is Rs. 25.49 lacs and Rs. 18.54 lacs respectively. Similarly Surat People's Bank also has more branches, hence average rent paid is Rs. 17.18 lacs. Remaining seven banks are having average rent, rates and taxes around Rs. 10 lacs. There is sudden increase in rent, rates and taxes of Baroda People's Bank i.e. during the year 1988-89 and 1996-97. At the end of the year 1990-91, rent, rate, and taxes stood at Rs. 2.09 lacs and rose by 4 times to Rs. 8.89 lacs at the end of the year 1991-92. Similarly for the year ended on 31st March 1995 rent, rates, and taxes paid were Rs. 5.22 lacs which drastically increased to Rs. 18.60 lacs for the year 1995-96. The extreme values of this banks are Rs. 2.02 lacs in the year 1987-88 and Rs. 29.24 lacs in the year 1996-97 which in turn affect the average rents, rates and taxes which amounts to Rs. 8.29 lacs. with standard deviation of 8.92 and shoots the CV to 107.64. This doubling of CV is due to expansion i.e. opening of new branches, which requires hiring of premises. The Sarvodya Nagarik Bank's expenditure of rent, rates and taxes is observed stable, the average is Rs. 1.52 lacs with standard deviation of 0.86 only.

TABLE 5.10

RENTS, RATES AND TAXES EXPENSE AS AN ELEMENT OF FIXED COST

Sr. No.	*Name of the Bank*	*87-88*	*88-89*	*89-90*	*90-91*	*91-92*	*92-93*	*93-94*	*94-95*	*95-96*	*96-97*	*AVG*	*SD*
1	The Kalupur Bank	16.75	15.40	18.99	21.59	15.26	22.88	23.58	32.82	36.16	51.47	25.490	11.515
2	Rajkot Nagrik Bank	6.08	7.15	8.70	13.97	14.51	16.95	22.50	31.63	30.52	33.42	18.543	10.400
3	Anyona Saharakri Bank	4.45	6.06	5.82	4.54	5.26	8.43	16.80	10.19	16.05	25.14	10.274	6.911
4	Surat People's Bank	12.82	9.48	12.57	11.12	7.46	13.62	20.68	24.05	31.37	28.58	17.175	8.394
5	Natpur Co-Op Bank	1.85	1.87	1.81	1.88	1.94	2.68	4.18	3.97	6.96	8.58	3.572	2.412
6	Anand Mercantile Bank	1.01	1.53	1.43	1.47	2.05	2.73	3.35	4.81	9.65	13.70	4.173	4.220
7	Dahod Urban Bank	1.79	1.95	2.48	2.53	1.96	3.40	3.48	3.91	6.64	7.29	3.543	1.945
8	Sarvodya Nagrik Bank	0.57	0.85	0.95	1.03	1.14	1.21	1.97	2.19	1.83	3.44	1.518	0.856
9	Baroda People's Bank	2.02	2.22	2.02	2.09	8.89	6.20	6.41	5.22	18.60	29.24	8.291	8.924
10	Sardar Bhiladwala Bank	1.75	2.45	3.95	4.44	4.17	7.17	5.85	7.26	7.98	11.35	5.637	2.884

Legal Fees

It is the legal expenses and the fees paid to the Bank's advocates. These charges will increase due to number of suits filed by the banks against the defaulters or Banks' customers who have filed against the Bank. It has no direct connection with the amount of deposits or advances of Banks. Hence legal expenses are taken as a fixed cost.

Disputes with Banks or Banks are dragged to the court of Law for which Bank would have to engage the Lawyer and to pay the fees and incur the expenses to get the justice. This legal fee becomes the Banking service cost. Table 5.11 indicates such legal charges of selected Urban Co-operative Banks in Gujarat. Average legal fees of ten years paid by The Kalupur Commercial Bank amounts to Rs. 1.77 lacs. During ten years, the legal fee paid by The Kalupur Commercial Bank is highly fluctuating. In the year 1995-96, it was at the tune of Rs. 6.056 lacs and dropped to only Rs. 2800 for the year 1996-97. Rajkot Nagarik Bank has not shown Legal fees separately in its Profit and Loss Account for four years i.e. from 1987-88 to 1990-91. Similarly two years and one year's legal fees of Sarvodaya Bank and Baroda People's Bank respectively are not available. Lower average legal fees of other Banks amounting to Rs. 78000 is paid by Dahod Urban bank except Kalupur Commercial Bank. No bank has paid more than Rs. 64000 on an average of legal fees during ten years. Standard deviation with average of each Bank for ten years is very low, therefore the legal fees paid by selected Urban Banks is stable during the period of study.

Audit Fees

Bank audit is mandatory. Auditor is appointed for this purpose with some fixed amount of fees payable. Audit fees of selected Urban Co-operative Banks in Gujarat for ten years is analysed as follows:

As is said earlier, it is fixed cost component. It remains

TABLE 5.11

LEGAL FEES

Sr. No.	Name of the Bank	87-88	88-89	89-90	90-91	91-92	92-93	93-94	94-95	95-96	96-97	AVG	SD
1	The Kalupur Bank	0.000	0.728	0.700	0.988	1.301	2.189	1.797	3.894	6.056	0.028	1.768	1.894
2	Rajkot Nagrik Bank	0.000	0.000	0.000	0.000	1.307	2.379	1.629	0.277	0.453	0.000	0.604	0.859
3	Anyona Saharakri Bank	0.158	0.402	0.312	0.020	0.289	0.058	0.091	0.186	0.143	0.096	0.175	0.123
4	Surat People's Bank	0.075	0.082	0.181	0.117	0.172	0.055	0.130	0.354	0.631	1.432	0.323	0.427
5	Natpur Co-Op Bank	0.054	0.080	0.045	0.074	0.026	0.122	0.583	0.384	0.342	0.627	0.234	0.232
6	Anand Mercantile Bank	0.060	0.023	0.075	0.045	0.110	0.427	0.190	0.312	0.276	0.317	0.133	0.141
7	Dahod Urban Bank	0.038	0.072	0.061	0.113	0.038	0.071	0.030	0.105	0.129	0.125	0.078	0.037
8	Sarvodya Nagrik Bank	0.035	0.018	0.040	0.105	0.153	0.311	0.000	0.000	0.083	0.326	0.107	0.121
9	Baroda People's Bank	0.208	0.118	0.193	0.160	0.022	0.228	0.000	0.193	0.628	1.017	0.277	0.311
10	Sardar Bhiladwala Bank	0.314	0.363	0.230	0.031	0.113	0.349	0.440	0.314	0.432	0.050	0.264	0.151

unchanged even Banks' deposits and advances are increasing. As per Table 5.12, audit fees of The Kalupur Commercial Bank from 1987-88 to the year 1994-95 except in the year 1992-93 has remained constant i.e. about Rs. 20,000. And then for next two years, it has increased heavily because of new branches opened all over Gujarat. For last two years i.e. 1995-96 and 1996-97, audit fee is Rs. 1.55 lacs and Rs. 1.60 lacs respectively. This has affected the average from Rs. 20,000 to Rs. 50,000. Average audit fee's standard deviation is 0.573.

The Annyonya Sahayakari Bank's audit fees paid, ranges between Rs. 7,000 and Rs. 25,000 having average over ten years of Rs. 11,000 with standard deviation of 0.05 per cent which indicates that the Audit fee is stable throughout the ten year period.

Similar is the case with Natpur Co-operative Bank, Anand Mercantile Bank and Dahod Urabn Bank, their average audit fees paid are Rs. 15,000, Rs. 21,000 and Rs. 25,000 respectively. The standard deviation stands 0.03, 0.07 and 0.06 respectively and least standard deviation 0.02 is of Sarvodaya Nagrik Bank. Overall every Banks' standard divination is very low. Therefore it can be concluded that the audit fees as expense of selected Urban Co-operative Banks is constant and not varies from its average audit fees i.e. remains fixed.

CV is calculated for all the Banks which allows the inter bank comparison. Lowest CV is 21.97 of Sarvodya Nagrik Bank.

Depreciation

Bank owns premises and furniture as a fixed asset. Under straight-line method or reducing balance method depreciation is provided annually. Depreciation amount is depending upon written down value of fixed asset and percentage of depreciation on it. The amount of deposits or advances in no way change the amount of depreciation, it remains constant. So it is a fixed cost to the banks' activities.

TABLE 5.12

AUDIT FEES AS AN ELEMENT OF FIXED COST

Sr. No.	*Name of the Bank*	*87-88*	*88-89*	*89-90*	*90-91*	*91-92*	*92-93*	*93-94*	*94-95*	*95-96*	*96-97*	*AVG*	*SD*
1	The Kalupur Bank	0.18	0.16	0.20	0.20	0.21	0.41	0.20	0.26	1.55	1.60	0.497	0.573
2	The Rajkot Nagrik Bank	0.45	0.45	0.56	0.50	0.51	0.61	1.14	0.84	0.80	0.90	0.676	0.232
3	Anyona Saharakri Bank	0.25	0.12	0.10	0.08	0.07	0.10	0.10	0.10	0.10	0.10	0.112	0.050
4	The Surat People's Bank	0.22	0.30	0.60	0.60	0.30	0.75	0.40	0.25	0.70	0.85	0.497	0.230
5	The Natpur Co-Op Bank	0.16	0.17	0.19	0.10	0.11	0.16	0.15	0.13	0.18	0.10	0.145	0.033
6	Anand Mercantile Bank	0.18	0.19	0.19	0.24	0.20	0.15	0.18	0.10	0.27	0.35	0.205	0.069
7	Dahod Urban Bank	0.22	0.19	0.16	0.20	0.23	0.24	0.24	0.29	0.34	0.36	0.247	0.064
8	Sarvodya Nagrik Bank	0.04	0.10	0.08	0.10	0.11	0.10	0.10	0.10	0.11	0.10	0.094	0.021
9	Baroda People's Bank	0.05	0.10	0.18	0.16	0.15	0.15	0.26	0.23	0.12	0.46	0.186	0.114
10	Sardar Bhiladwala Bank	0.05	0.34	0.32	0.37	0.24	0.28	0.10	0.10	0.10	0.20	0.210	0.117

Depreciation is provided on fixed asset like premises and furniture of the Banks. Depreciation is depending upon variation in fixed assets. Table 5.14 shows the fixed assets of selected Urban Co-operative Banks and Table 5.13 reveals the depreciation on it. Because of branch expansion, the fixed assets of Kalupur Bank had increased unevenly during 1989-90, 1994-95 and onwards. The Surat People's Bank's fixed asset increased to Rs. 202.24 lacs at the end of the year 1992-93, which increased abnormally to Rs. 332.13 lacs in the year 1993-94. Such abnormal increase observed in all ten banks. It must be due to purchase of new assets. The reduction in fixed assets in any year will obviously be due to depreciation provided on fixed assets or sale of fixed assets. Fixed assets amounting to Rs. 807.10 lacs of The Surat People's Bank for the year 1996-97 compared to Rs. 471.67 lacs for the year 1995-96, nearly the rise is doubled. This may be due to opening of new branches in the year 1996-97. And to open new branches, purchase of new premises and furniture is obvious.

The rise in fixed asset will increase the depreciation but depreciation will not increase or decrease due to change in the volume of Banks' deposits or advances.

Average depreciation of Kalupur Bank is Rs. 34.66 lacs with standard deviation of 31.82. The Sarvodya Nagarik Bank had average depreciation of Rs. 84,000 with standard deviation of 0.21. Within the span of ten year, depreciation remained relatively constant, which reflected no addition to the fixed assets by Sarvodaya Nagarik Bank. The CV of 130.94 of Dahod Urban Bank indicates less consistency than the other Banks.

Printing, Stationery, Advertisement etc.

This expenditure has got both the elements fix as well as variable. Some amount for stationery and printing is required regularly but over and above, higher the Bank business higher the requirement of printing and stationery. Portion of printing

TABLE 5.13

DEPRECIATION AS AN ELEMENT OF FIXED COST

Sr. No.	Name of the Bank	87-88	88-89	89-90	90-91	91-92	92-93	93-94	94-95	95-96	96-97	AVG	SD
1	The Kalupur Bank	16.38	17.49	14.91	14.43	13.72	19.76	25.28	41.44	77.31	105.89	34.661	31.825
2	The Rajkot Nagrik Bank	8.91	12.54	12.52	13.63	10.49	18.23	20.65	24.51	30.85	32.60	18.493	8.454
3	Anyona Saharakri Bank	0.76	1.13	0.95	0.98	0.89	3.42	4.25	2.95	6.16	8.24	2.973	2.591
4	The Surat People's Bank	19.10	17.61	16.19	21.32	18.35	34.76	37.00	48.58	67.53	65.43	34.587	19.845
5	The Natpur Co-Op Bank	3.33	2.95	3.87	4.28	5.29	5.33	7.65	11.82	13.72	17.20	7.544	4.974
6	Anand Mercantile Bank	2.80	3.15	2.84	2.87	2.60	3.54	3.95	5.84	7.28	8.59	4.346	2.134
7	Dahod Urban Bank	0.48	0.64	0.63	0.54	0.68	0.63	0.61	3.66	5.86	0.35	1.408	1.844
8	Sarvodya Nagrik Bank	0.59	0.67	0.72	0.78	0.58	0.76	1.10	1.03	1.05	1.07	0.835	0.207
9	Baroda People's Bank	1.90	1.16	1.33	2.28	5.14	6.02	4.21	3.80	4.66	22.78	5.328	6.355
10	Sardar Bhiladwala Bank	3.23	4.30	8.65	5.68	9.15	10.76	12.43	12.98	14.20	26.04	10.742	6.535

TABLE 5.14

FIXED ASSETS

Sr. No.	Name of the Bank	87-88	88-89	89-90	90-91	91-92	92-93	93-94	94-95	95-96	96-97	AVG	SD
1	The Kalupur Bank	69.60	76.57	102.76	118.78	124.30	117.44	112.50	194.61	361.25	495.96	177.377	140.238
2	The Rajkot Nagrik Bank	108.35	115.59	139.54	179.55	212.70	255.65	264.58	293.04	315.86	364.12	224.934	88.043
3	Anyona Saharakri Bank	4.62	9.12	8.30	8.67	10.76	13.56	13.49	19.896	66.19	69.11	22.371	24.218'
4	The Surat People's Bank	152.63	139.38	128.20	168.70	204.23	202.24	332.13	345.21	471.67	807.10	295.149	211.466
5	The Natpur Co-Op Bank	45.50	42.09	83.16	84.65	79.87	79.28	95.03	138.92	128.88	118.22	189.560	32.134
6	Anand Mercantile Bank	63.78	61.29	58.83	57.35	54.98	59.45	63.04	78.78	87.85	136.15	72.150	24.73
7	Dahod Urban Bank	4.34	5.80	5.72	5.91	6.16	5.75	5.49	16.13	22.06	20.18	9.654	6.932
8	Sarvodya Nagrik Bank	14.02	14.95	16.91	16.44	15.89	15.22	16.20	15.34	15.947	15.07	15.601	0.844
9	Baroda People's Bank	7.71	7.52	6.84	17.68	35.66	22.83	21.63	24.38	31.67	35.63	21.155	11.193
10	Sardar Bhiladwala Bank	17.07	16.83	16.41	16.00	38.94	39.10	38.12	86.91	100.71	110.42	48.051	37.115

and stationery is fixed and remaining variable which can be treated as semi variable.

The expenses on printing and stationery as stated in the Table 5.15 of selected Urban Co-operative Bank. The Sarvodaya Nagarik Bank's printing, stationery and advertisement is amounting to Rs. 1.53 lacs which was minimum amongst 10 Banks. Surat People's Bank paid Rs. 29.76 lacs on printing and stationery for the year 1996-97, which stands highest. The Surat People's Bank's average expense on stationery and printing was Rs. 15.70 lacs with standard deviation of 8.14. More consistent expense within 10 years was of Sarvodaya Nagrik Bank as the standard deviation is just 0.54 only. Co-efficient of variation of Rajkot Nagarik Bank for printing and stationery expenses was lowest i.e. 26.49. Annyonya Bank's CV is on higher side i.e. 76.28.

For the purpose of comparison, the fixed cost of Urban Co-operative Banks' and other than Urban Co-operative Banks' are presented in the Table 5.16.

Percentages of fixed cost to total cost of banking services are indicated in the following Table 5.16. The fixed cost of four broad groups of banks like State Bank of India (SBI), Nationalised Banks (NB), Private Sectors Banks (PSB) and Foreign Banks (FB) is shown in Table 5.16.

The ratio is calculated as - Fixed cost $\div$ Total cost $\times$ 100

There is a sharp decline in the fixed cost of foreign Banks from 53.42 per cent for the year 1980 to 43.64 per cent in the year 1990-91 which shows steady decline in the fixed cost and also observed in State Bank of India Group's Banks as well as Nationalised Banks. But ups and downs are revealed in the fixed cost as a percentage of total cost for Private Sector Banks.

TABLE 5.15

PRINTING AND STATIONERY EXPENSE AS AN ELEMENT OF FIXED COST

Sr. No.	*Name of the Bank*	*87-88*	*88-89*	*89-90*	*90-91*	*91-92*	*92-93*	*93-94*	*94-95*	*95-96*	*96-97*	*AVG*	*SD*
1	The Kalupur Bank	13.31	14.55	15.39	17.78	14.29	14.70	11.11	19.59	27.60	24.11	17.243	5.155
2	The Rajkot Nagrik Bank	7.20	10.59	10.93	11.32	8.50	16.99	16.39	14.79	13.53	14.89	12.513	3.315
3	Anyona Saharakri Bank	2.23	2.08	2.53	2.57	2.88	4.03	4.24	5.17	13.63	8.24	4.760	3.631
4	The Surat People's Bank	4.94	7.12	8.11	15.57	11.18	16.53	17.97	19.70	26.14	29.76	15.702	8.137
5	The Natpur Co-Op Bank	1.69	1.86	2.79	2.80	2.47	2.96	4.54	4.87	4.82	5.02	3.382	1.299
6	Anand Mercantile Bank	3.00	4.88	3.95	4.20	4.39	7.02	8.44	4.58	4.27	4.94	4.967	1.590
7	Dahod Urban Bank	1.80	1.12	1.18	2.25	1.89	3.74	3.77	3.61	5.87	2.99	2.822	1.472
8	Sarvodya Nagrik Bank	0.73	1.40	1.00	1.11	1.89	2.50	1.25	1.67	1.62	2.12	1.529	0.541
9	Baroda People's Bank	1.42	1.97	2.76	5.44	5.00	9.79	8.47	8.54	9.88	10.42	6.369	3.483
10	Sardar Bhiladwala Bank	3.34	4.10	6.25	5.61	7.26	7.23	7.35	7.34	8.27	9.41	6.616	1.844

TABLE 5.16

FIXED COST AS A PERCENTAGE OF TOTAL COST

Year	*SBI Group*	*Nationalised Banks*	*Private Sector Banks*	*Foreign Banks*
1979-80	35.72	32.24	40.98	53.42
1980-81	32.86	31.04	41.35	55.16
1981-82	31.63	30.37	40.34	56.84
1982-83	32.76	31.03	39.19	52.01
1983-84	34.36	31.22	39.32	47.06
1984-85	35.13	30.99	38.20	47.50
1985-86	34.13	30.30	37.46	45.54
1986-87	33.03	29.33	36.05	48.10
1988-89	33.35	28.46	35.53	39.47
1989-90	31.05	28.63	36.97	35.73
1990-91	31.39	27.38	36.31	34.64
1991-92	43.93	33.38	43.67	39.72

Sources: Financial Analysis of Banks Volumes I and II , IBA Bombay and computed from data given to Banks for relevant years.

Dr. P. V. Ramana Murthy, Dr. Suresh Chand Garg, Shri Kishore C. Raut, Shri Santosh D. Das, Shri S. K. Verghese and some others have named the fixed cost as establishment expenses for staff and other establishment expenses.

Total Fixed Cost

Audit Fees, Postage and Telegrams, Printing and Stationery, Depreciation, Director's fees, Salaries and Allowances, Rent, Rates and Taxes and the Legal Fees as a components of fixed cost are added to get the total fixed cost. Table 5.17 shows the total fixed cost of selected Urban Co-operative Banks for the year 1987-88 to the year 1996-97. As discussed earlier, total fixed cost is also called as establishment expenses for staff and other. The average fixed cost of Kalupur Commercial Bank is Rs. 332.18 lacs with standard deviation of 165.80. The range of fixed cost is Rs. 161.43 lacs to Rs. 643.10 lacs but it has sharply increased during the year 1992-93 to 1996-97. The average fixed cost of Surat People's Bank is Rs. 392.52 lacs with the higher standard deviation of 210.43. The Kalupur Commercial Bank's and The Surat People's Bank's fixed cost declined during the year 1991-92 to Rs. 205 lacs and 249 lacs respectively. The Rajkot Nagrik Bank had average fixed cost of Rs. 316.33 lacs with a standard deviation of 135.37. During ten years, the fixed cost of Rajkot Nagrik Bank had sharply increased from Rs. 227.04 lacs for the year 1991-92 to Rs. 337.98 lacs for the year 1992-93. It was Rs. 463.78 lacs in the year 1995-96, which increased sharply to Rs. 549.91 for the year 1996-97. The Kalupur Commercial Bank and The Rajkot Nagrik Bank both are scheduled Banks and have got the branch network at State level. So by opening every new branch their fixed cost is supposed to increase. The first position for lowest co-efficient of variation is of Rajkot Nagrik Bank and the second position is of Anand Mercantile Bank having C.V. 42.79 and 48.93 respectively.

Element of Fixed Cost to Total Fixed Cost

As per Table 5.18, a share of audit fees in total fixed cost for all the banks and for all the ten years is less than 1 per cent, so it is insignificant. According to Table 5.19 proportion of expenses on postage and telegrams as a component of total fixed cost for all the Banks is less than 4 per cent for all the ten years, so again it is considered to be insignificant. But the expenses incurred by selected Urban Co-operative Banks on printing and stationery seems to be significant as they are minimum 2 per cent and highest 15 per cent to the total fixed cost.

Table 5.20 shows share of printing and stationery as element of fixed cost to the total fixed cost. The expenses on printing and stationery of Anand Mercantile Bank are showing higher proportion to total fixed cost. It is 11.93 per cent for the year 1987-88 and rose to 16.47 per cent for the year 1988-

TABLE 5.17

TOTAL FIX COST

Sr. No.	Name of the Bank	87-88	88-89	89-90	90-91	91-92	92-93	93-94	94-95	95-96	96-97	AVG	SD
1	The Kalupur Bank	161.43	185.27	228.69	260.59	205.79	301.46	335.23	447.59	570.29	643.13	333.946	166.725
2	The Rajkot Nagrik Bank	151.25	172.70	196.51	263.39	228.35	340.36	379.33	423.29	464.23	549.91	316.931	135.482
3	Anyona Saharakri Bank	49.73	57.26	62.76	83.33	67.55	107.90	132.77	151.83	201.89	248.30	116.331	67.165
4	The Surat People's Bank	160.19	174.44	237.57	270.27	249.21	376.44	467.62	581.44	728.40	682.85	392.843	210.747
5	Natpur Co-Op Bank	20.92	24.93	31.30	36.76	31.87	49.08	58.37	72.26	100.09	109.85	53.545	31.375
6	Anand Mercantile Bank	25.15	29.62	30.88	37.46	33.46	46.13	54.69	61.45	83.94	115.39	51.816	28.658
7	Dahod Urban Bank	22.35	24.17	35.65	36.89	32.29	50.38	56.01	74.90	87.22	87.01	50.687	24.787
8	Sarvodya Nagrik Bank	15.06	18.88	22.64	25.99	27.36	43.04	50.50	65.42	74.22	84.63	42.773	24.894
9	Baroda People's Bank	23.55	27.14	37.49	46.81	51.33	76.98	77.73	118.72	146.70	200.75	80.720	57.974
10	Sardar Bhiladwala Bank	59.34	81.41	119.35	100.26	86.57	154.96	173.94	190.24	221.00	312.34	149.943	77.440

TABLE 5.18

PROPORTION OF AUDIT FEES WITH TOTAL FIX COST

Sr. No.	Name of the Bank	87-88	88-89	89-90	90-91	91-92	92-93	93-94	94-95	95-96	96-97	AVG	SD
1	The Kalupur Bank	0.001	0.001	0.001	0.001	0.001	0.001	0.001	0.001	0.003	0.002	0.001	0.001
2	The Rajkot Nagrik Bank	0.003	0.003	0.003	0.002	0.002	0.002	0.003	0.002	0.002	0.002	0.002	0.001
3	Anyona Saharakri Bank	0.005	0.002	0.002	0.001	0.001	0.001	0.001	0.001	0.000	0.000	0.001	0.001
4	Surat People's Bank	0.001	0.002	0.003	0.002	0.001	0.002	0.001	0.000	0.001	0.001	0.001	0.001
5	The Natpur Co-Op Bank	0.008	0.007	0.006	0.003	0.003	0.003	0.003	0.002	0.002	0.001	0.004	0.002
6	Anand Mercantile Bank	0.007	0.006	0.006	0.006	0.006	0.003	0.003	0.002	0.003	0.003	0.005	0.002
7	Dahod Urban Bank	0.010	0.008	0.004	0.005	0.007	0.005	0.004	0.004	0.004	0.004	0.006	0.002
8	Sarvodya Nagrik Bank	0.003	0.005	0.004	0.004	0.004	0.002	0.002	0.002	0.001	0.001	0.003	0.001
9	Baroda People's Bank	0.002	0.004	0.005	0.003	0.003	0.002	0.003	0.002	0.001	0.002	0.003	0.001
10	Sardar Bhiladwala Bank	0.001	0.004	0.003	0.004	0.003	0.002	0.001	0.001	0.000	0.001	0.002	0.001

TABLE 5.19

PROPORTION OF POSTAGE AND TELEGRAMS WITH TOTAL FIX COST

Sr. No.	*Name of the Bank*	*87-88*	*88-89*	*89-90*	*90-91*	*91-92*	*92-93*	*93-94*	*94-95*	*95-96*	*96-97*	*AVG*	*SD*
1	The Kalupur Bank	0.014	0.015	0.014	0.013	0.013	0.013	0.014	0.014	0.012	0.013	0.013	0.001
2	The Rajkot Nagrik Bank	0.034	0.039	0.038	0.031	0.030	0.025	0.030	0.029	0.026	0.021	0.030	0.006
3	Anyona Saharakri Bank	0.011	0.012	0.010	0.010	0.013	0.010	0.010	0.010	0.010	0.010	0.011	0.001
4	The Surat People's Bank	0.008	0.010	0.007	0.010	0.010	0.009	0.007	0.007	0.005	0.007	0.008	0.002
5	The Natpur Co-Op Bank	0.025	0.026	0.023	0.023	0.020	0.017	0.020	0.016	0.014	0.014	0.020	0.004
6	Anand Mercantile Bank	0.032	0.027	0.038	0.029	0.024	0.023	0.020	0.021	0.013	0.010	0.024	0.008
7	Dahod Urban Bank	0.016	0.015	0.011	0.014	0.014	0.013	0.018	0.014	0.014	0.015	0.014	0.002
8	Sarvodya Nagrik Bank	0.029	0.038	0.042	0.039	0.029	0.028	0.017	0.027	0.020	0.017	0.029	0.009
9	Baroda People's Bank	0.031	0.050	0.031	0.038	0.025	0.025	0.025	0.018	0.017	0.014	0.027	0.011
10	Sardar Bhiladwala Bank	0.022	0.019	0.014	0.024	0.025	0.017	0.015	0.014	0.017	0.016	0.018	0.004

89. There is a sharp decline from the year 1993-94 i.e.15.43 per cent to 7.45 per cent for the year 1994-95. The proportion further declined by 5 per cent in the year 1995-96. For all the Banks, normally a declining trend is observed. As discussed earlier, depreciation depends upon the fixed assets and the rate of depreciation but here depreciation as a element of fixed cost and a part of total fixed cost are indicated in the Table 5.21. The share of depreciation in total fixed cost is not negligible as it was with audit fees and postage and telegrams. It is almost more than 5 per cent for all the Banks in the sample with some exceptions. The higher depreciation proportion to total fixed cost is reflected in the case of Natpur Co-operative Bank, it is ranging between 10.86 per cent and 16.36 per cent. While the Rajkot Nagrik Bank and Dahod Urban bank are on the lower side in providing the depreciation during ten years of study.

According to Table 5.22, a share of directors' fees in total fixed cost is not more than 0.5 per cent in any one of the 10 sample banks during all ten years of study, so we can consider it as insignificant.

Table 5.06 shows salaries and allowances forming a major part of the total fixed cost of selected Urban Co-operative Banks during ten years. 7 out of 10 selected Banks are spending 80 per cent or more for salaries and allowances of total fixed cost i.e. higher than any other element of fixed cost. In the year 1995-96, Sarvodaya Nagrik Bank's proportion of salaries to total fixed cost is 91.66 per cent whereas during all ten years Baroda Peoples Bank's salaries to total fixed cost proportion has remained on lower side. The lowest proportion was 59.44 per cent for the year 1992 and it was at the peak i.e. 82.77 per cent in the year 1994-95. As such, there is no sudden increase or decrease with any Banks in any year for the Salaries and Allowances to total fixed cost.

Table 5.23 shows a share of rent, rate, taxes etc. in the total fixed cost of selected Urban Co-operative Banks. Baroda

TABLE 5.20

PROPORTION OF PRINTING AND STATIONERY WITH TOTAL FIX COST

Sr. No.	*Name of the Bank*	*87-88*	*88-89*	*89-90*	*90-91*	*91-92*	*92-93*	*93-94*	*94-95*	*95-96*	*96-97*	*AVG*	*SD*
1	The Kalupur Bank	0.082	0.079	0.067	0.068	0.069	0.049	0.033	0.044	0.048	0.037	0.058	0.018
2	The Rajkot Nagrik Bank	0.048	0.061	0.056	0.043	0.037	0.050	0.043	0.035	0.029	0.027	0.043	0.011
3	Anyona Saharakri Bank	0.045	0.036	0.040	0.031	0.043	0.037	0.032	0.034	0.068	0.033	0.040	0.011
4	The Surat People's Bank	0.031	0.041	0.034	0.058	0.045	0.044	0.038	0.034	0.036	0.044	0.040	0.008
5	The Natpur Co-Op Bank	0.081	0.075	0.089	0.076	0.078	0.060	0.078	0.067	0.048	0.046	0.070	0.014
6	Anand Mercantile Bank	0.119	0.165	0.128	0.112	0.131	0.152	0.154	0.075	0.051	0.043	0.113	0.043
7	Dahod Urban Bank	0.081	0.046	0.033	0.061	0.059	0.074	0.067	0.048	0.067	0.034	0.057	0.016
8	Sarvodya Nagrik Bank	0.048	0.074	0.044	0.043	0.069	0.058	0.025	0.026	0.022	0.025	0.043	0.019
9	Baroda People's Bank	0.060	0.073	0.074	0.116	0.097	0.127	0.109	0.072	0.067	0.052	0.085	0.026
10	Sardar Bhiladwala Bank	0.056	0.050	0.052	0.056	0.084	0.047	0.042	0.039	0.037	0.030	0.049	0.015

TABLE 5.21

PROPORTION OF DEPRECIATION WITH TOTAL FIX COST

Sr. No.	Name of the Bank	87-88	88-89	89-90	90-91	91-92	92-93	93-94	94-95	95-96	96-97	AVG	SD
1	The Kalupur Bank	0.101	0.094	0.065	0.055	0.067	0.066	0.075	0.093	0.136	0.165	0.092	0.035
2	Rajkot Nagrik Bank	0.059	0.073	0.064	0.052	0.046	0.054	0.054	0.058	0.066	0.059	0.058	0.008
3	Anyona Saharakri Bank	0.015	0.020	0.015	0.012	0.013	0.032	0.032	0.019	0.031	0.033	0.022	0.009
4	Surat People's Bank	0.119	0.101	0.068	0.079	0.074	0.092	0.079	0.084	0.093	0.096	0.088	0.015
5	Natpur Co-Op Bank	0.159	0.118	0.124	0.116	0.166	0.109	0.131	0.164	0.137	0.157	0.138	0.022
6	Anand Mercantile Bank	0.111	0.106	0.092	0.077	0.078	0.077	0.072	0.095	0.087	0.074	0.087	0.014
7	Dahod Urban Bank	0.021	0.026	0.018	0.015	0.021	0.013	0.011	0.049	0.067	0.004	0.024	0.019
8	Sarvodya Nagrik Bank	0.039	0.035	0.032	0.030	0.021	0.018	0.022	0.016	0.014	0.013	0.024	0.009
9	Baroda People's Bank	0.081	0.043	0.035	0.049	0.100	0.078	0.054	0.032	0.032	0.113	0.062	0.030
10	Sardar Bhiladwala Bank	0.054	0.053	0.072	0.057	0.106	0.069	0.071	0.068	0.064	0.083	0.070	0.016

TABLE 5.22

PROPORTION OF DIRECTORS' FEES WITH TOTAL FIX COST

Sr. No.	Name of the Bank	87-88	88-89	89-90	90-91	91-92	92-93	93-94	94-95	95-96	96-97	AVG	SD
1	The Kalupur Bank	0.000	0.000	0.000	0.000	0.000	0.000	0.000	0.000	0.000	0.000	0.000	0.000
2	The Rajkot Nagrik Bank	0.001	0.001	0.001	0.000	0.000	0.000	0.000	0.000	0.000	0.000	0.000	0.000
3	Anyona Saharakri Bank	0.004	0.007	0.006	0.002	0.005	0.005	0.004	0.002	0.002	0.003	0.004	0.002
4	The Surat People's Bank	0.000	0.000	0.000	0.001	0.000	0.001	0.001	0.000	0.000	0.001	0.000	0.000
5	The Natpur Co-Op Bank	0.000	0.000	0.000	0.000	0.000	0.000	0.000	0.000	0.000	0.000	0.000	0.000
6	Anand Mercantile Bank	0.006	0.004	0.004	0.003	0.005	0.005	0.005	0.004	0.003	0.003	0.004	0.001
7	Dahod Urban Bank	0.009	0.006	0.004	0.006	0.005	0.004	0.004	0.003	0.002	0.002	0.005	0.002
8	Sarvodya Nagrik Bank	0.000	0.000	0.000	0.000	0.000	0.000	0.000	0.000	0.000	0.000	0.000	0.000
9	Baroda People's Bank	0.008	0.008	0.006	0.009	0.007	0.006	0.005	0.003	0.003	0.002	0.006	0.002
10	Sardar Bhiladwala Bank	0.007	0.007	0.000	0.000	0.002	0.000	0.000	0.000	0.000	0.000	0.002	0.003

Peoples Co-operative Bank's rent, rate taxes, expenditure were 4.40 per cent in the year 1994-95 which sharply increased to 12.68 per cent in the year 1995-96. It further increased to 14.57 per cent for the year 1996-97. Obviously this sudden increase is due to opening of new branches and hiring of new premises during the year 1995-96 and 1996-97. Similarly for the same Bank, it was 4.46 per cent rent, rate and taxes of total fixed cost for the year 1991 and sharply increased to 17.32 per cent for the year 1991-92 i.e. again an incidence of opening of a new branch in Baroda. Overall table reflects declining trend during ten years of rent, rate and taxes to the total fixed cost.

Table 5.26 indicates legal fees as a proportion of total fixed cost. This table shows that the proportion is insignificant because none of the selected banks and in any of the years it crosses the limit of even 1 per cent.

Share of Total Fixed Cost in Total Cost

Earlier, establishment cost for staff and for others was considered as a fixed cost. This total fixed cost for State Bank of India Group, Nationalised Banks, Private Sector Banks and Foreign Banks is calculated as percentage to total expenditure of the Banks i.e. the proportion of fixed cost to total cost for the Banks other than the Urban Co-operative Banks is reflected in Table 5.16. Now here in the table, the fixed cost to total cost is less than 30 per cent. But as per Table 5.24 the Urban Co-operative Banks' proportion of fixed cost to total cost is no way more than 30 per cent of total fixed cost. A ratio of fixed cost to total cost is on the higher side for Sarvoday Nagrik Bank. Its lowest proportion is 18.93 per cent for the year 1987-99, it has reached to the peak i.e. 27.93 per cent for the year 1994-95 i.e. highest in the entire table. The Rajkot Nagrik Bank having large deposits but its expenses on establishments are less compare to other Banks in the sample. For the entire period of ten years it has remained between 7.77 per cent and 10.48 per cent for the year 1989-90 and the year 1993-94 respectively. The trend of proportion of fixed cost to total cost is consistent during the entire period of study for Rajkot Nagrik Bank. The Kalupur Commercial Bank's total fixed cost is fluctuating between 11.25 per cent for the year 1996-97 and 19.23 per cent in the year 1990-91. Similarly fixed expenses of Sardar Bhiladwada Bank as a share of total cost were on the higher side ranging from 15.63 per cent in the year 1988-89 to 24.04 per cent in the year 1996-97.

Proportion of Fixed Cost with Total Average Deposits

For the purpose of above comparison, average total deposit is calculated based on the opening balance and closing balance of deposits for a year. The total deposit includes fixed deposits, saving deposits and current deposits. Similarly the fixed cost includes the establishment expenses for staff and other establishment expenses. There are eight elements of fixed cost which are taken into consideration viz. — i) Audit fees ii) Postage and telegrams, iii) printing and stationery, iv) Depreciation on fixed assets, v) Directors' fees vi) Legal fees, vii) Salaries and Allowances and viii) Rent, Rate and Taxes. Table 5.25 gives fixed cost as a proportion of total average deposits. Baroda People's Bank's fixed cost is 4.49 per cent of total deposits for the year 1987-88 whereas it is at the peak i.e. 6.46 per cent for the year 1996-97. Baroda People's Bank is the only Bank, which has such a highest proportion. The Graph 5.01 to 5.10 show the trend in proportions of fixed cost with total average deposits. During the years i.e., 1987-88 to 1988-89 there is a decline but till 1990-91 it is rising whereas it sharply declines from 1992-93 to 1993-94 but again from 1994-95 it has sharply increased till two years and then for last two years it has became stable. Comparatively the average deposits of Baroda People's Co-operative Bank are ranging between Rs. 524.96 lacs and Rs. 3106.57 lacs for the years 1987-88 and 1996-97 respectively.

Theoretically the fixed cost is assumed to be constant

TABLE 5.23

PROPORTION OF RENT, RATES AND TAXES WITH TOTAL FIX COST

Sr. No.	Name of the Bank	87-88	88-89	89-90	90-91	91-92	92-93	93-94	94-95	95-96	96-97	AVG	SD
1	The Kalupur Bank	0.104	0.083	0.083	0.083	0.074	0.076	0.070	0.073	0.063	0.080	0.079	0.011
2	The Rajkot Nagrik Bank	0.040	0.041	0.044	0.053	0.064	0.050	0.059	0.075	0.066	0.061	0.055	0.011
3	Anyona Saharakri Bank	0.089	0.106	0.093	0.054	0.078	0.078	0.127	0.067	0.079	0.101	0.087	0.021
4	The Surat People's Bank	0.080	0.054	0.053	0.041	0.030	0.036	0.044	0.041	0.043	0.042	0.047	0.014
5	The Natpur Co-Op Bank	0.088	0.075	0.058	0.051	0.061	0.055	0.072	0.055	0.070	0.078	0.066	0.012
6	Anand Mercantile Bank	0.040	0.052	0.046	0.039	0.061	0.059	0.061	0.078	0.115	0.119	0.067	0.029
7	Dahod Urban Bank	0.080	0.081	0.070	0.069	0.061	0.067	0.062	0.052	0.076	0.084	0.070	0.010
8	Sarvodya Nagrik Bank	0.038	0.045	0.042	0.040	0.042	0.028	0.039	0.033	0.025	0.041	0.037	0.006
9	Baroda People's Bank	0.086	0.082	0.054	0.045	0.173	0.081	0.082	0.044	0.127	0.146	0.092	0.044
10	Sardar Bhiladwala Bank	0.029	0.030	0.033	0.044	0.048	0.046	0.034	0.038	0.036	0.036	0.038	0.007

TABLE 5.24

PROPORTION OF TOTAL FIX COST WITH TOTAL COST

Sr. No.	*Name of the Bank*	*87-88*	*88-89*	*89-90*	*90-91*	*91-92*	*92-93*	*93-94*	*94-95*	*95-96*	*96-97*	*AVG*	*SD*
1	The Kalupur Bank	0.129	0.146	0.152	0.192	0.158	0.184	0.145	0.128	0.135	0.112	0.148	0.025
2	The Rajkot Nagrik Bank	0.089	0.092	0.078	0.103	0.100	0.102	0.105	0.105	0.088	0.089	0.095	0.009
3	Anyona Saharakri Bank	0.184	0.188	0.180	0.207	0.207	0.208	0.236	0.246	0.234	0.200	0.209	0.023
4	The Surat People's Bank	0.177	0.175	0.191	0.194	0.160	0.188	0.204	0.239	0.240	0.170	0.194	0.027
5	The Natpur Co-Op Bank	0.125	0.154	0.162	0.168	0.161	0.154	0.164	0.179	0.184	0.133	0.158	0.018
6	Anand Mercantile Bank	0.159	0.139	0.116	0.115	0.104	0.099	0.127	0.137	0.129	0.136	0.126	0.018
7	Dahod Urban Bank	0.102	0.098	0.127	0.117	0.109	0.113	0.113	0.139	0.123	0.095	0.114	0.014
8	Sarvodya Nagrik Bank	0.189	0.184	0.212	0.210	0.231	0.225	0.214	0.279	0.263	0.203	0.221	0.030
9	Baroda People's Bank	0.203	0.167	0.184	0.183	0.210	0.193	0.147	0.218	0.215	0.211	0.193	0.023
10	Sardar Bhiladwala Bank	0.179	0.156	0.270	0.204	0.196	0.225	0.227	0.216	0.226	0.240	0.214	0.032

throughout the period, therefore, the unit cost is required to reduce as the output is increasing. This principle is proving true in case of Kalupur Commercial Bank. The proportion of fixed cost to total average deposit is 4.13 per cent in the year 1987-88 that is gradually declining year after the year and lastly in the year 1996-97 it is 1.63 per cent. The Graph 5.01 shows the trend of the ratio between fixed cost and total average deposits of Kalupur Commercial Bank. The curve either is falling steadily, sharply or it is remaining steady. For the purpose of ideal situation, i.e., fixed cost per unit of deposit shows decline in case of Kalupur Commercial Bank. The average total deposit of this Bank is showing sharp growth during the period of 1987-88 to 1986-87. Average total deposits for the year 1996-97 were amounting to Rs. 39,349.91 lacs as compared to Rs. 3,910.24 lacs for the year 1987-88 which are highest in all the sample Banks. On one side the deposits are rapidly increasing while the total fixed cost of Kalupur Commercial Bank per unit of deposit is continuously declining which is an ideal situation.

The Rajkot Nagrik Bank's proportion of fixed cost with total average deposits is showing continuous steady trend that is ranging between 1.42 per cent and 1.94 per cent, whereas the average total deposits have increased from Rs. 10,083.73 lacs to Rs. 30,554.73 lacs for the year 1987-88 and the year 1996-97 respectively. There is no sharp increase in the average deposits of Rajkot Nagrik Bank but they are increasing slowly, same is the situation of the proportion of fixed cost to the total average deposits. The Graph 5.02 of Rajkot Nagrik Bank reveals the consistent trend for the said ratio.

Annyonya Sahayakari Bank's ratio for fixed cost to total deposits is ranging between 2.0 per cent and 3.27 per cent. The Graph 5.03 shows the fluctuations in the trend of said proportion from the year 1987-88 to 1989-90. It is more or less stable, but till 1991 it has slowly increasing. Subsequently for the year 1991-92 there is sudden decline but again similar amount of increase is reflected for the year 1992-93. Further

TABLE 5.25

PROPORTION OF TOTAL FIX COST WITH TOTAL AVERAGE DEPOSITS

Sr. No.	Name of the Bank	87-88	88-89	89-90	90-91	91-92	92-93	93-94	94-95	95-96	96-97	AVG	SD
1	The Kalupur Bank	0.041	0.040	0.037	0.034	0.025	0.026	0.015	0.014	0.016	0.016	0.026	0.011
2	The Rajkot Nagrik Bank	0.015	0.014	0.015	0.018	0.014	0.019	0.019	0.019	0.018	0.018	0.017	0.002
3	Anyona Saharakri Bank	0.025	0.025	0.025	0.028	0.020	0.029	0.031	0.031	0.033	0.029	0.028	0.004
4	Surat People's Bank	0.026	0.024	0.027	0.027	0.023	0.030	0.031	0.035	0.038	0.028	0.029	0.005
5	The Natpur Co-Op Bank	0.019	0.019	0.020	0.020	0.016	0.021	0.022	0.023	0.024	0.019	0.020	0.002
6	Anand Mercantile Bank	0.032	0.031	0.025	0.024	0.017	0.021	0.020	0.020	0.021	0.023	0.023	0.005
7	Dahod Urban Bank	0.015	0.014	0.019	0.018	0.014	0.020	0.020	0.023	0.022	0.017	0.018	0.003
8	Sarvodya Nagrik Bank	0.034	0.035	0.035	0.035	0.033	0.046	0.048	0.056	0.059	0.057	0.044	0.011
9	Baroda People's Bank	0.045	0.040	0.045	0.048	0.046	0.054	0.045	0.064	0.063	0.065	0.051	0.009
10	Sardar Bhiladwala Bank	0.021	0.025	0.031	0.023	0.018	0.029	0.028	0.026	0.026	0.031	0.025	0.004

TABLE 5.26

PROPORTION OF LEGAL FEES WITH TOTAL FIX COST

Sr. No.	Name of the Bank	87-88	88-89	89-90	90-91	91-92	92-93	93-94	94-95	95-96	96-97	AVG	SD
1	The Kalupur Bank	0.000	0.004	0.003	0.004	0.006	0.007	0.005	0.009	0.011	0.000	0.005	0.003
2	The Rajkot Nagrik Bank	0.000	0.000	0.000	0.000	0.006	0.007	0.004	0.001	0.001	0.000	0.002	0.003
3	Anyona Saharakri Bank	0.003	0.007	0.005	0.000	0.004	0.001	0.001	0.001	0.001	0.000	0.002	0.002
4	The Surat People's Bank	0.000	0.000	0.001	0.000	0.001	0.000	0.000	0.001	0.001	0.002	0.001	0.001
5	The Natpur Co-Op Bank	0.003	0.003	0.001	0.002	0.001	0.002	0.010	0.005	0.003	0.006	0.004	0.003
6	Anand Mercantile Bank	0.002	0.001	0.002	0.001	0.003	0.009	0.003	0.005	0.003	0.003	0.003	0.002
7	Dahod Urban Bank	0.002	0.003	0.002	0.003	0.001	0.001	0.001	0.001	0.001	0.001	0.002	0.001
8	Sarvodya Nagrik Bank	0.002	0.001	0.002	0.004	0.006	0.007	0.000	0.000	0.001	0.004	0.003	0.002
9	Baroda People's Bank	0.009	0.004	0.005	0.003	0.000	0.003	0.000	0.002	0.004	0.005	0.004	0.003
10	Sardar Bhiladwala Bank	0.005	0.004	0.002	0.000	0.001	0.002	0.003	0.002	0.002	0.000	0.002	0.002

till 1995-96, the curve is showing steady trend but thereafter it has started declining in the year 1996-97. Comparatively, the average total deposit of Annyonya Sahayakari Bank is continuously increasing at a steady rate but there is a sharp increase in the year 1995-96 and 1996-97. The average deposits of Annyonya Sahayakari Bank for the year 1995-96 were Rs. 6167.98 lacs which rapidly gone upto Rs. 8420.32 lacs for the year 1996-97. But surprisingly, in the year of increase, in average deposits the proportion of fixed costs to total average deposits has gone down. This situation can be concluded, as the rate of growth in deposits is very high compare to the increase in total fixed cost.

The Surat People's Bank's average deposits have increased by four times during the period of ten years of the study. The average deposits in the year 1987-88 amounted to Rs. 6,155.38 lacs which gradually increased to Rs. 19,341.51 lacs in the year 1995-96. But there is a sharp rise to Rs. 24,513.53 lacs in the year 1996-97, whereas a proportion of total fixed cost with total deposits of Surat People's Bank is ranging between 2.27 per cent and 3.77 per cent. The Graph 5.04 shows the proportion of fixed cost with total average deposits, showing steady trend from the year 1987-88 to till 1991-92, but it is increasing continuously till the year 1995-96 and suddenly declined in the year 1996-97.

The Natpur Co-operative Bank's proportion of fixed cost with total average deposits shown in the table 5.25 is very much stable during the period of study with the exception. It has fallen from 2.02 per cent for the year 1990-91 to 1.55 per cent in the year 1991-92. But then again it has reached to 2.10 per cent in the year 1992-93. It has declined from 2.35 per cent in the year 1995-96 to 1.99 per cent for the year 1996-97. For other years, the curve in the Graph 5.05 shows a straight line curve

The Anand Mercantile Bank's average deposits were Rs. 778.14 lacs for the year 1987-88 growing to Rs. 3981 lacs for the year 1995-96. In these years, it is continuously increasing in some years at a low growth rate and in some years at high growth rate but there is a sharp increased by Rs. 1,000 lacs between the year 1995-96 and 1996-97. The average deposits reached to the peak of Rs. 4945.73 lacs in the year 1996-97. The Table 5.25 of proportion of fixed cost with the average deposit showing Anand Mercantile Bank's range between 1.70 per cent and 3.23 per cent. Looking at the Graph 5.06, the curve is continuously falling from the year 1987-88 till the year 1991-92 but it has marginally increased in the year 1992-93 and then it is constant throughout.

Table 5.25 reveals the range of proportion of fixed cost with total deposits of Dahod Urban Bank i.e. minimum 1.40 per cent to maximum of 2.32 per cent. The Graph 5.07 shows the trend in the proportion of fixed cost with total average deposits of Dahod Urban Bank, which is fluctuating during the year 1987-88 to the year 1991-92. But the fluctuations are very meager, it is almost steady but the curve is rising till the year 1994-95 and onwards it is falling till the year 1996-97. We can conclude that the curve is almost stable.

Eventually the Sarvodaya Nagrik Bank has not mobilized much deposit compared to any other Banks in the sample. The growth rate of average total deposits is also very low but the proportion of fixed cost with total deposits is at the second highest position. The proportion ranges from 3.33 per cent to 5.94 per cent during the period of study, so we can conclude that the Sarvoday Nagrik Bank pays higher fixed cost compared to other Banks in the sample. The Graph 5.08 of Sarvodaya Nagrik Bank showing almost the straight line between the years 1987-88 to 1991-92 but thereafter a sharp rise noticed till the year 1995-96 which is against the principle of falling fixed cost per unit over a period of time if the output is increasing.

This is the another bank alongwith Baroda People's Bank, The Graph 5.09 shows unusual curve of proportions between fixed cost and average total deposits, which indicates these both banks must have reduced their establishment expenses to survive in the forthcoming era of competition.

The Sardar Bhiladwala Bank's Graph 5.10 for the proportions between fixed cost and total average deposits shows continuous fluctuations during the year of study but still it ranges between 1.83 per cent and 3.10 per cent comparatively again it is third bank having the higher fixed cost as compared to its average deposits.

Earlier, at several places, it has been stated that the elements of fixed cost are independent with the volume of bank business. In other words, there is insignificant variation in the fixed cost elements but this aspect is not proved logical by any statistical tool. Statistical tool can support the logical explanations made for each element. The sample size of our study is ten banks i.e.. n =10. There are 8 elements of fix cost i) Salaries and Allowances ii) Directors fee iii) Audit fees iv) Legal fees v) Printing and Stationery vi) Rents, Rates, and Taxes vii) Postage and Telegram viii) Depreciation. Each element of cost is taken from 10 samples banks with values of ten years, i.e., from the year 1987-88 to 1996-97. Therefore it is the case of Multivariate analysis.

"Analysis of Variance (ANOVA), in its simplest form is a general procedure for isolating the source of variability in a set of measurements. The purpose is to determine the extent to which the effect of an independent variable as a major component."

Multivariate Analysis of Variance

ANOVA versus MANOVA

"Recent studies suggest that there is no clear advantage to either the Univariate or Multivariate approach. Indeed, for some sets of data, the Univariate approach is more powerful, whereas in other instances with spherically violated, the Multivariate approach may be more powerful. If variability is great, small effects may be hidden by the Univariate Test, in which case the multivariate approach is more powerful."[1]

The Multivariate Analysis of Variance (MANOVA), yields significant F ratio. It is useful to estimate the extent to which the total variability in measurement can be attributed to be dependent. In other words, analysis yielding insignificant F ratio is useful to estimate the extent to which total variability in measurement can be attributed to be independent variable.

MANOVA is also called as Multivariate Tests of significance. There are different approaches to test the Hypothesis H_0. Name of the tests are i) Pillais test ii) Hotellings test iii) Wilks test and iv) Roys test.

Suppose μ_t , it is the average cost for the t year. Then H_0 is $m_t = m$ for all $_t$ is to be tested. If H_0 is true then the probability of observing higher values of F are more than 5 per cent. For all eight elements of fixed cost, eight Hypothesis of H_0 are framed. Null Hypothesis H_0 for all elements of fixed cost m_t is average fixed cost of each element of fixed cost for all ten year.

i) $H_0 = \mu^1{}_t$ is average legal fees paid during ten years by selected 10 Urban Co-operative Banks in Gujarat which remains constant.
ii) $H_0 = \mu^2{}_t$ is average Audit fees paid by the selected Urban Co-operative Banks which remains constant during ten years.
iii) $H_0 = \mu^3{}_t$ is average Postage and telegram expenses paid by ten selected Urban Co-operative Banks which remains constant during ten years.
iv) $H_0 = \mu^4{}_t$ is average Printing and Stationary expenses paid by ten selected Urban Co-operative Banks which remains constant during 10 year.
v) $H_0 = \mu^5{}_t$ is average Depreciation provided on fixed assets by ten selected Urban Co-operative Banks which remains constant during ten years.

vi) $H_o = \mu^6{}_t$ is average Directors fees paid by 10 selected Urban Co-operative Banks which remains constant during ten years.

vii) $H_o = \mu^7{}_t$ is average Salaries and allowance paid by ten selected Urban Co-operative Banks which remains constant during ten years.

viii) $H_o = \mu^8{}_t$ is average Rent Rates and Taxes expenses paid by ten selected Urban Co-operative Banks during ten years.

Eight null Hypothesis are tested under MANOVA

Table 5.27 shows the results of the Pillais test of significance

Multivariate Analysis of Variance (MANOVA)

i) Accepted value F = 0.229 - Null Hypothesis for legal fees indicates probability of observing F value at 22.9 per cent which is more than 5 per cent, therefore H_o is accepted at 5 per cent level of significance. We conclude that average legal fees paid by Urban Co-operative Banks remains constant with respect to period of ten year.

ii) Null hypothesis for Audit fees is accepted significance of F is at 40 per cent higher than 5 per cent therefore H_o is accepted at 5 per cent level of significance. We conclude that average audit fees paid by Urban Co-operative Banks remains constant with respect to the period of ten years.

Similarly the result H_o for average:

— Postage and Telegram expenses
— Printing and Stationery expenses
— Depreciation
— Salaries and Allowance and
— Rent Rates and Taxes expense

TABLE 5.26.A

VALUES OF "F" AT DEGREES OF FREEDOM

Sr. No.	*Variable*	*Value*	*Approx. Calculated Observed Value of F*	*Degrees of Freedom*	*Error Degrees of Freedom*	*Significance of F*	*At Per cent Level*
1	Legal fees	0.99008	11.09202	9.00	1.00	0.229	5 per cent
2	Audit fees	0.96829	3.39235	9.00	1.00	0.400	5 per cent
3	Postage and Telegram	0.93460	1.58786	9.00	1.00	0.552	5 per cent
4	Printing and Stationery	0.98751	8.78835	9.00	1.00	0.256	5 per cent
5	Depreciation	0.87152	0.75369	9.00	1.00	0.721	5 per cent
6	Directors' fees		12.49	9.00	1.00	0.006	
7	Salaries	0.89117	0.90982	9.00	1.00	0.678	5 per cent
8	Rent, Rates and Taxes	0.89221	0.91971	9.00	1.00	0.676	5 per cent

Value of F indicated in table 5 is greater than 5 per cent at 5 per cent level of significance. Hence it is concluded that the above mentioned average expenses remains constant with respect to the period of ten years as mentioned in the Table 5.27. It also shows the value of F and level of significance at 5 per cent level.

TABLE 5.27

VALUES OF F FOR ELEMENT OF FIXED COST AND LEVEL OF SIGNIFICANCE AT 5 PER CENT

Sr. No.	*Variable*	*F values Pillais test*	*Level of significance at 5 per cent*
1	Legal fees	22.9 per cent	Not significant
2	Audit fees	40.00 per cent	Not significant
3	Postage and telegram	55.20 per cent	Not significant
4	Printing and stationery	25.60 per cent	Not significant
5	Depreciation	72.00 per cent	Not significant
6	Director's fees	0.6 per cent	Significant
7	Salaries and allowancse	67.80 per cent	Not significant
8	Rent, Rates and Taxes	67.76 per cent	Not significant

The null hypothesis is rejected when only average Director fees paid by ten Urban Co-operative Banks. Value of F is 0.6 per cent i.e. less than 5 per cent.

The Table 5.26.A showing directors fees' for all ten years are not available and for the few years, directors fees of Sardar Bhiladwala Banks is also not available. Hence value of F is less than 5 per cent.

REFERENCE

1. Ref.: Ellen R. Girden Nova University ANOVA Repeated measures 1992 Sage Publications, New Delhi pp. 1 and 25.

GRAPH 5.01

TRENDS IN RATIOS OF FIXED COST TO AVERAGE DEPOSITS OF THE KALUPUR BANK

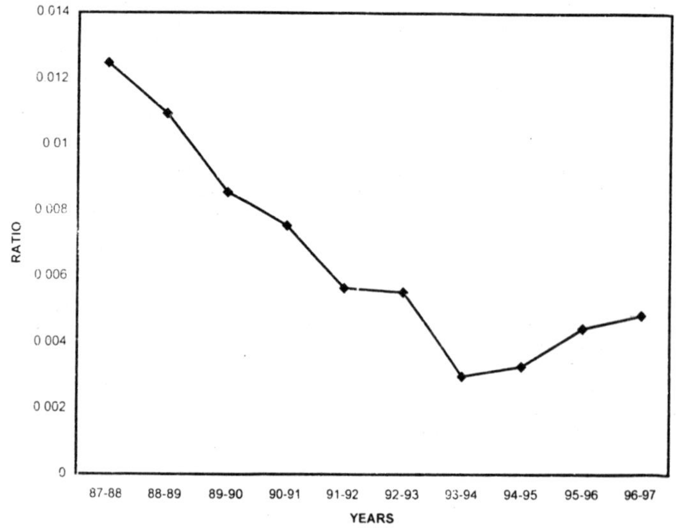

GRAPH 5.02

TRENDS IN RATIOS OF FIXED COST TO AVERAGE DEPOSITS OF THE RAJKOT NAGARIK BANK.

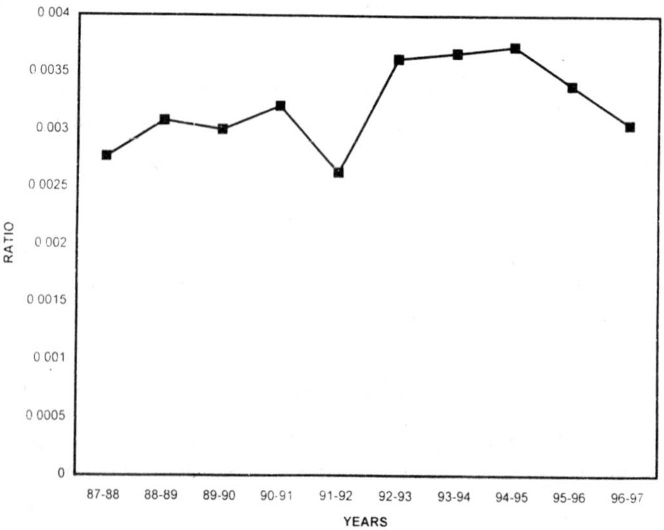

GRAPH 5.03

TRENDS IN RATIOS OF FIXED COST TO AVERAGE DEPOSITS OF THE ANYONYA SAHAYAKARI BANK

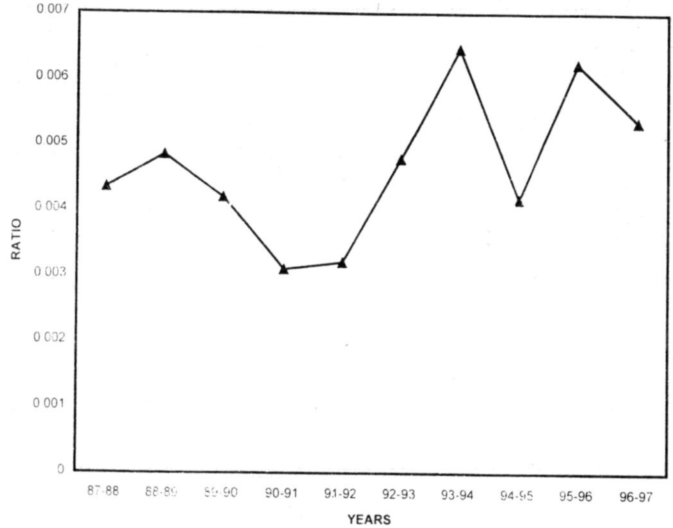

GRAPH 5.04

TRENDS IN RATIOS OF FIXED COST TO AVERAGE DEPOSITS OF THE SURAT PEOPLE'S BANK

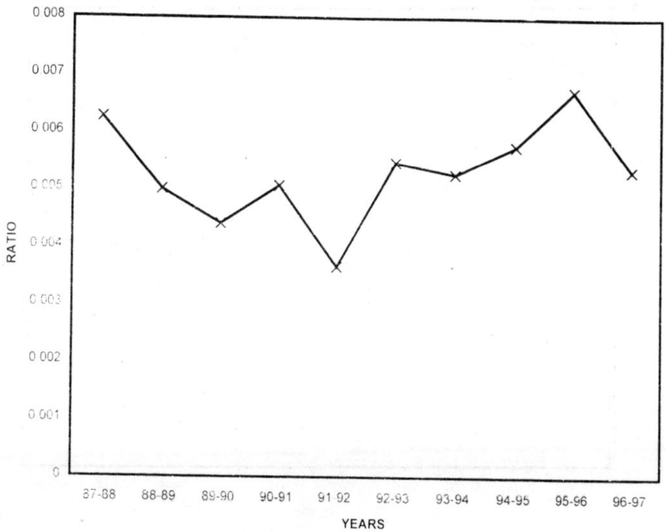

GRAPH 5.05

TRENDS IN RATIOS OF FIXED COST TO AVERAGE DEPOSITS OF THE NATPUR BANK

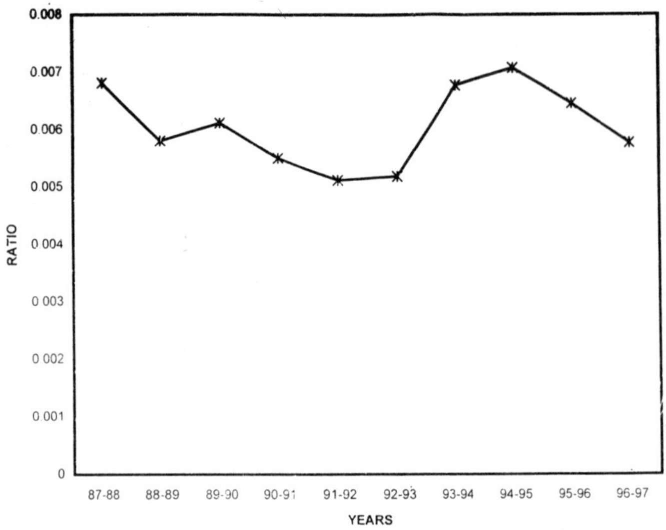

GRAPH 5.06

TRENDS IN RATIOS OF FIXED COST TO AVERAGE DEPOSITS OF THE ANAND MERCANTILE BANK

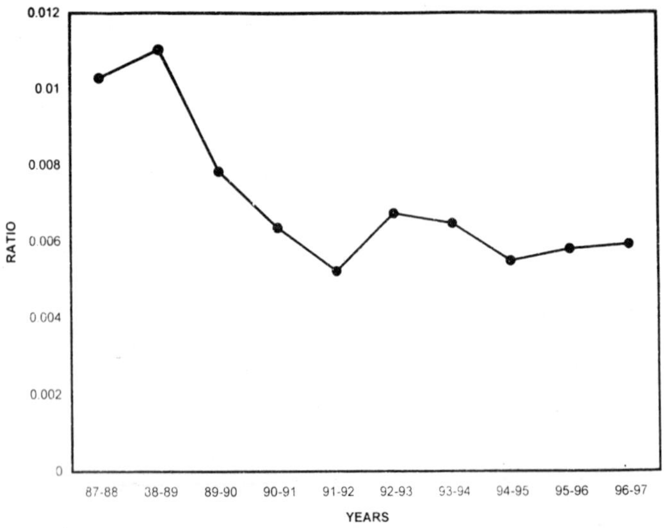

GRAPH 5.07

TRENDS IN RATIOS OF FIXED COST TO AVERAGE DEPOSITS OF THE DAHOD URBAN BANK

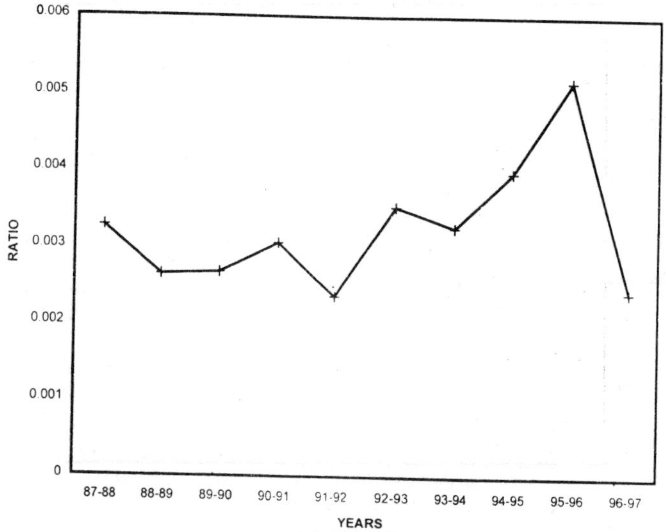

GRAPH 5.08

TRENDS IN RATIOS OF FIXED COST TO AVERAGE DEPOSITS OF THE SARVODYA BANK

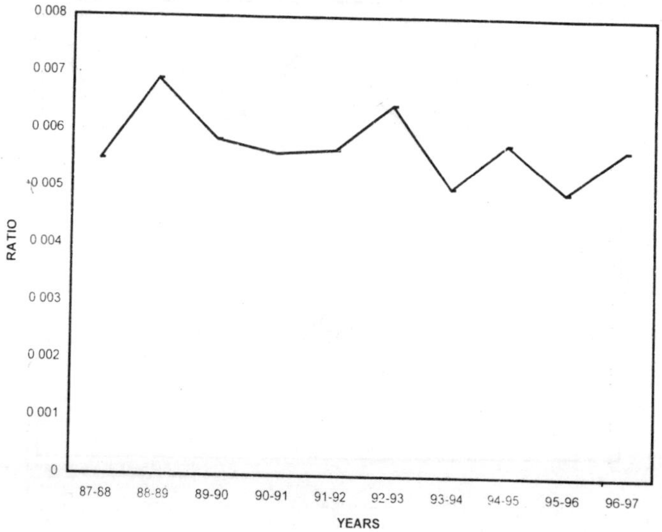

GRAPH 5.09

TRENDS IN RATIOS OF FIXED COST TO AVERAGE DEPOSITS OF THE BARODA PEOPLE'S BANK

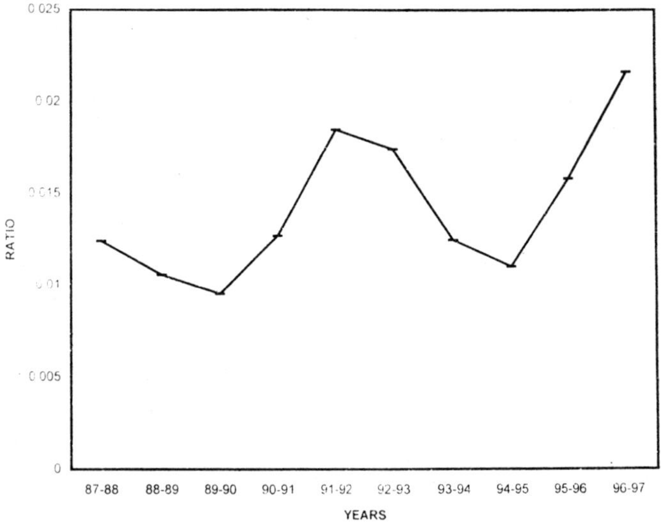

GRAPH 5.10

TRENDS IN RATIOS OF FIXED COST TO AVERAGE DEPOSITS OF THE SARDAR BHILADWALA BANK

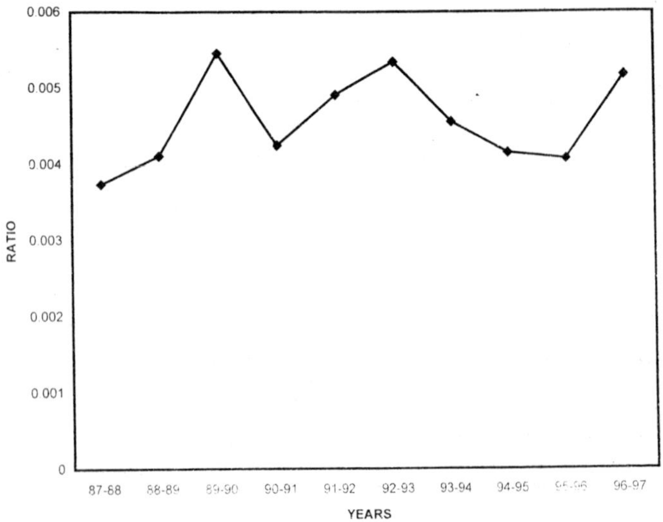

6

Deposits: Variable Cost

Variable Cost Defined

Kohler has defined variable cost as "An operating expense, or operating expenses as a class, that vary directly, sometimes proportionately, with sales, or production volume, facility utilization, or other measure of activity, example:- Material consumed, direct labour, power factory supplies, depreciation (on production basis) sales commission etc."[1]

Variable cost is termed as a marginal cost, direct cost, activity cost, volume cost or out of pocket cost. Fixed cost as discussed in earlier chapter remains constant in total but they vary per unit with output rate. Costs that are proportionately variable in total are constant per unit. Variable cost may be confined to those that do vary as a continuous function of output and fixed costs to those that do not vary. Which costs item are fixed and which are variable depends upon the degree of adaptation of costs to output rate. An increase in the output means the proportionate increase in total variable costs and decrease in output results in a proportionate decline in total variable costs. There is a direct relationship between output and variable cost.

Methods of Classifying Cost into Variable and Fixed Cost

There are three methods of classifying costs into fixed and variable cost that are:

i) High and Low point method,

ii) Scattered Diagram method
iii) Least Square method

High and Low Point Method

Variable cost per unit can be derived as:

$$\text{Variable cost per unit} = \frac{\text{Total cost of High Vol.} - \text{Total cost of Lower Vol.}}{\text{Higher output} - \text{Lower output}}$$

On the basis of variable cost per unit, variable cost of any level of output can be decided.

Then total fixed cost can be determined.

Total fixed cost = Total Cost – Total Variable Cost

Scattered Diagram Method

Total cost for various level of output is plotted on a graph. Total cost is measured on "Y" axis and the output on "X" axis. A single straight line is drawn by visual inspection in such a manner that the graph-line can be nearer to all the plotted points in the Graph and coverage's on the "Y" axis. From that point, at which it merges with the "Y"-axis, draw a horizontal graph-line to "X" axis. This graph-line decides the fixed cost for all the level of outputs.

Least Square Method

Variable cost can be calculated by following steps.

i) Calculate the difference between total cost at each level of output and average cost.
ii) Calculate difference in actual output and average output.
iii) Multiply difference between costs and output respectively.
iv) Get division of above multiplication in 'c' by squares in 'b', which will give variable cost.

The above calculations are based on equation of straight line

Y = a + bX. Where a = fixed cost, b = Variable cost per unit, and X = number units

Eventually, known variable cost for the banking activity is interest. Interest has direct relation with deposits and advances. Every increase in volume of deposit will result into increase in the amount of interest on advances, therefore, it is necessary to understand the concept of interest.

Interest

Interest Defined

"Interest is simply defined as the cost of using someone else's money or viewed from the other end, as the price to be charged for allowing someone else to use your money (clearly one person's cost is someone else's income). Just as it is possible to hire a car for a period, paying the car hiring company, a rental which varies with the length of the period of hire, so it is possible to 'hire' sum of money in return for payment of an agreed interest charge. Thus, although interest is often referred to as 'the price of money', it would really be more accurate to call it the price for the 'use of money." [2]

Interest Rates

Till the year 1958, interest rates were not controlled. The banks were allowed to offer and charge the interest rates by themselves. In October 1958, banks voluntarily decided to maintain the certain maximum limit of interest rates offered on deposits. From 1964, Reserve Bank of India started administering interest rates on deposits. Reserve Bank of India began to control the lending rates from 1960. Since the nationalization of Commercial Banks in 1969, regulation of deposits and lending rates supplemented by detailed guidelines on distribution of credit to priority sectors were issued.

The purpose behind the administrative control on interest rate structure was largely to direct implicit subsidy to certain sectors and enable them to obtain funds at concessional rate of interest. An element, subsidy i.e. providing loans and advances at a concessional rate is nothing but to charge higher rate to other non-concessional borrowers. The regulation of interest rates on lending has led to the regulation of the deposits' rates, mainly to keep the cost of funds of banks at a reasonable relation to the rates at which they are required to advance.

Criticism of Interest Rate Policy

The policy of regulated interest rates has been criticised on several grounds like:

i. Regulated interest rates has resulted into less interest rates for depositors which adversely affected in providing incentives for saving in the form of financial assets,
ii. Regulated interest rates were inflexible and not reflecting market trends,
iii. Lower interest rates on Government securities adversely affected banks' profitability,
iv. Credit to the priority sector gave rise to credit rationing which proved inefficient,
v. The rates on deposits do not allow for effective competition between banks and other institutions in view of price determination,
vi. The lending rate structure has become so complex with number of sub and main clauses,
vii. Concessional rates of interest appear to have allowed projects of doubtful viability to be undertaken.

Rational of prohibiting payment of interest on demand deposits and imposing ceiling on interest rates to be paid on fixed and saving deposits is based on two reasons:

i) Large money centered banks can be forestalled, which are aggressively bidding for deposits, which are coming from smaller communities. These deposits could help in meeting the local credit needs of the same communities.

ii) High interest rates on fixed deposits will force the bank to acquire high yielding risky assets in order to meet interest expenses.

"Interest rates on deposits and advances are generally subject to two types of regulations issued by monetary authorities, which are as follows:-

i) Overall regulation through monetary policy directed at controlling cost and supply of credit, and

ii) Detailed regulation of interest rates on deposits with the objective of preventing wasteful competition and of interest rates on different categories of advances. The objective in this case is to render assistance to the national economic policy by prescribing concessional low rates to priority sectors in the economy.

These regulations limits the freedom of action to be taken by banks in framing strategies for achieving profit objectives. Thus, liquidity requirements restrain the growth of risky assets while an upward revision of interest rates on advances increases the earning power of banks."[3]

A survey of the available information on cost in banking industry was carried out by the Banking Commission (1972), which revealed in its report the facts regarding interest paid on deposits during the years from 1961 to 1968 by scheduled commercial banks.

During these years, there is a sharp increase in interest cost as a whole but the proportion of interest paid to the volume of deposits shows rise at a very low growth rate or it is remaining constant. For the year 1966, the ratio of interest cost to deposit is 4.04 per cent and increases to 4.10 per cent but then again it has come down to 4.04 per cent in the year 1968.

TABLE 6.01

INTEREST ON DEPOSITS PAID BY SCHEDULED COMMERCIAL BANKS AND ITS PERCENTAGE TO THE DEPOSITS

Year	*Interest Paid on Deposits*	*Interest as Per cent of Deposits*
1961	36.2	2.30
1962	44.45	2.51
1963	50.20	2.62
1964	59.33	2.74
1965	86.24	3.52
1966	115.34	4.04
1967	132.35	4.10
1968	147.48	4.04

Interest Cost of Funds

Nationalised Bank

It is the total interest paid on the interest bearing liabilities i.e. deposits and borrowings. But, as it is discussed in earlier chapters, borrowings forms insignificant portion of banks' funds, therefore, major portion of interest paid is on deposits.

The following Table 6.02 illustrates interest cost of funds of Nationalised Banks in India.

Interest cost of fund = Interest paid ÷ Interest bearing liabilities × 100

The interest cost of deposits is just 2.30 per cent in the year 1961, which has reached the top of 6.24 per cent in the year 1979. Sometimes it has fallen but again it has increased. The fluctuations in cost of deposits are due to administrative control on rate of interest, in the interest of national development and changes in economic policies from time to time. As a part of change, in monetary policies, some fiscal and monetary measures are taken. Under these measures, interest on deposits regulated by the monetary authorities of India. Change in interest rates resulted into the change in interest cost of deposits.

TABLE 6.02

INTEREST COST OF FUNDS (DEPOSITS AND BORROWINGS) OF NATIONALISED BANKS

Year	*Cost as per cent*	*Year*	*Cost as per cent*
1970	3.69	1980	5.93
1971	3.98	1981	5.90
1972	4.08	1982	5.92
1973	4.36	1983	5.48
1974	5.51	1984	5.71
1975	5.86	1985	5.94
1976	6.52	1986	5.99
1977	6.40	1987	6.52
1978	6.03	1988-89	6.85
1979	6.23	1989-90	6.24

Source: Computed from statistical tables relating to banks in India, RBI Publication

It will be worthwhile to study the share of interest in the total expenditure of nationalised banks. Following Table 6.03 expresses the share of interest paid as a proportion of total expenses:

TABLE 6.03

TOTAL INTEREST PAID AS PROPORTION TO TOTAL EXPENSES:

Year	*Cost as per cent*	*Year*	*Cost as per cent*
1970	51.2	1982	69.63
1971	52.6	1983	68.97
1972	53.5	1984	68.78
1973	55.4	1985	69.01
1974	59.1	1986	69.70
1975	57.1	1987	70.67
1976	63.3	1988-89	71.54
1977	64.6	1989-90	71.35
1978	66.8	1990-91	72.62
1979	68.0	1991-92	66.62
1980	67.76	1995-96	58.68
1981	68.96	1996-97	64.34
		1997-98	65.22

Source: Statistical tables published by *RBI and Report on Trends and Progress of Banking in India*, 1997-98.

Initially during 1970 and 1975, share of interest cost of deposits grew steadily. In the year 1975, share of interest was 57.1 per cent then it suddenly increased up to 63.3 per cent. There is 7 per cent growth in the share of interest cost from the year 1976 to the year 1980 and reached to the tune of 57.76 per cent. Up to the year 1990-91, the share of interest cost to total expense was highest i.e. 72.65 per cent then it has sharply declined to 66.62 per cent. This sharp decline may be due to deregulation of interest rates. It further declined to 58.68 per cent in the year 1995.96. The Indian economic reforms had impact on this decline by way of withdrawing ceiling on interest rates.

Interest Cost of Funds : Other Banks

Following is the comparison among State Bank of India Group Banks (SBIG), Nationalised Banks (NB), Private Sector

Banks (PSB), Foreign Banks (FB) and All Scheduled Commercial banks (ASB) with regard to the share of interest cost to total expenditure:

SBI Group		*NB Group*		*PSB Group*		*FB Group*		*ASB Group*	
1995-96	1996-97	1995-96	1996-97	1995-96	1996-97	1995-96	1996-97	1995-96	1996-97
54.98	59.27	58.68	64.35	66.44	69.03	59.7	57.43	58.2	62.6

Source: Reported on Trends and progress of Banking in India 1996-97.

Earlier, in the Chapter IV – "Deposits performance of selected Urban Co-operative Banks in Gujarat", only the performance of deposits has been discussed for ten years, i.e. study period. Here in this chapter, the variable costs are matched with deposits, therefore, the actual deposits amounts are not taken as a base but the two years average of deposits are calculated to match the variable cost. The averages are calculated by adding the opening balance of deposits and closing balance of deposits of a year, then divided by two. These calculations are carried out for getting average current deposits; average saving deposits, average fixed deposits and average total deposits. It was noted earlier that the variable cost is the interest cost on deposits. As per RBI guidelines, interest on current deposits is refused. In other words, current deposits are interest free deposits. Obviously, remaining saving deposits and fixed deposits are interest bearing deposits. Therefore, while studying the variable cost of deposits, saving deposits and fixed deposits are to be matched with the interest cost.

Interest Rate on Saving Deposits

Earlier, it has been discussed about the interest rate structure. Reserve Bank of India had a full control on rate of interest but steadily and gradually the interest rate on term deposits was deregulated by Reserve Bank of India. Study period includes both the phases i.e. the regulated interest rate strucure and the deregulated interest rate structure. Urban Banks may find it difficult to manage its variable cost i.e.

interest rates in the changing scenario, in deregulated interest rate structure. Earlier RBI was regulating the interest rates, hence Urban Co-operative Banks were in protected environment.

The Reserve Bank of India has continued to regulate the interest rate on saving deposits. During the study period, the interest rate has fluctuated three times. From the year 1987-88, the interest on saving deposits was 5 per cent till the year 1990-91, then in the year 1991-92 it was 6 per cent per annum, again it was reduced to 4.5 per cent, from the year 1992-93 it has continued to be 4.5 per cent till the year 1996-97.

Interest Rate on Fixed Deposits

The maturity of term deposits was regulated by the Reserve Bank of India till 9th October, 1991. The different maturity periods were i) 15 to 45 days, ii) 46 to 90 days iii) 90 days to 6 months, iv) 6 months to 9 months. v) 9 months to 1 year, vi) 1 year to 2 years, vii) 2 years to 3 years, viii) 3 years to 5 years and ix) 5 years and above. For all these types of maturity, the interest rates were between 11 per cent and 13 per cent. Then Banks were free to choose and determine the maturity for term deposits. Maximum rate of interest was determined by the Reserve Bank of India on the fixed deposits having maturity between three and five years. The maximum interest in the year 1992 was 13 per cent which was reduced in 1993 to 11 per cent and further reduction took place in the year 1994 to the 10 per cent. Maximum interest 12 per cent was allowed for the maturity between 1year and 2 year in October, 1995. In the year 1996, the deposits up to one year maturity, the maximum interest was payable at 11 per cent but then from the year 1996, Reserve Bank of India lifted the total control on the interest rates on deposits. As a consequence, Urban Co-operative Banks were free to choose the interest rate on fixed deposits and the term of maturity.

In the third chapter, it has been discussed that the Urban

Co-operative Banks were allowed to pay 1 per cent higher interest to the depositors than what was paid by other banks. Depositors were attracted to deposit, their hard earned money with Urban Co-operative Banks, as they were getting 1 per cent more interest than that of Commercial Banks. This scene was under the administered rate of interest. Since 1996, Urban Co-operative Banks, not able to get the advantage of paying 1 per cent more rate of interest. This liberty of paying higher rate of interest on deposits is available with all the Banks from the year 1996. This may result into reduction of deposits with Urban Co-operative Banks, if the management of Urban Co-operative Banks do not match the costs with its deposits. The reasons are Commercial Banks and other non-banking institutions have professional and trained Managers to attract the deposits. There may be a severe competition, it is survival of the fittest. If Urban Co-operative Banks want to compete, then they will have to keep their rate of interest reasonably low, having considered the cost of such deposits.

Interest Cost Compared

Interest Cost Compared with Total Cost

Researchers' have studied this factor with respect to all Scheduled Commercial Banks, Nationalised Banks, Foreign Banks, State Bank of India Group Banks, Private Sector Banks and Public Sector Banks but no study so far is observed on this particular issue for Urban Co-operative Banks. As per Table 6.04, The Surat People's Bank amongst the selected Urban Co-operative Banks is found to be lowest in share of interest to total cost, its share of interest in total cost ranges between 48.44 per cent to 71.48 per cent. During the years 1987-88 to the year 1990-91, it is gradually declining for the year 1990-91 i.e. 67.40 per cent and sharply declined to 48.44 per cent for the year 1991-92 but then there was an increasing trend till the year 1994-95 i.e. 60.48 per cent. For the last two years, it has remained between 57 per cent and 58 per cent. Conversely the Anand Mercantile Bank seems to be on a

TABLE NO. 6.04

SHARE OF TOTAL INTEREST IN TOTAL COST

Sr. No.	*Name of the Bank*	*87-88*	*88-89*	*89-90*	*90-91*	*91-92*	*92-93*	*93-94*	*94-95*	*95-96*	*96-97*	*CV*	*AVG*
1	The Kalupur Bank	0.824	0.792	0.794	0.753	0.792	0.727	0.708	0.666	0.677	0.707	7.37	0.744
2	The Rajkot Nagrik Bank	0.786	0.632	0.653	0.564	0.554	0.527	0.553	0.530	0.501	0.465	16.02	0.577
3	Anyona Saharakri Bank	0.782	0.773	0.778	0.732	0.756	0.765	0.749	0.740	0.753	0.789	2.47	0.762
4	The Surat Peoples's Bank	0.715	0.710	0.675	0.674	0.484	0.602	0.620	0.605	0.574	0.586	11.32	0.624
5	The Natpur Co-Op Bank	0.856	0.827	0.818	0.795	0.798	0.803	0.803	0.787	0.790	0.835	2.73	0.811
6	The Anand Mercantile Bank	0.833	0.855	0.878	0.880	0.875	0.789	0.963	0.847	0.862	0.859	5.05	0.864
7	Dahod Urban Bank	0.752	0.755	0.719	0.706	0.657	0.690	0.701	0.699	0.703	0.730	4.12	0.711
8	Sarvodya Nagrik Bank	0.745	0.758	0.758	0.758	0.742	0.760	0.773	0.706	0.722	0.623	5.98	0.734
9	Baroda People's Bank	0.739	0.820	0.804	0.806	0.779	0.797	0.704	0.725	0.719	0.740	5.57	0.763
10	Sardar Bhiladwala Bank	0.750	0.797	0.737	0.743	0.746	0.714	0.723	0.682	0.707	0.679	4.84	0.728

TABLE NO. 6.05

PROPORTION OF TOTAL INTEREST WITH TOTAL ASSETS

Sr. No.	*Name of the Bank*	*87-88*	*88-89*	*89-90*	*90-91*	*91-92*	*92-93*	*93-94*	*94-95*	*95-96*	*96-97*	*CV*	*AVG*
1	The Kalupur Bank	0.110	0.094	0.086	0.063	0.059	0.056	0.042	0.052	0.054	0.068	31.31	0.068
2	The Rajkot Nagrik Bank	0.117	0.074	0.090	0.070	0.006	0.068	0.066	0.064	0.064	0.061	40.81	0.068
3	Anyona Saharakri Bank	0.079	0.079	0.078	0.073	0.056	0.077	0.073	0.069	0.074	0.083	10.27	0.074
4	The Surat Peoples's Bank	0.068	0.063	0.064	0.062	0.046	0.060	0.060	0.057	0.057	0.060	9.69	0.060
5	The Natpur Co-Op Bank	0.094	0.077	0.074	0.072	0.057	0.082	0.076	0.069	0.071	0.088	13.59	0.076
6	The Anand Mercantile Bank	0.070	0.068	0.079	0.078	0.065	0.081	0.089	0.074	0.077	0.097	12.40	0.078
7	Dahod Urban Bank	0.074	0.075	0.073	0.073	0.058	0.083	0.075	0.072	0.080	0.086	10 02	0.075
8	Sarvodya Nagrik Bank	0.077	0.088	0.080	0.077	0.066	0.092	0.104	0.090	0.093	0.105	14.18	0.087
9	Baroda People's Bank	0.069	0.080	0.084	0.086	0.067	0.089	0.083	0.079	0.070	0.078	9.63	0.079
10	Sardar Bhiladwala Bank	0.065	0.093	0.062	0.063	0.050	0.063	0.059	0.056	0.055	0.057	19.04	0.062

higher side with respect to the interest share to total cost, it has reached to the peak of 96.25 per cent in the year 1993-94, except 78.93 per cent in the year 1992-93, this Bank's interest to total cost has remained at 85 per cent or above. The Rajkot Nagrik Bank having large amount of deposits among the selected Urban Co-operative Banks has maintained the share of interest to total cost at lower level. During the period of 10 years, it has declined continuously, for the year 1987-88, it was 78.60 per cent whereas for the year 1996-97, it is ever lowest at 46.56 per cent. Such a lowest share of interest is not registered by any bank in any year among the sample banks. Remaining banks in the sample, have registered the interest share to the total cost on an average 70 per cent to 85 per cent as reflected in Table 6.04. The average share of interest cost was 58 per cent for Rajkot Nagrik Bank with coefficient of variation 16.02 per cent. It can be interpreted that the variation in interest cost was higher with the average of 58 per cent. At the second position, Surat People's Co-operative Bank has an average share of interest cost to total cost was 62 per cent with the co-efficient of variation with 11.32 per cent. This Bank has also high variation in its interest cost to total cost. The Dahod Urban Co-operative Bank stands at third position with average share of interest cost to total cost at 71 per cent with coefficient of variation at just 12.4 per cent then The Sarvoday Nagrik Bank and Sardar Bhiladwala Bank who have an average of 73 per cent and Kalupur Bank has 74 per cent., The Annonya Sahakari bank has maintained its average share of interest cost to total cost at 76 per cent with the lowest coefficient of 2.40 per cent, so almost it is negligible. The range of share of interest cost was between 74 per cent and 78.85 per cent. The Anand Mercantile Bank has 86 per cent average share of interest to the total cost with coefficient variation at 5.05 per cent. Similarly, the Natpur Co-operative Bank has 81 per cent average share of interest to total cost with 2.73 per cent of coefficient.

Interest Cost Compared with Total Assets

Table 6.05 reveals the ratio between the interest paid during the year and the total assets of the respective Urban Co-operative Banks. This aspect was applicable where the total assets of the Bank are compared to its expenditure. Researchers' have thrown the light on this ratio as expense bearing capacity of the total assets. Low ratio will reflect the sound position of the assets of the Bank whereas the higher ratio indicates the weak position of the total assets of the Bank in this aspect, The Surat People's Bank has obtained the ratio at 4.61 per cent in the year 1991-92. The Rajkot Nagrik Co-operative Bank has 11.71 per cent in the year 1987-88, which is the highest proportion between interest paid and total assets.

Interest Cost Compared with Working Capital

Working capital of Urban Co-operative Banks comprises of Banks' Share capital, Reserves, all types of Deposits and the Borrowings. In Table 6.06, the working capital is compared with the total interest paid by the selected Urban Co-operative Banks. The ratio is calculated by dividing total interest with working capital. The lowest proportion in this regard was with, The Surat People's Bank in the year 1987-88, the interest paid by the Bank is 7.34 per cent to working capital but then it was continuously declining. In the year 1990-91, the proportion was 6.65 per cent, which sharply declined to 4.79 per cent in the year 1991-92. From the year 1992-93, again it reached to 6 per cent and then it maintained till the year 1996-97. Second lowest proportion obtained by The Sardar Bhiladwala Bank but the fluctuations noticed in proportion during ten years. The lowest proportion was 5.31 per cent in the year 1991-92 whereas 10.34 per cent in the year 1988-89. The average proportion was 7 per cent during the ten years with 20.10 per cent coefficient variation. The highest fluctuation in the proportion of interest with working capital reflected by The Kalupur Commercial Bank.

TABLE 6.06

PROPORTION OF TOTAL INTEREST WITH WORKING CAPITAL

Sr. No.	*Name of the Bank*	*87-88*	*88-89*	*89-90*	*90-91*	*91-92*	*92-93*	*93-94*	*94-95*	*95-96*	*96-97*	CV	*AVG.*
1	The Kalupur Bank	0.124	0.103	0.099	0.069	0.062	0.062	0.055	0.056	0.059	0.073	31.30	0.076
2	The Rajkot Nagrik Bank	0.104	0.084	0.102	0.080	0.064	0.080	0.079	0.075	0.079	0.073	15.23	0.082
3	Anyona Saharakri Bank	0.091	0.083	0.084	0.079	0.059	0.085	0.078	0.074	0.085	0.095	12.12	0.081
4	The Surat Peoples's Bank	0.073	0.068	0.069	0.066	0.048	0.066	0.065	0.060	0.062	0.068	10.79	0.064
5	The Natpur Co-Op Bank	0.104	0.084	0.081	0.077	0.061	0.088	0.087	0.081	0.086	0.105	14.84	0.085
6	The Anand Mercantile Bank	0.076	0.092	0.094	0.094	0.075	0.089	0.097	0.084	0.097	0.105	10.41	0.090
7	Dahod Urban Bank	0.080	0.079	0.077	0.076	0.061	0.087	0.083	0.077	0.087	0.100	12.46	0.081
8	Sarvodya Nagrik Bank	0.085	0.094	0.085	0.084	0.069	0.100	0.109	0.092	0.102	0.113	13.99	0.093
9	Baroda People's Bank	0.078	0.092	0.091	0.095	0.073	0.099	0.093	0.083	0.081	0.088	9.50	0.087
10	Sardar Bhiladwala Bank	0.074	0.103	0.067	0.066	0.053	0.068	0.064	0.060	0.060	0.065	20.10	0.068

The average proportion is 8 per cent but the highest coefficient of variation among the selected banks, i.e., 31.30 per cent. The Rajkot Nagrik Bank, The Annonya Sahayakari Bank and The Dahod Urban Bank has got 8 per cent proportion, while the average proportion between interest paid and working capital was at 9 per cent which is narrated by The Natpur Co-operative Bank, The Anand Mercantile Bank, The Sarvoday Nagrik Bank and The Baroda People's Bank.

Interest Cost Compared with Total Deposits

Total deposits of Urban Co-operative Banks, includes the Current deposits, Saving deposits, Fixed deposits and Other deposits. The total interest paid includes the interest paid by the Urban Co-operative Banks on deposits and borrowings. In short, the total interest is paid on interest bearing liabilities. Earlier, in the first chapter, it was stated that the share of borrowings in the interest bearing liabilities was marginal. The total interest paid compared with the total deposits including borrowings as shown in Table 6.07. If the borrowing component neglected from the interest bearing liabilities then the table 6.08 reflects the interest cost of deposits, conveniently the table reveals the interest cost as a percentage of total deposits. The Kalupur Commercial Bank, for the initial three years shown higher interest cost of deposits i.e. 17.41 per cent, 14.92 per cent and 13.65 per cent in the year 1987-88, 1988-89 and 1989-90 respectively. Suddenly declined to 9.62 per cent in the year 1990-91 and further in the year 1993-94, it was ever lowest at 7.28 per cent but again in the year 1996-97 it showed the increase to 10.26 per cent. The Kalupur Commercial Bank got lot of fluctuations during the ten years revealed by coefficient variation, which was 32.39 per cent with the average interest cost at 11 per cent for ten years. Minimum interest cost with reasonably low fluctuation indicated by The Surat People's Bank, its lowest interest cost was 6.82 per cent in the year 1991-92 and maximum was 9.58 per cent in the year 1996-97. The average interest cost of ten years was 9 per cent with 9.88 per cent of coefficient variation.

TABLE 6.07

PROPORTION OF TOTAL INTEREST WITH TOTAL DEPOSIT (C+S+F+O) INCLUDING BORROWINGS

Sr. No.	Name of the Bank	87-88	88-89	89-90	90-91	91-92	92-93	93-94	94-95	95-96	96-97	CV	AVG.
1	The Kalupur Bank	0.167	0.145	0.134	0.094	0.087	0.087	0.071	0.072	0.078	0.100	32.07	0.104
2	The Rajkot Nagrik Bank	0.103	0.097	0.123	0.097	0.078	0.100	0.099	0.095	0.101	0.094	11.04	0.099
3	Anyona Saharakri Bank	0.107	0.104	0.105	0.099	0.074	0.107	0.099	0.093	0.105	0.116	11.05	0.101
4	The Surat Peoples's Bank	0.079	0.095	0.093	0.092	0.068	0.095	0.093	0.086	0.089	0.095	9.82	0.089
5	The Natpur Co-Op Bank	0.094	0.102	0.101	0.094	0.076	0.108	0.106	0.101	0.099	0.119	11.10	0.100
6	The Anand Mercantile Bank	0.111	0.107	0.109	0.103	0.083	0.098	0.110	0.097	0.110	0.115	9.18	0.104
7	Dahod Urban Bank	0.109	0.109	0.106	0.106	0.083	0.118	0.113	0.103	0.117	0.123	10.03	0.109
8	Sarvodya Nagrik Bank	0.126	0.132	0.121	0.115	0.093	0.133	0.145	0.126	0.139	0.151	12.84	0.128
9	Baroda People's Bank	0.114	0.111	0.110	0.116	0.090	0.125	0.150	0.133	0.105	0.112	13.92	0.117
10	Sardar Bhiladwala Bank	0.089	0.124	0.084	0.083	0.068	0.089	0.085	0.079	0.078	0.084	17.01	0.086

TABLE 6.08

PROPORTION OF TOTAL INTEREST WITH TOTAL DEPOSITS EXCLUDING BORROWINGS

Sr. No.	*Name of the Bank*	*87-88*	*88-89*	*89-90*	*90-91*	*91-92*	*92-93*	*93-94*	*94-95*	*95-96*	*96-97*	*CV*	*AVG.*
1	The Kalupur Bank	0.174	0.149	0.137	0.096	0.091	0.091	0.073	0.073	0.081	0.103	32.39	0.107
2	The Rajkot Nagrik Bank	0.103	0.097	0.123	0.097	0.078	0.100	0.099	0.095	0.101	0.094	11.04	0.099
3	Anyona Saharakri Bank	0.107	0.104	0.105	0.099	0.074	0.107	0.099	0.093	0.105	0.116	11.02	0.101
4	The Surat Peoples's Bank	0.079	0.095	0.093	0.092	0.068	0.095	0.093	0.086	0.089	0.096	9.88	0.089
5	The Natpur Co-Op Bank	0.094	0.102	0.102	0.095	0.077	0.109	0.106	0.101	0.099	0.119	10.85	0.100
6	The Anand Mercantile Bank	0.113	0.108	0.118	0.120	0.102	0.125	0.124	0.098	0.116	0.119	7.92	0.114
7	'Dahod Urban Bank	0.110	0.109	0.106	0.106	0.085	0.121	0.121	0.116	0.126	0.128	11.25	0.113
8	Sarvodya Nagrik Bank	0.129	0.134	0.121	0.123	0.103	0.150	0.167	0.137	0.143	0.157	13.75	0.136
9	Baroda People's Bank	0.115	0.111	0.110	0.116	0.092	0.128	0.156	0.143	0.111	0.117	15.13	0.120
10	Sardar Bhiladwala Bank	0.089	0.124	0.084	0.084	0.070	0.092	0.087	0.081	0.081	0.087	16.26	0.088

Similarly, The Sardar Bhiladwala Bank had lower average interest cost of deposits at 9 per cent but with the higher CV at 16.26 per cent i.e. the interest cost more fluctuating compared to The Surat People's bank. The lowest interest cost was 6.95 per cent in the year 1991-92 whereas the highest was 12.45 per cent in the year 1988-89. Among selected Urban Co-operative Banks, Sarvoday Nagrik Bank was showing maximum interest cost at the average of 14 per cent during ten years with 13.75 per cent CV. The minimum proportion was 10.35 per cent in the year 1991-92 whereas 16.67 per cent in the year 1993-94. The Baroda People's Bank also had higher interest cost at the average of 12 per cent, The Rajkot Nagrik Bank, The Annyonya Sahayakari Bank and The Natpur Commercial Bank had 10 per cent average interest cost. The Anand Mercantile Bank and The Dahod Urban Bank had average cost at 11 per cent with 7.92 per cent and 11.25 per cent coefficient of variation respectively.

Interest Cost Compared with Total Deposits including Borrowings

As stated in the earlier paragraphs, contribution of borrowing is negligible which is proved in the Table 6.07. Apart from the deposits including current, saving, fixed and other deposits, the borrowings are added with the total deposits and then the average of two years is calculated to get the ratio with interest. In Table 6.07, the proportion of interest with the total deposits and the ratio including borrowings were largely remaining stable. The average interest cost of interest bearing liabilities of The Kalupur Commercial Bank remains at 11 per cent but coefficient variation has declined to 32.07 per cent. The Rajkot Nagrik Bank has an average interest cost of interest bearing liabilities at 10 per cent with the coefficient variation of 11.04 per cent. When the borrowings are added to the total deposits, obviously, in calculation of the ratio between total interest and deposits with borrowings, the figure of denominator was increasing. Borrowings reported of The Kalupur Commercial Bank, The Natpur Co-operative

Bank, The Anand Mercantile Bank, The Dahod Urban Bank, The Baroda People's Bank and The Sardar Bhiladwala Banks; other Banks not reported any borrowings separately in their Annual Reports, therefore, only with these banks the ratio would decline. Average ratio of interest of The Kalupur Commercial Bank has declined from 11 per cent to 10 per cent as The Kalupur Commercial Bank had borrowings. Similarly, The Anand Mercantile Bank's average proportion decreased from 11 per cent to 10 per cent. The Sarvodaya Nagrik Bank's proportion declined from 14 per cent to 13 per cent.

Interest Cost Compared with Total Deposits Excluding Current Deposits

Certainly, current deposits do not bear any interest cost, in other words, they are interest free. In earlier paragraphs, the total interest is compared with the total deposits, which includes current deposits but it will be worth-noting the ratio of total interest to the total deposits excluding current deposits.

In the fourth chapter, titled, "Deposits Performance of selected Urban Co-operative Banks", studied the sample banks having more current deposits proportionately which are very few. Major Banks have insignificant shares of current deposits in the total deposits. Therefore, Table 6.09 shows the proportion of total interest with total deposits excluding current deposits, similar to Table 6.07 i.e. total interest with total deposits including current deposits. The Kalupur Commercial Bank, The Sarvoday Nagrik Bank, The Sardar Bhiladwada Bank, The Surat People's Bank have comparatively more current deposits than that of the other banks selected as a sample. Therefore, the interest cost of the deposits of The Kalupur Commercial Bank varies from 11 per cent to 13 per cent, The Surat People's Bank's interest costs increases from 9 per cent to 10 per cent. The Sarvoday Nagrik Bank's interest cost increases from 14 per cent to 15 per cent and lastly the interest

TABLE 6.09

PROPORTION OF TOTAL INTEREST WITH TOTAL DEPOSITS EXCLUDING CURRENT DEPOSIT

Sr. No.	Name of the Bank	87-88	88-89	89-90	90-91	91-92	92-93	93-94	94-95	95-96	96-97	CV	AVG.
1	The Kalupur Bank	0.202	0.173	0.166	0.116	0.109	0.111	0.099	0.097	0.095	0.123	29.06	0.129
2	The Rajkot Nagrik Bank	0.107	0.102	0.129	0.102	0.083	0.106	0.106	0.102	0.108	0.100	10.62	0.105
3	Anyona Saharakri Bank	0.110	0.107	0.108	0.102	0.077	0.112	0.104	0.097	0.109	0.121	10.98	0.105
4	The Surat Peoples's Bank	0.086	0.108	0.111	0.108	0.080	0.113	0.112	0.102	0.105	0.111	11.13	0.103
5	The Natpur Co-Op Bank	0.097	0.108	0.107	0.100	0.081	0.115	0.112	0.106	0.104	0.123	10.83	0.105
6	The Anand Mercantile Bank	0.121	0.116	0.126	0.128	0.109	0.133	0.134	0.107	0.123	0.125	7.69	0.122
7	Dahod Urban Bank	0.114	0.113	0.110	0.111	0.088	0.124	0.124	0.120	0.130	0.131	10.89	0.117
8	Sarvodya Nagrik Bank	0.134	0.140	0.128	0.130	0.110	0.160	0.179	0.149	0.155	0.169	14.47	0.145
9	Baroda People's Bank	0.118	0.114	0.113	0.119	0.094	0.135	0.171	0.151	0.113	0.119	17.70	0.125
10	Sardar Bhiladwala Bank	0.096	0.135	0.092	0.093	0.078	0.104	0.100	0.094	0.095	0.101	14.65	0.099

cost of The Sardar Bhiladwada Bank has increased from 9 per cent to 10 per cent. For remaining banks, the interest cost was either more or less remained unchanged.

Interest on Saving Deposits and on Fixed Deposits

The total interest paid by the selected Urban Co-operative Banks is divided in two parts, i.e.,

i) Interest on saving deposits, and
ii) Interest on fixed deposits including other deposits.

During the span of ten years of study, the interest rates on saving deposits were ranging between 4.5 per cent and 6 per cent. The Reserve Bank of India controls the interest rate on saving deposits. As observed above, in earlier paragraphs, "Interest rates on saving deposits", during the period from the year 1987-88 to 1990-91, average rate of interest on saving deposits was 5 per cent, for the year 1991-92 it was 6 per cent and from the year 1992-93 and afterwards it was 4.5 per cent. The average saving deposits of selected Urban Co-operative Banks shown in data bank.

REFERENCES

1. Kohler's Dictionary for Accounts, p. 533.
2. David Palfreman, Philip Ford, *Element of Banking Levels I and II*, Manchester.
3. *Report of Banking Commission*, Government of India, 1972.

7

Deposits: Social and Other Cost

Social Banking — Social Cost

Introduction

Banking is one of the industry, which touches the lives of millions directly or indirectly to every-one and/or anywhere. Banking industry is the heart of the financial system of our country. Right from 1950, India has been planning for a socialistic pattern of society. The Constitution of India has set forth the principles of promoting the welfare of the people by securing and protecting social order. The Institutions of the national life should be at achieving the goal for better living, self-confidence and dignity for the economically weaker sections of society. The British rulers ruined the precious wealth of the Indians. The political reaction after Independence had been taken place in the form of Nationalization of Reserve Bank of India in 1949 with fulfillment and commitment to serve the social and economic objectives of the country.

To promote the national objectives, 14 major Commercial Banks were nationalized in 1969. On the occasion of nationalization of banks, a statement tabled before the parliament says, "it will be one of the positive objective of nationalized banks to actively foster the growth of new and progressive enterprises, and to create fresh opportunities for hitherto neglected and backward areas in different parts of the country. Our sole concern has been to accelerate developments and thus make significant impacts on the problems of poverty and unemployment and to bring about progressive reduction of the disparities between the rich and the poor sections of our people and between the relatively advanced and backward areas of our country.

Indian banks were assigned the task of implementing Social Banking Schemes. The term social banking refers to a policy induced credit, delivered by banks to the priority sectors such as: agriculture, small scale industries, small business, professionals and self-employed retail traders, road and water transport operators, educationally and economically weaker sections of any communities. These sections of the societies had hardly any access to the banking system prior to nationalisation of banks. Thus so-called class banking has been replaced by a mass banking. "Credit or Finance is one of the strategic factors that determine the pace and pattern of socio-economic development. It facilitates as well as stimulates the development process."[1]

In order to enlarge the scope of social banking, the definition of weaker sections has been widened and following targets has been stipulated for Commercial Banks as per the recommendations of the Ghosh Committee:

i) 40 per cent in total advances should be for priority sectors,
ii) 18 per cent of the total advances should be for direct agriculture,
iii) 1 per cent of the previous year's advance should be under the Differential Rate of Interest (DRI) scheme,
iv) 40 per cent of the DRI advances should be lent to scheduled castes and scheduled Tribes,
v) 2/3 of the DRI advances or 25 per cent of the priority sector advances should be lent to the weaker sections.

With active involvement of banks in social banking, some operational problems had cropped up which are:

i) Problems of reporting and controlling due to vast expansion of branches,
ii) Adverse effect in income on advances due to high servicing cost of small accounts,
iii) Increasing establishment and operational costs,
iv) Problems in recycling of resources.

The Government and The Reserve Bank of India had taken various steps from time to time for strengthening the income of banks.

i) Increase in rate of interest on food credit,
ii) Increase in coupon rates on Central Government Securities,
iii) Increase in rate of interest on interest bearing portion of cash reserves,
iv) Rationalisation of service charges,
v) Consolidation of banking operations,
vi) Effective and timely monitoring of banking operations.

All India Social Banking—An Achievement

Social responsibility of banking sector in India are multidimensional in nature, involving —customers for wider, better and efficient service, Government for a fair return on capital and co-operative with Planning Commission, Monetary Authority and other Financial Institutions, Employee for Status, Participation and Fair remuneration, Society for Financial and Economic growth and themselves for asset and capital formation and organisational development.

An idea of extension of social responsibility of Indian banking can be had from the fact that while banks are open for 44 hours a week in Zurich and 40 hours a week in New

York but banks operate only for 22 hours a week in India.

If banking sector wishes to play a dynamic and effective role in the field of social obligations, they have to condition themselves towards development—oriented and customer—centered approach, liberalize credit policies, decentralised administration and participative management techniques. The guiding principle and creed of management philosophy of these financial institutions has to be a centralised policy, a decentralised adminstration but a joint appraisal.

Following facts will convince about the achievements in social banking:

Between June 1969 and March 1991, the total numbers of banks' offices were increased from 8262 to 60101 and the proportion of branches in rural areas rose from 22.2 per cent to 58.4 per cent.

Banks' credit to agriculture and allied activities rose from negligible level of Rs. 67 crores in March 1968 and 2.2 per cent of banks' total advances to Rs. 16756 crores in March 1991 or 15.3 per cent of their net credit. But the Banks' credit to agriculture sector declined from Rs. 4398 crore in the year 1996-97 to Rs. 3427 crores in the year 1997-98. It was 16.3 per cent of total advances in the year 1996-97 whereas the proportion of agricultural credit to total credit declined to 10.9 per cent in the year 1997-98 as compared to the year 1996-97.

The share of the weaker sections, comprising of Small and Marginal Farmers, Rural Artisan, Scheduled Castes and Scheduled Tribes etc. in total bank credit worked out to 11 per cent at the end of June 1990.

Priority sectors' lending in weaker sections including agriculture amounted to Rs. 1151 crores in the year 1996-97, which rose to Rs. 14627 crores in the year 1997-98. The share of priority sector lending in total bank credit was 15.8

per cent in the year 1996-97, which rose to 17.2 per cent in the year 1997-98. [2]

It seems from the year 1991, banks were consistently defaulting on priority sector lending target of 40 per cent of their net credit and also on sub target of credit to agriculture of 18 per cent. The share of priority sector advances declined nearly about 41 per cent in the pre-reform period to 37 per cent or so in 1995-96.

Urban Co-operative Banks in Gujarat – Social Banking

The responsibility of Co-operative Banks in meeting the social objectives is more, compared to other banks. Therefore the target stipulated by Reserve Bank of India and various Monetary Authorities of the country for the Urban Co-operative Banks were on higher side. The share of priority sector lending is 60 per cent of total advances as compared to 40 per cent of the other banks. The Urban Co-operative Banks of Gujarat had Rs. 39585.73 lacs lending to priority sector as against its total advances amounted to Rs. 66741.83 lacs in the year 1985. The proportion of priority sector advances stands at 59.31 per cent. In the year 1994, priority sector advances were Rs. 134448.68 lacs as against the total advances amounted to Rs. 236036.11 lacs, the proportion was 56.96 per cent. In priority sector, the weaker sections' advances of Urban Co-operative banks in Gujarat had Rs. 33551.81 lacs. i. e. 14.21 per cent of total Urban Co-operative Banks' credit. The weaker sections means Scheduled Caste and Scheduled Tribes' credit amounted to Rs. 4026.23 lacs in the year 1994 and women credit was 6015.76 lacs

Emerging Scenario

During the last 25 years' operation of social banking in the country has given a way to serious thinking of reforming it. Earlier social banking operated on a highly cross subsidized rate and lending rates which were determined on the basis of the type of borrowers and the purpose for which the credit is to be given. To bring about rationalised approach, the Central Monetary Authority has changed the lending rates under social banking based on the size of the limit. The lending rates up to Rs. 50,000 ranged from 11.5 per cent to 15.5 per cent, from Rs. 50,000 to Rs. 2 lacs it was 16.5 per cent and over Rs. 2.00 lacs it was 21.5 per cent. Thus the importance till the year 1990-91 was given to purpose of advance then the shift in importance in that purpose has given a way to size of the limit and the borrowers' ability to pay and some sort of rationalisation had been brought about in lending rates.

There is growing feeling that profitability is being totally sacrificed with greater emphasis on social lending and that the social lending and profitability are not compatible. Chakravarty Committee has commented that the administered interest rate system has grown to be unduly complex and contains features which have reduced the ability of the system to promote the effective use of credit at concessional rate of interest, appears to take projects of doubtful viability.

A World Bank study on the financial cost of lending in India confirms that the growth of non-performing loans have had a damaging effect on transaction costs. In the long run it will necessarily lower the credit rating of the banking institution and thereby restrict its access to deposits.

There are two major components of financial sector reforms: First, directed credit is bad hence required to be withdrawn and Second, interest rates should be market driven and there should not be cross subsidisation. Narasimham Committee had recommended that the share of priority sector advances should be brought down from present target of 40 per cent to 10 per cent of Commercial Banks. Priority sector should be redefined but RBI did not agree to it and left the target unchanged. Later on, RBI pointed out that present share of redefined priority sectors worked out to 30 per cent. The concessional element in lending rates was totally eliminated as a part of the reforms. For instance even a small borrower has to bear an interest rate of 12.5 per cent against 10 per cent in the pre-reform phase.

Two components of social cost emerged from the above discussions are:

i) Directed credit to priority sector and
ii) Concessional Rate of interest on priority sectors lending.

It will be worth noting that since 1994, concessional rate of interest scheme has been gradually withdrawn. Now the interest rates are fluctuating according to the quantum of lending. Higher the amount of advances higher is the rate of interest and for low amount of lending, interest rates charged are low. Urban banks are free to choose the interest rate for the advances for more than Rs. 2 lacs. According to RBI guidelines on advances for an amount up to or less than Rs. 2 lacs, interest rate should not be less than Prime Lending Rate (PLR).

Out of the study period of ten years i.e. 1987-88 to 1996-97; during the period from 1987-88 to 1993-94 Differential Rate of Interest (DRI) scheme was existing, in which the element of social cost was incurred by Urban Co-operative Banks. Income deficit i.e. difference between earning on regular advances and priority sector advances is termed as social costs. Urban Co-operative Banks had lent about 60 per cent of its total advances and Commercial Banks had lent about 40 per cent of its net advances to priority sector as directed credit and at subsidised rate of interest, thereby the banks have incurred the social costs. Since 1994, Central Monetary Authority continued the policy of directed credit for priority sector. But the subsidies in rate of interest have been withdrawn. Therefore the earnings from advances to priority sectors and other than priority sectors remained same. Urban Co-operative Banks have suffered the social costs on it's 60 per cent of advances to priority sector up to year 1994. From the year 1994-95 onward no such cost are required to be faced by Urban Co-operative Banks, hence calculation of opportunity cost of priority sector advances are avoided in this study.

The Urban Co-operative Banks continue to incur the social cost other than the priority sectors' advances such as donations to voluntary organisation and appropriating its profit by various welfare funds like general welfare, staff benefit, shareholder welfare fund, community welfare fund, education fund etc. These all funds do not contribute financial income to the bank ultimately it tends to fulfilling the objectives of Co-operative movement in India. These are the efforts Urban Co-operative Banks are making in upliftment of the members consequently the society. Ultimately it is the expenditure to Bank hence in present study it is considered as the cost of deposits rather it is an opportunity cost of the fund. Table 7.14 — shows the amount of funds allocated for the social purposes by the Urban Co-operative Banks i.e. the social cost of selected Urban Co-operative Banks. The Kalupur Commercial Bank has allocated more than Rs. 20 lacs during ten years whereas The Rajkot Nagrik Bank has allocated more than Rs. 10 lacs,The Annyonya Bank has more than Rs. 4 lacs. The Surat People's Bank comparatively less amount of such expenses. The Natpur Co-operative Bank as compared to its size of depoists allocating more than Rs.4 lacs. The Anand Mercantial, The Dahod Urban Bank and The Sarvoday Nagrik Bank, The Baroda People's Bank, The Sardar Bhiladwala Bank have negligible social cost except The Baroda People's Bank has started allocating more than Rs.5 lacs from the year 1992-93.

The Table 7.15 gives the proportion of social cost to the average deposits of selected Urban Co-operative Banks. The table reveals that the proportion of social cost in the form of donations are very insignificant throughout the period of ten years. We can conclude that when priority sector financing at a cross subsidiesed interest rate has been given up by the RBI then Urban Co-operative Banks must appropriate some more amount of its profit for social purposes.

Non-Performing Assets (NPA)

NPA Introduced

A Non-Performing Asset may be defined as a credit facility on which installments / interest have has remained 'past due' for specified period. An amount outstanding under any of the credit facilities is to be treated as 'past due' when it remained unpaid for 30 days i.e. beyond the due date. Thus receipt of installments / interest and non-availability of security or net worth of the borrower / guarantor will be the determining factor for treating a credit facility as NPA.

The criteria for treating credit as NPA is as follows:

Term Loan

For the years 1995-96 and 1996-97 a term loan account would be treated as NPA, if the interest there on remained 'past due' for the period of 4th and 3rd quarters respectively. From the year 1997-98 onwards, the account would be treated as NPA, if the interest and / or installments remained 'past due' for two out of four quarters. It may be noted that it is not necessary that these two should be for consecutive quarters. The quarters have to be calculated taking into account of 3 months from the date when an account becomes past due.

Cash Credit and Over Draft Account

A Cash Credit / Over Draft account is treated as NPA, if the account is 'out of order' for a period of 4th, 3rd and 2nd quarters, during the years ended on 31st March of 1995, 1996, 1997 and onwards, as the case may be. An account is treated as "out of order", if the balance outstanding in the account is continuously exceeds minimum sanctioned limits or drawing power or the outstanding balance in the principal operating account is less than the sanctioned limits or drawing power, but there are no credits continuously given for six months as on the date of balance sheet or credit are not enough to cover the interest debited during the same period.

The concept of "past due" for calculating the "out of order" status is not applicable for cash credit account now. In such cases the date from which the account has become out of order has to be taken into account.

Bills Purchased or Discounted

A bill is to be treated as NPA if it remains overdue and unpaid for a period of 4th , 3rd and 2nd quarters during the years ended on 31st March of 1995, 1996, 1997 and onwards as the case may be. Overdue interest should not be charged and taken into income account in respect of overdue bills, unless it is realized.

Other Credit Facilities

Any other credit facility is to be treated as NPA if it remains past due and unpaid for a period of 4th , 3rd and 2nd quarters during the year ended on 31st March of 1995, 1996, 1997 and onward as the case may be.

Credit Facilities backed by Government Guarantee

If the interest on a government guaranteed advances becomes 'past due' for the above-specified number of quarters, such advances should be treated as NPA for the purpose of income recognition and unrealized interest on such account should not be taken to income account. However there is no need to make any provision on such account.

Non-Performing Advances are non-yielding advances and they bring down the overall yield. Besides, it affects the bottom line, as provisions will have to be made as per prudential norms. It would therefore be necessary for the banks to take effective measures to reduce their NPA to the maximum possible extent. Steps should also be taken to upgrade the quality of such advances for performing status so that income on such assets can be transferred to profit and loss account and also to reduce provisioning requirements. Following table gives the Gross and Net Non-Performing Assets of Public Sector Banks in India and the proportion of NPA with total advances and assets.

TABLE 7.01

GROSS AND NET NON-PERFORMING ASSETS OF PUBLIC SECTOR BANK FROM 1993 TO 1998 (AMOUNT IN CRORES)

Year	*Gross NPA*	*Per cent to Gross Advance*	*Per cent to Total Asset*	*Net NPA*	*Per cent to Net Advance*	*Per cent to Total Assets*
1993	39253	23.2	11.8	NA	NA	NA
1994	41041	24.8	10.8	NA	NA	NA
1995	38385	19.5	8.70	17567	10.7	4.0
1996	41061	18.0	8.20	18297	8.9	3.6
1997	43557	17.8	7.80	20285	9.2	3.6
1998	45653	16.0	7.00	21232	8.2	3.3

Source: Report on Trend and Progress of Banking in India 1997-98.

Table 7.01 shows the quantum of gross NPAs as a percentage of gross advances of Public Sector banks declined from 17.8 per cent in 1997 to 16 per cent in the year 1998. Gross NPA as a proportion to total assets of public sector banks declined from 11.8 per cent in 1993 to 7.0 per cent in the year 1998. Provisions have been made for one half of gross NPA of public sector bank. The net NPA as a percentage of net advances also declined from 9.2 per cent in 1997 to 8.2 per cent in 1998. Net NPA to total assets declined from 4.0 per cent in 1995 to 3.3 per cent.

NPA of Bank in India

Table 7.02 shows Gross non-performing assets proportion with total advances of Urban Co-operative Banks who have reported.

TABLE 7.02

GROSS NON-PERFORMING ASSETS OF URBAN CO-OPERATIVE BANKS 1995 TO 1998

Year	*No. of Banks Reported*	*NPA As Proportion to Total Advance*
1995	832	13.9 per cent
1996	1161	12.9 per cent
1997	1363	13.3 per cent
1998	179	11.0 per cent

Sources: Report on Trends and Progress of Banking in India, 1997-98, RBI publication.

The gross non-performing asset of Urban Co-operative Banks marginally increases to 13.3 per cent in 1997 from 12.9 per cent in 1997. Which has come down to 11 per cent in 1998.

As discussed earlier, The Reserve Bank of India has given guidelines for consideration of Non-Performing Assets. Amongst ten selected Urban Co-operative Banks except one bank, no bank has shown the classification of Non-Performing Assets in their annual reports. But provision against such Non-Performing Assets have been made in their Profit and Loss Accounts and also shown in the Balance Sheets. Based on such information Table 7.03 is prepared, which reflect Non-Performing Assets of each selected Urban Co-operative Banks in the sample.

The Surat People's Bank is facing severe problem of Non-Performing Assets, compared to advances. Proportion of Non-Performing Assets is very high. For the year 1992-93, it stands at Rs.1265 lacs as against the advance of Rs.9000 lacs the proportion is 14 per cent which is highest in ten years shown in Table 7.04. For ten years the proportion of NPAs with advances stands nearly 8 and 21 per cent. NPAs of Surat People's Bank were at the peak of Rs.2600 lacs for

TABLE 7.03

NON-PERFORMING ASSETS (NPA)

Sr. No.	Name of the Bank	87-88	88-89	89-90	90-91	91-92	92-93	93-94	94-95	95-96	96-97
1	The Kalupur Bank	95.90	182.95	202.90	423.90	604.42	1113.74	771.41	1067.81	1067.84	1612.74
2	The Rajkot Nagrik Bank	127.79	348.00	300.00	350.00	350.00	500.00	500.00	575.00	700.00	1050.00
3	Anyona Saharakri Bank	34.78	44.78	58.00	80.57	90.00	100.00	235.62	249.57	313.57	358.15
4	The Surat Peoples's Bank	275.00	355.00	465.00	600.00	1000.00	1265.00	1450.00	1700.00	2050.00	2600.00
5	The Natpur Co-Op Bank	31.48	37.88	46.00	56.02	67.76	83.88	105.89	126.70	152.36	180.02
6	Anand Mercantile Bank	36.33	46.44	59.56	80.10	96.42	124.17	159.88	222.08	290.19	348.13
7	Dahod Urban Bank	7.00	11.00	4.00	3.00	5.00	17.00	11.50	2.50	11.00	30.00
8	Sarvodya Nagrik Bank	3.13	3.25	3.75	5.00	6.50	18.00	13.54	16.15	21.65	30.35
9	Baroda People's Bank	21.34	30.90	42.01	57.82	83.03	115.05	200.05	242.33	292.95	342.36
10	Sardar Bhiladwala Bank	94.13	114.52	136.54	158.70	183.78	250.48	306.52	347.10	403.49	496.06

the year 1996-97. The Rajkot Nagrik Bank and The Kalupur Commercial Bank's NPAs are proportionately low ranging between 1 and 4 per cent of their advances as revealed in Table 7.04. Among the ten selected Urban Co-operative Banks, both The Rajkot Nagrik Bank and The Kalupur Commercial Bank are scheduled banks and have the highest deposits and advances and lowest portion of Non-Performing Assets. It indicates that care is taken in lending process so the advances do not turn into Non-Performing Assets. The Surat People's Bank is also having the same type of status but it should take care in advancing.

The Annyonya Sahayakari Bank also have the higher proportions of NPA with advances. The proportion shows increasing trend from 1993-94 onwards. For the year 1996-97 NPAs of the Annyonya Sahayakari Bank were Rs.358.15 lacs. There is sharp rise in NPAs of The Anand Mercantile Bank from the year 1994-95 and continued till the year 1996-97. It was Rs.222.08 lacs in the year 1993-94 and Rs.348.13 lacs in 1996-97. The maximum average proportion of NPAs to total advances is 13.6 per cent of The Surat People's Bank and minimum is 0.45 per cent i.e. even less than 1 per cent with The Dahod Urban Co-operative Bank. 2.9 per cent NPAs to advances is remarkable performance of The Rajkot Nagrik Bank having been lent the huge advances, this bank is keenly watching with its crane's eyes on every rupee of advance.

Cost of NPA

The Non-Performing Assets are the advances on which installment/interest is not received for certain specified period. When out of those, some advance turn out as bad then ultimately it is the loss to the bank, which is debited to the Profit and Loss Accounts as financial loss. So far as the NPAs are concerned, on which installments / interests is not received then they incur the cost for the banks. NPA i.e the advances becoming non-yielding, idle assets if they would have been advanced else, here they would have earned the

TABLE 7.04

RATIO OF NPA TO ADVANCE

Sr. No.	*Name of the Bank*	*87-88*	*88-89*	*89-90*	*90-91*	*91-92*	*92-93*	*93-94*	*94-95*	*95-96*	*96-97*	*AVG*
1	The Kalupur Bank	0.01	0.02	0.02	0.05	0.06	0.1	0.05	0.05	0.03	0.04	0.0430
2	The Rajkot Nagrik Bank	0.01	0.04	0.03	0.03	0.02	0.03	0.03	0.03	0.03	0.04	0.0290
3	Anyona Saharakri Bank	0.02	0.03	0.04	0.05	0.04	0.04	0.1	0.1	0.1	0.08	0.0600
4	Surat Peoples's Bank	0.08	0.09	0.09	0.09	0.13	0.16	0.17	0.17	0.17	0.21	0.1360
5	The Natpur Co-Op Bank	0.03	0.03	0.03	0.03	0.04	0.05	0.05	0.05	0.05	0.04	0.0400
6	Anand Mercantile Bank	0.03	0.03	0.04	0.04	0.04	0.05	0.06	0.07	0.07	0.08	0.0510
7	Dahod Urban Bank	0.007	0.009	0.002	0.001	0.002	0.008	0.005	0.001	0.003	0.007	0.0045
8	Sarvodya Nagrik Bank	0.007	0.005	0.006	0.007	0.007	0.01	0.01	0.01	0.01	0.01	0.0082
9	Baroda People's Bank	0.04	0.04	0.04	0.05	0.05	0.06	0.08	0.09	0.08	0.07	0.0600
10	Sardar Bhiladwala Bank	0.04	0.04	0.04	0.04	0.04	0.06	0.06	0.07	0.07	0.07	0.0530

income. The advanced amount forming a part of NPA is certainly a part of deposits. Deposits have to be paid interest i.e the cost. Therefore NPA has cost of deposits. Cost of NPA is the interest that would have yielded as on normal advances. Interest amount on NPA is the amount of cost of NPA. The proportion of cost so calculated with average deposit is NPA cost of deposits. To ascertain such cost, following process has been adopted.

i) Proportion of the total interest earned by a particular bank on its average advances and investments is determined. The average proportions for ten years for each bank is calculated. Table 7.05 shows such Average Interest Rate on average advances and investments.

ii) The average rate of interest calculated as mentioned above is used to calculate the amount of interest on Non-Performing Assets per year. This amount of interest per year is non-receiving on NPA by a bank is assumed as the cost of deposits. Table 7.06 gives an amount of cost of NPA.

iii) The amount of interest so calculated on NPAs is compared with average deposits. The ratio between interest on NPA and average deposits is the NPA cost of deposits. Table 7.07 exibits cost of Non-Performing Assets to Average deposits.

iv) Ten years average of cost of NPA to average deposits is calculated for all ten banks. Table 7.08 reflects the average cost of NPA to deposits per Rs.100.

It was very difficult to process above mentioned four steps because the Urban Co-operative Banks have not followed the norms in preparing annual accounts prescribed by the Banking Regulation Act 1949. On 18.01.1991, the Government of India has issued a notification to make amendments to the third schedule to Banking Regulation Act 1949 incorporating and considering the recommendations of Ghosh Committee[3]

TABLE 7.05

PROPORTION OF TOTAL INTEREST RECEIVED WITH AVERAGE ADVANCES AND INVESTMENTS

Sr. No.	*Name of the Bank*	*87-88*	*88-89*	*89-90*	*90-91*	*91-92*	*92-93*	*93-94*	*94-95*	*95-96*	*96-97*	*AVG*
1	The Kalupur Bank	0.218	0.184	0.134	0.136	0.109	0.110	0.088	0.112	0.126	0.141	0.136
2	The Rajkot Nagrik Bank	0.237	0.222	0.256	0.220	0.167	0.211	0.179	0.184	0.184	0.184	0.204
3	Anyona Saharakri Bank	0.225	0.222	0.233	0.233	0.179	0.248	0.230	0.221	0.207	0.226	0.222
4	The Surat Peoples's Bank	0.297	0.294	0.294	0.257	0.272	0.271	0.196	0.165	0.176	0.168	0.239
5	The Natpur Co-Op Bank	0.218	0.199	0.195	0.193	0.183	0.277	0.224	0.200	0.168	0.199	0.206
6	The Anand Mercantile Bank	0.169	0.199	0.207	0.189	0.161	0.223	0.191	0.172	0.178	0.203	0.189
7	Dahod Urban Bank	0.229	0.215	0.190	0.187	0.154	0.222	0.184	0.164	0.177	0.181	0.190
8	Sarvodya Nagrik Bank	0.197	0.194	0.194	0.198	0.153	0.200	0.197	0.188	0.205	0.299	0.202
9	Baroda People's Bank	0.226	0.243	0.250	0.256	0.184	0.235	0.253	0.226	0.189	0.195	0.226
10	Sardar Bhiladwala Bank	0.195	0.212	0.156	0.161	0.162	0.206	0.185	0.193	0.167	0.185	0.182

TABLE 7.06

COST OF NON-PERFORMING ASSETS (NPA)

Sr. No.	Name of the Bank	87-88	88-89	89-90	90-91	91-92	92-93	93-94	94-95	95-96	96-97
1	The Kalupur Bank	12.467	23.7835	26.377	55.107	78.575	144.79	100.283	138.815	138.819	209.66
2	The Rajkot Nagrik Bank	25.558	69.6	60	70	70	100	100	115	140	210.00
3	Anyona Saharakri Bank	7.6516	9.8516	12.76	17.725	19.8	22	51.8364	54.9054	68.9854	78.79
4	The Surat Peoples's Bank	66	85.2	111.6	144	240	303.6	348	408	492	624.00
5	The Natpur Co-Op Bank	6.296	7.576	9.2	11.204	13.552	16.776	21.178	25.34	30.472	36.00
6	Anand Mercantile Bank	6.9027	8.8236	11.3164	15.219	18.32	23.592	30.3772	42.1952	55.1361	66.14
7	Dahod Urban Bank	1.33	2.09	0.76	0.57	0.95	3.23	2.185	0.475	2.09	5.70
8	Sarvodya Nagrik Bank	0.626	0.65	0.75	1	1.3	3.6	2.708	3.23	4.33	6.07
9	Baroda People's Bank	4.69	6.80	9.24	12.72	18.27	25.31	44.01	53.31	64.45	75.32
10	Sardar Bhiladwala Bank	16.9434	20.6136	24.5772	28.566	33.08	45.086	55.1736	62.478	72.6282	89.29

TABLE 7.07

COST OF NON PERFORMING ASSETS TO DEPOSITS

Sr. No.	*Name of the Bank*	*87-88*	*88-89*	*89-90*	*90-91*	*91-92*	*92-93*	*93-94*	*94-95*	*95-96*	*96-97*	*AVG*
1	The Kalupur Bank	0.002	0.004	0.003	0.005	0.007	0.011	0.004	0.004	0.004	0.005	0.005
2	The Rajkot Nagrik Bank	0.002	0.006	0.004	0.005	0.004	0.006	0.005	0.005	0.005	0.007	0.005
3	Anyona Saharakri Bank	0.004	0.004	0.005	0.006	0.006	0.006	0.012	0.011	0.011	0.009	0.007
4	Surat Peoples's Bank	0.008	0.011	0.012	0.014	0.022	0.024	0.023	0.024	0.025	0.025	0.019
5	The Natpur Co-Op Bank	0.004	0.006	0.006	0.006	0.007	0.007	0.008	0.008	0.007	0.006	0.006
6	Anand Mercantile Bank	0.006	0.005	0.006	0.006	0.007	0.008	0.009	0.011	0.011	0.011	0.008
7	Dahod Urban Bank	0.001	0.001	0.000	0.000	0.000	0.001	0.001	0.000	0.001	0.001	0.001
8	Sarvodya Nagrik Bank	0.001	0.001	0.001	0.001	0.002	0.004	0.002	0.003	0.003	0.004	0.002
9	Baroda People's Bank	0.006	0.006	0.006	0.007	0.009	0.010	0.018	0.019	0.015	0.013	0.011
10	Sardar Bhiladwala Bank	0.006	0.006	0.006	0.007	0.007	0.008	0.009	0.008	0.008	0.009	0.007

related to the formats of Balance Sheets and Profit and Loss Accounts. The old formats were not found suitable. As such, the suggestions were examined and fresh notification was issued on 19.12.1991 expressing government's intention to introduce revised formats. At last, the RBI issued circular as on 06.02.1992 to the Chief Executives of all the Banks in India to prepare and present their accounts under revised formats for the year ended on 31st March, 1992 and thereafter. The revised formats for Profit and Loss Accounts, Form - "B" gives the schedule no. 13 titled 'Interest Earned'. This schedule is to be prepared as prescribed:

Schedule 13 — Interest Earned

		Current year	*Previous year*
i)	Interest / discount on advances / bills	—	—
ii)	Income on investments	—	—
iii)	Interest on balances with RBI and other inter Bank Fund	—	—
iv)	Others	—	—

From the above schedule, it becomes very clear that every bank should show separately the interest on advances and interest on investments. Further more, the interest on balances with RBI and other Banks should be shown separately. But no Urban Co-operative Bank is preparing its Profit and Loss Accounts as per the revised formats prescribed by RBI on 06.02.1992. That means even after 6 years when the Banks' Annual Accounts are audited by a Chartered Accountant and placed before Annual General Meetings, the height of it is no objection has been raised by any. Therefore the interest on advances, discount on bills and interest on investments are inseparable because they are shown under one title as interest and discount. So I am left with no alternative but to calculate the interest rate earned by Urban Co-operative Banks during the year on average advances with average investments jointly.

Table 7.05 shows the proportion of total interest earned by a bank on its average advances and investments as mentioned above in the step no.1. Whereas Table 7.06 shows the average interest rate multiplied by the Non-Performing Assets of the Banks i.e. the result will be the amount of interest on Non-Performing Assets, it becomes the NPA cost for deposits that covers our step no.2. Table 7.07 shows the amount of interest on NPA divided by the average deposits. This gives the ratio between interest and average deposits, this is according to step no. 3. And the Table 7.08 i.e. the following table gives the average of the ratio between interests on NPA to average deposits i.e. nothing but the average cost of non-performing assets to deposits per Rs. 100. Following Table 7.08 shows the average NPA cost to the deposits of Rs.100:

TABLE 7.08

AVERAGE NPA COST OF DEPOSITS PER RS.100

Sr. No	*Name of the Banks*	*Average NPA Cost to Deposits of per Rs.100*
1	The Kalupur Commercial Bank	0.50
2	The Rajkot Nagarik Bank	0.49
3	The Anyonya Sahayakari Bank	0.75
4	The Surat People's Bank	1.89
5	The Natpur Co-operative Bank	0.65
6	The Anand Mercantile Bank	0.80
7	The Dahod Urban Co-operative Bank	0.07
8	The Sarvoday Nagarik Bank	0.22
9	The Baroda People's Bank	1.09
10	The Sardar Bhiladwala Bank	0.75

Cost of NPAs' per Rs. 100 of deposits of The Surat People's Bank is maximum amongst the selected ten sample banks. The Surat People's bank has a serious problem of NPA. The proportion of NPA to total advances is also high. Conversely The Dahod Urban Co-operative Bank is very careful in lending, its proportion of NPA to total advance is less than 1 per cent during 1987-88 to 1996-97. The NPA cost of deposit is just 7 paise per Rs. 100 deposit which is minimum in all selected ten banks. The Baroda People's Bank's NPA cost is considerably high i.e. Rs. 1.09 for per deposits Rs. 100. The proportion of NPA to advances is ranging between 4 per cent and 9 per cent during ten years. The Kalupur Commercial Bank and The Rajkot Nagrik Bank's performance is remarkable in quality of advances, for the year 1987-88, both the banks had proportion of just 1 per cent between NPA and total advances and this proportion in case of The Rajkot Nagarik Bank had remained less than 5 per cent during the ten years. Having huge business compared to other banks in the sample, both the banks are successful in limiting the NPA by careful advances. The NPA cost per Rs. 100 of deposits stand 50 paisa and 49 paisa for The Kalupur Commercial Bank and The Rajkot Nagarik Bank respectively.

SLR and CRR of Urban Banks

SLR and CRR Introduction

For the purpose of maintaining the liquidity of a bank and protection to depositors, The Reserve Bank of India adopted tools as Statutory Liquidity Ratio and The Cash Reserve Requirement. To understand the working of SLR and CRR, certain terms are required to be understood.

Bank Rate

The Reserve Bank of India has wide powers to control the credit of the commercial and all other banks. Similarly it can change the cost of credit by various tools which are within the power of RBI. As far as the Central Banks of the country is concerned, The Reserve Bank of India is the lender of the last resort to these banks. It provides accommodation to the Commercial and Co-operative Banks by rediscounting the eligible bills or at loans against approved securities. The rate of interest charged by The Reserve Bank of India on such advances is called as RBI Rate or in short the Bank Rate. Section 49 of The Reserve Bank of India Act 1934, defines this rate as the "Standard rate at which the Banks is prepared to buy or re-discount bills of exchange or other commercial paper (CP) eligible for purchase under the act." Bank rate happens to be the prime rate of interest in the money market. By bringing change in Bank Rate, the RBI intends to influence other rates of interest. Bank Rate machinery is used as a credit control device whereby the cost of credit to the borrower is increased or decreased.

Interest Rates on Advances

It is discussed earlier that The Reserve Bank of India used to administer the interest rate on deposits for various maturities. From 1996 RBI has deregulated the interest rate structure on deposits. Similarly RBI was used to determine the rate of interest on advances till the year 1994. The rate of interest charged by Commercial and Co-operative Banks to their borrower on advances is called the Advance Rate of Interest. The Reserve Bank of India used to prescribe various levels of rate of interest and changing it from time to time. The rate may vary according to the purpose and type of advance and the nature of securities offered by the borrowers. In past, Urban Co-operative Banks were giving only 4 per cent interest rate on advances to the weaker sections of the society under the differential rate of interest (DRI) schemes as per guidelines issued by RBI. Obviously it was less than the interest paid on deposits. Such deficit in interest becomes the variable cost for the banks. Higher the advances higher will be the variable cost and vise versa.

Credit Controls

The Reserve Bank of India has been given wide powers under The Banking Regulation Act 1949 and The Reserve Bank of India Act 1934 for the purpose of controlling credit granted by Commercial and Co-operative Banks. Various methods of credit control have been divided into two categories— 1) General and 2) Selective. The main difference between them is that general credit control measures the overall capacity of the bank to grant the credit is affected whereas under the selective credit control, credit given on the security of specific type of commodities only is regulated. Other advances are not at all affected by such control.

General Credit Control

The general credit control measures affect cost of credit and the availability of credit in general. The bank rate policy influences the cost of accommodation that The Reserve Bank of India grants to the banks. By restricting the quantum of its refinance to the bank, the central bank also reduces the capacity of the bank to grant credit. Moreover, by raising the cash reserve requirement and the statutory liquidity ratio for banks, The Reserve Bank of India reduces the lendable resources of the Commercial and Urban Co-operative Banks. By prescribing the minimum and maximum lending rates for Commercial and Urban Co-operative Banks, The Reserve Bank of India also varies the cost of credits to the ultimate borrowers.

The Selective Credit Control

The selective credit control affect the advances granted against specified commodities only. Such controls specify higher margins, lower ceiling limits for lending rates. These controls distinguish between advances for productive essential and non-productive non-essential and speculative purposes on the other hand. These controls are more flexible than general credit control.

SLR Defined

A bank receives deposits in the form of money from public and utilities, the same for the purpose of lending or investment. But bank must keep a part of the deposits in the form of liquid assets. Liquid assets are those assets, which can be easily and quickly converted into cash. The liquid assets safeguard the solvency of a bank and enable it to repay deposits as and when demanded by the depositors.

The Banking Regulation Act 1949 prescribes the minimum level of such liquid assets to be maintained by banks. According to section 24, every bank in India is required to maintain liquid assets in the form of cash, gold or approved securities. The amount of such shall not be less than 25 per cent on any closer of the day of the total of its demand and time liabilities in India. The ratio of these liquid assets to total liabilities in India is called Statutory Liquidity Ratio (SLR). The Reserve Bank of India is empowered to raise or reduce the ratio.

CRR Defined

Every bank is required to deposit a portion of its deposit liabilities in cash with RBI. Section 42 of The Reserve Bank of India Act 1934 state that every bank is required to maintain an average daily balance equal to at least 3 per cent of its demand and time liabilities with RBI. The term 'Average Daily Balance' means the average of balance held at the end of business on each day of the week. This requirement is called the Statutory Cash Requirement or Cash Reserve Requirement. The Reserve Bank of India is authorized to raise this ratio from 3 per cent to 15 per cent of the deposit liabilities.

Besides the above, the Reserve Bank of India Act also empowers the Central Banks to ask the bank for maintaining with it, in addition to above, an additional average daily balance at the rate specified by it. This additional daily balance is to be calculated on the basis of the additions to deposits after a specified date. The Reserve Bank of India directed the banks to maintain additional reserve of 10 per cent of the incremental deposits received by banks after 14 January 1971. The Reserve Bank of India pays interest on all these cash reserve maintained with it except on minimum cash reserve i.e. 3 per cent of deposit liabilities.

Narasimhan Committee on the financial system has recommended that as an interim measure, RBI should pay interest on the balance at the rate of equivalent to that applicable on one-year deposits. But the argument of RBI is that the rate of interest paid covers the average of cost funds to the industry. In USA concept of CRR was originated but their banks are not entitled for any compensation on CRR balances. In Philippines, interest on CRR is paid at the rate of 4 per cent, Bangladesh Banks earn 5 per cent on CRR.

CRR continued to be at the minimum level of 3 per cent till 1973. From June 1973 to 1983, cash reserve requirement changed 19 times. Then from 8 February CRR changed from 8.5 per cent to 9 per cent. CRR was made effective from 28 Feb. 1987 at a level of 9.5 per cent.

The Banking Regulation Act initially stipulated SLR at 20 per cent of demand and time liabilities, making no distinction between cash on hand and balances held with RBI to meet the CRR according to Section 42(1) of RBI Act. The objective of SLR was to impose some financial discipline on the banks and provide protection to the depositors and a cushion to Banks to cope-up with sudden withdrawal of deposits. In 1962, Banking Regulation Act was amended; therein the liquid assets were defined and also SLR was increased from 20 per cent to 25 per cent. This increase was made apparently due to bank failures in the late 1950's.

Revision in Cash Reserve Requirement

TABLE 7.09

RATE OF INTEREST PAID ON ADDITIONAL CRR OVER 3 PER CENT

With Effect From	*CRR at Present*	*Rate of Interest Paid on Additional CRR Over 3 per cent*
24.10.87	10.0	10.5
02.04.88	10.5	10.5
02.07.88	11.5	10.5
April, 89	11.0	10.5
July, 89	15.0	10.5
15.05.93	14.0	10.5
06.08.94	15.0	10.5
09.12.95	14.0	10.5
27.04.96	13.5	10.5
11.05.96	13.0	10.5
06.07.96	12.0	10.5
04.01.97	10.5	10.5
18.04.97	10	10.5
29.08.98	11	10.5

Although Banking Regulation Act have prescribed SLR 25 per cent of demand and time liabilities of bank, it was revised in upward direction 12 times during the period of 1970 to 1984. The rise in SLR started from the nationalisation of 14 major commercial banks in 1969 when there was no problem of bank failures.

"So far as SLR is concerned, there is some controversy about its objective. Though this technique was introduced initially to prevent the banks from offsetting the impact of the CRR by liquidating their government security holdings. It is now employed with the objective of restricting the expansionary trend in bank credit and for supporting the government borrowings."[4] "SLR has evolved principally into an instrument for supporting the governments market borrowing."[5] SLR and CRR as a tool of monetary control are proved very effective. But simultaneously they both have serious limitations of loss in bank income. Any increase in SLR or CRR may results in:

i) Certain portion of bank assets will earn NIL,
ii) Interest received on additional CRR and income on SLR may not cover the Fixed and Variable Cost of the Bank. It is overall reduction in bank's earning,
iii) Loss in prospective income,
iv) Profitability becomes less important than liquidity and security.

Basically bank should continue its income growth rate by upward revision in SLR and CRR banks are forced to cover the loss in their income.

TABLE 7. 10

REVISIONS IN STATUTORY LIQUIDITY RATIO (SLR)

With effect from	*Per cent of Demand and Time Liabilities*
25th April, 1987	37.5 per cent
2nd January, 1988	38 per cent
22nd September,1990	38.5 per cent
16th October, 1993	34.75 per cent
29th October, 1994	31.5 per cent
22nd October, 1997	25.0 per cent

Distribution of Deposit of Rs.100

Deposit of Rs.100 is assumed total loanable fund. Then according to prescribed rates of CRR / SLR as on 31st March 1997, the distribution of loanable fund would be—

Purpose	*Amount Rs.*
Loanable Funds	100.00
Less CRR	14.00 w.e.f.. 9/12/95
Less SLR	31.50 w.e.f. 29/10/94

Funds available for advances	54.50
60 per cent per cent for priority sector	32.70
Other advances	21.80

Determination of Cost of Cash Reserve Requirements (CRR)

The Cost of CRR would be calculated on the basis of transfer earnings. The Reserve Bank of India is not paying any interest on initial CRR of 3 per cent and on additional CRR at the rate of 10.5 per cent per annum.

Total CRR	Rs.14
Interest free CRR	Rs.03
Interest bearing CRR	Rs.11
Amount of Interest (At the rate of 10.5)	Rs.1.155 (Rs.11 × Rate 0.105)

Therefore earning on CRR of Rs.14 would be Rs.1.155 paid by the Reserve Bank of India. These Rs.14 are allowed to advances elsewhere at the rate of interest at which individual bank selected in the sample has earned at an average of ten years. Certainly that earning will be more than Rs.1.155 paid by the Reserve Bank of India.

Rate of interest on advances is calculated by dividing total interest received on advances and investment with average advances plus average investment of that particular year for each bank and for ten years.

Then the ten years average rate of interest is calculated for each bank, which is shown in following table.

TABLE 7.11

TEN YEARS' AVERAGE RATE OF INTEREST ON AVERAGE ADVANCES AND INVESTMENTS

Sr. No.	*Name of the Bank*	*Average Rate of Interest on Advances and Investments*
1	The Kalupur Commercial Bank	13.6
2	The Rajkot Nagarik Bank	20.4

3	The Anyonya Sahayakari Bank	22.2
4	The Surat People's Bank	23.9
5	The Natpur Co-operative Bank	20.5
6	The Anand Mercantile Bank	18.9
7	The Dahod Urban Co-operative Bank	19.0
8	The Sarvoday Nagarik Bank	20.2
9	The Baroda People's Bank	20.6
10	The Sardar Bhiladwala Bank	18.2
	Average Interest Rate of ten Banks	19.75

The difference between interest on Rs. 14 i.e. amount of CRR as general advance at the above rate and Rs. 1.155 interest paid by RBI is the cost of CRR to a bank. Following table shows the cost of CRR to each bank:

TABLE 7.12

COST OF CRR TO SELECTED URBAN CO-OPERATIVE BANKS IN GUJARAT

Sr. No.	*Name of the Bank*	*Earning at Normal Rate*	*Interest Paid by RBI*	*Cost of CRR, Deposits per Rs. 100*
1.	The Kalupur Comm. Bank	1.905	1.155	0.75
2.	The Rajkot Nagrik Bank	2.856	1.155	1.701
3.	The Anyonya Sahayakari Bank	3.108	1.155	1.953
4.	The Surat People's Bank	3.346	1.155	2.191
5.	The Natpur Co-op. Bank	2.87	1.155	1.715
6.	The Anand Mercantile Bank	2.646	1.155	1.491
7.	The Dahod Urban Co-op. Bank	2.66	1.155	1.505
8.	The Sarvoday Nagarik Bank	2.828	1.155	1.673
9.	The Baroda People's Bank	2.884	1.155	1.729
10.	The Sardar Bhiladwala Bank	2.548	1.155	1.393

The Surat People's Banks cost for CRR is maximum to Rs. 2.191 i.e. .for deposits of Rs. 100. Whereas minimum cost of CRR Rs. 0.75 for deposits of Rs. 100 is recorded by The

Kalupur Commercial bank. The interest on CRR paid by the Reserve Bank of India is consistent at Rs. 1.155. The bank is yielding high, interest on its advance shows high cost of CRR. Opportunity cost have been taken as a base to ascertain the cost of CRR therefore higher rate of interest earn on advance will reveal the higher cost of CRR. Conversely low interest earning bank will give low cost of CRR.

Average interest rate for all ten banks is Rs. 19.75 than the single figure cost of CRR as average cost for all banks could be—

	Rs.
Average interest on Advances	19.75
Transfer earning on CRR (Rs.14)	2.765
Earning on CRR from RBI	1.155
Cost of CRR (Opportunity cost)	1.610

Per hundred rupees of deposit, each bank is loosing Rs.1.61 as a cost of CRR. It is a loss of income to the Urban Co-operative Banks that ultimately reduces the profitability of the banks.

Cost of SLR

The Cost of SLR is also calculated similarly as is calculated for CRR i.e. on the basis of transfer earning. Here the interest earned on government securities and other approved securities is assumed at 12 per cent. The prescribed rate of SLR is 31.5 per cent of total time and demand liabilities of the bank. Actual income on government and other approved securities at 12 per cent on SLR of Rs. 31.50 will be amounted to Rs. 3.78. The cost of SLR would be the difference between interest earned on Rs. 31.5 as normal advance and Rs. 3.78.

Following table gives the cost of SLR for each Bank.

TABLE 7.13

COST OF SLR OF SELECTED URBAN CO-OPERATIVE BANKS IN GUJARAT

Sr. No	*Name of the Banks*	*Regular Income on Advance of Rs. 31.5*	*Income from Govt. Securities of Rs. 31.5*	*Cost of SLR*
1.	The Kalupur Comm. Bank	4.284	3.78	0.504
2.	The Rajkot Nagarik Bank	6.426	3.78	2.646
3.	The Anyonya Sahayakari Bank	6.993	3.78	3.213
4.	The Surat People's Bank	7.528	3.78	3.748
5.	The Natpur Co-op. Bank	6.457	3.78	2.677
6.	The Anand Mercantile Bank	5.953	3.78	2.173
7.	The Dahod Urban Co-op. Bank	5.985	3.78	2.205
8.	The Sarvoday Nagarik Bank	6.363	3.78	2.583
9.	The Baroda People's Bank	7.119	3.78	3.339
10.	The Sardar Bhiladwala Bank	5.733	3.78	1.953

The average rate of interest on advance for ten banks is 19.75 per cent. Then earning on SLR at the rate of 19.75 is—

Transfer earning on SLR Rs.31.5 At the rate of 19.75 per cent	6.22
Earning on Govt. Securities At the rate of Rs.12 per cent	3.78
Cost of SLR (Opportunity cost)	2.44

It could be concluded that cost of SLR under transfer earning turns out to Rs. 2.44 for deposits of Rs.100.

TABLE 7.14

TOTAL SOCIAL COST

Sr. No.	Name of the Bank	87-88	88-89	89-90	90-91	91-92	92-93	93-94	94-95	95-96	96-97
1	The Kalupur Bank	20.98	21.06	27.71	29.37	30.75	34.56	30.76	53.07	60.88	62.33
2	The Rajkot Nagrik Bank	11.74	18.25	18.47	9.95	16.62	22.67	33.74	41.25	51.89	65.09
3	Anyona Sahakari Bank	4.02	4.62	5.34	6.06	7.31	10.80	12.96	14.67	19.08	20.99
4	The Surat Peoples's Bank	0.00	0.01	0.03	2.31	6.64	12.02	16.76	9.69	0.79	0.69
5	The Natpur Co-Op Bank	4.70	7.52	7.88	14.56	17.63	15.17	24.59	28.27	30.81	41.61
6	Anand Mercantile Bank	0.55	2.79	3.56	3.68	4.12	4.89	5.25	5.05	4.14	5.53
7	Dahod Urban Bank	1.84	2.24	1.85	3.16	3.91	4.86	5.98	6.17	0.51	0.16
8	Sarvodya Nagrik Bank	0.20	0.06	0.26	0.51	0.49	2.35	4.99	5.99	6.99	0.00
9	Baroda People's Bank	0.74	1.56	3.41	0.88	2.79	5.12	12.03	25.51	35.51	57.94
10	Sardar Bhiladwala Bank	0.77	2.25	5.58	0.40	0.58	1.34	0.68	0.85	0.24	5.22

TABLE 7.15

THE PROPORTION OF TOTAL SOCIAL COST TO AVERAGE DEPOSITS

Sr. No.	*Name of the Bank*	*87-88*	*88-89*	*89-90*	*90-91*	*91-92*	*92-93*	*93-94*	*94-95*	*95-96*	*96-97*	*AVG*
1	The Kalupur Bank	0.004	0.003	0.003	0.003	0.003	0.003	0.001	0.002	0.002	0.002	0.002
2	The Rajkot Nagrik Bank	0.001	0.002	0.001	0.001	0.001	0.001	0.002	0.002	0.002	0.002	0.001
3	Anyona Saharakri Bank	0.002	0.002	0.002	0.002	0.002	0.003	0.003	0.003	0.003	0.002	0.002
4	Surat Peoples's Bank	0.000	0.000	0.000	0.000	0.001	0.001	0.001	0.001	0.000	0.000	0.000
5	The Natpur Co-Op Bank	0.003	0.006	0.005	0.008	0.009	0.006	0.009	0.009	0.007	0.007	0.007
6	Anand Mercantile Bank	0.000	0.002	0.002	0.002	0.001	0.002	0.002	0.001	0.001	0.001	0.001
7	Dahod Urban Bank	0.001	0.001	0.001	0.002	0.002	0.002	0.002	0.002	0.000	0.000	0.001
8	Sarvodya Nagrik Bank	0.000	0.000	0.000	0.001	0.001	0.002	0.005	0.005	0.005	0.000	0.002
9	Baroda People's Bank	0.001	0.001	0.002	0.000	0.001	0.002	0.005	0.009	0.008	0.010	0.004
10	Sardar Bhiladwala Bank	0.000	0.001	0.001	0.000	0.000	0.000	0.000	0.000	0.000	0.001	0.000

REFERENCES

1. Sir John Hicks — Capital and Growth, pp. 289-291.
2. Ref.: Indian Economic Survey 1998-99, RBI Publication, issue of February 1999.
3. A Ghosh, Dy. Governor, RBI.
4. Functions and Working, RBI Edition IV, Bombay, 1983, p. 79.
5. Rao D.C. 'The SLR, its Role and some Policy Issue, RBI Bulletin Bombay November 1980 p. 862.

8

Cost Management of Deposits: An Assessment

Introduction

Banking industry has occupied a key position in the Indian economy. It is difficult to imagine that how an economic system could function smoothly without banking services. Banking Industry adds to the wealth by their lending, investing and related activities, which facilitates the economic process of production, distribution and consumption. Thus banks constitute the core of financial structure of an economy. The development of Indian Banking Sector prior to nationalization was not quite satisfactory keeping in view of socio-economic requirements of the country. After nationalisation, banking sector in India has made remarkable progress in extending geographical spread and functional reach. After nationalisation, banks have been entrusted social responsibilities like financing to weaker sections of the society, development of priority sector and providing banking facilities to the neglected sectors. Despite significant progress in post nationalisation phase, certain serious problems of banking sector have emerged reflecting declining productivity and efficiency, which as a consequence has reduced the profitability. As greater thrust was given towards social banking, efficiency, productivity and profitability got neglected in pre-reform phase. Basically banks are commercial organisations dealing with public funds. Profitability is an index of operational efficiency of the banks and their performance is judged on this parameter. Therefore the profitability and viability of the banks are considerably important.

Urban Co-operative Banks cannot be separated for the above mentioned issues. To maintain profitability bank has to either reduce its cost or increase its income. As discussed in the first chapter, increasing income without increasing the volume of the business is not within the control of an individual bank as it is an external factor. However, cost being internal factor up to some extent is within the control of an individual bank.

After 1969 i.e. nationalisation of 14 major commercial banks, banking industry has passed through two phases (1) Pre reform phase and (2) Post reform phase. Obviously, Indian banks are still not acquainted with post reform phase as it has completed only a few years. Post reform phase is identified as de-regulation of interest rate structure, both on advances and on deposits. It means that the Central Monetary Authority or The Reserve Bank of India does not control the interest rates. Only control is remaining on pre-emption i.e. every bank has to make provision for cash reserve requirement (CRR) and statutory liquidity ratio (SLR). In this regard, the monetary authorities are seeming committed to reduce proportion of CRR as well as SLR. In pre-reform phase, once the CRR was at the peak of 15 per cent and SLR was at 38.5 per cent, but in the post-reforms phase it reduced to 10 per cent and 25 per cent CRR and SLR respectively. Another control of The Reserve Bank of India is on credit policy i.e. 30 to 40 per cent of credit is directed to the priority sector. In case of Urban Co-operative Banks 60 per cent of total credit is directed to the priority sector. But this directed credit control has less significance on the cost of the funds because opportunity cost does not exist on directed credit as the rate of interest on priority sector advances are similar to other than priority sectors advances. So as regard to CRR and SLR the opportunity cost exist because the interest paid on CRR by RBI is less than the interest rate prevailing on advances, similar is the case for SLR. The only difference is the rate of return on SLR investments is higher than the CRR earnings.

Ratio Analysis

Generally quantitative information fails to provide a clear understanding therefore the ratio analysis is used to identify the causes and changes in costs, profits and profitability over a period of time. For measuring the performance of Urban Co-operative Banks in terms of profitability, three sets of ratios have been used:

i) Spread Ratios,
ii) Burden Ratios,
iii) Gross Profit Ratios.

Spread Ratios

Spread is difference between interest on advances, investments and interest paid on the deposits. So spread is an amount available to the Urban Co-operative Banks for meeting their administrative, operative and other expenses, earlier termed as fixed costs. Every bank tries to increase the amount of spread so that it is sufficiently available to meet the non-interest expenses and the remainder would contribute to the profit volume. Proper management and deployment of funds is of great importance to increase the spread. Spread along with non-interest income termed as other income i.e. commission, brokerage, service charges etc. forms the total income.

Spread with Average Deposits

Table 8.1 reveals ratio between spread and average deposits of selected Urban Co-operative Banks. The average ratio of spread to deposits is highest with The Surat People's Bank at 8.48 per cent, The Rajkot Nagrik Bank with an average ratio of spread with deposits at 8.04 per cent occupies second position. During the period of ten years, the minimal spread

TABLE 8.01

PROPORTION OF SPREAD WITH AVERAGE DEPOSITS

Sr. No.	*Name of the Bank*	*87-88*	*88-89*	*89-90*	*90-91*	*91-92*	*92-93*	*93-94*	*94-95*	*95-96*	*96-97*	*AVG*
1	The Kalupur Bank	0.052	0.054	0.045	0.039	0.031	0.038	0.040	0.051	0.060	0.064	0.047
2	The Rajkot Nagrik Bank	0.033	0.063	0.071	0.081	0.068	0.096	0.086	0.089	0.105	0.113	0.080
3	Anyona Saharakri Bank	0.036	0.037	0.040	0.047	0.045	0.060	0.057	0.053	0.046	0.047	0.047
4	Surat Peoples's Bank	0.052	0.065	0.070	0.072	0.127	0.097	0.084	0.081	0.095	0.105	0.085
5	Natpur Co-Op Bank	0.041	0.058	0.060	0.062	0.063	0.079	0.068	0.072	0.062	0.065	0.063
6	Anand Mercantile Bank	0.051	0.042	0.047	0.035	0.036	0.063	0.034	0.046	0.037	0.043	0.043
7	Dahod Urban Bank	0.054	0.055	0.060	0.061	0.060	0.072	0.063	0.062	0.066	0.061	0.062
8	Sarvodya Nagrik Bank	0.054	0.055	0.054	0.054	0.048	0.070	0.058	0.066	0.068	0.139	0.067
9	Baroda People's Bank	0.069	0.052	0.057	0.056	0.052	0.063	0.103	0.089	0.064	0.058	0.066
10	Sardar Bhiladwala Bank	0.059	0.058	0.054	0.063	0.076	0.080	0.056	0.067	0.079	0.106	0.070

to average deposit proportion of The Rajkot Nagrik Bank is 3.33 per cent in the year 1987-88, but looking to remaining nine years it is an exceptional year i.e. 1987-88. For all remaining nine years the ratio has remained more than 6 per cent. The Surat People's Bank has the proportion of spread with average deposits between 5.18 per cent and 12.65 per cent during ten years. The Kalupur Commercial Bank having huge amount of deposits and advances, is comparatively on lower side with regards to the proportion of spread with average deposits. In the year 1991-92, the bank has spread of 3.06 per cent on average deposits. Percentage of spread to average deposits of The Kalupur Commercial Bank is 4.73 per cent. This bank stands at third lowest in the sample having second highest position for deposits. The Sarvodaya Nagrik Bank has shown a sharp increase in spread to deposits from 6.82 per cent to 13.90 per cent from the year 1995-96 to 1996-97. Average percentage is 6.88 which is influenced by last year's proportion.

Spread with Working Capital

The ratio of spread as a percentage of working fund is considered to be an important ratio, which indicates profitability of Urban Co-operative Banks. The ratio is calculated by taking difference between interest earned and interest paid divided by working capital.

Table 8.02 describes the ratio of spread as a percentage of working capital during 1991-92 to 1996-97, it can be seen that the ratio ranges between 2.1 per cent and 4.5 per cent and the average percentage is 3.40 per cent. The highest spread with working capital is 6.50 per cent for The Rajkot Nagrik Bank. In this regard, The Surat People's Bank witnesses the ratio between 4.7 per cent to 8.9 per cent whereas the average percentage is 6.10 per cent. The Natpur Co-operative Bank has the average of 5.3 per cent of spread with working capital during the ten years. The Sardar Bhiladwala Bank has a range between 4.3 per cent and 5.9 per cent with average of 5.4 per cent. The Kalupur Commercial Bank, The Anyonya

TABLE NO. 8.02

PROPORTION OF SPREAD WITH WORKING CAPITAL

Sr. No.	*Name of the Bank*	*87-88*	*88-89*	*89-90*	*90-91*	*91-92*	*92-93*	*93-94*	*94-95*	*95-96*	*96-97*	*AVG*
1	The Kalupur Bank	0.037	0.037	0.033	0.028	0.021	0.026	0.030	0.039	0.043	0.045	0.034
2	Rajkot Nagrik Bank	0.034	0.054	0.059	0.066	0.055	0.076	0.068	0.070	0.083	0.088	0.065
3	Anyona Saharakri Bank	0.031	0.030	0.032	0.038	0.036	0.047	0.045	0.042	0.037	0.039	0.038
4	Surat People's Bank	0.048	0.047	0.052	0.052	0.089	0.068	0.059	0.056	0.066	0.074	0.061
5	Natpur Co-Op Bank	0.046	0.048	0.048	0.050	0.050	0.064	0.056	0.058	0.054	0.057	0.053
6	Anand Mercantile Bank	0.035	0.036	0.037	0.028	0.027	0.045	0.026	0.039	0.031	0.038	0.034
7	Dahod Urban Bank	0.039	0.040	0.043	0.044	0.043	0.052	0.044	0.041	0.046	0.048	0.044
8	Sarvodya Nagrik Bank	0.036	0.038	0.038	0.037	0.032	0.046	0.038	0.044	0.049	0.099	0.046
9	Baroda People's Bank	0.047	0.043	0.047	0.046	0.041	0.049	0.061	0.052	0.047	0.043	0.048
10	Sardar Bhiladwala Bank	0.050	0.048	0.043	0.050	0.058	0.059	0.041	0.050	0.058	0.078	0.054

Sahayakari Bank and The Anand Mercantile Bank indicated lesser spread as compared with working capital.

Spread with Total Assets

This is one of the parameters to identify the profitability of the bank. Table no. 8.03 gives the percentage of spread with total assets of Urban Co-operative Banks during ten years. The Surat People's Bank has spread as a percentage of total assets at 5.70 per cent which stands highest in selected 10 Urban Co-operative Banks. The Anand Mercantile Bank has a lower spread as a percentage of total assets i.e. just 2.90 per cent. Second lowest average spread as a percentage of total assets of The Kalupur Commercial Bank is 3.1 per cent as an average for 10 years.

Burden Ratios

Burden is defined as a difference between non-interest expenses (establishment expenses, staff expenses and other expenses termed as fixed costs in the study) and non interest income (Consisting of commission, exchange, brokerage and other miscellaneous receipt) of Urban Co-operative Banks. It represents, the excess of non-interest expenses over non-interest income. In other words they are uncovered non-interest expenses by non-interest income. They remain to be covered by the spread to arrive at profit. Thus profit of Urban Co-operative Banks is the difference between spread and burden. If burden is more, it adversely affect the profit and vice versa, therefore Urban Co-operative Banks always try to maintain burden at minimum level to get the higher profit.

Burden with Average Deposit Ratio

Table 8.04 gives burden as a percentage of average deposits. Lower percentage of burden with average deposit is a favourable sign to Urban Co-operative Banks and vise versa. The Sarvodaya Nagrik Bank has the highest burden as a percentage of deposits during ten years i.e. 3.77 per cent

TABLE 8.03

PROPORTATION OF SPREAD WITH TOTAL ASSESTS

Sr. No.	*Name of the Bank*	*87-88*	*88-89*	*89-90*	*90-91*	*91-92*	*92-93*	*93-94*	*94-95*	*95-96*	*96-97*	*AVG*
1	The Kalupur Bank	0.033	0.034	0.028	0.025	0.020	0.023	0.023	0.036	0.040	0.043	0.031
2	The Rajkot Nagrik Bank	0.038	0.048	0.052	0.058	0.005	0.065	0.057	0.060	0.066	0.073	0.052
3	Anyona Saharakri Bank	0.027	0.028	0.030	0.035	0.034	0.043	0.042	0.039	0.032	0.034	0.034
4	The Surat Peoples's Bank	0.044	0.043	0.048	0.049	0.086	0.061	0.054	0.054	0.060	0.066	0.057
5	The Natpur Co-Op Bank	0.041	0.044	0.044	0.047	0.047	0.059	0.049	0.049	0.045	0.048	0.047
6	Anand Mercantile Bank	0.032	0.026	0.031	0.023	0.023	0.041	0.024	0.034	0.025	0.035	0.029
7	Dahod Urban Bank	0.036	0.038	0.041	0.042	0.041	0.049	0.039	0.038	0.042	0.041	0.041
8	Sarvodya Nagrik Bank	0.032	0.036	0.036	0.034	0.031	0.043	0.036	0.043	0.045	0.093	0.043
9	Baroda People's Bank	0.042	0.038	0.044	0.042	0.038	0.044	0.055	0.049	0.041	0.038	0.043
10	Sardar Bhiladwala Bank	0.044	0.043	0.040	0.047	0.054	0.055	0.038	0.046	0.053	0.069	0.049

whereas The Rajkot Nagrik Bank has lowest burden as a percentage of average deposits amongst ten selected Urban Co-operative Banks and The Anand Mercantile Bank stands at 1.38 per cent. Second lowest is The Kalupur Commercial Bank having 1.42 per cent of burden as a percentage of average deposits. The Anyonya Sahayakari Bank, The Surat People's Bank, The Baroda People's Bank and The Sardar Bhiladwala Bank has a burden as a percentage of average deposits for more than 2.2 per cent and less than 2.5 per cent.

Burden with Working Capital

This ratio indicates that how much of the working funds are engaged in burden. Again higher the ratio lower the profitability is the indication of this ratio. Table 8.05 shows highest burden as a percentage of working capital is of The Sarvodaya Nagrik Bank that stands at 2.60 per cent during 10 years whereas The Anyonya Sahayakari Bank has 2 per cent, The Baroda People's Bank and The Sardar Bhiladawala bank has burden with working capital ratio at 1.8 and 1.7 per cent respectively.

Burden with Total Assets

Table 8.06 indicates the ratio of burden with total assets for ten years and for ten banks. The Rajkot Nagrik Bank and The Kalupur Commercial Bank has an average proportion of less than 1 per cent whereas The Sarvodaya Nagrik Bank has the average proportion of burden with total assets for more than 2 per cent. Remaining banks have this proportion more than 1 per cent and less than 2 per cent.

Gross Profit Ratios

As a matter of fact, gross profit is the important barometer of the efficiency of the Urban Co-operative Banks, more over it is one of the important objectives for survival and the growth of Urban Co-operative Banks. Profit is the result of revenue and cost function. Any excess of revenue over expenditure forms a profit. Thus gross profit can be defined

TABLE 8.04

PROPORTION OF BURDEN WITH AVERAGE DEPOSITS

Sr. No.	Name of the Bank	87-88	88-89	89-90	90-91	91-92	92-93	93-94	94-95	95-96	96-97	AVG
1	The Kalupur Bank	0.021	0.021	0.019	0.017	0.012	0.014	0.009	0.008	0.011	0.010	0.014
2	The Rajkot Nagrik Bank	0.010	0.012	0.012	0.015	0.012	0.017	0.016	0.015	0.014	0.015	0.014
3	Anyona Saharakri Bank	0.023	0.024	0.023	0.026	0.019	0.027	0.028	0.028	0.026	0.026	0.025
4	The Surat Peoples's Bank	0.018	0.021	0.024	0.023	0.020	0.027	0.027	0.029	0.032	0.025	0.025
5	The Natpur Co-Op Bank	0.013	0.018	0.019	0.018	0.014	0.020	0.019	0.020	0.020	0.016	0.018
6	Anand Mercantile Bank	0.019	0.015	0.013	0.012	0.008	0.011	0.013	0.014	0.015	0.017	0.014
7	Dahod Urban Bank	0.012	0.013	0.017	0.016	0.012	0.018	0.015	0.018	0.016	0.013	0.015
8	Sarvodya Nagrik Bank	0.030	0.030	0.023	0.032	0.030	0.041	0.043	0.050	0.050	0.049	0.038
9	Baroda People's Bank	0.025	0.019	0.021	0.021	0.021	0.026	0.025	0.036	0.026	0.025	0.024
10	Sardar Bhiladwala Bank	0.019	0.020	0.028	0.020	0.015	0.025	0.024	0.022	0.022	0.027	0.022

TABLE 8.05

PROPORTION OF BURDEN WITH WORKING CAPITAL

Sr. No.	*Name of the Bank*	*87-88*	*88-89*	*89-90*	*90-91*	*91-92*	*92-93*	*93-94*	*94-95*	*95-96*	*96-97*	*AVG*
1	The Kalupur Bank	0.015	0.015	0.014	0.013	0.008	0.010	0.007	0.006	0.008	0.007	0.010
2	Rajkot Nagrik Bank	0.010	0.010	0.010	0.012	0.010	0.013	0.012	0.012	0.011	0.011	0.011
3	Anyona Saharakri Bank	0.020	0.019	0.018	0.021	0.015	0.021	0.022	0.022	0.021	0.021	0.020
4	The Surat Peoples's Bank	0.017	0.015	0.017	0.017	0.014	0.019	0.019	0.020	0.022	0.018	0.018
5	The Natpur Co-Op Bank	0.014	0.015	0.015	0.015	0.011	0.016	0.016	0.016	0.017	0.015	0.015
6	The Anand Mercantile Bank	0.013	0.013	0.010	0.010	0.006	0.008	0.011	0.012	0.013	0.015	0.011
7	Dahod Urban Bank	0.009	0.009	0.012	0.012	0.009	0.013	0.010	0.012	0.011	0.010	0.011
8	Sarvodya Nagrik Bank	0.020	0.021	0.016	0.022	0.020	0.027	0.028	0.034	0.035	0.035	0.026
9	Baroda People's Bank	0.017	0.016	0.017	0.017	0.016	0.020	0.015	0.021	0.019	0.019	0.018
10	Sardar Bhiladwala Bank	0.016	0.016	0.022	0.015	0.011	0.018	0.017	0.016	0.016	0.020	0.017

TABLE 8.06

PROPORTATION OF BURDEN WITH TOTAL ASSESTS

Sr. No.	*Name of the Bank*	*87-88*	*88-89*	*89-90*	*90-91*	*91-92*	*92-93*	*93-94*	*94-95*	*95-96*	*96-97*	*AVG*
1	The Kalupur Bank	0.013	0.013	0.012	0.011	0.008	0.009	0.005	0.006	0.007	0.006	0.009
2	Rajkot Nagrik Bank	0.011	0.009	0.009	0.011	0.001	0.011	0.010	0.010	0.009	0.009	0.009
3	Anyona Saharakri Bank	0.017	0.018	0.017	0.019	0.014	0.020	0.020	0.020	0.019	0.018	0.018
4	Surat Peoples's Bank	0.016	0.014	0.016	0.016	0.014	0.017	0.017	0.019	0.020	0.016	0.016
5	Natpur Co-Op Bank	0.013	0.013	0.014	0.014	0.011	0.015	0.014	0.014	0.014	0.012	0.013
6	Anand Mercantile Bank	0.012	0.009	0.009	0.008	0.005	0.007	0.010	0.010	0.010	0.014	0.009
7	Dahod Urban Bank	0.008	0.009	0.012	0.011	0.008	0.012	0.009	0.011	0.010	0.009	0.010
8	Sarvodya Nagrik Bank	0.018	0.020	0.015	0.020	0.019	0.025	0.027	0.033	0.032	0.033	0.024
9	Baroda People's Bank	0.015	0.014	0.016	0.015	0.015	0.018	0.014	0.020	0.016	0.017	0.016
10	Sardar Bhiladwala Bank	0.014	0.015	0.021	0.015	0.011	0.017	0.016	0.015	0.015	0.018	0.016

as difference between total income and total expenditure for any period. In other words, it is a difference between spread and burden for Urban Co-operative Banks. Profitability ratios are the common ratios required for judging the performance of the Urban Co-operative Banks because absolute profit can be increased by employing more resources without improving the profitability. Analysis of profitability ratio is highly important to the management to measure the efficiency of the bank. Again other interested parties like shareholders, borrowers and depositors need it. The judgement of growth, repayment capacity, trust of the public depends upon the profitability. Following profitability ratios have been analysed:

i) Gross profit as a percentage of average deposits,
ii) Gross profit as a percentage of working capital,
iii) Gross profit as a percentage of total assets.

Grofit Profit with Average Deposits

Table 8.07 gives profit as a percentage of average deposits. During the ten years from 1987 - 88 to 1996-97, The Kalupur Commercial Bank shows continuous decline in the ratio for first five years starting from 3.14 per cent to 1.88 per cent then in the remaining five years it shows continuous rise in the ratio starting from 2.32 per cent and reaching to the peak at 5.46 per cent. Somehow these two periods can be treated more or less as pre reform and post reform phase but such a distinction is not observed with other banks in the sample.

Deregulation of interest rates on deposits has been introduced in the year 1996. Banks were free to decide the interest rates on deposits. Selected ten banks are showing significant increase in the year 1996-97 in the ratio of profit as a percentage of average deposits.

Following figures of profit as a percentage of average deposits for the year 1995-96 and 1996-97 are self-explanatory.

TABLE 8.07

PROPORTION OF GROSS PROFIT WITH AVERAGE DEPOSITS

Sr. No.	*Name of the Bank*	*87-88*	*88-89*	*89-90*	*90-91*	*91-92*	*92-93*	*93-94*	*94-95*	*95-96*	*96-97*	*AVG*
1	The Kalupur Bank	0.031	0.033	0.026	0.021	0.019	0.023	0.031	0.043	0.049	0.055	0.033
2	Rajkot Nagrik Bank	0.023	0.051	0.059	0.066	0.055	0.079	0.070	0.074	0.092	0.098	0.067
3	Anyona Saharakri Bank	0.013	0.014	0.017	0.022	0.026	0.033	0.029	0.026	0.019	0.021	0.022
4	Surat Peoples's Bank	0.034	0.044	0.047	0.049	0.106	0.070	0.058	0.052	0.063	0.080	0.060
5	Natpur Co-Op Bank	0.028	0.040	0.041	0.043	0.049	0.060	0.049	0.052	0.043	0.048	0.045
6	Anand Mercantile Bank	0.032	0.027	0.034	0.023	0.028	0.052	0.020	0.032	0.022	0.026	0.030
7	Dahod Urban Bank	0.042	0.043	0.043	0.045	0.048	0.054	0.049	0.044	0.051	0.048	0.047
8	Sarvodya Nagrik Bank	0.024	0.025	0.031	0.022	0.018	0.029	0.015	0.016	0.019	0.090	0.029
9	Baroda People's Bank	0.044	0.033	0.036	0.036	0.031	0.037	0.077	0.054	0.039	0.033	0.042
10	Sardar Bhiladwala Bank	0.041	0.038	0.026	0.043	0.061	0.055	0.032	0.045	0.057	0.079	0.048

TABLE 8.07(A)

PROFIT AS A PERCENTAGE OF AVERAGE DEPOSITS

Sr. No	*Name of the Bank*	*1995-96*	*1996-97*
1	The Kalupur Bank	4.88	5.46
2	The Rajkot Nagrik Bank	9.10	9.82
3	The Anyonya Bank	1.95	2.13
4	The Surat People's Bank	6.32	8.00
5	The Natpur Bank	4.27	4.81
6	The Anand Bank	2.22	2.58
7	The Dahod Urban Bank	5.05	4.78
8	The Sarvodaya Bank	1.87	3.99
9	The Baroda People's Bank	3.27	3.87
10	The Sardar Bhiladwala Bank	5.65	7.86

From the above table it is evident that The Dahod Urban Bank is the only exception for reduction in the rate of gross profit to average deposits. The highest profit-earning bank as a percentage of average deposit is The Surat People's Bank having average of 8.03 per cent during ten years. The second position is obtained by The Rajkot Nagrik Bank by having average proportion of 6.06 per cent.

Gross Profit with Working Capital

Table 8.08 shows the profit as a percentage of working capital. Here The Rajkot Nagrik Bank has 5.4 per cent of profit as percentage of working capital as an average for ten years. The lowest percentage of profit as a percentage of working capital is obtained by The Anyonya Sahayakari Bank at 1.8 per cent during ten years as an average. The second highest profit-earning bank as a per cent of working capital is The Surat People's Bank with 4.3 per cent as an average of ten years. Here also nine banks i.e. other than Baroda People's Bank have shown increasing proportion from 1995-96 to 1996-97 of gross profit with working capital. Second lowest

TABLE 8.08

PROPORTION OF GROSS PROFIT WITH WORKING CAPITAL

Sr. No.	*Name of the Bank*	*87-88*	*88-89*	*89-90*	*90-91*	*91-92*	*92-93*	*93-94*	*94-95*	*95-96*	*96-97*	*AVG*
1	The Kalupur Bank	0.022	0.022	0.019	0.015	0.013	0.016	0.023	0.033	0.035	0.039	0.024
2	The Rajkot Nagrik Bank	0.024	0.044	0.049	0.054	0.045	0.063	0.056	0.058	0.072	0.077	0.054
3	Anyona Saharakri Bank	0.011	0.011	0.014	0.017	0.021	0.026	0.023	0.020	0.016	0.018	0.018
4	Surat Peoples's Bank	0.031	0.032	0.034	0.036	0.075	0.049	0.040	0.036	0.044	0.056	0.043
5	The Natpur Co-Op Bank	0.031	0.033	0.033	0.035	0.039	0.048	0.040	0.042	0.037	0.042	0.038
6	Anand Mercantile Bank	0.022	0.023	0.027	0.018	0.021	0.037	0.016	0.027	0.019	0.023	0.023
7	Dahod Urban Bank	0.030	0.031	0.031	0.032	0.035	0.039	0.033	0.029	0.035	0.037	0.033
8	Sarvodya Nagrik Bank	0.016	0.018	0.022	0.015	0.012	0.019	0.010	0.010	0.013	0.064	0.020
9	Baroda People's Bank	0.030	0.028	0.030	0.029	0.024	0.029	0.046	0.031	0.028	0.024	0.030
10	Sardar Bhiladwala Bank	0.034	0.031	0.021	0.034	0.046	0.041	0.024	0.033	0.042	0.058	0.037

proportion of profit with working capital is of The Sarvodaya Nagrik Bank.

Gross Profit with Total Assets

Table 8.09 gives proportion of profit with total assets of selected Urban Co-operative Banks.

This ratio is more than 4 per cent as an average for ten years obtained by The Rajkot Nagrik Bank and The Surat People's Bank whereas The Sarvodaya Nagrik Bank has less than 2 per cent. In this regard similar position is that of The Anyonya Sahayakari Bank. Remaining banks have more than 2 per cent profit as a percentage of total assets during the ten years.

Trend Analysis

Trend analysis basically is an indicator of quantitative changes in banking activities. It shows the direction of a variable over a period of time. Besides this, it highlights trend pattern which helps in knowing the development as well as the level of efficiency in banking operation over a time framed. This trend analysis has been undertaken through five indicators namely:

i) Income trends,
ii) Expenditure trend,
iii) Spread trend,
iv) Burden trend, and
v) Profit trend.

Total Income Trend

The main component of banks' income is an interest and discount, the other incomes are commission, brokerage, exchange and other miscellaneous income. Here the trend analysis has been made in aggregate. The aggregate trend provides an overall picture of the total income. Graph 8.01 shows the trend in total incomes of selected Urban Co-operative

TABLE 8.09

PROPORTATION OF GROSS PROFIT WITH TOTAL ASSESTS

Sr. No.	*Name of the Bank*	*87-88*	*88-89*	*89-90*	*90-91*	*91-92*	*92-93*	*93-94*	*94-95*	*95-96*	*96-97*	*AVG*
1	The Kalupur Bank	0.020	0.020	0.016	0.014	0.012	0.014	0.018	0.031	0.032	0.036	0.021
2	The Rajkot Nagrik Bank	0.027	0.038	0.043	0.047	0.004	0.053	0.046	0.050	0.058	0.063	0.043
3	Anyona Saharakri Bank	0.010	0.010	0.013	0.016	0.020	0.024	0.021	0.019	0.014	0.015	0.016
4	Surat Peoples's Bank	0.029	0.029	0.032	0.033	0.072	0.044	0.037	0.035	0.040	0.050	0.040
5	The Natpur Co-Op Bank	0.028	0.030	0.030	0.033	0.036	0.045	0.035	0.036	0.031	0.036	0.034
6	Anand Mercantile Bank	0.020	0.017	0.022	0.015	0.018	0.034	0.014	0.024	0.015	0.021	0.020
7	Dahod Urban Bank	0.028	0.029	0.029	0.031	0.033	0.037	0.030	0.027	0.032	0.032	0.031
8	Sarvodya Nagrik Bank	0.015	0.016	0.021	0.014	0.012	0.017	0.009	0.010	0.012	0.060	0.019
9	Baroda People's Bank	0.027	0.024	0.028	0.026	0.023	0.026	0.041	0.029	0.024	0.022	0.027
10	Sardar Bhiladwala Bank	0.030	0.028	0.019	0.032	0.044	0.038	0.022	0.031	0.038	0.051	0.033

TABLE 8.10

AVERAGE COSTS AS A PERCENTAGE OF AVERAGE DEPOSITS OF SELECTED URBAN CO-OPERATIVE BANKS

Sr. No	*Elements of cost*	*1*	*2*	*3*	*4*	*5*	*6*	*7*	*8*	*9*	*10*
1	**Interest paid (V Cost)**	**10.68**	**9.88**	**10.09**	**8.87**	**10.04**	**11.43**	**11.29**	**13.64**	**11.98**	**8.78**
2	Salaries and Allowances	1.56	1.33	2.30	2.27	1.38	1.16	1.49	3.59	2.21	2.11
3	Printing and Stationery	0.13	0.07	0.11	0.11	0.14	0.19	0.10	0.17	0.25	0.12
4	Postage and Telegrams	0.03	0.05	0.03	0.02	0.04	0.04	0.03	0.11	0.08	0.05
5	Rent and Taxes	0.17	0.09	0.24	0.13	0.13	0.11	0.13	0.15	0.28	0.10
6	Depreciation	0.18	0.10	0.06	0.24	0.27	0.15	0.05	0.09	0.19	0.18
7	Audit Fees	0.00	0.00	0.00	0.00	0.01	0.01	0.01	0.01	0.01	0.00
8	Directors' fees	0.00	0.00	0.01	0.00	0.00	0.01	0.01	0.00	0.02	0.00
9	Legal fees	0.01	0.00	0.01	0.00	0.01	0.01	0.00	0.01	0.01	0.01
10	**Total fixed cost**	**2.08**	**1.65**	**2.77**	**2.78**	**1.96**	**1.66**	**1.81**	**4.13**	**3.04**	**2.56**
11	**Total cost (V + F cost)**	**12.76**	**11.53**	**12.86**	**11.65**	**12.00**	**13.09**	**13.09**	**17.77**	**15.02**	**11.34**
12	Interest received	14.99	17.92	14.78	17.34	16.34	15.76	17.44	20.30	18.63	15.75
13	Other income	0.66	0.27	0.28	0.33	0.20	0.28	0.31	0.36	0.59	0.36
14	**Total income**	**15.64**	**18.20**	**15.06**	**17.67**	**16.54**	**16.04**	**17.76**	**20.66**	**19.22**	**16.10**
15	**Profit**	**2.89**	**6.66**	**2.20**	**6.03**	**4.54**	**2.95**	**4.66**	**2.89**	**4.20**	**4.76**

GRAPH 8.01

TREND OF TOTAL INCOME.

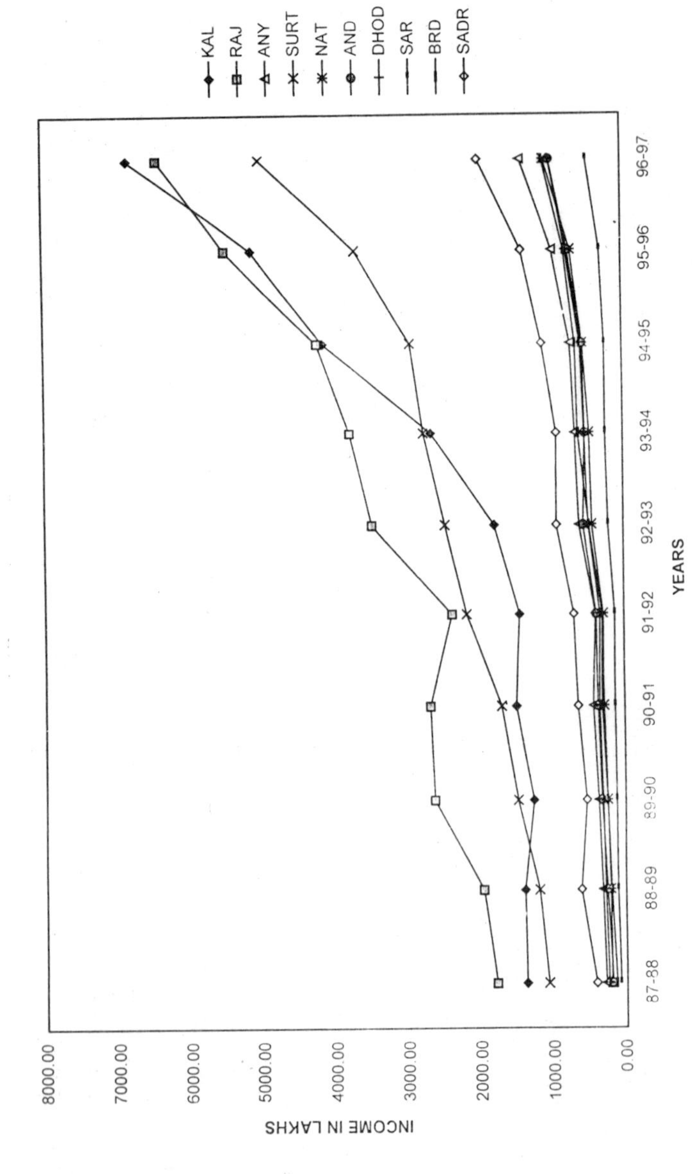

Banks. On "X" axis the selected 10 years is plotted whereas on "Y" axis the total income is plotted. All ten curves indicate the trend in total income for ten banks. The Kalupur Commercial Bank's total income remains constant from the year 1987-88 to 1991-92. From 1992-93, it is continuously showing sharp increase till the year 1996-97. The total income of The Kalupur Commercial Bank was Rs. 1795.5 lacs, which suddenly increased to Rs. 2662.57 lacs in the year 1993-94, which again sharply increased to Rs. 4150.3 lacs in the year 1994-95. For The Rajkot Nagrik Bank, the total income curve is increasing but not as it has increased for The Kalupur Commercial Bank.

Before the year 1992-93, the increase is gradual whereas from 1993-94 the increase is at a faster rate. The Surat People's Bank is having third position as regards to total income in the selected Urban Co-operative Banks. The only difference is for all ten years is that it is increasing, in no year it became stable. From the year 1994-95, the sharp increase is observed in the total income of The Surat People's Bank. Fourth position is obtained by The Sardar Bhiladwala Bank as regards to total income but it has never crossed the total income of Rs. 2000 lacs whereas The Surat People's Bank, The Rajkot Nagrik Bank and The Kalupur Commercial Bank have either reached to the total income of Rs. 5000 lacs or Rs. 6000 lacs or more for the year 1996-97. The total income of The Sarvodaya Nagrik Bank is at the bottom in selected banks and more or less it has remained stable during the ten years. The Anyonya Sahayakari Bank, The Natpur Co-operative Bank, The Dahod Urban Bank, The Anand Mercantile Bank and The Baroda People's Bank's total income trend is observed similar and shows a very low rate of growth in total income during ten years.

Total Expenditure Trend

The major items of expenditure are interest paid on deposits and other items are the establishment expenditure which remains fixed to a great extent. Before 1996 the rate of interest to be paid on deposits was pre-determined by The Reserve Bank of India. So Urban Banks have practically very less control on the interest expenditure. The interest expenditure was depending upon the mobilisation of deposits, higher the deposits mobilised higher will be the interest expenditure payable. But it does not mean that Urban Banks do not have any control on the volume of expenditure at all. The Management of the Urban Co-operative Banks can reduce the expenses by employing different cost reduction techniques like developing organisational structure, maximum utilisation of assets, introducing more sophisticated tools and machines. But still it is rather difficult for banks to reduce expenses like other business organisation. The total expenditure incurred by ten selected Urban Co-operative Banks during the period of 1987-88 to 1996-97 is plotted on the Graph 8.02. The trends in expenditure for The Kalupur Commercial Bank, The Rajkot Nagrik Bank and The Surat People's Bank are behaving similarly as observed in the trends of total income.

Here The Rajkot Nagrik Bank shows the sharp increase in the total expenditure from the year 1991-92 to 1992-93 and from 1995-96 to 1996-97 and for remaining years the growth rate in total expenditure was somewhat less as compared with the previous years. In case of The Kalupur Commercial Bank from the year 1986-87 to 1991-92, total expenditure is steady and not rising but from 1992-93 rising at a faster rate from Rs. 1635.67 lacs to Rs. 5716.8 lacs in the year 1986-87. The growth rate in expenditure for The Surat People's Bank till the year 1994-95 was less but then it is rising suddenly. For the year 1996-97 it has reached to the peak of Rs. 4000 lacs. Remaining seven banks' total expenditure trend is almost same ranging from more or less upto Rs. 1000 lacs and the growth rate is also less as compared to earlier three banks.

Trends in Spread

Graph 8.03 shows the trend in spread of selected Urban

GRAPH 8.02

TREND OF EXPENDITURE.

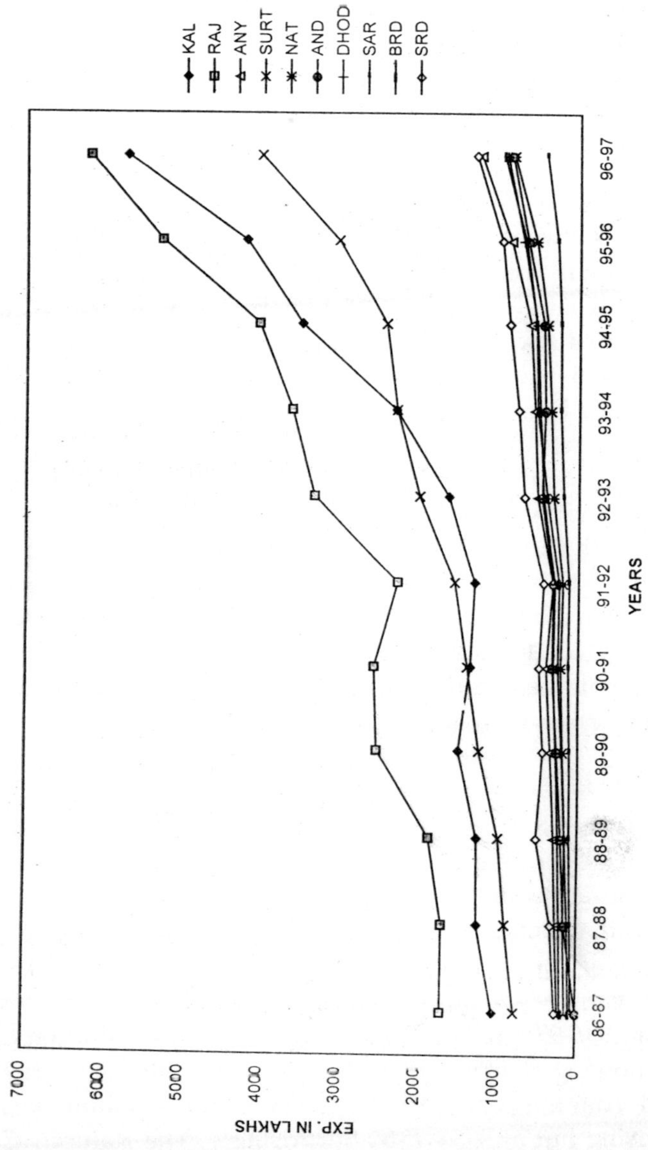

Co-operative Banks as it is a very important indicator as a matter of efficiency of the bank, every bank tries to keep it high as it can. The Rajkot Nagrik Bank is very much successful in increasing its spread at a faster rate than any other bank in the selected sample. The growth in year 1995-96 and 1996-97 is remarkable. It was just Rs. 2000 lacs at the end of the year 1994-95 and reached at the peak of Rs. 3500 in the year 1996-97. These results are found rare. In case of The Kalupur Commercial Bank, the spread has remained more or less stable between Rs. 300 lacs to Rs. 500 lacs but then from 1993-94 it was Rs. 900 lacs and achieved the spread of Rs. 1617 lacs for the year 1994-95. For the year 1996-97, it has remained Rs. 2531 lacs. Sudden increase in last four years observed for The Kalupur Commercial Bank. The Surat People's Bank's trend in spread is increasing at a higher growth rate from the year 1990-91 to 1991-92, then it has become steady upto the year 1993-94, then again it shows the sharp increase till the end of the year 1996-97. Same is the case with The Sardar Bhiladwala Bank, the spread has remained below 500 lacs in the beginning of 8 years of study period and then it has increased during last two years for more than Rs. 500 lacs. Remaining six banks' trend in spread is showing negligible increase during all ten years and they have remained more or less similar in case of spread.

Trends in Burden

Graph 8.04 presents the trend in burden of selected Urban Co-operative Banks. The highest burden is observed for The Surat People's Bank amongst the selected ten Urban Co-operative Banks. It looks uncontrolled establishment expenditure of The Surat People's Bank during the year 1990-91 till the year 1995-96 but then burden has become stable for the year 1996-97. For The Rajkot Nagrik Bank, the burden trend is showing sharp increase from the year 1991-92 to 1992-93 and from the year 1995-96 to 1996-97, for remaining years it is rising but at slow rate. Surprisingly, The Kalupur Commercial Bank's burden trend is showing sharp increase from

GRAPH 8.03

TREND OF SPREAD

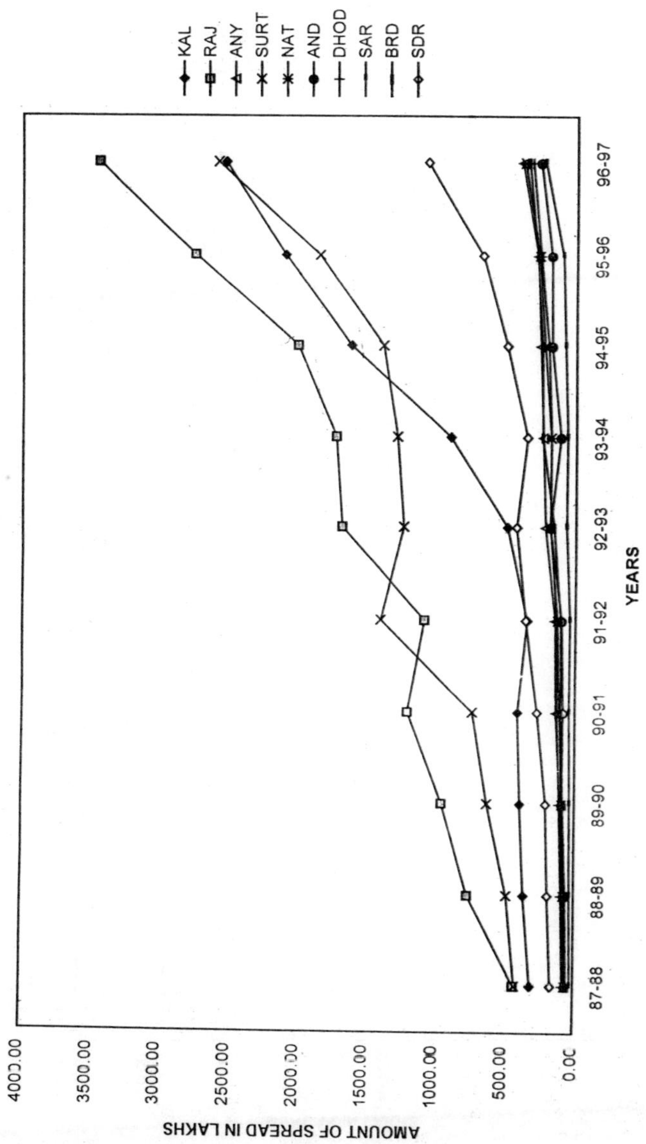

GRAPH 8.04

TRENDS OF BURDEN.

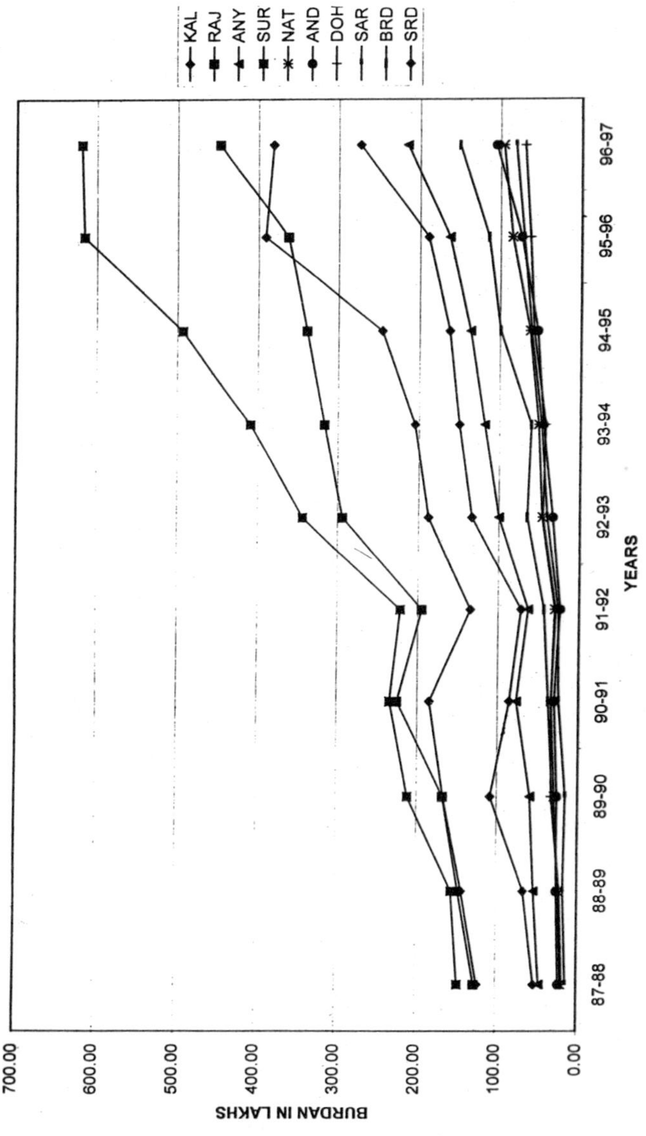

the year 1994-95 to 1995-96 and suddenly it shows decline in the burden for the year 1996-97. It is the only bank amongst selected Urban Co-operative Banks showing decline in the burden for two years i.e. for 1991-92 and 1996-97. For remaining banks, the burden trend is increasing but at a slow rate, The Baroda People's Bank, The Sarvodaya Nagrik Bank, The Dahod Urban Bank, The Anand Mercantile Bank and The Natpur Co-operative Bank are almost showing the similar trends in burden.

Trends in Gross Profit

Graph 8.05 presents trends in profit for selected Urban Co-operative Banks. Higher profit is achieved by The Rajkot Nagrik Bank during ten years amongst all selected Urban Co-operative Banks with exception for the year 1991-92. The profit of The Rajkot Nagrik Bank has reached to the peak of Rs. 3000 lacs for the year 1996-97. As it is observed in earlier graphs, there is a sharp increase in the profit of The Rajkot Nagrik Bank for the year 1995-96 and 1996-97. In case of the Kalupur Commercial Bank such a sharp increase is observed in profit during the year 1992-93 upto the year 1996-97, it was Rs. 304 lacs and Rs. 2150 lacs respectively. In the initial six years it was less than Rs. 300 lacs. The Surat People's Bank is at the third position in earning profit, it is also observed there is a sharp increase in profit for the last two years. The fourth position is achieved by The Sardar Bhiladwala Bank in earning the profit, for the year 1996-97 it has the profit of nearly Rs. 800 lacs.

The remaining six banks in earning profit are less than Rs. 250 lacs for all the ten years. Normally no significant increase is observed in profit for The Anyonya Shayakari Bank, The Natpur Co-operative Bank, The Anand Mercantile Bank, The Dahod Urban Bank, The Sarvodaya Nagarik Bank and The Baroda People's Bank.

GRAPH 8.05

TRENDS OF GROSS PROFIT.

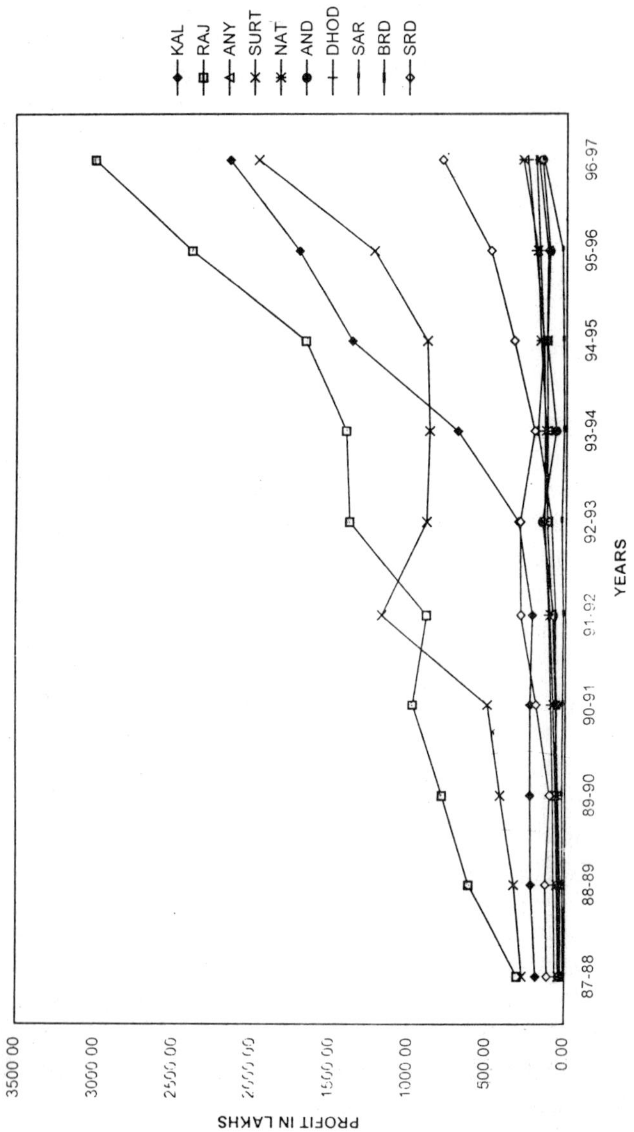

Economies of Scale in Urban Banks

Here the purpose is to investigate the existence of economies of scale in selected Urban Co-operative Banks. If there is any relationship between the total cost and size of deposits, an understanding of this relationship will enable to determine the most desirable size of deposits of a bank, at least in the form of cost. If the relationship is such that marginal cost is constant at all levels of output i.e. deposits, then it implies that there is no limit to the size of deposits. On the other hand if marginal cost is showing declining trend then the increase in deposits will bring reduction in the cost. It would be worth to estimate the total cost function of the selected Urban Co-operative Banks. From the estimated total cost function, the marginal cost curve can be derived and the average cost curve will enable to draw the conclusion on the impact of size of the deposits on the total cost.

Meaning of Economies of Scale

Any manufacturing unit normally finds that average cost per unit of their output declines as the volume of output increases. There are also situations where the larger volume of production increases the average cost per unit. In other words, the scale of production is often determinant of cost per unit. Consequently manufacturing industries tend to limit their size of operation whereby they could achieve the maximum advantage of economies arising out of scale considering demand of a product.

Economies or dis-economies of scale normally appear because of following reasons:

Economies

i) Increase in utilisation of machine capacity,
ii) Fairly huge amount of expenses in production,
iii) Specialization of a labour in production resulting in more and more output,

iv) Unused efficiency of plant and equipments at higher volume of production and

v) Reduction in purchase prices because of purchases in bulk.

Dis-economies

i) Inefficiencies arising out of meager management control,

ii) Due to communication gaps and because of that delays in operation and

iii) Labour turnover due to less motivation.

Though the economies of scale may be observed in capital incentive industry because of first and second factor in point "a" and all factors of dis-economies but they may be observed in labour intensive industry also. Therefore it would be worth to examine the economies of scale in banks. The existence of economies of scale can be identified in manufacturing industry merely by inspection of a data where unutilised plant and machinery capacity or huge amounts of fixed cost are present. Testing of economies or dis-economies due to increased or decreased efficiency of plant and machinery or labour as the volume of production changes. For a manufacturing unit producing single item, statistical cost output relationship can be estimated by way of using cost and connected output figures, assuming other influencing factors constant. The relationship so established would indicate the sensitivity of increase in output on cost but a multi-product manufacturing unit will face complexity in establishing the cost output relation as explained above. In case of multi-product unit, following data is required to be collected:

i) Direct cost of each product in order to investigate the scale of economies,

ii) Conversion of different product into units of equivalent cost and

iii) Preparing a product mix in the same ratio throughout the time of study.

Once information required is obtained, cost output relation can be established for single product manufacturing unit. Alternatively the total cost function can be estimated through statistical technique whereby all the outputs produced are produced as a separate variable.

For a multi-product manufacturing unit, the total cost can not be compared simply with one type of output because it will not show the economies of scale exist or not. For example, in the banking industry, the total cost and total deposit ratio should not show any relationship, if we look at the rate before compilation. However, the investigation in this study is showing a strong relationship between the size of bank measured by way of size of deposits and the total cost, if some factors are assumed constant. The size of deposits in Urban Co-operative Banks represents the level of activity in all other lines of business such as advances, discounting bills, remittances, letter of credits etc. and therefore it is decided to introduce only the level of deposits as a variable representing all other activities. The limitations of this approach are also to be understood. In this study the method implies that a change in advances will not have influence on the cost. In other words it is assumed that the amount of deposits determines the cost and ignores the other factors. Also, they are represented by behaviour in deposits as it finds difficult to obtain meaningful results by using the statistical tools if large number of closely related variables are used. Finally, it has been decided to introduce the amount of deposits rather than the number of accounts in the investigations. The Urban Co-operative Banks having identical total deposits may have different cost because of different deposits mix (current, saving and fixed deposits).

Analysis of Average Cost

Average Cost

The average cost is the cost per unit of deposits. To obtain the average cost, total cost is divided by total deposits of selected Urban Co-operative Banks and to obtain the average cost curve, the cost per unit of deposits so calculated for ten years for each bank is plotted on the graph.

Marginal Cost

The Chartered Institute of Management Accountant, England, defines the term marginal cost as follows:

"Marginal cost is the amount at any given volume of output by which aggregate cost are changed if the volume of output is increased or decreased by one unit. In this context, a unit may be a single article, a batch of articles, an order, and a stage of production capacity of a department. It relates to change in output in the particular circumstances under consideration." According to CIMA, "Terminology marginal costing is the ascertainment of the marginal cost and the effect on profit of a changes in volume or type of output by differentiating between fixed costs and variable costs."

Theoretically the equilibrium level of output can be identified where the marginal cost curve cuts the average cost curve from below i.e. the average cost and marginal cost becomes equal. At initial phase, the average cost curve falls sharply, then in the second phase it becomes steady; and in the third phase it starts rising. The shape of marginal cost curve is obtained in the "U" shape. Initially marginal cost is less than average cost, onwards when marginal cost curve cuts the average cost curve from below i.e. the level of output is at equilibrium/MC=AC, then the marginal cost curve rises sharply than that of the average cost curve. It can be interpreted that in the initial stage any addition to size of deposits will reduce the average cost. But when the marginal cost curve cuts the average cost curve from below, it is the level of output where the increase in the size of deposits will not reduce the average cost. Therefore it is the equilibrium level of deposits which Urban Co operative Banks can mobilise. The last phase is, marginal cost rises sharply than the average cost and it means that any addition to the size of deposits increases the average cost i.e. the dis-economies have started. Till the marginal cost curve intersects the average cost from below then there exist economies of scale.

The selected Urban Co-operative Banks considered under the study are not placed under the similar economic conditions. They have entered into the market at different point of time e.g.

Sr. No.	*Name of Banks*	*Established in the Year*
1	The Kalupur Commercial Bank	1970
2	The Rajkot Nagrik Bank	1953
3	The Anyonya Sahayakari Bank	1889
4	The Surat People's Bank	1922
5	The Natpur Co-operative Bank	1971
6	The Anand Mercantile Bank	1971
7	The Dahod Urban Bank	1936
8	The Sarvodaya Nagrik Bank	1977
9	The Baroda People's Bank	1965
10	The Sardar Bhiladwala Bank	1930

All the above selected Urban Co-operative Banks have the different geographical conditions. The size of deposits of each bank is different. The Management structure of the bank is different. The membership, social and economical conditions of members are different. The coverage in the Gujarat State for each bank is different. The composition of total deposits (current, saving and fixed) is different as is observed in the fourth chapter of this study. The purpose of advances i.e. advances mix for each bank is different. In short, they are facing dissimilar conditions i.e. heterogeneous character exist in the selected Urban Co-operative Banks. The social accountability of Urban Co-operative Banks is more than that of the Commercial banks or any other Banks. The high fluctuations in the marginal costs of individual selected bank(s) is/are observed in this study, therefore average cost principle as a yardstick of performance evaluation is considered. Moreover, the banks operating in imperfect market conditions and uncertainty regarding decision making variables, it would be more appropriate to use the average cost analysis rather than marginal cost analysis.

Graph 8.06 - is showing the average cost curve for 11 years of The Kalupur Commercial Bank from the year 1986-87 to 1996-97. The average cost curve is falling continuously from the year 1987-88 to till the year 1991-92 where the size of deposits is nearly Rs. 12000 lacs. Then for the year 1992-93, it became steady and then during 1993-94 it sharply reduced and for the year 1994-95 it again increased. If the fluctuation of 1993-94 is avoided then the average cost is remaining more or less constant for four years upto the year 1994-95 but then it started increasing.

The rise in average cost curve indicates that the dis-economies have started from the level of deposits of Rs. 33000 lacs onwards. So it can be concluded that for The Kalupur Commercial Bank, in existing circumstances, the size of deposits level amounting to Rs. 33000 lacs is optimum.

Graph 8.07 is showing the average cost curve for The Rajkot Nagrik Bank for 11 years from 1986-87 to 1996-97. From the year 1986-87 itself the average cost curve shows a steady increase in the average cost. It has sharply increased upto the year 1989-90 but then it is declining sharply till the year 1991-92, again there is a sharp increase in the year 1992-93. In totality, The Rajkot Nagrik Bank's average cost during the 11 years are rising but rising at a very slow rate. It is difficult to conclude the optimum level of deposits as 11

GRAPH 8.06

AVERAGE COST CURVE OF THE KALUPUR.BANK OF THE YEARS 1986-87TO 1996-97.

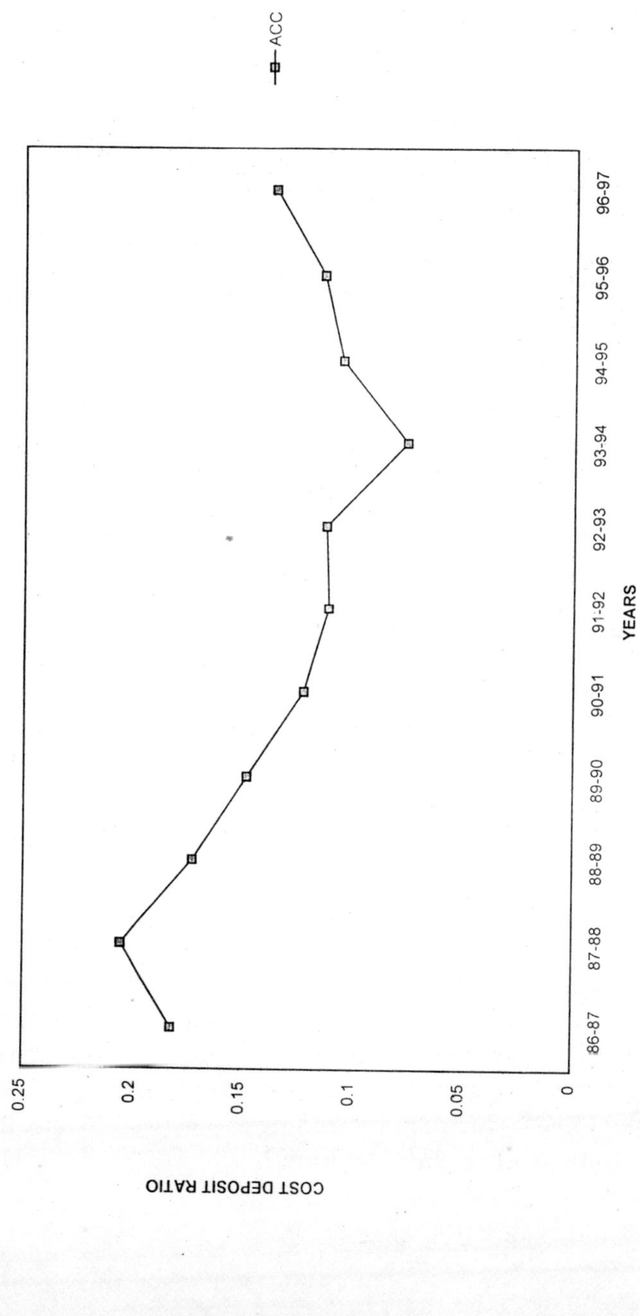

GRAPH 8.07

AVERAGE COST CURVE OF THE RAJKOT NAGARIK BANKS OF THE YEAR 1986-87 TO 1996-97.

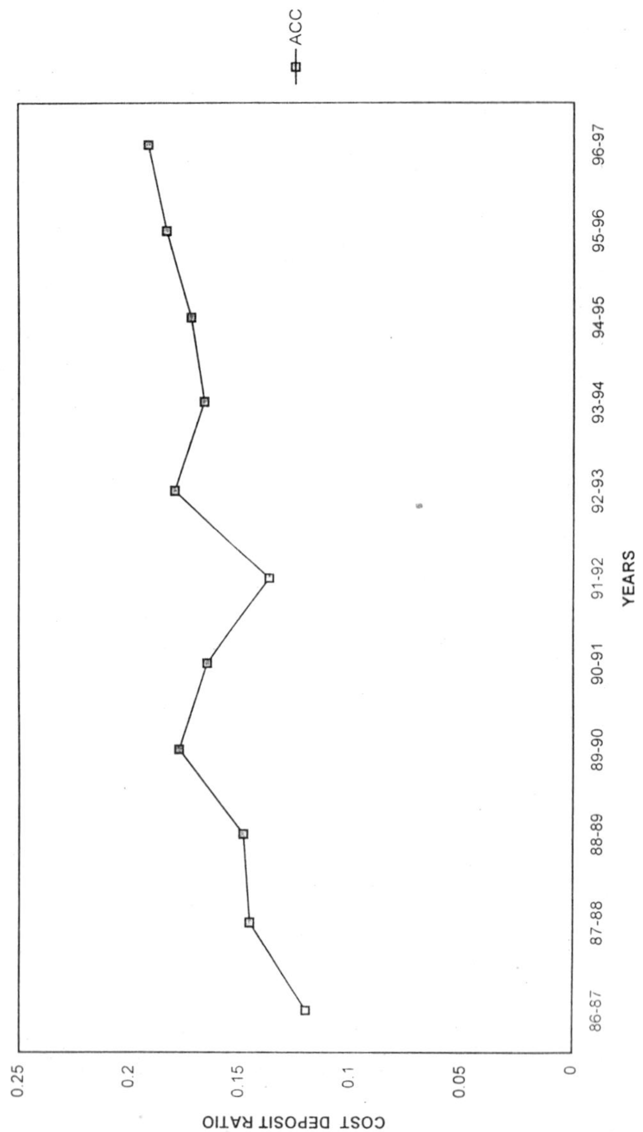

years is a short run for The Rajkot Nagrik Bank for concluding the optimum level of deposits.

Graph 8.08 is showing thc average cost curve for 11 years of The Anyonya Sahayakari Bank for the year 1986-87 to 1996-97. The average cost curve of this bank is placed on the higher side i.e. for all the 11 years it is ranging between 12 to 13 per cent of total deposits it means that the total cost as compared to total deposits is 12 to 13 per cent with exception of the year 1991-92 when it reduced to even less than 10 per cent. It can be concluded from the average cost curve that The Anyonya Sahayakari Bank can continue to increase its size of deposits even for more than Rs. 10000 lacs which was in the year 1996-97 as the curve is stable.

Graph 8.09 is showing the average cost curve for 11 years of The Surat People's Bank i.e. for the year 1986-87 to 1996-97. There is an unusual sharp rise in the year 1987-88 in the average cost from 8 per cent of total deposits to more than 13 per cent of total deposits. Then it declined during the year 1988-89 to 12 per cent. From the year 1991-92 it is more or less stable till the year 1996-97 moving around the 14 per cent of total deposits. Here also it can be concluded that The Surat People's Bank has yet to obtain the optimum level for size of deposits, it can increase the deposits for more than Rs.28000 lacs which were for the year 1996-97.

Graph 8.10 is showing the average cost curve for 11 years of The Natpur Co-operative Bank from the year 1986-87 to 1996-97. There is an uneven sharp rise of average cost from less than 8 per cent in the year 1986-87 to nearly 14 per cent for the year 1987-88. It is continuously declining till the year 1991-92 and reached to the lowest at 9 per cent of total deposits. Once again it is showing sharp increase during the year 1992-93, and reaching at the peak of nearly 13 per cent, then again the steady decline is observed till the year 1995-96 to the 10 per cent of total deposits. Overall fluctuations in the average cost of this bank are between 10 and 13 per

GRAPH 8.08

AVERAGE COST CURVE OF THE ANONYA SAHAYAKARI BANK OF THE YEAR 1986-87 TO 1996-97.

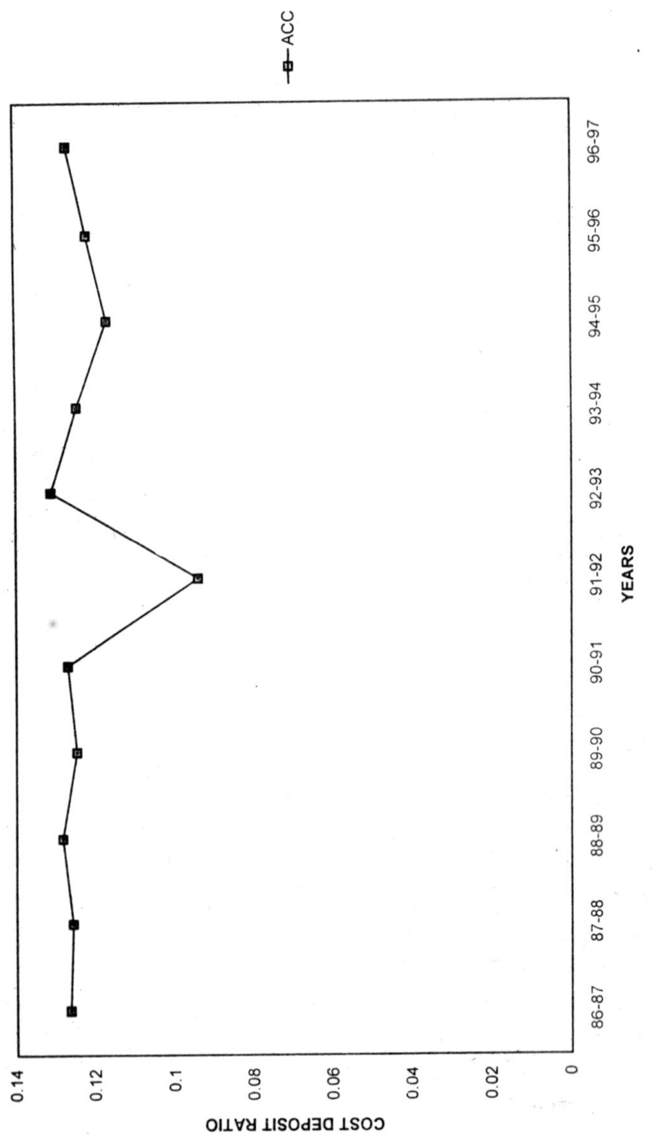

GRAPH 8.09

AVERAGE COST CURVE OF THE SURAT PEOPLE'S BANK OF THE YEAR 1986-87 TO 1996-97.

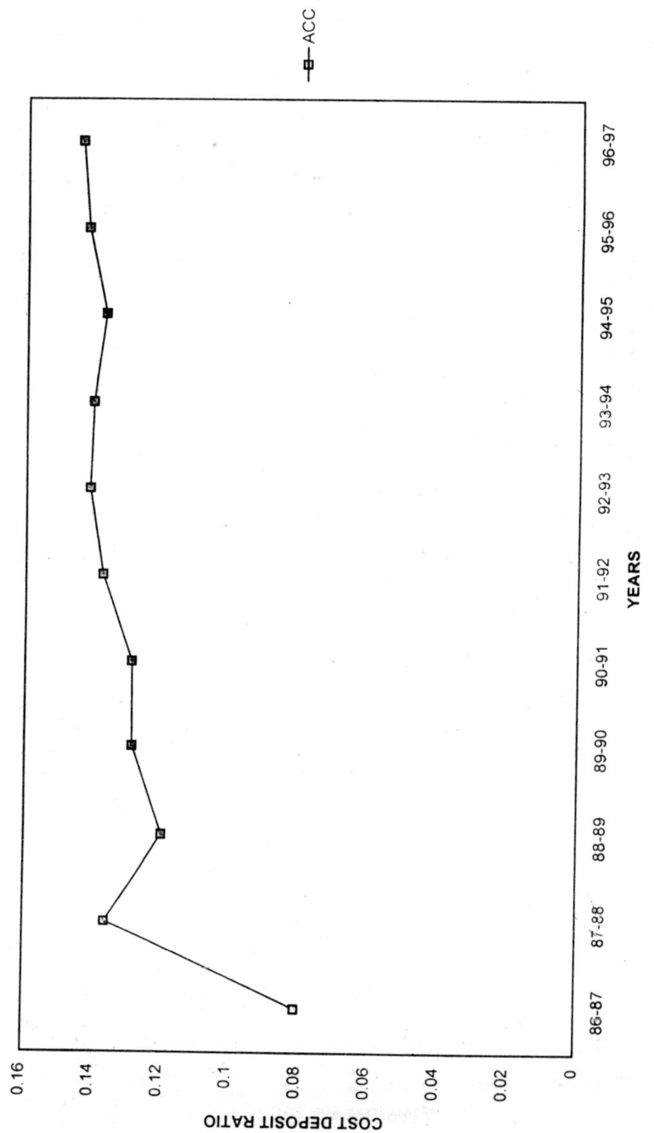

GRAPH 8.10

AVERAGE COST CURVE OF THE NATPUR BANKS OF THE YEAR 1986-87 TO 1996-97.

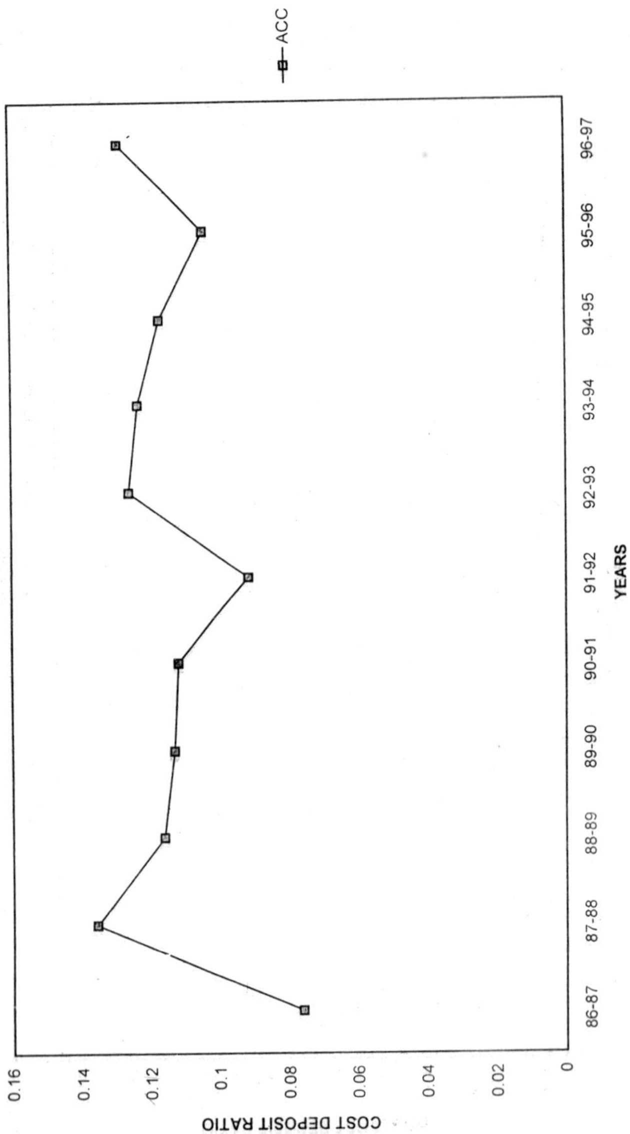

cent during the ten years but still it is hopeful for The Natpur Co-operative Bank to increase its deposits for more than Rs. 6500 lacs which are for the year 1996-97.

Graph 8.11 is showing the average cost curve for 11 years of The Anand Mercantile Bank from the year 1986-87 to 1996-97. Eventually it is the only bank which is showing the sharp decline in the average cost from 20 per cent to 10 per cent i.e. 50 per cent decline in the average cost of deposits during the year 1987-88 which is normally not observed by any other banks in the selected sample banks but then more or less it remained between 10 and 15 per cent for remaining years with the exception of sudden rise of 16 per cent during the year 1992-93 then again reduced sharply to 12 per cent in the year 1993-94, but the wide fluctuations in the average cost are observed.

Graph 8.12 is showing the average cost curve for 11 years of The Dahod Urban Co-operative Banks from the year 1986-87 to 1996-97. The average cost curve of this bank is placed at the higher position in the graph like The Anyonya Sahayakari Bank. More or less the average cost of this Bank is ranging between 14 to 16 per cent of the total deposits. The exceptional decline is during the year 1991-92 when it is nearly lowest at 12.25 per cent but then exceptional rise is observed during the year 1992-93 i.e. increased sharply to 17 per cent, average cost of deposits. Till the year 1996-97 it is showing decline at very slow rate at 15 per cent of total cost. Here also it can be concluded that there is a possibility to increase the deposits for more than Rs.6500 lacs.

Graph 8.13 is showing the average cost curve for 11 years of The Sarvodaya Nagrik Bank from the year 1986-87 to 1996-97. The average cost is around 15 per cent for five years starting from 1986-87 to 1990-91 but then in the year 1991-92 there is a marginal decline in the average cost nearly to 13 per cent but then for two consecutive years i.e. 1992-93 and 1993-94 there is a continuous increase in the average cost.

GRAPH 8.11

AVERAGE COST CURVE OF THE ANAND MERCANTILE BANK OF THE YEAR 1986-87 TO 1996-97.

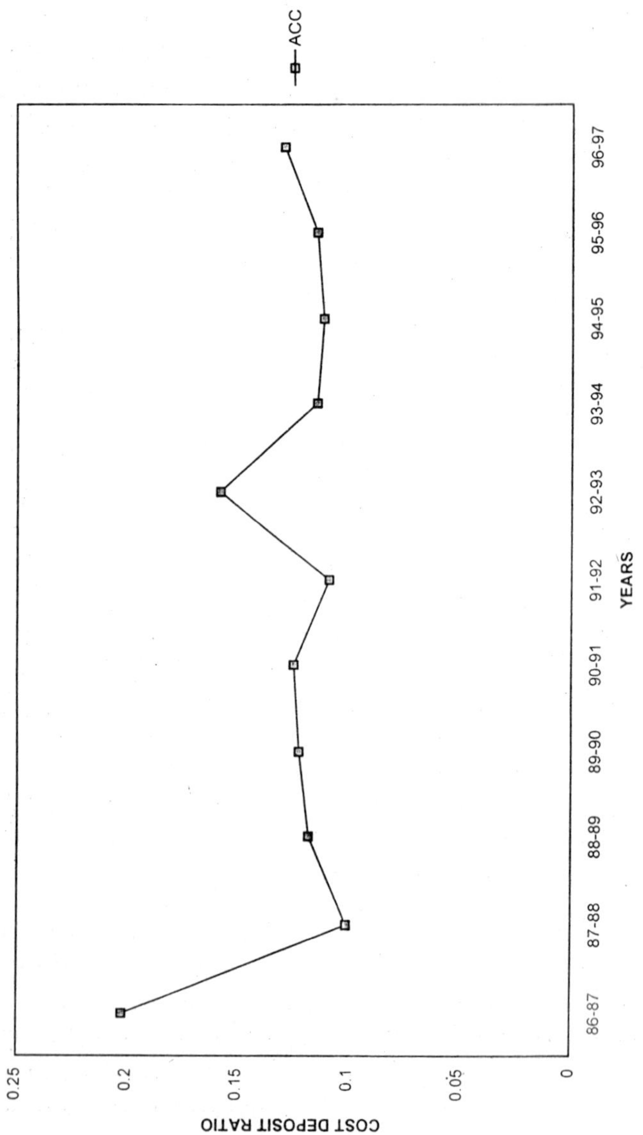

GRAPH 8.12

AVERAGE COST CURVE OF THE DAHOD URBAN BANK. OF THE YEAR 1986-87 TO 1996-97.

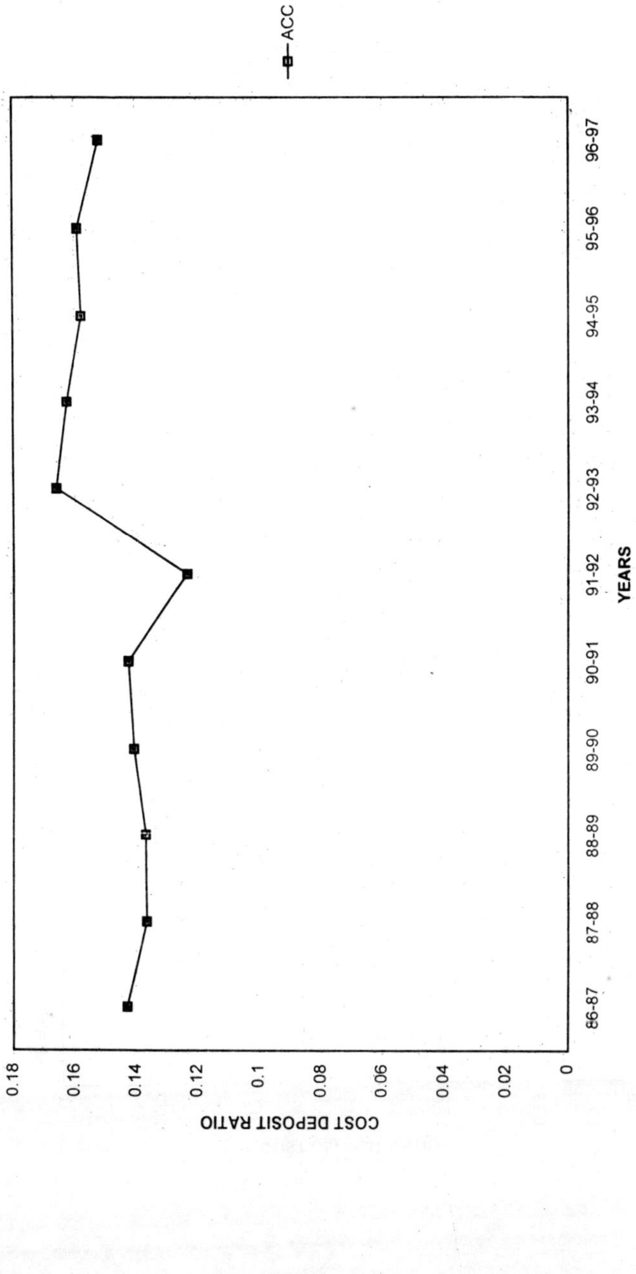

GRAPH 8.13

AVERAGE COST CURVE OF THE SARVODAYA BANK OF THE YEAR 1986-87 TO 1996-97.

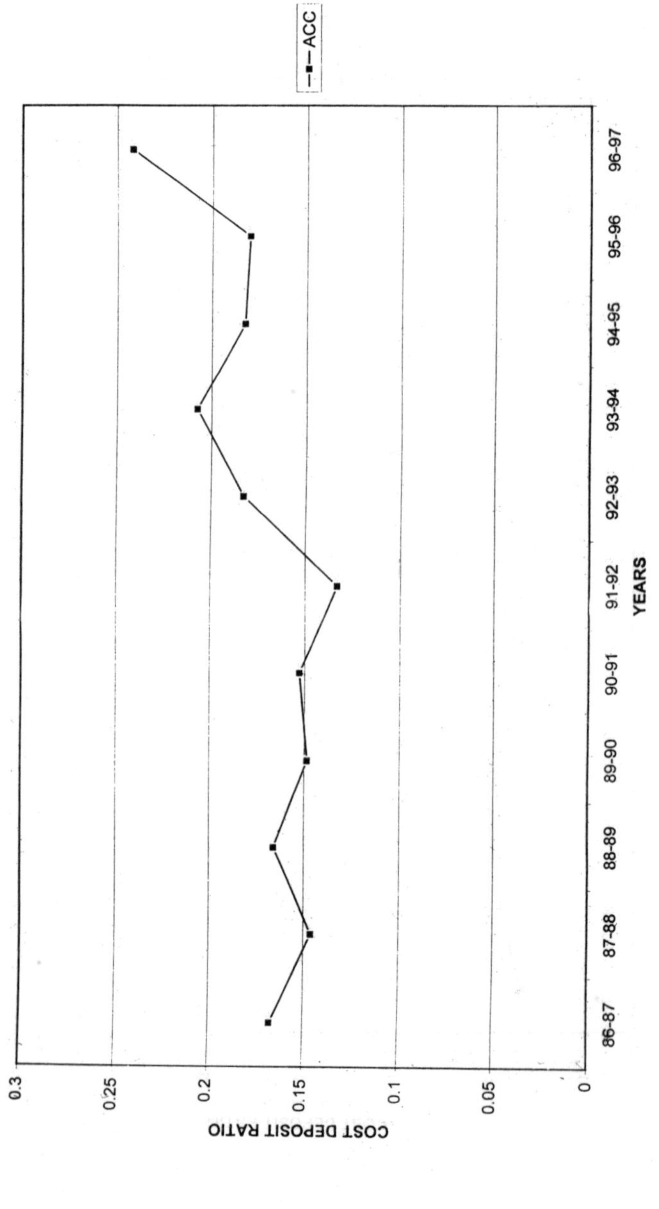

Similarly the sharp increase is observed during the year 1996-97 i.e. nearly to the peak of 25 per cent. Which is highest in the ten years of study. The overall average cost curve of The Sarvodaya Nagrik Bank is rising during 11 years but comparatively the total deposits of this bank is just Rs.1700 lacs which is the lowest one in the selected ten banks i.e. the lowest over deposits and higher average cost is alarming situation for this bank that there is something wrong with the management control.

Graph 8.14 is showing the average cost curve for 11 years of The Baroda People's Bank from the year 1986-87 to 1996-97. The average cost of this bank declines from 19 per cent to 12 per cent during the year 1987-88 then it became stable till the year 1991-92. The sharp rise is observed during the year 1992-93 in the average cost i.e. reached at the peak of nearly 27 per cent of the total deposits as total deposits are falling from Rs.2817 lacs in the year 1992-93 to Rs. 1954 lacs in the year 1993-94. This decline in total deposits is unusual during the ten years of study. As a matter of fact, the fixed cost never decline due to decline in business, hence the total cost unusually increased during the year 1993-94. But again it has sharply declined during the year 1994-95 and reached to 15 per cent. Similarly the reason is the total deposits have sharply increased from Rs. 1954 lacs in the year 1993-94 to Rs. 3570 lacs in the year 1994-95. So the sharp increase in deposits i.e. nearly doubled, has sharply reduced the average cost nearly half way, except this unusual situation the average cost of this bank has ranged between 10 and 15 per cent of total deposits. So it can be concluded that there is possibility of reducing the average cost by increasing the volume of deposits.

Graph 8.15 is showing the average cost curve for 11 years of The Sardar Bhiladwala Bank from the year 1986-87 to 1996-97. The average cost curve is more or less observed between 10 and 12 per cent during the 11 years. With the

GRAPH 8.14

AVERAGE COST CURVE OF THE BARODA PEOPLE'S BANKS OF THE YEAR 1986-87 TO 1996-97.

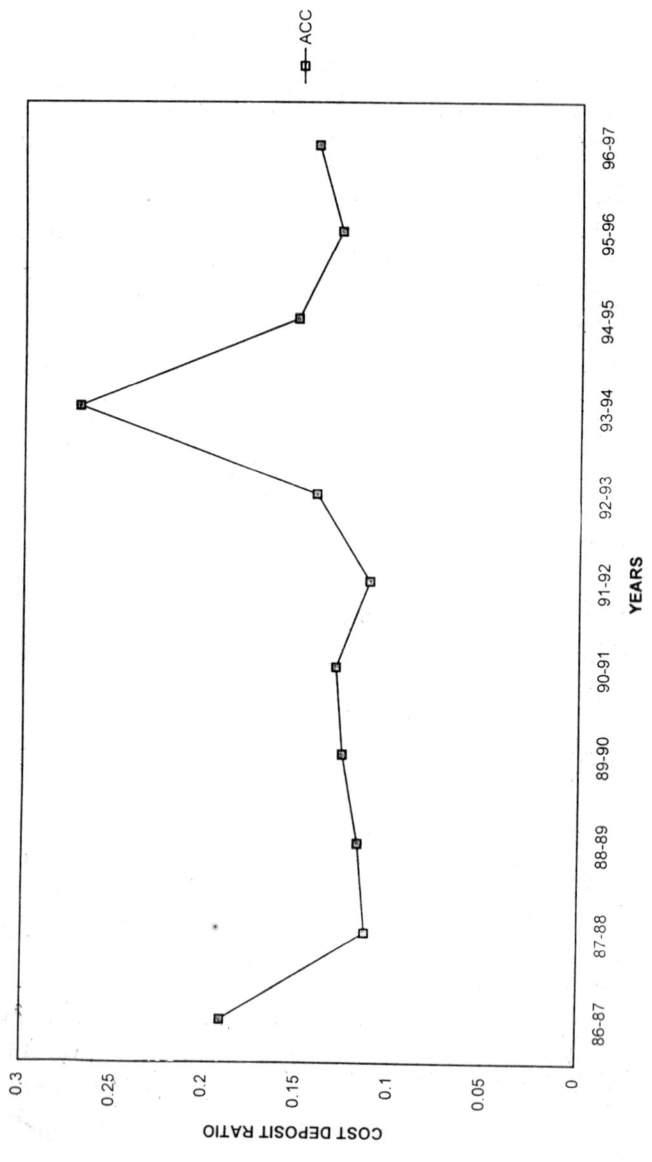

GRAPH 8.15

AVERAGE COST CURVE OF THE SARDAR BHILADWALA BANK OF THE YEAR 1986-87 TO 1996-97.

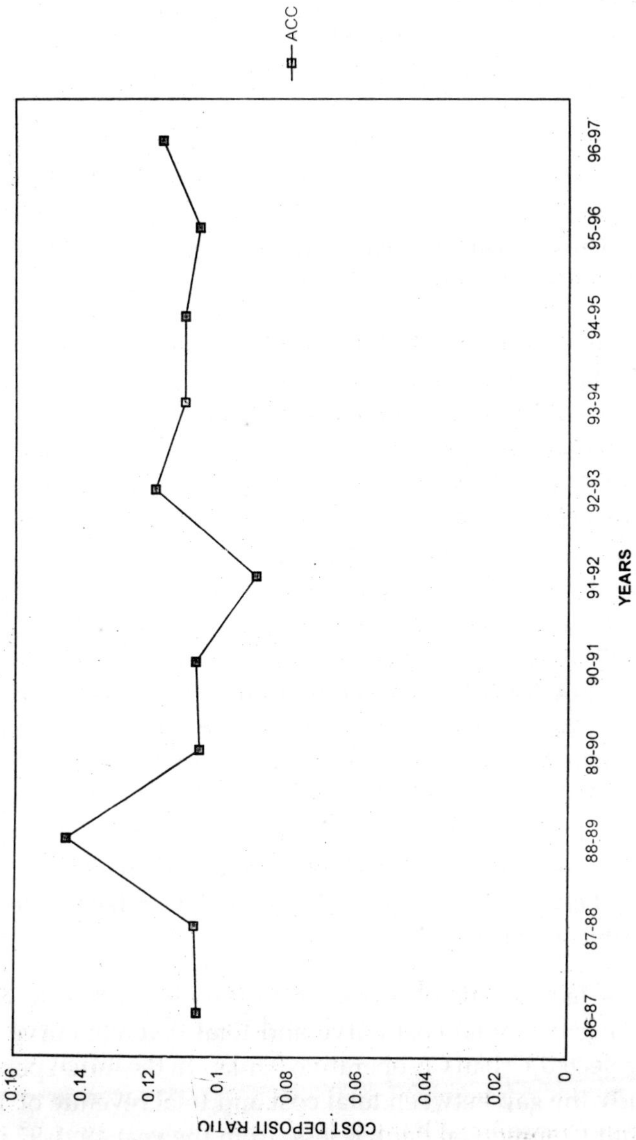

exception for the year 1988-89 it has increased from 10.8 per cent to 14.2 per cent but here the reason for increase is not decline in total deposits because total deposits have increased from Rs. 3000 lacs to Rs. 3500 lacs during the year 1988-89. So the reason for increase in average cost is other than deposits. Similarly it sharply reduced again to 10.5 per cent during the year 1889-90 and remained stable in the year 1990-91. There is a sharp increase during the year 1992-93 to 12 per cent. The overall average cost curve looked stable between 10 and 12 per cent during 11 years. Hence, there is a scope for this bank to reduce its average cost by increasing in the volume of deposits for more than Rs. 11000 lacs.

Analysis of Total Cost and Total Revenue Curve

Earlier in the discussion of analysis of average cost to total deposits the establishment of selected Urban Co-operative Banks have been mentioned. No bank is established after the year 1977. The bank like The Anyonya Sahayakari Bank, the year of establishment is 1889. In the initial year from the establishment, amount of fixed costs is higher. Obviously the total cost will be higher in comparison to the size of deposits. The Sarvodaya Nagrik Bank is established in the year 1977 since then the ten years may be considered to cover the fixed overheads for reaching to the Break Even Level of deposits, therefore the question doesn't arise for the remaining banks which were established earlier to this bank. So it is assumed that all selected Urban Co-operative Banks have attained the Break Even Point. Therefore every increase in total deposits will bring the additional spread. In other words, the gap between total cost and total revenue will be widened year after the years.

The fact can be observed from the Graph 8.16 to 8.25 regarding the total cost curve and total revenue curve for each selected Urban Co-operative Banks. In the initial period of study the gap between total cost and total revenue of The Kalupur Commercial Bank is less, from the year 1991-92 it is continuously widening and the highest gap is observed for the year 1996-97; the spread for the year 1996-97 Rs. 2531 lacs i.e. the highest during the ten years. Similarly for The Rajkot Nagrik Bank, the gap between total cost and total revenue is steadily increasing from the year 1991-92 and it is highest for the year 1996-97 i.e. Rs. 3448 lacs. The case of The Anyonya Sahayakari Bank is not different, this bank is also having minimal gap between total cost and total revenue till the year 1991-92 and then it has been observed that the gap between total cost and total revenue is almost uniform, for the year 1996-97 the spread is Rs. 395 lacs. For The Surat People's Bank, the gap between total cost and total revenue is continuously increasing from 1987-88 itself, in no year it has been reduced like The Rajkot Nagrik Bank and The Kalupur Commercial Bank. The gap is showing the healthy sign and the progress of The Surat People's Bank, the growth in the spread is from Rs. 421 lacs to Rs. 2586 lacs for the year 1987-88 and the year 1996-97 respectively. In case of The Natpur Co-operative Bank, the gap between total cost and total revenue is fluctuating but both the curves are showing the gap which may be concluded as uniform from the year 1991-92, the growth rate in spread is very low during the year 1987-88 to 1991-92. For the year 1996-97, the gap between total cost and total revenue is Rs. 376 lacs. Similar is the case of The Anand Mercantile Bank, the gap between total cost and total revenue is narrow throughout the study period of ten years with exception for the year 1993-94 The spread for the year 1996-97 is Rs. 262 lacs. For Dahod Urban Co-operative Bank and The Sarvodaya Nagrik Bank's gap between total cost and total revenue is observed marginal throughout the ten years, i.e. Rs. 319 lacs and Rs. 228 lacs for the year 1996-97 respectively. The Baroda People's Bank's gap between total cost and total revenue is marginal in the year 1987-88 but gradually it is increasing till the year 1992-93; for the year 1993-94 there is a highest gap between total cost and total revenue curve then onwards it has started narrowing down. The spread for the year 1996-97 is Rs. 346 lacs. The Sardar

Bhiladwala Bank's gap between total cost and total revenue curve is narrow for the year 1987-88 and ideally there is a constant increase in the gap between total cost and total revenue curve for all the ten years. There is a highest gap in the year 1996-97 amounting to Rs. 1070 lacs.

Average Cost as Percentage of Average Deposits

It will be interesting to note the major determinants of the total cost of deposits of selected Urban Co-operative Banks. For this purpose, costs sheet with actual values for each bank for all ten years is prepared then the ratio between each cost element and average total deposits is calculated. Thereafter ratios converted into the cost per element for per Rs. 100 of total deposits. In other words, cost per element as a percentage of average deposits is calculated for each bank selected for all ten years. Further the average of each element of cost for ten years is calculated to derive the conclusions about the behaviour of average cost of each element of cost. Table 8.10 reflects the results of above mentioned calculations. All ten columns of individual selected Urban Co-operative Banks reveal the average cost as a percentage of average total deposits for the element of variable cost, fixed cost, total cost, the revenue and the profit.

For all ten selected banks, the major determinant of total cost is a variable cost component i.e. interest paid on deposits. Here it is observed that the interest paid on deposits by The Sarvodaya Nagrik Bank is highest i.e.13.64 per cent whereas The Sardar Bhiladwala Bank has lowest variable cost at 8.78 per cent of deposits. The second lowest interest paying bank is The Surat People's Bank. It has the interest cost at 8.88 per cent of deposits whereas remaining banks are ranging between 10 to 12 per cent of total deposits. In case of Salaries and Allowances, the lowest cost is incurred by The Anand Mercantile Bank is at 1.16 per cent of deposits whereas again The Sarvodaya Nagrik Bank pays the highest salaries as a percentage of deposits. Interest and Salaries are having highest

GRAPH 8.16

TOTAL COST, TOTAL REVENUE CURVE OF THE KALUPUR BANK

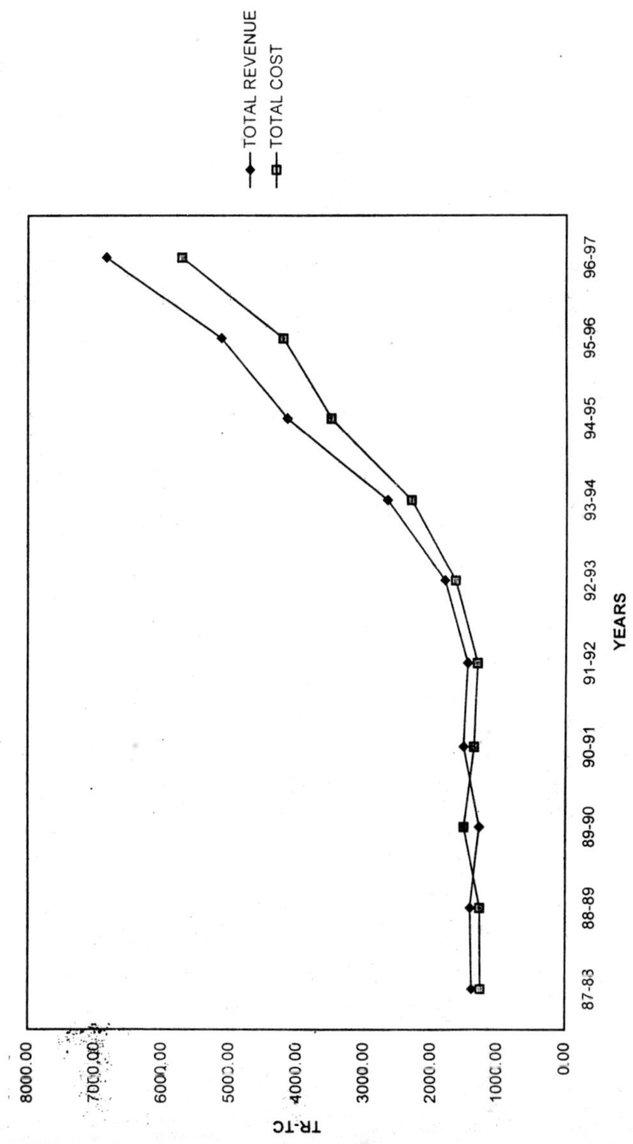

GRAPH 8.17

TOTAL COST, TOTAL REVENUE CURVE OF THE RAJKOT NAGARIK BANK.

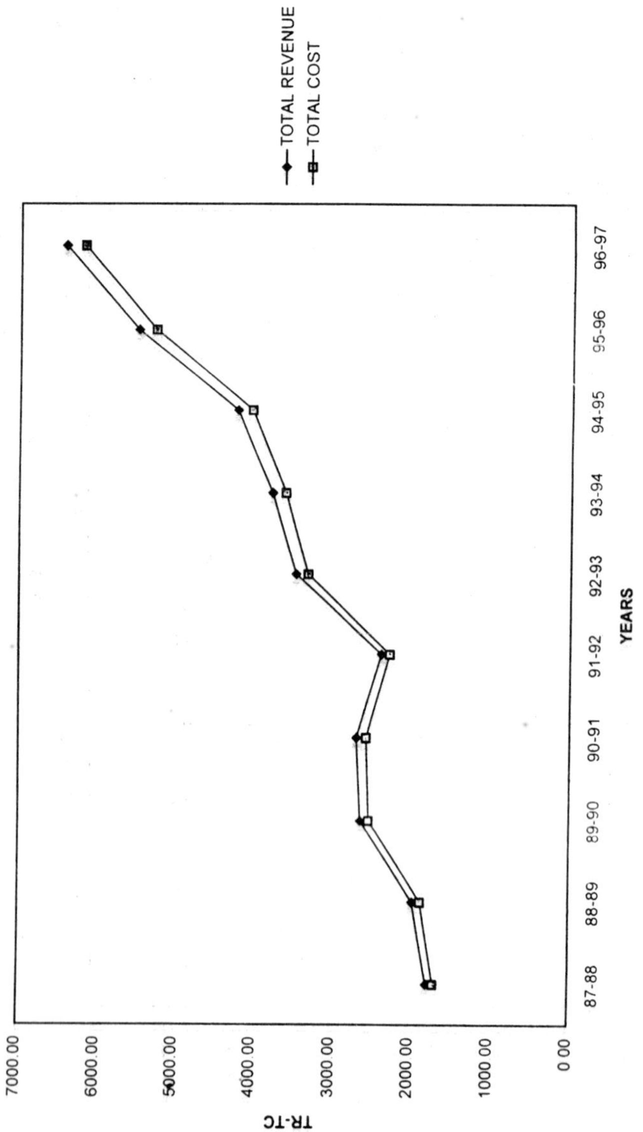

GRAPH 8.18

TOTAL COST, TOTAL REVENUE CURVE OF THE ANYONYA SAHAKARI BANK.

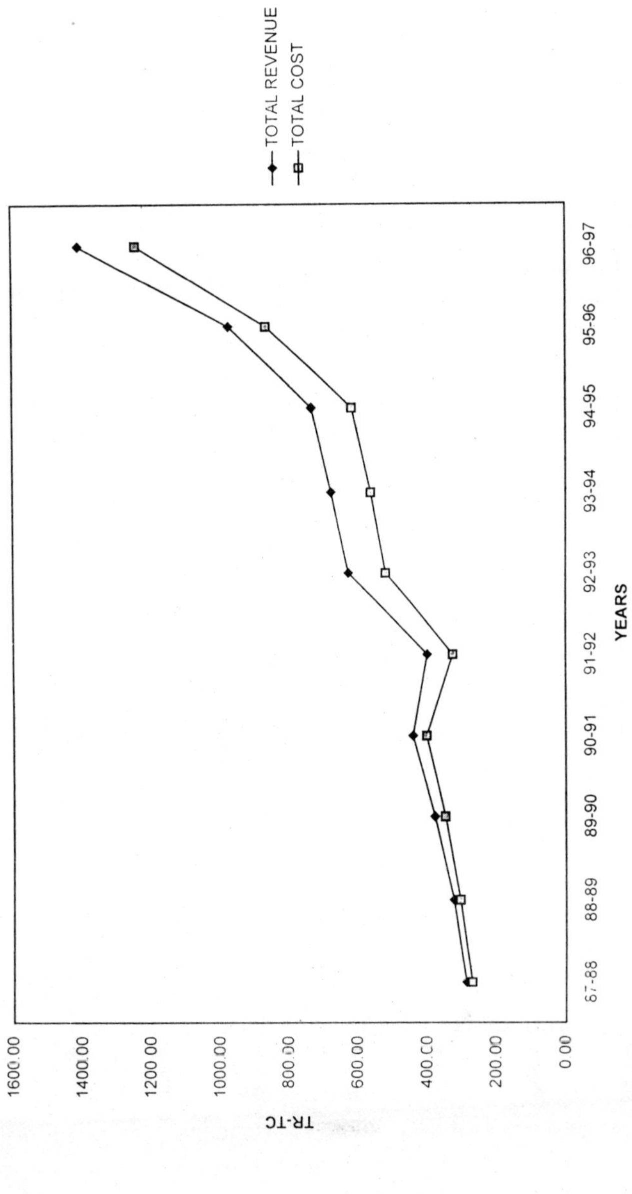

GRAPH 8.19

TOTAL COST, TOTAL REVENUE CURVE OF THE SURAT PEOPLE'S BANK

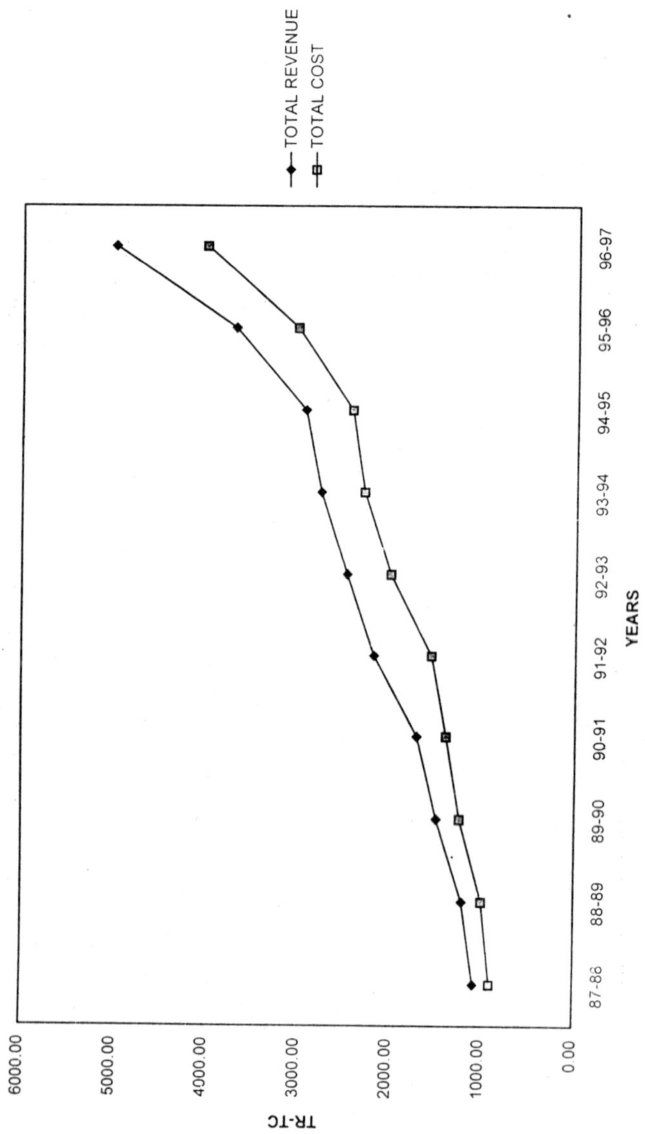

GRAPH 8.20

TOTAL COST, TOTAL REVENUE CURVE OF THE NATPUR BANK

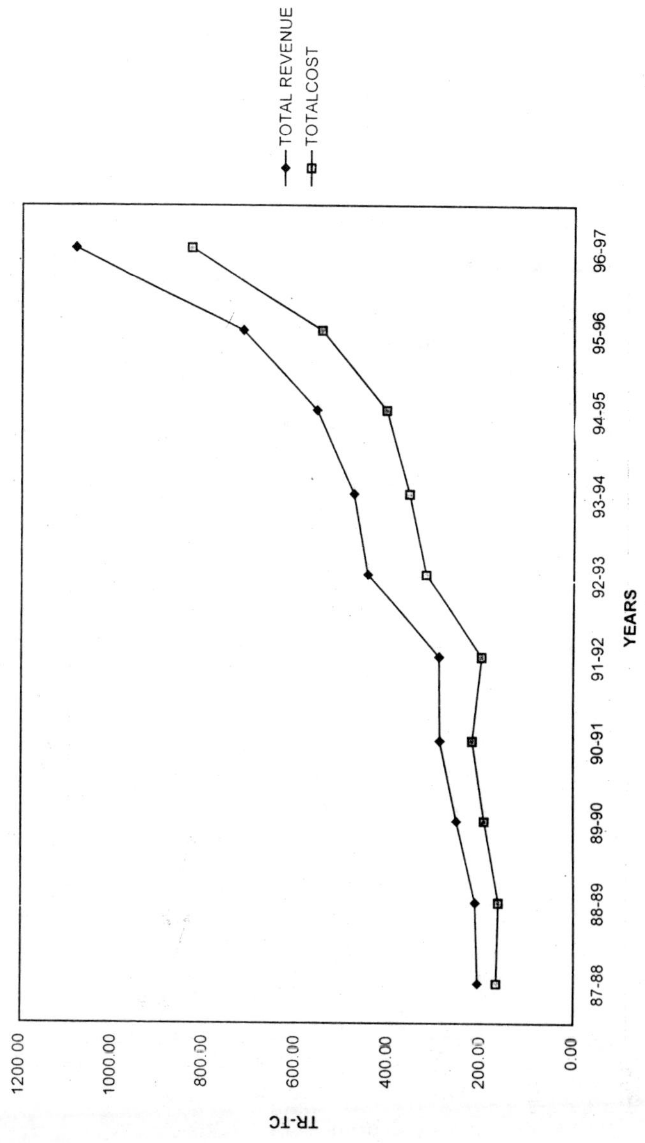

GRAPH 8.21

TOTAL COST, TOTAL REVENUE CURVE OF THE ANAND MERCANTILE BANK

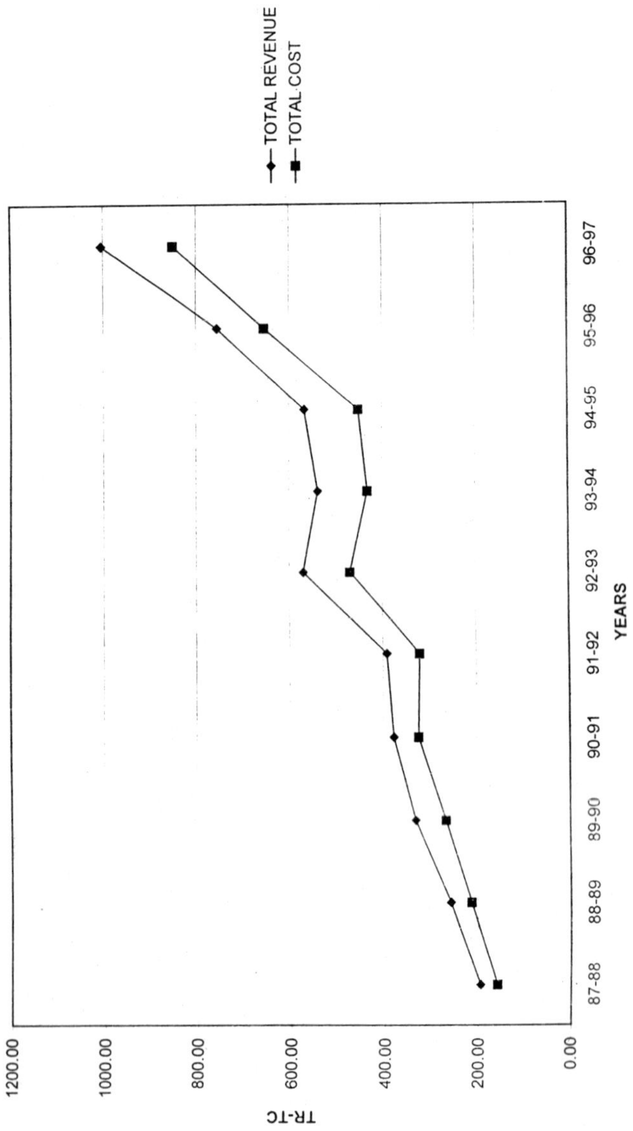

GRAPH 8.22

TOTAL COST, TOTAL REVENUE CURVE OF THE DAHOD URBAN BANK

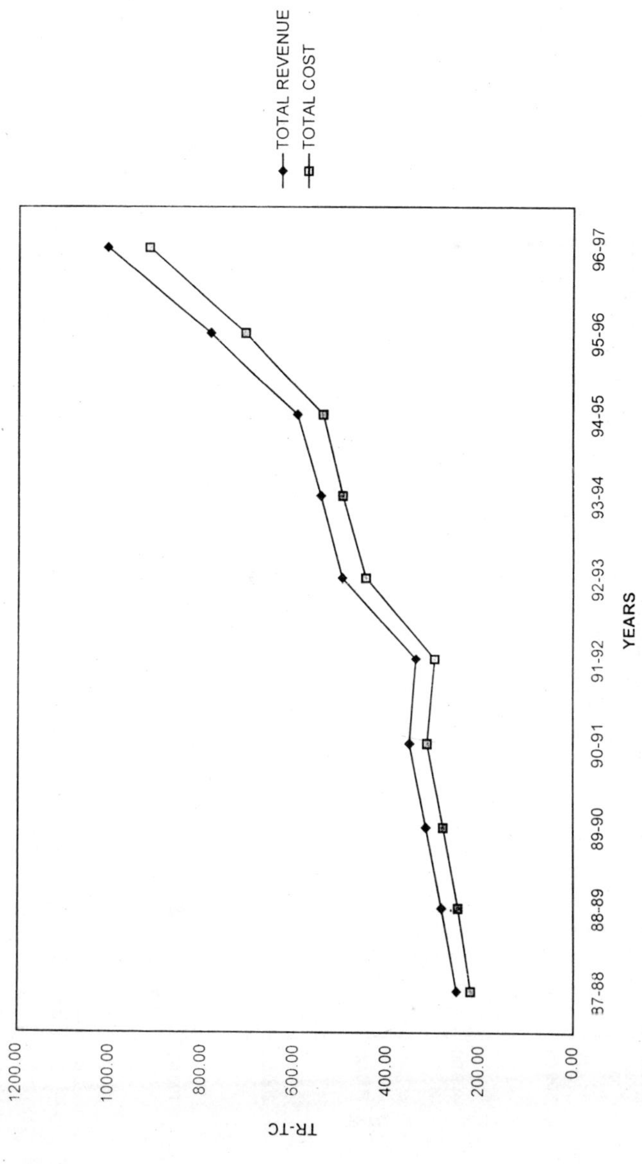

GRAPH 8.23

TOTAL COST, TOTAL REVENUE CURVE OF THE SARVODAYA NAGARIK BANK.

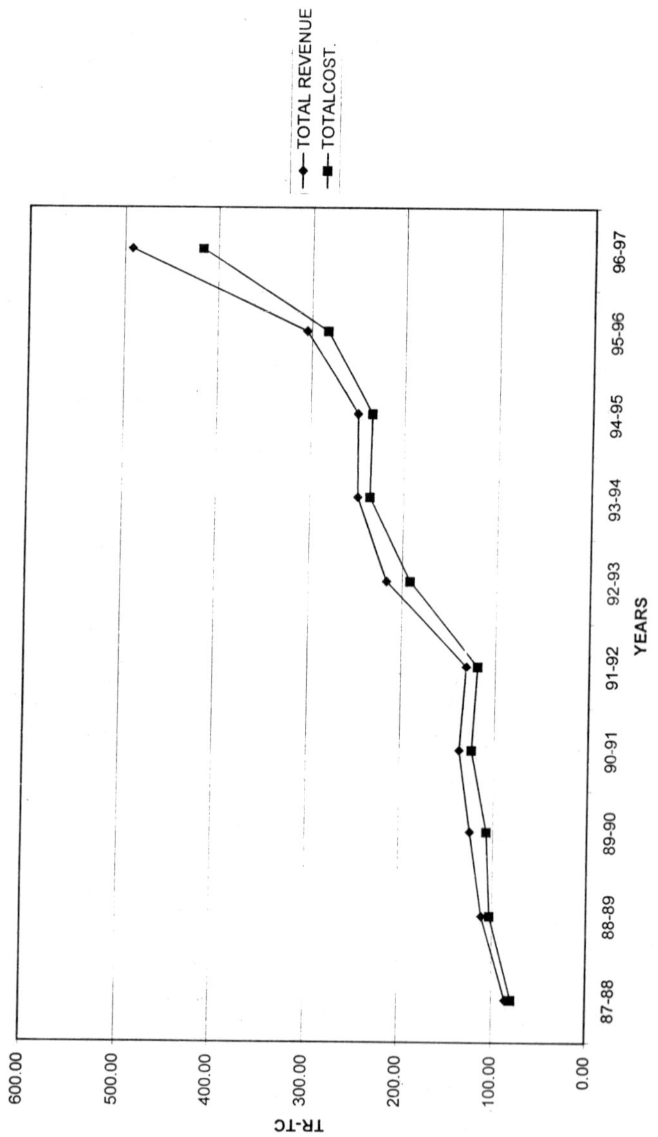

GRAPH 8.24

TOTAL COST TOTAL REVENUE CURVE OF THE BARODA PEOPLE'S BANK.

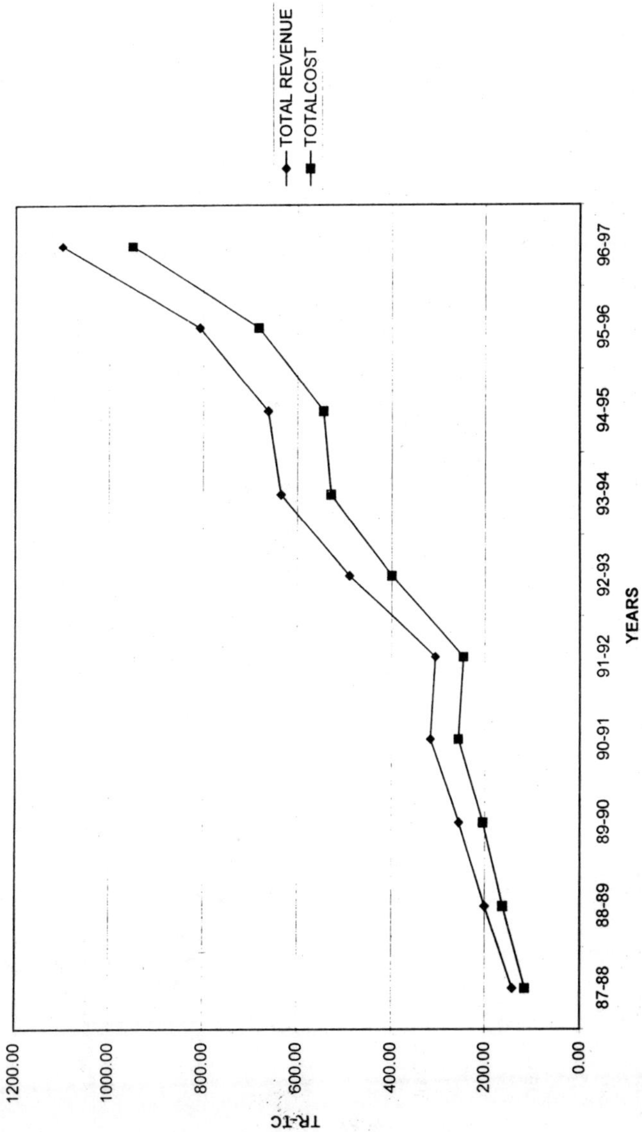

GRAPH 8.25

TOTAL COST TOTAL REVENUE CURVE OF THE SARDAR BHILADWALA BANK

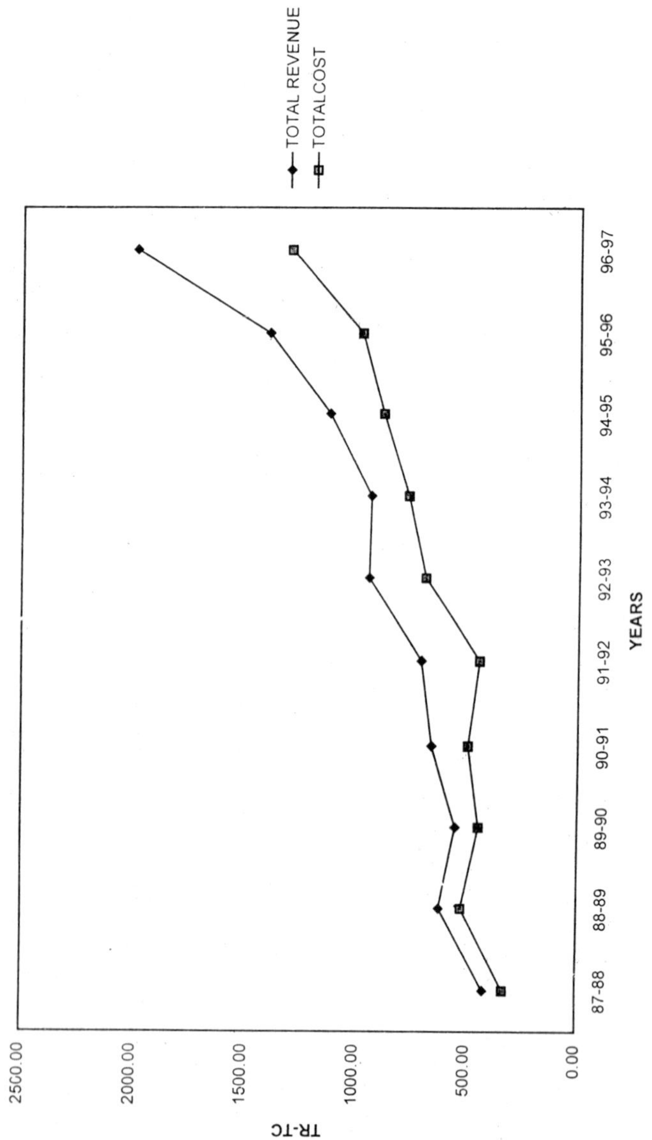

share in total cost for both of them, The Sarvodaya Nagrik Bank is on the top. So obviously it must reduce its interest as well as the salary cost. For reduction in interest, the technique of deposit mix can be utilised. The Sarvodaya Nagrik Bank should attract more current and saving deposits. Similar is the case of The Baroda People's Bank which is incurring nearly 12 per cent interest cost on deposits and also requires to adopt the deposit mix by attracting more current and saving deposits so that interest cost can be minimised. The reasonable salaries and allowances cost is incurred by The Kalupur Commercial Bank, The Rajkot Nagrik Bank, The Natpur Co-operative Bank and The Dahod Urban Bank but The Sardar Bhiladwala Bank, The Surat People's Bank, The Anyonya Sahayakari Bank and The Sarvodaya Nagrik Bank should reduce their cost and salaries which can be possible by introducing the computer services in banking activities. So increase in deposits will not increase the staff and consequently the salaries and allowances.

In case of printing and stationery, highest expenses is incurred by The Baroda People's Bank (0.25 per cent of the deposits); the second highest position is attained by The Anand Mercantile Bank with 0.19 per cent of deposits. The Rajkot Nagrik Bank have a statewide network of branches, but incurs the lowest expenses on printing and stationery and is successful in controlling the cost of printing and stationery (0.07 per cent of total deposits). The second lowest cost on printing and stationery is incurred by The Anyonya Sahayakari Bank and The Surat People's Bank. In this case, The Anyonya Sahayakri Bank is neither scheduled bank nor has any branch outside Vadodara city whereas The Surat People's Bank being scheduled bank and having its branches outside the Surat city is successful in controlling its expenses on printing and stationery.

Again The Surat People's Bank has the lowest cost on postage and telegram amongst the selected Urban Co-operative

Banks which is just at 0.022 per cent of total deposits. The maximum expenditure on postage and telegrams amongst selected ten Urban Co-operative Banks is incurred by The Sarvodaya Nagrik Bank is at 0.113 per cent of deposits. So this is the third element of cost on which The Sarvodaya Nagrik Bank in incurring the highest cost.

In paying the rent and taxes, the highest cost is incurred by The Baroda People's Bank (0.275 per cent of total deposits). Whereas The Rajkot Nagrik Bank being scheduled bank and having statewide branch network is successful in keeping its cost of rent and taxes lowest at 0.093 per cent of total deposits. The second highest position in paying rent and taxes is attained by The Anyonya Sahayakari Bank having the cost of rent and taxes at 0.024 per cent.

In making provision for depreciation on fixed assets, The Natpur Co-operative Bank is highest at 0.268 per cent of total deposits whereas The Dahod Urban Bank has the lowest provision of depreciation at 0.047 per cent of total deposits. Other three elements of fixed costs like Audit Fees, Directors' Fees and Legal fees, they are very much insignificant as observed from the table. In case of total fixed cost, The Sarvodaya Nagrik Bank has highest at 4.133 per cent of total cost whereas the second highest position is secured by The Baroda People's Bank by incurring 3.036 per cent of total fixed cost. Conversely The Rajkot Nagrik Bank has secured the ideal position by incurring the lowest fixed cost at 1.65 per cent of total deposits which can be considered as remarkable control over the total fixed cost which the other banks fails in controlling the fixed cost.

In case of total cost, The Sarvodaya Nagrik Bank has highest per cent (17.773 per cent of total deposits) and the lowest total cost is incurred by the Sardar Bhiladwala Bank (11.341 percent). The second lowest position in incurring total cost is achieved by The Rajkot Nagrik Bank (11.553 per cent of total deposits).

An interesting relationship is observed in case of total cost and the profit. The Bank incurring lowest cost has the highest profit, incurring higher cost has the lowest profit amongst the selected Urban Co-operative Banks. Following Table 8.16 shows the comparison between total cost and profit of selected Urban Co-operative Banks:

TABLE 8.16

COST PROFIT COMPARISON OF SELECTED URBAN CO-OPERATIVE BANKS

Sr. No.	*Name of the Banks*	*Total Cost as a Percentage of Total Deposits*	*Profit as a Percentage of Total Deposits*
1	The Kalupur Commercial Bank	12.758	2.886
2	The Rajkot Nagrik Bank	11.533	6.664
3	The Anyonya Sahayakari Bank	12.856	2.201
4	The Surat People's Bank	11.646	6.027
5	The Natpur Co-operative Bank	11.997	4.540
6	The Anand Mercantile Bank	13.088	2.955
7	The Dahod Urban Bank	13.095	4.660
8	The Sarvodaya Nagrik Bank	17.773	2.886
9	The Baroda People's Bank	15.019	4.198
10	The Sardar Bhiladwala Bank	11.341	4.762

A Significant lower total cost is 11.341 per cent and 11.533 per cent of The Sardar Bhiladwala Bank and The Rajkot Nagrik Bank respectively. If we get the third lowest total cost incurring bank then The Surat People's Bank has 11.646 per cent of total cost as a percentage of total deposits. The profit is 6.664 per cent, 6.027 per cent, 4.762 per cent of total deposits are observed with The Rajkot Nagrik Bank, The Surat People's Bank and The Sardar Bhiladwala Bank respectively. So it can be concluded that lowering the cost will increase the profit.

Standard Cost Introduced

A standard cost has been defined by the Chartered Institute of Management Accountants, London as, "A pre-determined calculations of how much costs should be under the specified working conditions."

Eric L. Kohler has defined the standard costs as, "A standard cost is a forecast or pre-determination of what actual costs should be under projected conditions, serving as a cost control and as a measure of production efficiency or standard of comparison when ultimately aligned against the actual costs. It furnishes a medium by which the effectiveness of current results can be measured and the responsibility for deviation can be placed."

Standard cost is a very important cost control technique. It is important to determine what a product should cost. If the actual cost is more than the determined cost, then it is a matter to be understood. Standard costing aims at eliminating the waste and increasing efficiency in performance through setting up the standards for production expenses and production performance. A Standard costs system can provide useful information, which cannot be given by an actual or absorbing costs system. When the standard costs are used for the purpose of cost control the technique is known as standard costing. Its application is to measure the variation from actual cost and analysing the causes of variation with a view to maintain maximum efficiency. Standard costing comprises of:

i) Ascertainment of standard cost under each element of cost,

ii) Measurement of actual cost,

iii) Comparison of actual cost with standard cost to find out the variance and

iv) Analysis of variance for the purpose of ascertaining the reasons of variance for taking the appropriate actions wherever necessary so that maximum efficiency may be achieved.

Standard Costs for Leading Banks

This study proposes the first step mentioned above i.e. ascertainment of standard cost. Table 8.17 — has shown the behaviour of average cost as a percentage of average total deposits. For all ten selected Urban Co-operative Banks the cost incurred on each element of costs as a percentage of total deposits is calculated and presented in the table which is discussed earlier in this chapter. The lowest cost incurred on each element of costs is assumed as the standard cost for such element. Following standard costs for each element of cost are suggested:

TABLE 8.17

STANDERDISED COSTING FORMAT FOR ELEMENT OF TOTAL COST

Sr. No.	*Element of Costs*	*Per cent*
1	Interest paid as a variable cost	8.779
2	Salaries and allowances	1.335
3	Printing and stationery	0.070
4	Postage and telegrams	0.022
5	Rent and taxes	0.093
6	Depreciation	0.096
7	Audit fees	0.002
8	Directors' fees	0.001
9	Legal fees	0.002
10	Total fixed cost	1.621
11	Total cost	10.4

In ascertainment of standard cost the banks having deposits less than Rs. 10000 lacs for the year 1996-97 are not considered because above mentioned standard costs for each element of costs are lowest averages for ten banks and for ten years. These lowest averages of each element of costs observed lowest with The Kalupur Commercial Bank, The Rajkot Nagrik Bank, The Surat People's Bank and The Sardar Bhiladwala Bank. Out of above-mentioned banks The Kalupur Commercial Bank, The Rajkot Nagrik Bank and The Surat People's Bank are scheduled banks. All above mentioned four banks had mobilise the deposits for more than Rs. 10000 lacs during the year 1996-97. Hence the above mentioned standard costs would be suitable for the banks leading with respect to deposits mobilisation.

Standard Costs Middle or Lower Middle Banks

The Urban Co-operative banks having deposits less than Rs. 10000 lacs are more in number in Gujarat. Fixed Costs pre unit reduces for higher amount of business, but the banks having less deposits face difficulties in covering the fixed costs. Hence there average costs are higher. The standard costs proposed for the banks mobilising less deposits are as under:

TABLE 8.18

STANDERDISED COSTING FORMAT FOR ELEMENT OF TOTAL COST

Sr. No.	*Element of Costs*	*Per cent*
1	Interest paid as a variable cost	10.67
2	Salaries and allowances	1.94
3	Printing and stationery	0.14
4	Postage and telegrams	0.05
5	Rent and taxes	0.15
6	Depreciation	0.15
7	Audit fees	0.01
8	Directors' fees	0.01
9	Legal fees	0.01
10	Total fixed cost	2.46
11	Total cost	13.13

The standard costs mentioned above are the averages of each element of costs for ten years of the study. The averages are always influenced by the extreme values, it means the average takes care of lowest as well highest values in the data. Here in the study the banks selected in the sample has mobilise the deposits even for more than Rs. 30000 lacs i.e. a peack conversely the banks mobilise the deposits even less than Rs. 2000 lacs. Therefore the averages of each element of costs are proposed as the standard costs.

9

Conclusions

Introduction

This chapter presents summary of the preceding chapters including the major findings of the study, policy implication of the findings, general observations and suggestions and areas for further research.

During 1930 to 1975, world at large has witnessed the activism of governments in terms of their development policies and in particular banking policies. In USA, President Ronald Reagan was really responsible for introducing supply side economics replacing demand management policy. Their policy package was an offshoot of market driven economic policy. Later on in UK, Prime Minister Margaret Thatcher also introduced a policy package that defined the role of government. The economic reforms in our country were also designed and implemented in the same direction. The financial sector reforms were basically introduced to make financial sector more competitive and more vibrant. All kinds of regulation in terms of interest rate structure and distribution of credit were largely given up by the government.

Liberalisation in banking industry may be:

i) Increasing competition in banking and easy entry to new financial institutions and improvement in banking services,
ii) Deregulation in advances and investments,

iii) Deregulation in interest rates,
iv) Entire change in RBI control,
v) Transparency in working results (Balance Sheet and Profit and Loss Account).

In the new area, The Urban Co-operative Banks have to change their policy and even attitude drastically. They need to accept one fact that globalisation is a fact and not an option. They have to tighten-up their belt and compete with organised banking sector, private banks and even foreign banks. Their old-age procedures and documentation have to be changed or modified in line with new technology introduced in banking industry.

Banking industry may face the following difficulties due to liberalisation:

i) Accept changes and prepare for the same.
ii) Competition within financial institutions.
iii) Reduction in interest rates in turn reducing income and profit. To avoid this situation, banks have to increase loans and advances by charging less interest.
iv) Increase in non-performing assets due to increase loans and advances.

In the recent past, nearly 37000 Non-Banking Institutions had entered into the financial market. These non banking financial institutions are now competing with the banks in mobilising deposits and lending advances, due to competition more advances at lower rates of interest and flexible terms of lending has created more overdues.

Planning for profit tends to control cost of banking services. Controlled costs will earn more and more profits to the banks. Therefore Urban Co-operative banks will be at ease in fulfilling its social objectives.

Profitability and cost structure of banking industry has been attracting the researchers. In 1993, Amandeep studied profitability of commercial banks using multivariate analysis and concluded that the efficient management of burden plays a major role in deciding the profitability. Inspite of lots of control on few determinants of burden, it is only an efficient management of the burden can significantly improve the profitability.[1] J. Singh in 1993 concluded that profitability largely depends upon cost consciousness.[2]

Rajgopalan opined profitability and productivity that depends on various factors like reduction in costs and recovery of overdues. He also indicated that establishment expenses play a key role in profitability of the banks, therefore to reduce the establishment cost attention should be paid on staffing pattern.[3]

Varsha Varde and Sampat Singh employed the model spread and burden to determine the profitability of commercial banks.[4] The work of Paul Mampilly and Gerg had focussed on cost and profitability of banking industry as a whole rather than individual bank.[5]

The Reserve Bank of India, Indian Banks' Association and National Institution of Bank Management have conducted several studies on cost and profitability of the banks. The study analysed the cost structure and profitability of Indian Commercial Banks for different times of interval. Up-till now we have not observed any significant research in the area of cost and profitability of Urban Co-operative Banks in India. The present work is definitely a first of it's kind in terms of analysis of cost with regard to deposits for Urban Co-operative Banks in India.

In Gujarat, Urban Co-operative Banks have completed their 110 years of banking services and Vadodara and Jambusar are two birthplaces of Urban Co-operative Banks. Now they have become more popular in their working areas. They are successful in achieving their social objectives. The growth of Urban Co-operative Banks is much faster as compared to commercial banks in mobilising the deposits. The Anyonya Sahayakari Bank which had deposits of Rs. 763 in the year 1889 and now has deposits of Rs. 1,26,05,22,258 at the end of the year 1997-98. Average deposits mobilised per bank office is 27 crores in India and Rs. 1617 lacs in Gujarat for the year 1997-98; in terms of membership, advances and reserves they have reached at the peak. The reserves of Urban Co-operative Banks are more than their share capital. The working capital of Urban Co-operative Banks in India for the year 1996-97 is observed at Rs. 34472 crores. The profitability of Urban Co-operative Banks in Gujarat in terms of percentage of working capital is reducing continuously. It was 2.45 per cent in the year 1983-84, 1.78 per cent in the year 1991-92 and 1.67 per cent in the year 1997-98, obviously this may be due to increasing costs.

Regional imbalance in progress of Urban Co-operative Banks in Gujarat is observed. Nearly 55 per cent of the Urban Co-operative Banks are located alone in central Gujarat region which covers 44 per cent of the total urban population of Gujarat State whereas only 1 per cent of the population is covered by Urban Co-operative Banks in Kutch District. However, Urban Co-operative Banks with respect to its objectives, method of working, location and credit policy have been preferred by public as compared to commercial banks.

After nationalisation of 14 major commercial banks, the resources of the banks are used in national development. Every Commercial Banks have to advance 40 per cent to the priority sector and Urban Co-operative Banks have to share 60 per cent of its total advances to the priority sector like Agriculture, Small Scale Industries etc. To satisfy the credit needs, banks require more funds which are obtained in the form of deposits. Because of financial sector reforms, now banks are facing a lot of competition from non banking financial institutions. Banks' deposits are mainly depending upon public savings, it is observed that the gross domestic savings for the year 1998-99 were 23.1 per cent as a percentage of GDP and deposits were 50.5 per cent of the national income. The average annual growth rate of deposits and domestic savings during the period of 1991 to 1995 were 17.54 per cent and 16.74 per cent respectively. Banking sector as a whole might be facing the competition in mobilising the deposits but the deposits mobilised by Urban Co-operative Banks are growing at the rate of 20.2 per cent, 27.1 per cent and 25.3 per cent for the financial years 1995-96, 1996-97 and 1997-98 respectively. The deposits mobilised per bank office in Gujarat during the year 1997-98 were Rs. 1617.60 lacs. Up to the year 1983, deposits mobilised per bank office by Commercial Banks in India were greater than the deposits mobilised per bank office by Urban Co-operative Banks in Gujarat. But from the year 1984 the deposits mobilised by Urban Co-operative banks were more than the deposits mobilised by commercial bank per office. During the ten years of study period the Kalupur commercial bank, and Baroda peoples bank have increased their deposit mobilisation by five times. For rest of the banks the increase in the deposits mobilised were reported to be more than 200 percentage for the decade. The Urban Co-operative banks are facing the problem of deposit mix. The fixed deposits are costlier than current and saving deposits respectively. A share of fixed deposits in total deposits is observed for more than sixty percentage whereas the current deposits are interest free deposits i.e. they are cheaper. The share of current deposits in the total deposit is observed to be less than ten percentage in eight out of ten banks.

Fixed Cost

Kohler has defined the fixed cost as cost for long-term assets, which is already incurred and hence cannot be changed. Fixed cost remains constant regardless of changes in volume. There is an inverse relationship between volume and fixed costs under the present study elements of fixed cost which were reported from the profit and loss account of the final accounts of selected Urban Co-operative Banks. They were Salaries and allowances, Directors fees, Legal fees, Audit fees, Printing and stationery, Rent and taxes, Postage & telegrams, and Depreciation on fixed assets.

Salaries and Allowances

Normally this cost remains stable with an exception in the case of Promotion, Yearly increment, and Revisions in pay scales.

The bank employees salaries may increase because of Expansion of Banks' branches, Increase in banks' services, and Increase in bank business over a period of time.

The salaries and allowances remained stable, therefore they are taken as an element of fixed cost. Highest average salaries are paid by The Surat People's Banks (Rs. 321.54 lacs during ten year). The Share of Salaries and Allowances in the total fixed cost is observed to be the highest (approximately 65-85 per cent of fixed cost). The ratio of salaries to total assets is observed to be between 8 to 25 per cent during the period of 1987-88 and 1996-97. The Average salary cost as a percentage of deposits of The Kalupur Commercial Bank is 1.562 per cent, for The Rajkot Nagrik Bank it is 1.335 per cent, for The Anyonya Sahayakari Bank it is 2.301 per cent, for The Surat Bank it is 2.27 per cent, for The Natpur Co-operative Bank it is 1.38 per cent, for The Anand Mercantile Bank it is 1.16 per cent, for The Dahod Urban Bank it is1.49 per cent, for The Baroda People's Bank it is 2.21 per cent and for The Sardar Bhiladwala Bank it is 2.12 per cent. The highest salaries and allowances were paid by the Sarvodaya Bank (3.6 per cent of total deposits).

Directors Fees

The members of the Board of Urban Co-operative Banks are paid fees or conveyance allowances which formed a cost to the banks. But the Directors' fees as an element of fixed cost forms a negligible part i.e. even less than 1 per cent of fixed cost as observed mostly for all the banks and for all the ten years. The average Directors' fees for ten years as a percentage of deposits for The Rajkot Nagrik Bank is observed to be 0.001 per cent, for The Anyonya Sahayakari Bank it is 0.01 per cent, while for The Anand Mercantile Bank it is 0.07 per cent.

Postage and Telegrams

The expenses on postage and telegrams paid by selected Urban Co-operative Banks are ranging between 1 per cent and 4 per cent of the total fixed cost. The average postage and telegram expenses of ten years as a percentage of deposits for The Kalupur Commercial Bank it is 0.028 per cent, for The Rajkot Nagrik Bank it is 0.05 per cent, for The Anyonya Bank it is 0.03 per cent, for The Surat People's Bank it is 0.03 per cent, for The Natpur Co-operative Bank it is 0.04 per cent, for The Anand Mercantile Bank it is 0.04 per cent, for The Dahod Urban Bank it is 0.03 per cent, for The Baroda People's Bank it is 0.08 per cent, for The Sardar Bhiladwala Bank it is 0.05 per cent whereas The Sarvodaya Nagrik Bank has the highest expenses on postage and telegrams in the selected sample (0.11 percentage).

Rent and Taxes

The rent and taxes are paid by Urban Co-operative Banks for the use of premises to its owner on regular basis The Rajkot Nagarik Bank and The Kalupur Commercial Bank have statewide branch network. At each branch place, these banks may not have their own premises. They hire the premises by paying rent. The share of rent in the total fixed cost for The Kalupur Commercial Banks is observed to be 8 to 10 per cent. The Anyonya Sahayakari Bank paid 10 to 12 per cent of fixed cost for rents and taxes. The average rent and taxes expenses of ten years as a percentage of deposits paid by The Kalupur Commercial Bank is 0.17 per cent, for The Rajkot Nagrik Bank it is 0.09 per cent, for The Anyonya Sahayakari

Bank it is 0.24 per cent, for The Surat People's Bank it is 0.13 per cent, for The Natpur Bank it is 0.13 per cent, for The Anand Mercantile Bank it is 0.11 per cent, for The Dahod Urban Bank it is 0.13 per cent, for The Sarvodaya Nagrik Bank it is 0.15 per cent and for The Sardar Bhiladwala Bank it is 0.1 per cent whereas the highest expenses on rent and taxes are incurred by The Baroda People's Bank (0.28 per cent).

Legal and Audit Fees

Legal and Audit fees are insignificant expenses in total fixed cost. The average Audit fees for the ten years as a percentage of deposits is 0.004 per cent for The Rajkot Nagrik Bank, The Anyonya Sahayakari Bank and The Surat People's Bank. While The Anand Mercantile Bank and The Baroda People's Bank have 0.008 per cent of fixed cost as legal and audit fees. The Kalupur Commercial Bank has reported legal and audit fees to be 0.002 per cent of total fixed cost. The highest legal fees I paid by The Sarvodaya Nagrik Bank and The Baroda People's Bank (0.011 per cent).

The lowest legal and audit fees is paid by The Rajkot Nagrik Bank (0.003 per cent).

Depreciation

Banks can own only premises and furniture required for banking business, and these are the only fixed assets of the Urban Co-operative Banks. Depreciation is provided under Fixed Installment Method or Reducing Balance Method. Depreciation has no influence on volume of banks business. The Kalupur Commercial Bank provides highest depreciation of Rs. 105 lacs in the year 1996-97. Proportion of depreciation in fixed cost is highest of The Natpur Co-operative Banks i.e. nearly 15 per cent and The Dahod Urban Co-operative Banks is on lower side i.e. nearly 2 per cent. The average depreciation of ten years as a percentage of total deposits incurred by The Kalupur Commercial Bank stood at 0.19 per cent, for The Rajkot Nagrik Bank it is 0.1 per cent, for The Anyonya

Sahayakai Bank it is 0.06 per cent, for The Surat People's Bank it is 0.24 per cent, for The Anand Mercantile it is 0.15 per cent, for The Dahod Urban Bank it is 0.05 per cent, for The Sarvodaya Nagrik bank it is 0.09 per cent, for The Baroda People's Bank it is 0.19 per cent and for The Sardar Bhailadwala Bank it is 0.18 per cent. The highest depreciation is provided by the Natpur Co-operative bank (0.244 per cent).

Printing and Stationery

Certain banks like The Kalupur Commercial Bank and The Anand Mercantile Bank have a greater share of printing and stationery in total fixed costs. This cost contributes nearly less than 10 per cent of the fixed cost whereas its proportion to the total cost is observed negligible i.e. even less than 2 per cent. The average printing and stationery expenses for ten years as a percentage of deposits paid by The Kalupur Commercial Bank stood at 0.13 per cent, for The Rajkot Nagrik Bank it is 0.07 per cent. The Anyonya Sahayakari Bank and The Surat People's Bank have reported it to be 0.11 per cent. The Natpur Co-operative Bank printing and stationary expenditure as a percentage of total fixed cost is observed to be 0.14 per cent, for The Anand Mercantile Bank it is 0.19 per cent, for The Dahod Urban Bank it is 0.1 per cent, for The Sarvodaya Nagrik Bank it is 0.17 per cent, for The Sardar Bhiladwala Nagrik Bank it is 0.12 per cent. The highest expenses on printing and stationery is paid by The Baroda People's Bank (0.25 per cent).

The average total fixed cost for ten years as a percentage of the average total deposits for The Kalupur Commercial Bank is found to be 2.08 per cent, for The Rajkot Nagrik Bank it is 1.65 per cent, for The Anyonya Sahayakari Bank it is 2.77 per cent, for The Surat People's Bank it is 2,78 per cent, for The Natpur Co-operative Bank it is 1.96 per cent, for The Anand Mercantile Bank it is 1.86 per cent, for The Dahod Urban Bank it is 1.81 per cent. The highest average fixed cost is observed for The Sarvodaya Nagrik Bank (4.133 per cent.)

Next to The Sarvodaya Nagrik Bank, The Baroda People's Bank also reported their average cost as a percentage of the average total deposit at 3.04 per cent. Finally The Sardar Bhiladwala Bank has reported it to be 2.65 per cent.

The results of multivariate analysis of variation (MANOVA) have yielded positively in the study. The hypothesis for all 8 elements of fixed cost remaining stable during ten years were accepted. The behavior of the above mentioned eight elements of the total fixed costs of banking services is as per our expectations

Variable Cost

It is an operating expense or operating expense as a class, that vary directly sometimes proportionately with the volume of output. It is also termed as marginal cost. Their different method of classifying the total cost into fixed cost and variable cost such as:

i) High and low point method,
ii) Scattered diagram method and
iii) Least square method.

Interest has a direct relation with volume of deposits. The interest vary with the volume of deposit. Therefore interest cost is termed as variable cost. The interest is the cost of using someone's money or the price to be charged for allowing the use of somebody's money.

The Interest rates were not at all controlled in India till 1958. From 1964 the RBI started administering interest rates on deposits. Then the interest rate policy was criticised on various grounds. In pre-nationalisation period, interest paid on deposits by scheduled commercial banks ranged between 2.30 per cent to 4.04 per cent for the year 1961 and 1968 respectively. During two decades, from the nationalisation of commercial banks i.e. from 1970 to 1990 interest paid on deposits were to the tune of 3.69 per cent to 6.24 per cent.

Interest — Total Cost

Interest has a major share in total cost of banking services but it is not the only determinant of the total cost. In the present study, share of interest in total cost of nationalised banks is observed continuously rising from the year 1970 to 1990.

Year	*Share of Interest in Total Cost*
1970	51.2
1975	57.5
1980	67.76
1985	69.01
1990	71.35

Suddenly proportion of interest in total cost reduced to 58.68 per cent in the year 1995-96 and 62.22 per cent in the year 1997-98.

The Reserve Bank of India has given up the control over the interest rates on the term deposits from 1996. But still continued to regulate the interest rates on savings deposits at 4.5 per cent. Now it will be interesting to observe the share of interest in total cost i.e. in regulated interest rate structure Urban Co-operative Banks were allowed to pay 1 per cent more interest on deposits but since deregulation, commercial and other banks can compete with Urban Co-operative Banks in paying interest on deposits.

During ten years, interest as a percentage of total cost for selected Urban Co-operative Banks is ranging between 58 per cent and 86 per cent i.e. for The Rajkot Nagarik Bank and The Anand Mercantile Co-operative Bank respectively. The Natpur Co-operative Bank's share of interest to total cost is also very high at 81 per cent during ten years. It is necessary for The Anand Mercantile Bank and The Natpur Co-operative Bank to control the interest cost by keeping the low rates of interests.

Interest — Total Assets

The average proportion of interest as a percentage to total assets of selected Urban Co-operative Banks is ranging between 6 per cent and 9 per cent for The Surat People's Bank and The Sarvodaya Nagarik Bank during the period from 1987-88 to 1997-98.

Interest — Working Capital

Similarly the average proportion of interest paid to working capital of selected Urban Co-operative Banks during the period of 1987-88 to 1996-97 is maximum at 9 per cent and minimum at 6 per cent i.e. for The Sarvodaya Nagarik Bank and The Surat People's Bank respectively.

Interest — Cost of Deposits

The variable cost of deposits is determined in this chapter by calculating the interest paid as a percentage of total deposits. Total interest paid includes the interest paid on borrowings. Following table shows average interest cost of interest bearing liabilities and deposits for ten selected banks.

From the above table it becomes very clear that except The Kalupur Commercial Bank, Anand Mercantile Bank and The Sarvodaya Nagarik Bank other banks have negligible borrowing throughout the study period. The selected Urban Co-operative Banks, representing Urban Co-operative Banking sector in Gujarat, projects 10.4 per cent interest cost as variable cost of total deposits as an overall average. Total deposits include current deposits and they do not bear any interest cost. Therefore if current deposits are excluded from the total deposits to get the interest cost on interest bearing liabilities then the average interest cost of deposits excluding current deposits turns out to be 8.779 per cent and other wise it is reported to be is 13.64 per cent.

Costing of Banking Services

The Costing as a technique is very useful not only in

manufacturing but in banking sector as well. One should understand the characteristics of costs in bank. The cost strongly influences the viability of a bank.

TABLE 9.01

INTEREST COST AS A PERCENTAGE OF INTEREST BEARING LIABILITIES AND DEPOSITS

Sr. No.	*Name of the Bank*	*Interest Cost as per cent of Interest Bearing Liabilities*	*Interest Cost as per cent of Deposits*
1.	The Kalupur Com. Bank	11	10
2.	The Rajkot Nagarik Bank	10	10
3.	The Anyonya Sahayakari Bank	10	10
4.	The Surat People's Bank	09	09
5.	The Natpur Co-operative Bank	10	10
6.	The Anand Mercantile Bank	11	10
7.	The Dahod Urban Co-operative Bank	11	11
8.	The Sarvodaya Nagarik Bank	14	13
9.	The Baroda People's Bank	12	12
10.	The Sardar Bhiladwala Bank	09	9

Costing Methods and Techniques

The researchers while costing the banks' services applied various methods and technique. Process costing is a form of operation costing where product passes through two or more process before it becomes finished product. Operation costing determines the cost of standerdised services. Operation costing is used for costing on Transport, Supply, Social and Municipal services but banks do not provide the standerdised services. Ex Governor of RBI, Shri C. Rangarajan also feels that if is difficult to determine the costs of banks' services because number of variables is quite large. Uniform costing is not a costing technique in itself, it simply suggest uniformity in following the costing principles and practices. "Manual on costing in private sector and Urban Co-operative Banks" published by RBI, suggested to implement the uniform costing and to establish the 'costing cell' in the head offices of the banks. Direct costing is popularly known as marginal costing in which total cost is distributed into two parts i.e. fixed cost and variable cost. Incremental costing relates to differential cost represented by increase or decrease in total cost resulting from variation in operation. It measures the change in total cost that results from alternate course of action. These costs are generally variable costs.

Full or Traditional cost method is termed as absorption costing, in which fixed and variable costs are taken into account. It is a technique by which all costs are assigned to a product cost or cost of services rendered.

Banking Commission setup by Government of India analysed the cost data of Urban Co-operative Banks and brought out the cost of various types deposits. The Reserve Banks of India had constituted a standing advisory committee in January 1983 for studying norms for viability of Urban Co-operative Banks and its branches. It has represented the fixed and variable cost of banking services.

The Commercial Banks were asked to advance 40 per cent of its total credit to priority sector whereas the Urban Co-operative Banks have required to advance 60 per cent of its total credit to priority sector. It was not just a directed credit by The Reserve Bank of India but the priority sector credit was credit at concessional rate of interest. In turn the opportunity cost of such advances; the Urban Co-operative Banks were supposed to bear. Under the differential rate of interest (DRI) scheme, financing to priority sector was continued. From 1994, such subsidy has been withdrawn by the Reserve Bank of India but till that time the Urban Co-operative Banks has incurred the opportunity cost on such advances. The credit facility on which the installments / interest remained 'past due' for some specified period then The Reserve Bank of India has issued the guideline to consider such credit as non-performing assets (NPA). The Non-Performing Assets' percentage to the total advances in public sector banks were very high at 23.2 per cent in 1993 which declined to 16 per cent in the year 1998 whereas the non-performing assets of the Urban Co-operative Banks as a percentage of total advances were 13.9 per cent in the year 1995 and declined to 11 per cent in the year 1998. The Surat People's Bank in the present study is found to be having very high level of Non-Performing Assets, for the year 1996-97 it has got Rs. 2600 as NPAs. The opportunity cost of Non-Performing Assets calculated in this study for the deposits of Rs. 100 for commercial bank it was 50 paise, The Rajkot Nagrik Bank 49 paise, The Anyonya Sahayakari Bank 75 paise, The Surat People's Bank has highest cost of NPA for the deposit of Rs. 100 i.e. Rs. 1.89. The Natpur Co-operative Bank had NPA cost of deposit has 65 paise, The Anand Mercantile Bank 80 paise, The lowest NPA cost is observed with The Dahod Urban Bank i.e. just 7paise. The Sarvodaya Nagrik Bank 22 paise, The Baroda People's Bank has the second highest position in NPA cost of deposits Rs. 1.09. The Sardar Bhiladwala Bank has 75 paise as a cost of NPA to deposits. The Reserve Bank of India has prescribed the statutory liquidity ratio and cash reserve requirement which has fluctuated during the study period, the highest CRR was 15 per cent and lowest was 10 per cent whereas the SLR was highest at 38.5 per cent and lowest at 25 per cent of demand and time liabilities of Urban Co-operative Banks. The opportunity cost for SLR calculated stood at Rs. 2.44 for a deposit of Rs. 100 whereas the cost of CRR calculated stood at Rs. 1.61 for a deposit of Rs. 100.

Spread burden and gross profit ratios are analysed for selected Urban Co-operative Banks for ten years from 1987-88 to 1996-97. The spread average for ten banks in proportion with the total deposits is showing continuous rise from 5 per cent to 7.2 per cent i.e. from the year 1987-88 to the year 1992-92. Then it has marginally declined to 6.5 per cent in the year 1993 94 then onwards it shows the rising trend and reached to the peak of 8 per cent during the year 1996-97. The average burden of ten banks as a proportion to total deposits is fluctuating between 1.6 per cent to 2.4 per cent. In the year 1991-92 it is observed lowest at 1.6 per cent and the highest average burden was 2.4 per cent in the year 1994-95. The gross profit ratios with the deposits as an average for 10 banks is constantly rising from 3.1 per cent to 4.9 per cent from the year 1987-88 to the year 1992-93, then marginally it has declined to 4.3 per cent in the year 1993-94, again from 1994-95 they are rising and observed at the peak of 5.8 per cent. Total income trends during the ten years are showing continuous rise similarly the total expenditure trends are also showing the growth. The economies of scale are observed on the basis of average cost curve of individual ten banks during the ten years with few exceptions the average cost curve is observed falling or remaining stable. It can be concluded that since average cost curve is declining there is a scope of scale economies. Similarly when the average cost curve remaining stable, the incremental deposits will not increase the average cost so long the average cost curve is stable. The analysis of total cost and total revenue curve shows that all the banks have passed through the break-even-point and now they are widening the gaps between total cost and total revenue curves. In certain banks the gap is very marginal, therefore it can be concluded that these banks are required to reduce their cost. Ultimately in chapter 8, the standard cost of various expenses are derived from amongst the ten banks' lowest average expenditure.

Findings

The analysis of cost and management of cost of selected Urban Co-operative Banks revealed following broad findings of the study:

i) Average interest paid by ten selected banks declined from 11.13 per cent to 8.4 per cent from the year 1987-88 to 1991-92 respectively. Then in the year 1992-93 there was a substantial increase in the interest cost by 2.78 per cent i.e. the interest cost of deposits in the year 1992-93 observed at 11.17 per cent. Marginally it has increased to 11.25 per cent in the year 1993-94 and became stable to 11.36 per cent in the year 1996-97. The average interest cost of deposits for all ten years was 10.67 per cent.

ii) Ten banks' average salaries and allowance as an element of fixed cost was 1.67 per cent in the year 1987-88 for a deposit of Rs. 100, which revealed the increase up to the year 1990-91 at 1.87 per cent. But for the year 1991-92 it has reduced to 1.47 per cent, then in the year 1992-93 it has sharply increased to 2.08 per cent. It was marginally fluctuating up to the year 1996-97. In the year 1996-97 it stood at 2.09 per cent. The average for all ten years salary cost was Rs. 1.94 for the deposits of Rs. 100.

iii) The average printing and stationery expenses as an element of fixed cost was observed fluctuating during the period of 9 years from the year 1987-88 to the year 1995-96 between 0.127 per cent to 0.174 per cent but for the year 1996-97 it showed sudden decline and reached at the bottom for 0.09 per cent. The average printing and stationery cost for the deposit of Rs. 100 was 14 paise.

iv) The average expenditure incurred on postage and telegram for a deposit of Rs. 100 in the year 1987-88 was 0.049 per cent, which was fluctuating during ten years between 0.036 per cent and 0.05 per cent. No trend was observed in expenses paid by the selected Urban Co-operative Banks for postage and telegram. The average cost of deposit of Rs. 100 about postage and telegram for ten years was around 5 paise.

iv) The rent and taxes as an average for ten banks during the year of study was ranging between 0.12 per cent to 0.197 per cent. It was 0.143 per cent in the year 1994-95. It was increasing during three years up to 1996-97, i.e., 0.197 per cent. For remaining seven years it did not show any trend but marginally fluctuating. Average rent cost for deposits of Rs. 100 for ten years was 15 paise.

vi) Average depreciation provided by selected Urban Co-operative Banks in the year 1987-88 0.16 per cent which was reducing continuously upto the year 1990-91 at 0.121 per cent. Then it showed rising trend continuously from the year 1991-92 from 0.127 per cent to 0.188 per cent for the year 1996-97. The average depreciation for ten years was 0.15 per cent i.e. the depreciation cost of deposit of Rs. 100 as an average for ten years for all ten banks was 15 paise.

vii) Average audit fees of ten banks for the year 1987-88 was 0.008 per cent which remained more or less stable upto the year 1990-91 then from the year 1991-92 it is falling from 0.006 per cent to 0.004 per cent in the year 1996-97. Ten years' average audit fees cost is observed even less than 1 paise i.e. 0.006 per cent.

viii) Directors' fees as an average of ten banks in the year 1987-88 was the highest at 0.08 per cent of deposits then it was continuously falling during remaining nine years and in the year 1996-97, it was at the lowest at 0.003 per cent. The average Directors' fees for all ten years was 0.005 per cent.

ix) An average legal fees for ten banks in the year 1987-88 is 0.07 per cent which has remained stable upto 1991-92 with exception in the year 1990-91 but then in the year 1992-93 there was a sudden increase by 0.004 per cent and reached to 0.01 per cent. Again there was a sharp decline during the year 1993-94 to 0.05 per cent i.e. exactly 50 per cent less than the previous year which continued in the year 1994-95 and increased by 0.01 per cent for the year 1996-97 the .Average legal fees was again less than 1 paise for the deposit of Rs. 100 i.e. 0.006 percent

x) The average total fixed cost for the year 1987-88 is Rs. 2.19 for the deposit of Rs. 100 which was showing an increase upto the year 1989-90 i.e. Rs. 2.36 paise. Marginally it declined in the year 1990-91 to Rs. 2.33 then there was a sudden decline in the year 1991-92 where the total fixed cost has reduced to the lowest of Rs. 1.92. The year 1992-93 showing sharp rise in the total fixed cost by Rs. 0.7 and reaching to Rs. 2.616. There was a marginal decline in the year 1993-94 by just 1 paise. In the year 1994-95 the fixed cost was observed the highest i.e. Rs. 2.824 which declined to Rs. 2.614 for the year 1996-97. The average fixed cost for ten years as a cost of deposits of Rs. 100 was Rs. 2.44.

xi) The average total cost of selected ten banks was the lowest in the year 1991-92 is Rs. 10.32 for the deposits of Rs. 100 whereas it was maximum in the year 1996-97 at Rs. 13.97. Total cost was not showing any trend during ten years of study. The average total cost for ten years for deposits of Rs. 100 was observed Rs. 13.11.

xii) The average interest income on advances and investments for ten banks in the year 1987-88 was 16.16 per cent of total deposits which increased to 18.35 per cent in the year 1992-93 again increased to 19.36 per cent in the year 1996-97. The average total interest received for ten years and for ten banks was16.92 per cent.

xiii) The incomes other than interest as an average for

ten banks were fluctuating between 0.29 per cent to maximum of 0.46 per cent during ten years. The average other incomes of the Urban Co-operative Banks were 0.36 per cent of total deposits.

xiv) The average total income which included the interest received and other incomes as an average of 10 banks during ten years not showing any increasing or declining trend, but from the year 1994-95 to the year 1996-97 it was increased from 17.43 per cent to 19.74 per cent respectively. The average total income of selected Urban Co-operative Banks is 17.29 per cent of deposits.

xv) The average profit was increasing from 3.14 per cent to 5.77 per cent during the year 1987-88 to the year 1996-97. The average profit for ten years was 4.18 per cent of the total deposits.

xvi) The average spread i.e. the gap between total income and total expenditure as an average for ten banks for the year 1987-88 was 0.05 per cent of the total deposits which showed continuous increase after the year 1992-93 at 0.072 per cent. There was a marginal decline during the year 1993-94, the spread was 0.065 per cent, which remained stable at 0.068 per cent for the year 1994-95 and 1995-96, then it increased by 0.012 per cent and reached at the peak of 0.08 per cent in the year 1996-97. The average spread was 0.063 per cent of total deposits.

xvii) The average burden was the difference between the expenditure other than interest and the other incomes. As an average of ten banks for the year 1987-88 was 0.019 per cent which reached to 0.02 per cent upto the year 1990-91, then there was a fall in the year 1991-92 to 0.016 per cent, then it was fluctuating between 0.022 per cent to 0.024 per cent. Keeping the average burden for ten years at 0.021 per cent.

xviii) Urban Co-operative Banks were providing directed credit to the priority sectors upto the year 1994 at concenssional rate and was incurring the opportunity cost on such advances but since then the subsidies in interest rate have been withdrawn by the Reserve Bank of India. So from 1994 the opportunity cost on priority sectors advances were not incurred by the Urban Co-operative Banks.

xix) Non-Performing Assets was going to become a crucial problem for Urban Co-operative Banks in the years to come. The Surat People's Bank was observed the highest Non-Performing Assets whereas The Baroda People's Bank was the next. The average cost of Non-Performing Assets based on calculations of opportunity cost was Rs. 0.72 for the deposits of Rs. 100.

xx) The average cost for SLR calculated on the basis of opportunity cost was Rs. 2.44 for the deposit of Rs. 100.

xxi) The average cost for CRR calculated on the basis of opportunity cost was Rs. 1.61 for the deposit of Rs. 100.

xxii) Share of total interest paid in total cost of selected Urban Co-operative Banks was 73 per cent.

xxiii) The proportion of total interest paid with total assets of selected Urban Co-operative Banks was observed at 0.073.

xxiv) The proportion of total interest paid with working capital of selected Urban Co-operative Banks was observed at 0.08.

xxv) The lowest cost for each element of cost incurred by any one of the selected Urban Co-operative Banks considered as a standard cost for that particular element. Accordingly standard interest cost 8.78 per cent, salaries and allowances cost 1.33 per cent, printing and stationery 0.07 per cent, postage and telegram 0.022 per cent, rent and taxes 0.093 per cent, depreciation 0.096 per cent, audit fees 0.002 per cent, directors' fees 0.001 per cent, legal fees 0.002 per cent, total fixed cost 1.621 per cent which makes the total of all as a total standard cost 10.4 per cent of total deposits.

xxvi) The Urban Co-operative banks mobilising deposits less than Rs. 10,000 lacs. The standard cost are expected to incur standard total cost of Rs 13.11 for deposits of Rs. 100. The above mentioned standard cost of Rs. 13.11 can be segregated in to different elements as under:

Sr. No.	*Element of Cost*	*Amount in Rs.*
1.	Interest cost	10.67
2.	Salaries	1.93
3.	Printing and stationery	0.13
4.	Postage and telegram	0.05
5.	Rents and taxes	0.15
6.	Depreciation	0.15
7.	Audit Fees	0.01
8.	Director Fees	0.01
9.	Legal Fees	0.01

General Observations

i) Certain Urban Co-operative Banks are functioning amongst selected classes of the community.

ii) Numbers of banks are not increasing but only branches of the banks' are increasing. Therefore new leadership is not getting the ground to grow in the field of Urban Co-operative Banks. The Urban Co-operative Banks have been managed by the same leadership for years together. This has merits as well as demerits. The Sardar Nagrik Co-operative Bank, Vadodara is the example of such demerits.

iii) Some of the Urban Co-operative Banks are not

keeping their offices open before and after office timings. So urban people find the timings inconvenient.

iv) The facility of remittance of funds is not available in some of the Urban Co-operative Banks.

v) Women and People from weaker sections are less attracted by the Urban Co-operative Banks' for membership, borrowings and deposits.

vi) Cash Reserve Ratio and Statutory Liquidity Ratio are very high which restricts loaning operations of the Banks.

vii) The loans and advances per borrower are still high.

viii) Though credit deposit ratio is high, Urban Co-operative Banks experienced the unproductive funds lying with them.

ix) Some Urban Co-operative Banks have made remarkable progress in certain spheres of activities but others are lagging far behind. Some are not viable according to Marathe Committee's norms of viability in terms of Share Capital Reserves, Deposits, Advances and Working Capitals.

x) Some of the Urban Co-operative Banks are lagging behind in their contribution to the development of Indian economy, as they have not achieved the target of advancing to priority sectors.

xi) The Urban Co-operative Banks are still providing credit to priority sector.

xii) Advances to Small Scale and Cottage Industries are comparatively less.

xiii) Some of the Urban Co-operative Banks are not complying with the amendments to The Banking Regulation Act 1949 with respect to publishing annual accounts according to revised formats.

xiv) High inconsistency is seen with regard to administrative expenses.

xv) Lack of training, i.e., Refresher Courses to the Staff of Urban Co-operative Banks.

xvi) Some Urban Co-operative Banks are less equipped as regards to banking facilities.

xvii) There is need for in-house training programme for developing attitudinal change in outlook of professional management personnel.

Suggestions

i) There is a need for a comparative study of behaviour of cost in nationalised banks and Co-operative banks.

ii) All studies including the present one have analysed either costs or profits. There is a need to analyse comprehensively both the sides of a Balance Sheet of a bank.

iii) Performance appraisal for the banking sectors' employees should also be attempted as a part of core research programme.

iv) Activity based costing should really be applied to the banking industry and one must try and make banking sector more cost conscious.

v) Co-operative Banks should really try and undertake pilot studies in the areas where they are not operating today but they may operate tomorrow.

vi) In a liberal financial sector importance of training of the personnel is really most essential input which should really be emphasised at all level in the banking industry.

REFERENCES

1. Amandeep, *Profit and Profitability in Commercial Banks,* Deep and Deep publication, Delhi 1993.
2. J. Singh, *Profit Planning in Banks,* Deep and Deep Publication Delhi 1993.
3. A.V. Rajgopalan, *Productivity in Banks—A Overview,* 1993.
4. NIBM 1983.
5. "Innovations in Banking" by Paul Mampilly 1980 and Suresh Gerg, *"Indian Banking: Cost and Profitability,"* Anmol Publications Pvt. Ltd., 1982.

Bibliography

Donald D. Hester, AP of Economics, Yale University Indian *Banks their Portfolios: Profits and Policy,* University of Bombay, 1964.

S. Kr. Paul, *Company Accounts,* New Central Book Agency, 1993.

Radhe Shyam and O.P. Agrawal, Proceedings, 'Workshop on Profit Planning Bankers Training College, RBI, Bombay, 1988.

Vipin Shah, *Cost and Efficiency in Banking,* Printwell Publishers, Jaipur, 1987.

S. K. Verghese, *Profit and Profitability of India Commercial Banks in Seventies,* National Institute of Banking Management, Bombay, 1993.

Dr. Dhruvalata and D. Bhatt, *Bank Deposits in India,* Himalaya Publishing House, Bombay, 1993.

Kishore C. Raut and Santosh K. Das*'Commercial Bank in India—Profitability, Growth and Development',* Kanishka Publisher and Distrubuters, New Delhi, 1996.

Dr. Kiran Chopra, *Managing Profits, Profitability and Productivity in Public Sector Banking,* ABS Publications, Jalandhar, 1987.

Narendra Jadhav, *Challenges to Indian Banking,* Mecmillan India Limited, New Delhi, 1996.

Suresh Chand Garg, *Indian Banking Cost and Profitability,* Anmol Publications Pvt. Ltd., New Delhi, 1989.

Dr. P. V. and Ramanan Murty, *Cost and Profitability of Public Sector Banks,* Mohit Publication, New Delhi, 1996.

Raj Kapila and Uma Kapila *Banking and Financial Sector Reforms in India,* Academic Foundation, New Delhi, 1997.

Varsha Varde and Sampat P. Singh, *For Costing in Banking Industry,* National Institute of Banking Management, Bombay, 1992.

R. M. Shrivastava, *Financial Management and Policy,* Himalaya Publishing House, Mumbai, 1997.

A. S. Kanatawala, *Management Accounting Techniques for Lending Decisions by Banks,* M.S. University of Baroda.

A. S. Chawla, K. K. Uppal and Keshav Malhotra, *Indian Banking Towards 21th Century,* Deep and Deep Publications, New Delhi 1998.

N. K. Prasad, *Principles and Practice of Cost Accounting,* Book Syndicate Pvt. Ltd. Calcutta, 1997.

S. P. Arora and T. S. Soni, *Cost Accounting,* Petamber Publishing Company, New Delhi 1981.

M. G. Patkar, *Costing Methods and Technicues,* Nirali Prakashan, Pune.

Sumiudding, Mahfoozar Rehman and Hifzar Rehman, *Co-operative Accounting and Auditing,* Himalaya Publishing House, Bombay.

Chairman, *Urban Co-operative Banks in India,* Ferdration of Urban Co-operative Banks, Inter India Publications New Delhi.

President, Cost *Accounting in Commercial Banking,* The Institute of Cost and Works Accountant of India, Calcutta.

Chairman, *Technical Studies,* Prepared for the Banking Commission, RBI, Bombay, 1972.

JOURNALS

State Bank of India Monthly Review, SBI of Economic Research Dept., Bombay.

Punjab National Bank Monthly Review, PNB, Management Advisory and Service Division, New Delhi.

Journal of Gujarat Urban Co-operative Banks, Federations', Ahemadabad.

A Pre-budget 1999-2000 Document "Indian Economic Survey 1998-99", New Delhi.

Prajnan, Journal of Social and Management Sciences, National Institute of Bank Management, Pune.

Sahyog, Journal of Udaybhansinhji, Institute of Co-operative Management, Ghandhinagar.

The Journal of Banking Studies, Bankers' College, New Delhi.

The Journal of Indian Institute of Bankers, Mumbai.

'IBA Bulletin' Indian Banks Association, Mumbai.

Manual on Costing Exercises in Commercial Banks', RBI, Management Service Department, Bombay.

The Chartered Accountant, Journal of the Institute of Chartered Accountants of India, New Delhi.

The Management Account, Journal of the Institute of Cost and Works Accounts of India, Calcutta.

Indian Journal of Banking and Finance, The Dept. of Business, Financial Management and Economics, University of Jodhpur, Jodhpur.

Manual for Urban Co-operative Banks, Reserve Bank of India, Bombay, 1984.

'Chartered Secretary' The Journal of Corporate Executives The Institute of Company Secretaries of India, New Delhi.

REPORTS

Report of standing Advisory Committee for Urban Co-operative Bank, RBI, Bombay.

Report of Banking Commission, Govt. of India, 1972.

Reforms in Indian Banking—Agenda for Action, 'Banking Economist Conference' 92, Bank of Baroda, Baroda.

'Work shop on Profit, Planning, Proceedings' Banking Training Collage, RBI, Bombay.

'Programme of Business Development and Profit planing for Officers of Primary Co-operative Banks,' RBI, College of Agricultural Banking, Pune.

Programme on Branch Management for Urban Co-operative Banks (including internal control and House Keeping), RBI, College of Agriculture Banking, Pune.

ARTICLES/CASE STUDY

'How innovators use target costing to leverage value creation', Kavasseri V. Ramanathan, *The Management Accountant*, August 1999.

'A Brief note on the Implection of the Treget of 60 precent credit deposit ratio for 'Rural'and semi-urban' branches, S.L. Shetty, A framework of national credit plan.

'Bank deposits and Interest rates', C Rangarajan, A Framework of national credit plan.

'Assets-liabilities management for banks in a deregulated Enviroment', Ganti Subrahnonyam, *'Prajnan'*, vol. XXIII, No.1, 1994-95.

'Costing in Banks', R.M. Deole, Joint Conference of Office Bearers, Directors and Chief Executive Officers of Urban Co-operative Banks, 3rd November, 1996, Khandala.

"Importance of Co-operative Banks under the Changed Banking Scenario", Dr. C. Rangarajan, The Banker, 17th September, 1997.

"Financial Management of Urban Co-operative Banks—Framework and Application." A case study of Vasai Vikas Urban Co-operative Bank Ltd, R.S. Deshpande, Vaikunth Mehta, National Institute of Co-operative Management, Pune.

"Marketing of Banking Services by the Mehsana Urban Co-operative Ltd., Mehsana", A.K. Asthana, *The Banker*, 25th January, 1998.

"Some Aspects of Interest Rate Policy in India" M.K. Datar, *National Bank News Review*, July- September, 1996

"Interest Rate Policy Management under Liberalisation" — The Indian Experience and Outlook", V.R. Gundannavar National Bank, *New Review*, July-September, 1996.

'Banking Sector Reforms, Rational and Relevance", C. Rangarajan, Fourth SICOM Silver Jubilee Memorial Lecture, July, 1996.

"Global Perspective", P.G. Kakodkai, *The Banker*, 26 November-December, 1996.

Appendices

TABLE 1

WORKING CAPITAL OF SELECTED URBAN CO-OPERATIVE BANKS IN GUJARAT

Sr. No.	Name of the Bank	1987-88	88-89	89-90	90-91	91-92	92-93	93-94	94-95	95-96	96-97
1	The Kalupur Bank	9161.50	10403.31	13618.40	15815.23	17281.93	20798.64	38478.83	44366.78	52601.55	58840.32
2	Rajkot Nagrik Bank	13378.53	14864.24	17410.80	18989.99	20637.97	23360.68	27435.30	29997.10	36657.68	41675.58
3	Anyona Saharakri Bank	2668.71	2964.62	3465.56	3963.13	4353.47	5029.92	5750.90	6542.31	8795.29	11711.72
4	Surat Peoples's Bank	9525.71	11204.39	13155.91	15099.67	16372.39	20231.78	23612.52	25784.37	30634.37	39032.16
5	Natpur Co-Op Bank	1430.67	1751.29	2124.42	2413.35	2791.83	3042.54	3533.01	4314.49	5733.84	7472.71
6	Anand Mercantile Bank	1730.05	2228.69	2736.33	3354.18	4107.34	4194.27	4314.42	4733.32	6816.00	7147.23
7	Dahod Urban Bank	2214.66	2488.23	2757.33	3044.34	3369.39	3729.41	4609.95	5210.37	6176.98	7182.04
8	Sarvodya Nagrik Bank	772.05	886.35	1010.48	1217.82	1330.13	1591.70	1755.83	1830.19	2160.43	2449.31
9	Baroda People's Bank	1236.07	1652.24	1944.72	2404.54	2838.97	3574.07	4454.53	5021.61	7028.68	9006.44
10	Sardar Bhiladwala Bank	3577.42	4449.05	5213.25	5835.09	6601.86	7821.66	9340.77	10783.95	12304.80	14986.49

TABLE 2

PROFIT OF SELECTED URBAN CO-OPERATIVE BANKS IN GUJARAT

Sr. No.	Name of the Bank	1987-88	88-89	89-90	90-91	91-92	92-93	93-94	94-95	95-96	96-97
1	The Kalupur Bank	127.40	140.44	145.28	153.08	148.27	159.83	360.41	650.92	918.92	1119.16
2	Rajkot Nagrik Bank	90.96	100.02	110.27	124.00	105.28	151.06	170.52	188.64	225.09	240.03
3	Anyona Saharakri Bank	17.10	18.93	30.66	39.82	32.55	51.91	56.20	61.63	86.34	165.98
4	Surat Peoples's Bank	175.49	211.84	254.64	317.57	633.22	472.54	472.98	513.16	108.86	165.98
5	Natpur Co-Op Bank	40.02	50.03	60.47	70.05	92.65	126.15	120.01	151.13	170.95	252.93
6	Anand Mercantile Bank	36.60	44.07	65.31	53.36	70.00	101.01	105.98	116.56	101.74	153.35
7	Dahod Urban Bank	30.77	36.63	37.73	38.87	40.70	52.00	47.50	56.00	76.00	90.00
8	Sarvodya Nagrik Bank	6.01	8.60	12.20	13.25	12.12	24.92	13.08	15.41	22.23	30.00
9	Baroda People's Bank	26.22	37.74	51.22	60.79	61.03	89.34	106.42	119.00	126.13	149.64
10	Sardar Bhiladwala Bank	89.90	101.54	103.85	163.03	262.01	251.83	167.14	244.19	417.59	691.76

TABLE 3

TOTAL COST OF SELECTED URBAN CO-OP. BANKS IN GUJARAT

Sr. No.	Name of the Bank	1987-88	88-89	89-90	90-91	91-92	92-93	93-94	94-95	95-96	96-97
1	The Kalupur Bank	1254.79	1266.78	1502.52	1355.28	1305.82	1635.67	2305.17	3499.4	4210.72	5716.8
2	Rajkot Nagrik Bank	1701.25	1874.27	2528.46	2566.63	2277.16	3333.06	3619.53	4044.32	5274.72	6186.54
3	Anyona Saharakri Bank	269.95	304.16	347.78	402.08	325.57	519.12	562.09	616.36	863.49	1240.33
4	Surat People's Bank	903.33	996.65	1241.65	1393.89	1556.77	2004.22	2294.39	2431.54	3034.1	4017.01
5	Natpur Co-Op Bank	166.76	162.33	192.83	218.48	197.98	318.46	354.91	404.81	544.76	828.62
6	The Anand Mercantile Bank	158.49	212.93	266.61	324.55	321.24	468.16	430.91	450.11	652.56	850.54
7	Dahod Urban Bank	219.35	246.54	279.73	314.03	297.28	446.29	495.93	538.58	706.38	916.25
8	Sarvodya Nagrik Bank	79.51	102.65	106.78	123.66	118.49	191.64	235.52	234.27	282.75	416.25
9	Baroda People's Bank	116.03	162.14	203.57	255.38	244.74	399.41	528.01	544.51	681.35	950.51
10	Sardar Bhiladwala Bank	331.48	520.79	442.27	491.62	442.16	687.42	765.18	879.01	977.08	1299.3

TABLE 4

AVERAGE TOTAL DEPOSITS OF SELECTED URBAN CO-OPERATIVE BANKS IN GUJARAT

Sr. No.	Name of the Bank	1987-88	88-89	89-90	90-91	91-92	92-93	93-94	94-95	95-96	96-97
1	The Kalupur Bank	3910.24	4663.18	6228.45	7705.59	8392.46	11531.55	22281.09	31671.78	34950.73	39349.91
2	The Rajkot Nagrik Bank	10083.74	12163.61	13434.63	14899.76	16103.81	17574.13	20144.52	22626.51	26129.80	30554.73
3	Anyona Saharakri Bank	1977.51	2250.27	2555.12	2951.59	3304.73	3696.74	4219.31	4883.67	6167.98	8420.32
4	The Surat People's Bank	6155.38	7268.33	8949.43	10180.91	10985.88	12655.80	15155.88	16848.04	19341.51	24513.53
5	The Natpur Co-Op Bank	1114.95	1305.73	1541.06	1817.18	2050.60	2340.73	2696.62	3163.13	4255.57	5744.22
6	The Anand Mercantile Bank	778.14	969.49	1244.29	1577.46	1967.40	2247.65	2700.87	3133.63	3981.01	4945.73
7	Dahod Urban Bank	1495.36	1702.19	1892.43	2092.86	2305.09	2549.96	2871.48	3234.07	3929.13	5237.68
8	Sarvodya Nagrik Bank	437.02	544.02	640.24	736.15	822.07	938.92	1050.87	1162.62	1250.15	1491.40
9	Baroda People's Bank	524.97	673.61	825.83	968.41	1125.96	1419.01	1738.94	1856.80	2333.41	3106.57
10	Sardar Bhiladwala Bank	2782.46	3320.11	3866.45	4359.79	4733.17	5323.33	6322.81	7410.52	8537.50	10083.01

TABLE 5

BORROWINGS OF SELECTED URBAN CO-OPERATIVE BANKS IN GUJARAT

Sr. No.	*Name of the Bank*	*1986-87*	*87-88*	*88-89*	*89-90*	*90-91*	*91-92*	*92-93*	*93-94*	*94-95*	*95-96*	*96-97*
1	The Kalupur Bank	450.00	76.00	310.00	0.00	500.00	500.00	500.00	5.00	500.00	210.00	0.00
2	The Rajkot Nagrik Bank	0.00	0.00	0.00	0.00	0.00	0.00	0.00	0.00	0.00	0.00	0.00
3	Anyona Saharakri Bank	0.00	0.00	0.00	0.00	9.00	18.65	3.84	0.00	2.16	40.99	0.00
4	The Surat Peoples's Bank	0.00	0.00	0.00	0.00	0.00	0.00	0.00	0.00	0.00	0.00	380.33
5	The Natpur Co-operative Bank	0.00	0.27	0.04	31.88	4.49	54.52	0.00	0.00	0.00	0.00	0.00
6	The Anand Mercantile Bank	0.00	26.15	22.64	318.20	459.23	815.71	819.55	0.00	101.37	445.32	0.00
7	Dahod Urban Bank	22.00	4.08	2.00	6.50	6.00	81.73	56.28	352.12	464.94	168.37	238.22
8	Sarvodya Nagrik Bank	0.00	20.23	0.00	0.00	97.00	94.10	160.00	160.00	45.00	35.00	100.00
9	Baroda People's Bank	0.00	5.41	0.00	0.00	0.00	85.06	32.86	159.20	247.94	255.60	276.17
10	Sardar Bhiladwala Bank	0.00	0.00	0.00	15.61	35.99	147.26	149.86	180.71	147.76	363.12	303.12

TABLE 6

'TOTAL INTEREST ON ADVANCES AND INVESTMENTS OF SELECTED URBAN CO-OPERATIVE BANKS IN GUJARAT

Sr. No.	*Name of the Bank*	*1987-88*	*88-89*	*89-90*	*90-91*	*91-92*	*92-93*	*93-94*	*94-95*	*95-96*	*96-97*
1	The Kalupur Bank	1343.63	1365.22	1215.52	1432.49	1382.56	1681.48	2532.38	3948.75	4950.02	6574.11
2	Rajkot Nagrik Bank	1767.6	1949.02	2609.62	2652.68	2349.08	3437.61	3727.33	4149.04	5398.3	6323.31
3	Anyona Saharakri Bank	283.3	319.14	374.35	435.25	394.95	618.8	661.73	717.3	933.1	1373.38
4	Surat Peoples' Bank	1067.54	1190.04	1466.85	1675.69	2153.98	2444.05	2709.00	2856.16	3589.79	4942.4
5	Natpur Co-Op. Bank	205.54	210.56	250.34	286.12	288.28	441.5	467.73	546.21	700.69	1067.65
6	The Anand Mercantile Bank	192.44	252.79	326.65	369.94	381.05	555.95	527.16	558.17	743.92	993.44
7	Dahod Urban Bank	245.46	280.54	314.23	349.49	334.47	492.01	529.81	577.42	757.91	988.6
8	Sarvodya Nagrik Bank	84.1	109.7	116.91	135.23	128.55	213.41	245.5	244.98	301.55	488.23
9	Baroda People's Bank	137.41	195.42	248.57	306.45	297.29	476.52	617.21	641.84	774.99	1049.81
10	Sardar Bhiladwala Bank	414.48	607.09	535.37	640.2	689.32	918.06	908.38	1097.29	1364.17	1952.27

TABLE 7

TOTAL ADVANCES SELECTED URBAN CO-OPERATIVE BANKS IN GUJARAT OF 11 YEARS

Sr. No.	Name of the Bank	1987-88	88-89	89-90	90-91	91-92	92-93	93-94	94-95	95-96	96-97
1	The Kalupur Bank	5000.81	6095.87	7073.71	8089.13	8113.21	10016.6	10992.14	17112.49	23751.87	34899.01
2	The Rajkot Nagrik Bank	6677.04	7695.63	8724.38	10229.06	12399.73	14284.4	15184.88	16916.9	18219.81	24899.01
3	Anyona Saharakri Bank	1135.66	1194.23	1381.93	1470.3	1747.29	2009.62	2264.87	2348.54	2622.42	3619.89
4	The Surat Peoples's Bank	3386.5	3409.75	4187.08	5271.24	7193.67	7922.02	7407.98	8810.87	10983.68	12739.95
5	The Natpur Co-op. Bank	920.45	920.45	1159.08	1361.39	1566.67	1551.24	1597.85	2076.56	2342.12	3736.78
6	The Anand Mercantile Bank	1121.85	1121.85	1351.13	1617.74	2114.53	2406.1	2307.81	2964.24	3287.13	4108.59
7	Dahod Urban Bank	918.13	960.65	1239.81	1484.09	1943.45	2000.56	1965.43	2200.48	2552.7	3505.59
8	Sarvodya Nagrik Bank	301.32	551.31	579.19	625.66	736.93	941.42	1187.15	1297.34	1299.81	1472.99
9	Baroda People's Bank	450.31	586.24	813.31	902.35	1274.47	1690.26	2094.15	2459.39	2884.77	4072.86
10	Sardar Bhiladwala Bank	1802.59	2227.51	2732.27	3320.06	3739.23	3884.64	4165.43	4594.98	4948.93	5610.12

TABLE 8

INCOME OTHER THAN INTEREST OF SELECTED URBAN CO-OPERATIVE BANKS IN GUJARAT

Sr. No.	Name of the Bank	1987-88	88-89	89-90	90-91	91-92	92-93	93-94	94-95	95-96	96-97
1	The Kalupur Bank	38.55	42.01	61.91	75.86	71.52	114.02	130.19	201.55	179.2	261.85
2	Rajkot Nagrik Bank	24.61	25.27	29.11	37.96	33.35	46.52	62.73	83.92	101.55	103.26
3	Anyona Saharakri Bank	3.74	3.96	4.19	6.65	4.96	7.99	14.71	15.65	39.25	32.92
4	Surat Peoples's Bank	12.49	18.43	25.96	35.76	27.18	32.68	58.76	88.52	112.96	63.82
5	Natpur Co-op. Bank	1.24	1.79	2.6	3.4	2.35	3.11	7.19	9.77	15.03	13.89
6	Anand Mercantile Bank	2.65	4.2	5.24	7.97	10.19	13.22	9.72	8.51	10.37	10.45
7	Dahod Urban Bank	4.65	2.64	3.12	3.41	4.01	5.37	13.61	17.15	24.47	17.63
8	Sarvodya Nagrik Bank	1.42	1.55	7.42	1.69	2.07	3.15	3.11	4.7	3.44	3.71
9	Baroda People's Bank	4.84	4.46	6.26	9.75	8.52	12.19	17.25	19.73	32.65	50.33
10	Sardar Bhiladwala Bank	6.9	15.25	11.2	14.93	15.16	21.57	24.41	28.05	31.67	38.79

TABLE 9

TOTAL INVESTMENT OF SELECTED URBAN CO-OPERATIVE BANKS IN GUJARAT

Sr. No.	Name of the Bank	1987-88	88-89	89-90	90-91	91-92	92-93	93-94	94-95	95-96	96-97
1	The Kalupur Bank	626.78	817.58	1478.52	2424.11	3565.73	4757.88	14609.74	14688.65	9998.23	14012.85
2	Rajkot Nagrik Bank	275.99	585.09	730.21	732.21	734.71	1585.36	4730.36	4984.16	7761.43	9761.43
3	Anyona Saharakri Bank	96.86	151.94	177.55	256.22	331.55	356.55	566.32	755.88	1378.78	1781.78
4	Surat Peoples's Bank	194.15	245.95	254.95	283.25	358.25	1369.34	5731.46	7364.50	8534.78	17015.40
5	Natpur Co-Op Bank	20.45	20.45	20.45	20.45	20.45	20.45	255.45	515.00	1141.50	1615.47
6	The Anand Mercantile Bank	16.55	36.55	91.55	91.55	102.55	133.55	123.55	120.45	491.45	697.45
7	Dahod Urban Bank	134.01	202.76	291.43	157.13	199.26	236.46	792.55	1143.72	1244.91	1473.52
8	Sarvodya Nagrik Bank	1.00	1.00	1.00	2.00	2.00	4.00	4.00	4.05	84.45	83.45
9	Baroda People's Bank	90.01	105.01	135.01	110.01	135.01	135.01	166.26	172.56	617.56	649.06
10	Sardar Bhiladwala Bank	115.10	389.60	414.56	439.64	439.10	438.47	532.38	908.41	2874.71	4069.18

TABLE 10

CRR OF SELECTED URBAN CO-OPERATIVE BANKS IN GUJARAT

Sr. No.	Name of the Bank	1987-88	88-89	89-90	90-91	91-92	92-93	93-94	94-95	95-96	96-97
1	The Kalupur Bank	594.00	706.00	1310.00	1590.00	1707.00	1966.00	3138.00	4762.00	4906.00	5516.00
2	The Rajkot Nagrik Bank	1294.00	1277.00	2015.00	2234.00	2415.00	2638.00	2822.00	3393.00	3658.00	4277.00
3	Anyona Saharakri Bank	198.00	237.00	387.00	447.00	497.00	556.00	593.00	734.00	866.00	1182.00
4	The Surat Peoples's Bank	814.00	784.00	1345.00	1533.00	1659.00	1912.00	2135.00	2554.00	2733.00	3443.00
5	The Natpur Co-op. Bank	152.00	138.00	232.00	274.00	308.00	351.00	377.00	474.00	607.00	815.00
6	Anand Mercantile Bank	117.00	177.00	298.00	357.00	415.00	442.00	469.00	582.00	678.00	857.00
7	Dahod Urban Bank	149.00	179.00	284.00	314.00	346.00	382.00	402.00	485.00	550.00	733.00
8	Sarvodya Nagrik Bank	46.00	61.00	100.00	114.00	127.00	145.00	153.00	181.00	200.00	230.00
9	Baroda People's Bank	74.00	125.00	223.00	267.00	310.00	374.00	334.00	414.00	619.00	839.00
10	Sardar Bhiladwala Bank	279.00	350.00	581.00	655.00	712.00	501.00	888.00	1115.00	1199.00	1420.00

TABLE 11

SLR OF SELECTED URBAN CO-OPERATIVE BANKS IN GUJARAT

Sr. No.	Name of the Bank	1987-88	88-89	89-90	90-91	91-92	92-93	93-94	94-95	95-96	96-97
1	The Kalupur Bank	2227.00	2555.00	3320.00	4083.00	4382.00	5046.00	7788.00	10001.00	11039.00	12411.00
2	The Rajkot Nagrik Bank	4851.00	4622.00	5105.00	5736.00	6199.00	6773.00	7006.00	7127.00	8231.00	9625.00
3	Anyona Saharakri Bank	735.00	858.00	980.00	1146.00	1275.00	1428.00	1471.00	1543.00	1948.00	2625.00
4	The Surat Peoples's Bank	3054.00	2838.00	3409.00	3934.00	4259.00	4907.00	5299.00	5364.00	6150.00	7746.00
5	The Natpur Co-op. Bank	569.00	498.00	588.00	702.00	790.00	901.00	937.00	996.00	1366.00	1835.00
6	Anand Mercantile Bank	440.00	639.00	754.00	917.00	1066.00	1136.00	1165.00	1222.00	1527.00	1929.00
7	Dahod Urban Bank	561.00	647.00	719.00	806.00	888.00	982.00	998.00	1018.00	1237.00	1650.00
8	Sarvodya Nagrik Bank	172.00	220.00	253.00	294.00	327.00	373.00	379.00	381.00	450.00	518.00
9	Baroda People's Bank	280.00	453.00	565.00	686.00	796.00	961.00	829.00	870.00	1394.00	1889.00
10	Sardar Bhiladwala Bank	1047.00	1267.00	1472.00	1681.00	1827.00	2056.00	2204.00	2342.00	2699.00	3195.00

TABLE 12

COST SHEET OF THE KALUPUR COMMERCIAL BANK

Sr. No.	*Cost Elements*	*1987-88*	*88-89*	*89-90*	*90-91*	*91-92*	*92-93*	*93-94*	*94-95*	*95-96*	*96-97*
1	VARIABLE COST	1034.05	1002.92	1193.27	1020.28	1033.81	1189.60	1631.15	2331.38	2850.23	4042.12
2	SALARIES	112.59	134.18	175.35	202.30	158.26	237.75	268.71	343.53	414.96	451.95
3	PRINTING AND STNRY.	13.31	14.55	15.39	17.78	14.29	14.70	11.11	19.59	27.60	24.11
4	POSTAGE AND TELE.	2.22	2.76	3.15	3.30	2.75	3.77	4.55	6.06	6.65	8.08
5	RENTS	16.75	15.40	18.99	21.59	15.26	22.88	23.58	32.82	36.16	51.47
6	DEPRECIATION	16.38	17.49	14.91	14.43	13.72	19.76	25.28	41.44	77.31	105.89
7	AUDIT FEES	0.18	0.16	0.20	0.20	0.21	0.41	0.20	0.26	1.55	1.60
8	DIRECTORS' FEES	0.00	0.00	0.00	0.00	0.00	0.00	0.00	0.00	0.00	0.00
9	LEGAL FEES	0.00	0.73	0.70	0.99	1.30	2.19	1.80	3.89	6.06	0.03
10	TOTAL FIX COST	161.43	185.27	228.69	260.59	205.79	301.46	335.23	447.59	570.29	643.13
11	TOTAL COST	1195.48	1188.19	1421.96	1280.87	1239.60	1491.06	1966.38	2778.97	3420.52	4685.25
12	INT. RECEIVED	1343.63	1365.22	1215.52	1432.49	1382.56	1681.48	2532.38	3948.75	4950.02	6574.11
13	OTHER INCOME	38.55	42.01	61.91	75.86	71.52	114.02	130.19	201.55	179.20	261.85
14	TOTAL INCOME	1382.18	1407.23	1277.43	1508.35	1454.08	1795.50	2662.57	4150.30	5129.22	6835.96
15	PROFIT	186.70	219.04	-144.53	227.48	214.48	304.44	696.19	1371.33	1708.70	2150.71

TABLE 13

COST SHEET OF THE RAJKOT NAGRIK BANK

Sr. No.	*Cost Elements*	*1987-88*	*88-89*	*89-90*	*90-91*	*91-92*	*92-93*	*93-94*	*94-95*	*95-96*	*96-97*
1	VARIABLE COST	1337.11	1184.88	1651.23	1447.74	1261.44	1757.36	2000.87	2143.10	2643.33	2876.73
2	SALARIES	123.30	135.18	156.12	215.55	186.01	276.70	305.34	338.91	375.64	456.64
3	PRINTING AND STNRY.	7.20	10.59	10.93	11.32	8.50	16.99	16.39	14.79	13.53	14.89
4	POSTAGE AND TELE.	5.18	6.67	7.56	8.29	6.92	8.36	11.53	12.17	12.26	11.28
5	RENTS	6.08	7.15	8.70	13.97	14.51	16.95	22.50	31.63	30.52	33.42
6	DEPRECIATION	8.91	12.54	12.52	13.63	10.49	18.23	20.65	24.51	30.85	32.60
7	AUDIT FEES	0.45	0.45	0.56	0.50	0.51	0.61	1.14	0.84	0.80	0.90
8	DIRECTORS' FEES	0.13	0.12	0.12	0.13	0.10	0.14	0.15	0.16	0.18	0.18
9	LEGAL FEES	0.00	0.00	0.00	0.00	1.31	2.38	1.63	0.28	0.45	0.00
10	TOTAL FIX COST	151.25	172.70	196.51	263.39	228.35	340.36	379.33	423.29	464.23	549.91
11	TOTAL COST	1488.36	1357.58	1847.74	1711.13	1489.79	2097.72	2380.20	2566.39	3107.56	3426.64
12	INT. RECEIVED	1767.60	1949.02	2609.62	2652.68	2349.08	3437.61	3727.33	4149.04	5398.30	6323.31
13	OTHER INCOME	24.61	25.27	29.11	37.96	33.35	46.52	62.73	83.92	101.55	103.26
14	TOTAL INCOME	1792.21	1974.29	2638.73	2690.64	2382.43	3484.13	3790.06	4232.96	5499.85	6426.57
15	PROFIT	303.85	616.71	790.99	979.51	892.64	1386.41	1409.86	1666.57	2392.29	2999.93

TABLE 14

COST SHEET OF THE ANYONYA SAHAYAKARI BANK

Sr. No.	Cost Elements	1987-88	88-89	89-90	90-91	91-92	92-93	93-94	94-95	95-96	96-97
1	VARIABLE COST	211.04	235.03	270.73	294.13	246.05	396.97	421.21	456.13	650.05	978.04
2	SALARIES	41.13	46.35	52.04	74.18	56.95	90.22	105.50	131.47	163.43	203.21
3	PRINTING AND STNRY.	2.23	2.08	2.53	2.57	2.88	4.03	4.24	5.17	13.63	8.24
4	POSTAGE AND TELE.	0.53	0.70	0.63	0.80	0.88	1.09	1.29	1.49	2.07	2.47
5	RENTS	4.45	6.06	5.82	4.54	5.26	8.43	16.80	10.19	16.05	25.14
6	DEPRECIATION	0.76	1.13	0.95	0.98	0.89	3.42	4.25	2.95	6.16	8.24
7	AUDIT FEES	0.25	0.12	0.10	0.08	0.07	0.10	0.10	0.10	0.10	0.10
8	DIRECTORS' FEES	0.22	0.42	0.38	0.16	0.33	0.55	0.50	0.27	0.31	0.80
9	LEGAL FEES	0.16	0.40	0.31	0.02	0.29	0.06	0.09	0.19	0.14	0.10
10	TOTAL FIX COST	49.73	57.26	62.76	83.33	67.55	107.90	132.77	151.83	201.89	248.30
11	TOTAL COST	260.77	292.29	333.49	377.46	313.60	504.87	553.98	607.96	851.94	1226.34
12	INT. RECEIVED	283.30	319.14	374.35	435.25	394.95	618.80	661.73	717.30	933.10	1373.38
13	OTHER INCOME	3.74	3.96	4.19	6.65	4.96	7.99	14.71	15.65	39.25	32.92
14	TOTAL INCOME	287.04	323.10	378.54	441.90	399.91	626.79	676.44	732.95	972.35	1406.30
15	PROFIT	26.27	30.81	45.05	64.44	86.31	121.92	122.46	124.99	120.41	179.96

TABLE 15

COST SHEET OF THE SURAT PEOPLES' BANK

Sr. No.	Cost Elements	1987-88	88-89	89-90	90-91	91-92	92-93	93-94	94-95	95-96	96-97
1	VARIABLE COST	645.72	707.46	837.72	939.49	754.15	1206.56	1422.35	1470.58	1740.85	2355.47
2	SALARIES	121.68	138.08	198.16	218.66	209.04	307.19	387.86	484.42	598.44	551.87
3	PRINTING AND STNRY.	4.94	7.12	8.11	15.57	11.18	16.53	17.97	19.70	26.14	29.76
4	POSTAGE AND TELE.	1.33	1.75	1.73	2.68	2.60	3.31	3.34	3.88	3.41	4.51
5	RENTS	12.82	9.48	12.57	11.12	7.46	13.62	20.68	24.05	31.37	28.58
6	DEPRECIATION	19.10	17.61	16.19	21.32	18.35	34.76	37.00	48.58	67.53	65.43
7	AUDIT FEES	0.22	0.30	0.60	0.60	0.30	0.75	0.40	0.25	0.70	0.85
8	DIRECTORS' FEES	0.02	0.02	0.03	0.20	0.11	0.22	0.24	0.21	0.18	0.42
9	LEGAL FEES	0.08	0.08	0.18	0.12	0.17	0.06	0.13	0.35	0.63	1.43
10	TOTAL FIX COST	160.19	174.44	237.57	270.27	249.21	376.44	467.62	581.44	728.40	682.85
11	TOTAL COST	805.91	881.90	1075.29	1209.76	1003.36	1583.00	1889.97	2052.02	2469.25	3038.32
12	INT. RECEIVED	1067.54	1190.04	1466.85	1675.69	2153.98	2444.05	2709.00	2856.16	3589.79	4942.40
13	OTHER INCOME	12.49	18.43	25.96	35.76	27.18	32.68	58.76	88.52	112.96	63.82
14	TOTAL INCOME	1080.03	1208.47	1492.81	1711.45	2181.16	2476.73	2767.76	2944.68	3702.75	5006.22
15	PROFIT	274.13	326.57	417.52	501.69	1177.80	893.73	877.79	892.66	1233.50	1967.90

TABLE 16

COST SHEET OF THE NATPUR CO-OPERATIVE BANK

Sr. No.	*Cost Elements*	*1987-88*	*88-89*	*89-90*	*90-91*	*91-92*	*92-93*	*93-94*	*94-95*	*95-96*	*96-97*
1	VARIABLE COST	142.69	134.30	157.65	173.80	158.02	255.82	284.92	318.46	430.35	691.63
2	SALARIES	13.32	17.34	21.88	26.77	21.39	36.98	40.13	49.91	72.67	76.77
3	PRINTING AND STNRY.	1.69	1.86	2.79	2.80	2.47	2.96	4.54	4.87	4.82	5.02
4	POSTAGE AND TELE.	0.52	0.66	0.72	0.86	0.64	0.85	1.14	1.18	1.40	1.55
5	RENTS	1.85	1.87	1.81	1.88	1.94	2.68	4.18	3.97	6.96	8.58
6	DEPRECIATION	3.33	2.95	3.87	4.28	5.29	5.33	7.65	11.82	13.72	17.20
7	AUDIT FEES	0.16	0.17	0.19	0.10	0.11	0.16	0.15	0.13	0.18	0.10
8	DIRECTORS' FEES	0.00	0.00	0.00	0.00	0.00	0.00	0.00	0.00	0.00	0.00
9	LEGAL FEES	0.05	0.08	0.04	0.07	0.03	0.12	0.58	0.38	0.34	0.63
10	TOTAL FIX COST	20.92	24.93	31.30	36.76	31.87	49.08	58.37	72.26	100.09	109.85
11	TOTAL COST	163.61	159.23	188.95	210.56	189.89	304.90	343.29	390.72	530.44	801.48
12	INT. RECEIVED	205.54	210.56	250.34	286.12	288.28	441.50	467.73	546.21	700.69	1067.65
13	OTHER INCOME	1.24	1.79	2.60	3.40	2.35	3.11	7.19	9.77	15.03	13.89
14	TOTAL INCOME	206.78	212.35	252.94	289.52	290.63	444.61	474.92	555.98	715.72	1081.54
15	PROFIT	43.17	53.12	63.99	78.96	100.74	139.71	131.63	165.26	185.28	280.06

TABLE 17

COST SHEET OF THE ANAND MERCANTILE BANK

Sr. No.	Cost Elements	1987-88	88-89	89-90	90-91	91-92	92-93	93-94	94-95	95-96	96-97
1	VARIABLE COST	132.09	182.16	234.20	285.54	281.22	369.53	414.76	381.46	562.55	730.60
2	SALARIES	17.15	18.93	21.11	27.40	23.16	30.98	37.19	44.23	60.81	86.06
3	PRINTING AND STNRY.	3.00	4.88	3.95	4.20	4.39	7.02	8.44	4.58	4.27	4.94
4	POSTAGE AND TELE.	0.80	0.79	1.18	1.10	0.79	1.05	1.12	1.31	1.11	1.14
5	RENTS	1.01	1.53	1.43	1.47	2.05	2.73	3.35	4.81	9.65	13.70
6	DEPRECIATION	2.80	3.15	2.84	2.87	2.60	3.54	3.95	5.84	7.28	8.59
7	AUDIT FEES	0.18	0.19	0.19	0.24	0.20	0.15	0.18	0.10	0.27	0.35
8	DIRECTORS' FEES	0.15	0.13	0.11	0.13	0.16	0.23	0.27	0.27	0.27	0.29
9	LEGAL FEES	0.06	0.02	0.07	0.05	0.11	0.43	0.19	0.31	0.28	0.32
10	TOTAL FIX COST	25.15	29.62	30.88	37.46	33.46	46.13	54.69	61.45	83.94	115.39
11	TOTAL COST	157.24	211.78	265.08	323.00	314.68	415.66	469.45	442.91	646.49	845.99
12	INT. RECEIVED	192.44	252.79	326.65	369.94	381.05	555.95	527.16	558.17	743.92	993.44
13	OTHER INCOME	2.65	4.20	5.24	7.97	10.19	13.22	9.72	8.51	10.37	10.45
14	TOTAL INCOME	195.09	256.99	331.89	377.91	391.24	569.17	536.88	566.68	754.29	1003.89
15	PROFIT	37.85	45.21	66.81	54.92	76.56	153.51	67.43	123.77	107.80	157.90

TABLE 18

COST SHEET OF THE DAHOD URBAN BANK

Sr. No.	Cost Elements	1987-88	88-89	89-90	90-91	91-92	92-93	93-94	94-95	95-96	96-97
1	VARIABLE COST	164.97	186.12	201.16	221.77	195.33	308.09	347.78	376.37	496.61	669.01
2	SALARIES	17.47	19.69	30.61	30.52	26.89	41.41	46.66	62.04	66.91	74.36
3	PRINTING AND STNRY.	1.80	1.12	1.18	2.25	1.89	3.74	3.77	3.61	5.87	2.99
4	POSTAGE AND TELE.	0.36	0.36	0.38	0.53	0.44	0.68	1.00	1.06	1.26	1.33
5	RENTS	1.79	1.95	2.48	2.53	1.96	3.40	3.48	3.91	6.64	7.29
6	DEPRECIATION	0.48	0.64	0.63	0.54	0.68	0.63	0.61	3.66	5.86	0.35
7	AUDIT FEES	0.22	0.19	0.16	0.20	0.23	0.24	0.24	0.29	0.34	0.36
8	DIRECTORS' FEES	0.19	0.15	0.15	0.21	0.16	0.21	0.22	0.22	0.21	0.21
9	LEGAL FEES	0.04	0.07	0.06	0.11	0.04	0.07	0.03	0.11	0.13	0.13
10	TOTAL FIX COST	22.35	24.17	35.65	36.89	32.29	50.38	56.01	74.90	87.22	87.01
11	TOTAL COST	187.32	210.29	236.81	258.66	227.62	358.47	403.79	451.27	583.83	756.02
12	INT. RECEIVED	245.46	280.54	314.23	349.49	334.47	492.01	529.81	577.42	757.91	988.60
13	OTHER INCOME	4.65	2.64	3.12	3.41	4.01	5.37	13.61	17.15	24.47	17.63
14	TOTAL INCOME	250.11	283.18	317.35	352.90	338.48	497.38	543.42	594.57	782.38	1006.23
15	PROFIT	62.79	72.89	80.54	94.24	110.86	138.91	139.63	143.30	198.55	250.21

TABLE 19

COST SHEET OF THE SARVODAYA NAGRIK BANK

Sr. No.	Cost Elements	1987-88	88-89	89-90	90-91	91-92	92-93	93-94	94-95	95-96	96-97
1	VARIABLE COST	59.24	77.81	80.90	93.76	87.90	145.67	182.08	165.45	204.07	259.33
2	SALARIES	12.65	15.12	18.89	21.85	22.69	36.97	45.23	58.68	68.03	76.11
3	PRINTING AND STNRY.	0.73	1.40	1.00	1.11	1.89	2.50	1.25	1.67	1.62	2.12
4	POSTAGE AND TELE.	0.44	0.72	0.96	1.01	0.80	1.19	0.85	1.75	1.50	1.46
5	RENTS	0.57	0.85	0.95	1.03	1.14	1.21	1.97	2.19	1.83	3.44
6	DEPRECIATION	0.59	0.67	0.72	0.78	0.58	0.76	1.10	1.03	1.05	1.07
7	AUDIT FEES	0.04	0.10	0.08	0.10	0.11	0.10	0.10	0.10	0.11	0.10
8	DIRECTORS' FEES	0.00	0.00	0.00	0.00	0.00	0.00	0.00	0.00	0.00	0.00
9	LEGAL FEES	0.04	0.02	0.04	0.11	0.15	0.31	0.00	0.00	0.08	0.33
10	TOTAL FIX COST	15.06	18.88	22.64	25.99	27.36	43.04	50.50	65.42	74.22	84.63
11	TOTAL COST	74.30	96.69	103.54	119.75	115.26	188.71	232.58	230.87	278.29	343.96
12	INT. RECEIVED	84.10	109.70	116.91	135.23	128.55	213.41	245.50	244.98	301.55	488.23
13	OTHER INCOME	1.42	1.55	7.42	1.69	2.07	3.15	3.11	4.70	3.44	3.71
14	TOTAL INCOME	85.52	111.25	124.33	136.92	130.62	216.56	248.61	249.68	304.99	491.94
15	PROFIT	11.22	14.56	20.79	17.18	15.36	27.85	16.03	18.81	26.70	147.98

TABLE 20

COST SHEET OF THE BARODA PEOPLE'S BANK

Sr. No.	Cost Elements	1987-88	88-89	89-90	90-91	91-92	92-93	93-94	94-95	95-96	96-97
1	VARIABLE COST	85.71	132.98	163.75	205.96	190.60	318.47	371.91	394.92	489.69	703.11
2	SALARIES	17.03	20.01	29.62	34.51	30.51	52.25	56.06	98.27	109.85	133.59
3	PRINTING AND STNRY.	1.42	1.97	2.76	5.44	5.00	9.79	8.47	8.54	9.88	10.42
4	POSTAGE AND TELE.	0.72	1.35	1.16	1.77	1.27	1.89	1.91	2.09	2.49	2.79
5	RENTS	2.02	2.22	2.02	2.09	8.89	6.20	6.41	5.22	18.60	29.24
6	DEPRECIATION	1.90	1.16	1.33	2.28	5.14	6.02	4.21	3.80	4.66	22.78
7	AUDIT FEES	0.05	0.10	0.18	0.16	0.15	0.15	0.26	0.23	0.12	0.46
8	DIRECTORS' FEES	0.20	0.21	0.23	0.40	0.35	0.45	0.41	0.38	0.47	0.45
9	LEGAL FEES	0.21	0.12	0.19	0.16	0.02	0.23	0.00	0.19	0.63	1.02
10	TOTAL FIX COST	23.55	27.14	37.49	46.81	51.33	76.98	77.73	118.72	146.70	200.75
11	TOTAL COST	109.26	160.12	201.24	252.77	241.93	395.45	449.64	513.64	636.39	903.86
12	INT. RECEIVED	137.41	195.42	248.57	306.45	297.29	476.52	617.21	641.84	774.99	1049.81
13	OTHER INCOME	4.84	4.46	6.26	9.75	8.52	12.19	17.25	19.73	32.65	50.33
14	TOTAL INCOME	142.25	199.88	254.83	316.20	305.81	488.71	634.46	661.57	807.64	1100.14
15	PROFIT	32.99	39.76	53.59	63.43	63.88	93.26	184.82	147.93	171.25	196.28

TABLE 21

COST SHEET OF THE SARDAR BHILADWALA BANK

Sr. No.	Cost Elements	1987-88	88-89	89-90	90-91	91-92	92-93	93-94	94-95	95-96	96-97
1	VARIABLE COST	248.68	415.08	325.80	365.41	329.99	490.62	553.37	599.20	690.46	881.82
2	SALARIES	48.95	67.78	98.25	81.76	63.35	126.54	145.15	159.51	186.29	260.22
3	PRINTING AND STNRY.	3.34	4.10	6.25	5.61	7.26	7.23	7.35	7.34	8.27	9.41
4	POSTAGE AND TELE.	1.29	1.54	1.70	2.37	2.15	2.63	2.62	2.74	3.73	5.07
5	RENTS	1.75	2.45	3.95	4.44	4.17	7.17	5.85	7.26	7.98	11.35
6	DEPRECIATION	3.23	4.30	8.65	5.68	9.15	10.76	12.43	12.98	14.20	26.04
7	AUDIT FEES	0.05	0.34	0.32	0.37	0.24	0.28	0.10	0.10	0.10	0.20
8	DIRECTORS' FEES	0.42	0.54	0.00	0.00	0.14	0.00	0.00	0.00	0.00	0.00
9	LEGAL FEES	0.31	0.36	0.23	0.03	0.11	0.35	0.44	0.31	0.43	0.05
10	TOTAL FIX COST	59.34	81.41	119.35	100.26	86.57	154.96	173.94	190.24	221.00	312.34
11	TOTAL COST	308.02	496.49	445.15	465.67	416.56	645.58	727.31	789.44	911.46	1194.16
12	INT. RECEIVED	414.48	607.09	535.37	640.20	689.32	918.06	908.38	1097.29	1364.17	1952.27
13	OTHER INCOME	6.90	15.25	11.20	14.93	15.16	21.57	24.41	28.05	31.67	38.79
14	TOTAL INCOME	421.38	622.34	546.57	655.13	704.48	939.63	932.79	1125.34	1395.84	1991.06
15	PROFIT	113.36	125.85	101.42	189.46	287.92	294.05	205.48	335.90	484.38	796.90

TABLE NO 22

AVERAGE OF EACH ELEMENTS OF COST OF SELECTED URBAN CO-OPERATIVE BANKS IN GUJARAT

Sr. No.	*Name of the Bank*	*1987-88*	*88-89*	*89-90*	*90-91*	*91-92*	*92-93*	*93-94*	*94-95*	*95-96*	*96-97*	*Avg.*
1	VARIABLE COST	11.13	11.35	10.99	10.27	8.40	11.17	11.25	10.23	10.52	11.36	10.667
2	SALARIES	1.67	1.69	1.88	1.87	1.47	2.08	2.07	2.33	2.24	2.09	1.939
3	PRINTING AND STNRY.	0.14	0.15	0.14	0.15	0.13	0.17	0.15	0.13	0.13	0.09	0.139
4	POSTAGE AND TELE.	0.05	0.06	0.05	0.05	0.04	0.05	0.04	0.05	0.04	0.04	0.047
5	RENTS	0.15	0.14	0.13	0.12	0.14	0.15	0.17	0.14	0.18	0.20	0.152
6	DEPRECIATION	0.16	0.14	0.13	0.12	0.13	0.15	0.15	0.16	0.17	0.19	0.151
7	AUDIT FEES	0.01	0.01	0.01	0.01	0.01	0.01	0.01	0.00	0.00	0.00	0.006
8	DIRECTORS' FEES	0.01	0.01	0.00	0.00	0.00	0.01	0.00	0.00	0.00	0.00	0.005
9	LEGAL FEES	0.01	0.01	0.01	0	0.01	0.01	0.01	0.01	0.01	0.01	0.006
10	TOTAL FIX COST	2.19	2.21	2.36	2.33	1.92	2.62	2.59	2.82	2.77	2.61	2.444
11	TOTAL COST	13.32	13.56	13.35	12.6	10.32	13.79	13.84	13.06	13.3	13.97	13.111
12	INT. RECEIVED	16.16	16.74	16.14	15.97	14.44	18.35	17.73	16.99	17.36	19.36	16.924
13	OTHER INCOME	0.3	0.29	0.38	0.33	0.29	0.36	0.40	0.44	0.46	0.38	0.364
14	TOTAL INCOME	16.46	17.03	16.52	16.31	14.73	18.71	18.14	17.43	17.82	19.74	17.289
15	PROFIT	3.14	3.47	3.17	3.71	4.41	4.92	4.30	4.37	4.52	5.77	4.178